THE UNITED NATIONS AND GLOBAL SECURITY

Edited by

Richard M. Price and Mark W. Zacher

THE UNITED NATIONS AND GLOBAL SECURITY
© Richard M. Price and Mark W. Zacher, eds., 2004

First published 2004 by
PALGRAVE MACMILLAN™
175 Fifth Avenue, New York, N.Y. 10010 and
Houndmills, Basingstoke, Hampshire, England RG21 6XS.
Companies and representatives throughout the world.

PALGRAVE MACMILLAN is the global academic imprint of the Palgrave Macmillan division of St. Martin's Press, LLC and of Palgrave Macmillan Ltd. Macmillan® is a registered trademark in the United States, United Kingdom and other countries. Palgrave is a registered trademark in the European Union and other countries.

ISBN 1–4039–6390–8 hardback
ISBN 1–4039–6391–6 paperback

Library of Congress Cataloging-in-Publication Data
The United Nations and global security/edited by Richard Price and Mark W. Zacher.
    p. cm.
    Includes bibliographical references and index.
    ISBN 1–4039–6390–8 (hbk)—ISBN 1–4039–6391–6 (pbk)
    1. Security, International. 2. United Nations. I. Price, Richard (Richard MacKay), 1964– II. Zacher, Mark W.

JZ5588.U55 2004
341.7'2—dc22   2003060876

A catalogue record for this book is available from the British Library.

Design by Newgen Imaging Systems (P) Ltd., Chennai, India.

First edition: March 2004
10 9 8 7 6 5 4 3 2 1

Printed in the United States of America.

On August 19, 2003, the UN headquarters in Baghdad was bombed with the loss of life of 22 people and injuries to dozens of others. Among those seriously injured was one of this book's contributors, Gil Loescher, who was consulting about how best to manage Iraqi refugee issues. Gil has spent his academic life working on humanitarian and political issues surrounding refugees and has influenced the thinking of many people on how to improve the lives of refugees. His commitment to a better understanding of humanitarianism, and to the translation of that understanding so that it can improve the lives of others is a model for us all. We dedicate this book to him and his successful recovery.

CONTENTS

Foreword

Throughout my career I have worked both within the United Nations as a consultant and employee and outside as an academic analyst and critic to try to make the UN better and more effective at serving the most vulnerable. For the past 20 years, I have traveled to numerous refugee camps in Africa, Asia and Central America to assess the work of UN humanitarian agencies.

In August 2003, I went to Iraq to report on the human cost of the war. The attack on the UN headquarters in Baghdad on August 19, 2003 left 23 dead and scores of people injured. This event had a huge impact on my life and the life of my family. As the only survivor in the most devastated part of the building, I lost both my legs above the knees, severely damaged my right hand, and suffered numerous shrapnel wounds to my body. I am incredibly lucky to still be alive.

The Baghdad attack was also a devastating and cathartic event for the UN. The world changed instantaneously for this international organization and its staff.

For the past decade the UN has worked in highly politicized and militarized environments, from Bosnia to East Timor. In many of these settings UN and NGO humanitarian actions were used as a substitute for unsuccessful political and military interventions. In the midst of bitter intrastate conflicts, the traditional separation between military and humanitarian operations disappeared. Consequently, in the eyes of the local combatants, the UN became closely identified either with one side or the other, or with the intervening forces. The attack on the UN in Baghdad brought a new and unprecedented degree of anti-UN hostility to the surface, probably changing forever the way the UN and others view the security context in which they have to conduct their operations.

This dangerous new environment raises several old but now extremely pressing questions for the UN and the international community. How can the UN and NGO humanitarian agencies avoid being too closely identified with the military forces of intervening and occupying forces? How can the UN better balance the necessity of engaging in life saving operations in war zones with the risk such actions pose to its staff? Do the UN and the international community need to greatly bolster multilateral humanitarian and human rights norms even if this involves a restraint on the national interests of states? While policy solutions will not be clear-cut or easy to obtain, these questions need to be addressed by both governments and the UN.

Since the August attack, it is also evident that in postconflict settings like Iraq and Afghanistan the role of the UN in responding to chronic sources of instability and conflict is essential to international and regional security. Yet, as this excellent book demonstrates, states still remain a long way from helping the United Nations realize its full potential in the realm of international security. In the same way I have grown stronger and more determined, I hope the same will prove true of the United Nations.

Gil Loescher

ACKNOWLEDGEMENTS

There are many people who have been very helpful in the development of this volume. The director of the Centre of International Relations at the University of British Columbia, Brian Job, has been very helpful with administrative assistance and funding. A major source of financial assistance came from the Canadian Centre for Foreign Policy Development in the Department of Foreign Affairs and International Trade. We are particularly indebted to its director, Steven Lee, for financial and advisory assistance.

A conference to discuss the drafts was held in Vancouver in January 2003. The authors benefited from the comments of many attendees. Two individuals in particular—namely, David Malone, President of the International Peace Academy and Professor Michael Barnett of the Department of Political Science at the University of Wisconsin—provided an invaluable service by evaluating the conference papers, and all of the authors benefited from their insightful comments. We are most grateful for the efforts of David Pervin at Palgrave who facilitated the acceptance and publication of the study. At the University of British Columbia Adam Bower has done excellent work in editing the manuscripts, and Suzy Hainsworth has provided very helpful administrative assistance for the project. An earlier version of the chapter by Andrew Mack and Asif Khan, "UN Sanctions: A Glass Half Full?" was published in *Security Dialogue* as "The Efficacy of UN Sanctions," *Security Dialogue* 31, no. 3 (September 2000), pp. 279–92. It appears with permission of the publisher.

PREFACE

Students of international security are interested in the role of the United Nations because it is at the center of global collaboration to control international violence. Even when they are pessimistic about what the UN has done and can do, they are interested in grappling with the forces that influence its roles. At the time of the United Nations' founding in 1945, there was at best guarded optimism concerning its ability to make major contributions to a reduction in the incidence and severity of war. Some observers predicted that serious conflict between the Western allies and the Soviet Union would seriously hinder the UN's roles, and they were, of course, very prescient. The Cold War did have a major impact in constraining collaboration through the UN, but it did not completely preclude the evolution of some important roles. During this period the UN was involved in promoting decolonization, preventing and reversing Western military incursions in Third World states, and facilitating arms control accords.

Since the end of the Cold War in 1989, opportunities for the UN have increased significantly, but this is not to say that the UN has assumed a dominant role in world security politics. In its post-1989 manifestation, the UN has become much more active in intervening in civil conflicts, a new and largely unique role in its history. Also, it has been active in promoting the criminalization of mass killing, especially through its creation of the tribunals for the former Yugoslavia and Rwanda and its sponsorship of the meetings that led to the creation of the International Criminal Court. It has played some important roles in terminating a number of cases of interstate violence, in particular the Gulf War of 1990–91 and the conflicts in the former Yugoslavia between 1992 and 1995. On the other hand, it failed to stem the progress of humanitarian interventions that certainly challenged traditional international laws of aggression—the most notable case being the Kosovo crisis of 1999. More recently, the United Nations has been drawn into the international conflicts concerning terrorism and facilitated multilateral interventions in Afghanistan to stem the activities of al-Qaeda. The UN, however, then failed to control the U.S. intervention in Iraq in 2003—hence throwing significant doubt on the UN's ability to manage the international conflicts emanating from U.S. strategic concerns.

The chapters in this volume focus on major international security issues in which the UN has played important or not so important roles, and it is organized into four sections. First, there are sections on arms control, conflict prevention and resolution, managing international aggressions, military interventions, and institutional reform. The volume closes with an essay specifically looking at the recent Iraqi conflict in terms of its implications for global security multilateralism.

Few people would have expected in the late 1940s that the UN would play a major role with regard to the control of weapons of mass destruction, but this is exactly what has happened. Nina Tannenwald in her chapter on "The United Nations and Debates over Weapons of Mass Destruction" probes both what the UN has done and what it might do as a negotiating forum, an agent (e.g., an overseer of weapons inspectors), and especially a promoter of norms and rules. Its activities have evolved significantly in recent decades from focusing on East-West to North-South conflicts. While the Third World and some Western states want to strengthen multilateral controls, the great powers (especially the United States) are preaching that possession of the weapons by the five major nuclear powers is a bastion of international stability and that the real problem is to keep weapons of mass destruction (WMD) out of the hands of Third World states (especially so-called "rogue" regimes) and nongovernmental groups. In fact, the United States has taken certain steps to make its nuclear weapons more useable. The future of the regimes for weapons of mass destruction is certainly problematic in light of such developments.

While the United Nations has facilitated the development of legal regimes concerning weapons of mass destruction, quite different outcomes have evolved with regard to the development of international standards and norm setting in the case of small arms. These outcomes of UN activities in the realm of small arms control are the focus of Keith Krause's chapter, "Facing the Challenge of Small Arms: the UN and Global Security Governance." Krause stresses that the United Nations should be seen, most importantly, as a central participant in a transnational policy-making network. States and international organizations are part of this network but so are nongovernmental groups and individuals. Since the mid-1990s the United Nations has been a crucial actor in facilitating deliberations within the policy network, and while legally binding conventions have not developed, important normative developments have been quite prominent. It is definitely a policy sphere where major breakthroughs in formulating international conventions are unlikely, but, on the other hand, it is a sphere where very important learning of new values and practices takes place.

A unique sphere of arms control concerns the imposition of bans on the shipment of arms to states that are threatening particular UN member countries. Andy Knight addresses this sphere of arms control in "Improving the Effectiveness of UN Arms Embargoes." Knight notes that since 1948 the UN Security Council has imposed 14 mandatory and six nonmandatory arms embargoes—numbers that are considerably larger than most observers would anticipate. He notes that there have been some marked differences in the successes of the embargoes and that these differences are rooted in a variety of factors. These factors are (1) the degree of specificity of the mandates approved by the Security Council, (2) the comprehensiveness of the embargoed items, (3) the ability to impose sanctions on arms dealers and brokers, (4) the pattern of national legislation that facilitates the imposition of arms embargoes, (5) the ability of states to sell natural resources such as diamonds in order to purchase arms, and (6) the nature of the monitoring and enforcement mechanisms. States have learned a great deal about the use of arms embargoes, but they are still frequently faced with situations in which it is very difficult to adopt effective policies given the interests among states and private financial actors.

One of the most important areas for controlling the international use of armed force is to alter those conditions that lead to hostilities. This is commonly referred to as conflict prevention. Andrew Mack and Kathryn Furlong in their chapter "When Aspiration Exceeds Capability: the UN and Conflict Prevention" focus on the organizational and physical capabilities of the UN system. In explaining why the UN has not been a major force in conflict prevention, they focus on a variety of factors—including the actual character of the UN. With regard to such UN characteristics, they note that the UN lacks a strong research culture and possesses a strong commitment to state sovereignty. Next, they comment on the fragmented character of the UN system and the turf wars among bureaucratic departments that have different spheres of expertise and strategic predilections. Departments that focus on political and economic development issues particularly tend to adopt inconsistent and conflicting stances concerning conflict prevention. Last, they focus on the lack of physical and financial capabilities to address conflict prevention in a serious way—resources that are at the disposal or organizations such as the World Bank and the major donor states. Given this lack of financial capabilities, they call on the UN to focus on the promotion of normative changes that are necessary for conflict prevention.

The UN is often associated with mediatory strategies for the termination of armed conflicts. In his chapter "Can the UN Still Mediate?" Fen Hampson explores the success of the UN as a mediator in recent decades and the factors that have influenced its successes and failures. The record of the UN has been spotty as a mediator, whether done by the Secretary-General or one of his representatives, but it has also had some successes. Hampson focuses on a number of influential factors, including the strong support of the Security Council and especially its permanent members, their sharing of a coherent strategic approach to a conflict, the choice of the right personality as a mediator, and the UN's past record of success. Hampson also focuses on William Zartman's concept of "ripeness for settlement." This concept concerns particularly the existence of conditions whereby the conflicting parties are suffering because of the absence of an accord. In such situations the parties are willing to make sacrifices that they were not willing to make prior to this suffering and subsequent "ripeness."

The UN is often associated with deterring, reversing, and punishing aggressions. There are many subjects that could fall under this multifaceted rubric, but we have limited our foci to economic sanctions, the criminalization of mass killing, and action to control terrorism. Few security issues have been more controversial in the UN than that addressed by Andrew Mack and Asif Khan in "UN Sanctions: A Glass Half-Full?" In particular, economic sanctions have frequently been accused of ineffectiveness in ensuring compliance and in some cases producing increased suffering among the civilian populations of the target states. These well-publicized failures are exacerbated by the lack of resources within the UN system to properly evaluate past sanctions experiences. Despite the noted problems, some headway has been made in the recent development of so-called "targeted" or "smart" sanctions, which seek to ameliorate the more troubling aspects of traditional sanctions regimes. However, while in strict terms sanctions have largely proved ineffective in promoting positive action by defiant states, critics often fail to recognize the other (and perhaps more subtle) ways in which sanctions alter the nature of the international system: whether by stigmatizing violations or acting as a means of prevention and deterrence.

Richard Price and Joanne Lee's chapter, "International Tribunals and the Criminalization of International Violence" investigates one of the most revolutionary developments in international law—namely, the criminalization of interstate and civil violence. The first important steps were the launching of the crimes tribunals for the former Yugoslavia and Rwanda in the early 1990s. They were followed soon by the creation of an International Criminal Court (ICC) in 1998. Its central provisions stipulate that the ICC has jurisdiction over the actions of citizens of parties to the convention and actions on the territory of parties to the convention. The United States opposed many of the provisions of the Rome Treaty and has refused to become a signatory to it. It would prefer that the ICC be subject to the mandates of the UN Security Council. Price and Lee explore a number of the strengths and weaknesses of the ICC but are firm in their judgment as to its dramatic and positive impact on the international legal order with regard to violence. Most important, the changes embody some major shifts in the norms of international society.

Few issues are more prominent on the security agenda of the UN today than terrorism—an issue that is addressed in Edward Luck's "Another Reluctant Belligerent: The United Nations and the War on Terrorism." The UN system, and particularly several specialized agencies, were involved deeply in conventions dealing with air and maritime terrorism in the 1960s and 1970s. They enjoyed moderate success, but they were concerned with limited aspects of terrorism. The entire terrorist agenda changed dramatically with the events of 9/11 in 2001. The UN did respond by supporting the efforts of the United States and its allies in Afghanistan, but the UN membership did not succeed with regard to formulating a general convention on terrorism. Without peace in the Middle East, the attempts to develop a comprehensive convention are unlikely to be successful. At the moment, the United States sees the balance of forces with regard to terrorism as being more favorable outside the UN rather than within the organization, and therefore it is not likely to exert significant pressure to achieve a grand accord within the UN.

The one significant institutional change concerning terrorism within the UN was the establishment of the Counterterrorism Committee within the Security Council, but given its reliance on unanimity among the permanent five members, it does not represent a major move forward.

One of the most important issues in international security politics now involves military intervention by external actors, generally international organizations, in the domestic politics of countries. The conduct of such interventions is often aimed at promoting long-term domestic and international order, but they engender considerable controversy. The first chapter that confronts this general question is Allen Sens's "From Peace-keeping to Peace-building: The United Nations and the Challenge of Intrastate War." Sens delves into the development of peace building since the 1990s and finds that the record is certainly uneven and very unsuccessful in some cases. He focuses on the many obstacles that hinder the success of international efforts at peace building. One is the UN's reliance on liberal political prescriptions, which can, in fact, produce more cleavages and conflict within societies than they do reconciliation and order. Additional obstacles include the fact that there are no formal, comprehensive peace-building policies within the UN, no institutional home for the development of peace-building strategies and operations, the lack of coordination within UN bureaus that deal with peace building, and the lack of UN capabilities to restructure societies. Successful peace-building requires considerable economic resources, and the UN quite simply does not possess them. This does not mean that it cannot make contributions to peace building because of the roles of UN peace-keeping operations and because of the legitimacy that the UN brings to the restructuring of societies; but there are dramatic obstacles to major progress at the present time.

A great deal of the public and diplomatic dialogue with regard to intervention today focuses on what is generally called "humanitarian intervention." Two of the articles in this volume deal specifically with this issue: "Authorizing Humanitarian Intervention" by Jennifer Welsh and "Developing Countries and the Intervention-Sovereignty Debate" by Ramesh Thakur. Welsh sets her discussion of humanitarian intervention against the backdrop of the report of the International Commission on Intervention and State Sovereignty (ICISS) of 2002. The central argument of the commission was that in situations of threats to national populations, governments have a "responsibility to protect." When governments do not exercise that authority, the international community has a responsibility to consider providing protection on its own. The report did not state clearly the conditions under which this might occur, but it did rest the legitimacy of humanitarian intervention on the support of the Security Council. The proviso of the need for Security Council authorization, of course, puts considerable obstacles in the way of any interventionist action by the UN. Welsh particularly investigates the reasons why Council opposition is so important. The first is a prudential argument that Great Power support will make operations easier to carry out. The second is an ideational argument that focuses on the aura of legitimization that Security Council backing provides. And, finally, there is a power argument based on the likelihood of effectiveness in the case of backing from the five Great Powers. One of her key points relates to the fact that contrary to the views of some observers, the promotion of humanitarian intervention and counterterrorism are not contradictory. Assisting "failed states" is often seen as a strategy for undercutting terrorism, and promoting strong UN roles in each area can assist strong roles in the other.

Ramesh Thakur, who served on the International Commission for Intervention and State Sovereignty, focuses on the tension between developing and developed countries with regard to humanitarian intervention. He highlights the fears of the developing countries that a right of humanitarian intervention will give an opportunity to developed countries to establish a new colonial order. On the other hand, the Western developed states often possess a strong commitment to human rights for both ideational and strategic reasons and do not want to close the door on humanitarian intervention. In a sense, the developing countries lean much more toward a rules-based order grounded in the UN Charter. There is today, and there will likely be for some time, a fierce normative contestation concerning humanitarian intervention between developed and developing countries. Thakur does believe that all states would benefit by respecting the principles recommended by the ICISS.

The final article in this section concerning intervention is "Refugee Protection and State Security: Towards a Greater Convergence" by Gil Loescher. Refugee issues in the immediate post-1945 decades concerned asylum and resettlement for people who were politically persecuted—largely in Eastern Europe. In the last two decades, the increase of civil violence in many Third World countries, particularly in Africa, has brought about a very different kind of refugee problem. The refugees from these civil wars have caused considerable disorder and insecurity within countries, but they have also posed comparable problems for neighboring states. Since 1991 the United Nations has become deeply involved in these problems in areas such as Rwanda, Sierra Leone, the Congo, Yugoslavia, Somalia, Iraq, Afghanistan, and East Timor. In dealing with these civil wars, the UN's ability to contribute to stability and a mitigation of the refugee flows has been significantly curtailed by developing countries' traditional notions of state sovereignty, but the UN has also been hindered by the political and security concerns of developed countries. The refugee issue has taken on a new dimension since the mid-1990s as result of the increasing support for "human security," or the need to protect the welfare of individuals throughout the world. In response to this greater humanitarian concern, the UN High Commission for Refugees developed "the ladder of options" for assisting refugees and countries that are confronted by refugee flows. The UN has been significantly circumscribed in what is has been able to do because of limited support from governments and the UN bureaucracy, and this is only likely to change when the developed states see refugee assistance as supporting their strategic interests.

The last major section in the volume concerns institutional reform. In "The Conundrums of International Power Sharing: The Politics of Security Council Reform," Mark Zacher notes that no other UN institutional reform issue has attracted as much attention as the membership and voting rules of the UN Security Council. In 1966 there was a small increase in the number of nonpermanent members in the Council as a result of Third World pressure, but the larger issues concerning the veto and the possible addition of new permanent members could not be tackled during the Cold War period. The end of the Cold War in 1989 opened the door to deliberations about Security Council reform in a General Assembly committee from 1995 to 1997. The failure of these deliberations is often viewed as a product of stonewalling by the five permanent members of the Council, but their obstinacy on certain issues does not explain most of the dynamics and outcomes of the talks. The central factor that killed reform on the increase in the Council was the rivalries that existed among states within individual regions. Significant Security Council reform is going to require a concatenation of a variety of political developments that are hard to project at this time.

In "The UN, Regional Organizations, and Regional Conflict: Is There a Viable Role for the UN?" Brian Job explores the question of whether the UN will be able to sustain a central role in future peace enforcement operations, having throughout the 1990s depended increasingly on regional organizations and coalitions to mount such missions and accordingly having seen its role as the global legitimating authority for the use of force substantially eroded as well. His chapter begins by exposing the ambivalent relationship between regional organizations and the UN established in the Charter. It proceeds next to highlight the manner in which the Secretary-General sought to recast this relationship in light of the dilemmas confronting the UN as the "new world order" collapsed. The record of peace operations is reviewed, noting the three phases of peace operations of the 1990s. Finally, considerable attention is devoted to analyzing the viability of the tradeoffs inherent in a capability-legitimacy "bargain" between the UN and regional organizations. In this regard, the future for the UN is clouded, dependent upon developing effective "hybrid" arrangements with regional institutions and upon its capacity to overcome the erosion of its role as the sole legitimizing agency for the use of force in the international order.

Brian Job argues that the UN has in fact been looking to regional organizations to assume a greater role in conflict management, with the condition of prior consent from the Security Council. Job states that while this model of conflict management depends on the presence, legitimacy, and capacity of the regional organizations in question, its effectives lies in the increased trend toward regionalization that has led to the creation of organizations in Europe, Latin America, and Africa.

Lloyd Axworthy discusses the increase in a concern for human security as an opportunity for substantive UN reform. Axworthy points to the unprecedented transparency and diversity of entities participating within the Security

Council during the February 1999 debate on "the protection of civilians in armed conflict" in order to show how the human security agenda has served as a medium for procedural UN reform. The proposed UN reforms would allow greater democratization of the Assembly as well as an increased ability to conduct preventative missions, investigate security concerns in specific areas, enforce compliance with disarmament resolutions, and provide greater protection to UN humanitarian workers operating in conflict areas. In the Iraq crisis Axworthy notes that the centrality of the UN was simultaneously promoted by the human security concerns of global civil society and dismissed by the actions of certain states. The results are clear to see. However, he is a strong believer in the ability of the global body to be strengthened by a growing backing for human security.

The final section and chapter of the book concerns the implications of the US-led invasion of Iraq on UN multilateralism. In "The League of Nations Redux?" Richard Price discusses the role of the UN as a forum for expression and a provider of legitimacy for international security initiatives. Price states that U.S. unilateralism during the Iraq war has not necessarily undermined the role of the UN to the extent that some have argued. Instead, the inability to reconcile UN multilateralism and U.S. unilateralism in the case of Iraq proved damaging for both parties, as the Security Council's authority was seriously undermined and U.S. power in conducting the operation was diminished by the lack of international support and the absence of burden-sharing during the conflict. The reconciliation of U.S. security strategies and most UN member states' multilateralist approaches constitutes a central issue on the UN security agenda.

PART I

ARMS CONTROL

CHAPTER 1

THE UN AND DEBATES OVER WEAPONS OF MASS DESTRUCTION

Nina Tannenwald*

INTRODUCTION

Controlling the risks posed by weapons of mass destruction (WMD)—nuclear, chemical, and biological weapons—has been high on the agenda of the United Nations (UN) since its inception. Despite the fact that the UN Charter places little emphasis on arms control and disarmament, the very first General Assembly resolution in January 1946 called for the new UN Atomic Energy Commission to make proposals for "the elimination from national armaments of atomic weapons and of all other major weapons adaptable to mass destruction."[1] Since then, the UN has viewed reducing the risks to peace and security posed by these especially destructive weapons as one of its major tasks.

Traditionally, the major debates on WMD have focused on three dominant issues: First, how best to prevent destabilizing arms races and the use of such weapons? Is it through disarmament, arms control (including nonproliferation regimes), prohibitions on use, or deterrence? The second issue concerns which states contribute most to the dangers posed by these weapons: Is it the existing nuclear powers or future nuclear powers? The third issue concerns the type of inspection and monitoring regimes necessary to enforce any agreements: How can acceptable monitoring schemes be developed in the face of dual-use technologies?

Once very much an East-West issue, with the end of the Cold War debates over WMD became predominantly North-South issues. The central problem is how to balance the legitimate demands of developing countries for access to advanced technologies with the legitimate interests of the international community in controlling the spread of these weapons. On a more fundamental level, the WMD issue is also tied into debates over status and identity in the international community. Who has access to the identity of "responsible state" and, as such, can possess nuclear weapons, for example? To put it more bluntly, what right does the United States (and by extension the other "responsible" nuclear powers) have to possess nuclear weapons while other countries do not?

The latter issue has been raised in particularly acute fashion in recent years by the highly unilateralist policies of the Bush administration in the United States. U.S. leaders appeared to pursue new roles for nuclear weapons in counterproliferation strategies and the fight against terrorism, while expressing active disdain for the UN and international treaties and advocating a new doctrine of preemptive use of military force to prevent acquisition of WMD by others. Since these views are not widely shared by the rest of the world, debates over how to manage the problem of WMD have, in recent years, taken the somewhat startling form of the United States versus most of the rest of the world.

These debates reflect two different views of the nature of the global security problem. The first, expressed by the Bush administration, is that with the end of the superpower conflict, the world confronts a fundamentally different proliferation problem. Arms control and disarmament agreements negotiated during the Cold War do not work for holdout states (and nonstate actors) who refuse to adopt the norms of the regimes' founders. In this view, security is best achieved by preserving unfettered freedom of action and reliance on self-help and military strength. The second view is that in the wake of the 9/11 attacks, the political will to constrain proliferation has never been stronger, and multilateral cooperation is essential to keep WMD from falling into the wrong hands. The latter view prevails in most member states (although the UN itself favors WMD in the hands of no one). However, the United States has put increasing pressure on the UN in recent years to demonstrate that WMD regimes can be effective in preventing proliferation even in the hard cases involving those it identifies as recalcitrant states, such as Iran, North Korea, and Iraq before the 2003 war. Developing countries, while agreeing, also tend to view the nuclear powers as recalcitrant states.

This chapter briefly reviews the UN's role with respect to nuclear, chemical, and biological weapons. It also examines the important case of "coercive disarmament" against Iraq. It concludes with an evaluation of the UN's contribution to controlling WMD, some of the constraints it faces, and the prospects for its effectiveness in an era of American power.

NUCLEAR WEAPONS

Contemporary debates over nuclear weapons have focused on several highly contentious issues, including implementation of the Nuclear Nonproliferation Treaty (NPT), the nuclear programs of India, Israel, and Pakistan, and the lack of compliance with nonproliferation commitments by Iraq, North Korea, and Iran. The NPT, opened for signature on July 1, 1968, is the centerpiece of efforts to control the spread of nuclear weapons. It divides the world into two groups of states: those who possessed nuclear weapons at the time the treaty was negotiated and those who did not. Its immediate objective is to halt the spread of nuclear weapons to new states while promoting the peaceful uses of nuclear energy, but its ultimate objective is complete nuclear disarmament.

A total of 187 countries have joined the treaty. India and Pakistan, which conducted nuclear weapons tests in May 1998, both refused to join the regime. Cuba joined in fall 2002, leaving only India, Pakistan, and Israel outside the regime. North Korea's announcement in January 2003 that it would withdraw was the first time a signatory would pull out of a pact that aims for total nuclear disarmament.

The core of the NPT is a complex "bargain" in which the nonnuclear states agreed to forgo nuclear weapons in exchange for the Article VI commitment by the declared nuclear powers (the United States, Britain, Russia, France, and China) to pursue total nuclear disarmament. This bargain is crucial to the legitimacy of this highly asymmetric treaty. Even if the actual achievement of nuclear disarmament remains far in the future, it is of crucial symbolic importance for the nonnuclear states—and hence for the long-term stability and effectiveness of the treaty—that the nuclear powers show evidence of pursuing disarmament in good faith. The nuclear powers and their allies have thus long faced demands from an antinuclear weapons coalition of nonaligned states, a global grassroots antinuclear movement, and the UN to engage in nuclear disarmament.

Developments in recent years have cast severe doubt on the nuclear powers' commitment to disarmament. In particular, U.S. policies appear to be re-legitimizing the use of nuclear weapons. U.S. counterproliferation strategies call for new roles and missions for nuclear weapons, creating needs for new types of "bunker-busting" warheads. In the early 1990s the Pentagon drew up targeting plans for "rogue states." By 1996 this had been extended to "non-state actors," making terrorists legitimate targets for nuclear weapons. The U.S. Nuclear Posture Review—leaked in March 2002—stated that the United States would feel free to use nuclear weapons to prevent use of chemical and biological weapons by other states, naming Syria, North Korea, Iraq, Iran, and others as possible targets.[2]

Debates in the UN on nuclear weapons and disarmament in recent years have thus reflected deep, if sometimes muted, dissatisfaction on the part of a large majority of states. Many of the "thirteen steps" toward nuclear disarmament agreed to at the 2000 NPT review conference—viewed by many states as important indicators of the nuclear powers' commitment to nuclear disarmament—have either been abandoned or postponed indefinitely. Those abandoned include the 1972 Antiballistic Missile (ABM) Treaty and the US-Russian Strategic Arms Reduction Treaty (START II), while those postponed indefinitely include the entry into force of the UN-facilitated 1996 Comprehensive Test Ban Treaty (CTBT).[3]

In the wake of 9/11, nonnuclear states' ongoing demands for disarmament have been pitted against the nuclear powers' heightened concern with the spread of weapons to so-called rogue states. Many nonnuclear countries worry that concern with terrorist threats of WMD are subsuming broader questions of disarmament and even overriding them with a narrow focus on terrorist issues. Thus at an April 2002 meeting of NPT member states, the United States predictably placed heavy emphasis on keeping nuclear weapons and materials out of the hands of terrorists and on compliance issues, citing violations of nonproliferation agreements by Iraq and North Korea, while fending off disarmament issues. The latter included a call by the New Agenda Coalition—a group of seven nonnuclear states (Brazil, Egypt, Ireland, Mexico, New Zealand, South Africa, and Sweden)—for the nuclear-weapon states to provide legally binding security assurances and make no-first-use commitments.[4]

Arms control, for the time being, thus appears to have trumped disarmament, although the nonnuclear states' determination to reassert the importance of disarmament remains strong. Still, the voting coalitions in the First Committee of the General Assembly, which deals with disarmament, often do not break down neatly. A decade after the end of the Cold War, former Soviet bloc states often ally with the United States in votes. The United States has a long record of either abstaining or voting against resolutions, especially on nuclear issues. The First Committee is often regarded as an ineffective talk shop, debating and approving more than fifty resolutions each year. Nevertheless, it is one of the few public international forums that legitimizes the idea of nuclear disarmament.

The non-nuclear states tolerated the inequity of the NPT during the special circumstances of the Cold War. But they have become increasingly impatient as the nuclear powers show little willingness to give up their nuclear arsenals. Thus in August 1996, India, a longtime and outspoken advocate of nuclear disarmament, sought to block approval of the CTBT, objecting to the fact that the treaty did not include provisions prescribing a "time-bound framework" for the global elimination of nuclear weapons. India's veto was eventually circumvented only by moving the debate from the Conference on Disarmament to the General Assembly, where decisions are made by majority rather than consensus.[5] India went on to test nuclear weapons two years later (quickly followed by Pakistan), suggesting that a likely effect of the nuclear powers' continued reliance on nuclear deterrence is to sustain the interest of others in acquiring such weapons.[6]

Most states of the world are not on the verge of tossing out the NPT or pursuing a nuclear capability because they view the UN nonproliferation regime, despite its shortcomings, as serving their security interests. It is with respect to those states wavering on the margins of the regime—the North Koreas and Iraqs—that the signals by the nuclear powers about the usefulness and prestige of nuclear weapons are likely to make the most difference. If such states were to succeed in acquiring nuclear weapons, neighboring states might reconsider their nonnuclear status, and the nonproliferation regime could unravel, region by region.

CHEMICAL WEAPONS

Contemporary debates over chemical weapons focus primarily on the implementation and enforcement of the 1993 Chemical Weapons Convention

(CWC), a treaty negotiated in the UN's Conference on Disarmament. This treaty, which settled fundamental debates over whether states may possess these weapons, is significant testimony to the pivotal role of the UN in developing the chemical weapons (CW) prohibition. Still, although 152 states had ratified the convention by June 2003 (with 25 signatories yet to ratify), a group of mostly Middle Eastern hold-out states maintained that they would not agree to eliminate CW until other states eliminated their nuclear weapons.[7] The continued possession of nuclear weapons by others is a double standard they find unacceptable.

The remaining debates center on how best to monitor vigorously the presence and destruction of chemical weapons and their facilities while still protecting proprietary commercial knowledge of legitimate chemical industry activities. The dual-use nature of many pharmaceuticals makes this a difficult task. Major chemical exporters, generally developed nations, want to protect their commercial secrets while developing nations do not want their industrial development unnecessarily restricted by export controls on needed chemicals. The CWC has set up an elaborate system of controls and verification that seeks to balance these interests. Nevertheless, the implementation of the treaty got off to a shaky start, in part because the United States, after vigorously championing the adoption of the treaty, has been only lukewarm in implementing it.

The implementation of the convention has been plagued by controversies over the operation and financing of the Organization for the Prohibition of Chemical Weapons (OPCW), the official agency set up by the members of the treaty and charged with inspecting and verifying compliance with the convention. It is formally independent of the UN but cooperates with it. The United States delayed the implementing legislation until 1999, nearly three years behind schedule. This put it in violation of the treaty, since inspections of U.S. industry under the treaty could not begin until industries had made their declarations. When the U.S. Congress finally passed the legislation, it contained exemptions that opened loopholes for circumventing the intent of the treaty and severely weakened the CWC's verification regime. The exemptions included provisions to block challenge inspections on security grounds and prevent samples from being analyzed in other countries. These provisions created loopholes for other nations to shield activities banned by the treaty, leaving the United States in a poor position to demand strict compliance by other states with the CW regime.[8]

In addition, in initial inspections of U.S. facilities, the United States set a poor example of cooperation with inspectors. As for financing, states were behind in reimbursing OPCW for the costs of the verification process.[9] Late payments from the four states that possess chemical weapons—the United States, Russia, India, and South Korea—were a major strain on the budget. Due to financial crisis, OPCW was forced to scale back its verification activities. Only 200 of the 293 inspections planned for 2001 took place. In 2002 OPCW carried out 55 percent of planned visits.[10]

The irony was that with or without the CWC, the United States was already destroying its chemical weapons in accordance with a law passed by Congress in November 1985. The poor U.S. track record regarding CWC implementation also contrasted sharply with U.S. officials' vigorous proclamation of the CW threat and support for the free and unfettered access of weapons inspectors in Iraq. In short, the most ambitious, and to date successful, disarmament treaty in history has nevertheless had to wrestle with the dilemmas of the dissatisfaction of some WMD "have-nots" and the Bush administration's retreat from multilateralism.

BIOLOGICAL WEAPONS

Things were even grimmer in the area of biological weapons. Debates over biological weapons in recent years have focused primarily on whether and how to strengthen the 1972 Biological and Toxins Weapons Convention (BTWC) by giving it a verification system. This has involved questions about the relative utility of national versus international mechanisms for preventing proliferation, including whether international verification of germ weapon activity is even feasible and about whether new treaty mechanisms are needed.

The United States and the Soviet Union led the initial 1972 ban, which 146 nations had joined by March 2003 (with 18 signatories yet to ratify). The treaty, which bans the possession, development, and stockpiling of biological weapons, was agreed to without verification measures since at the time it was negotiated most governments considered use of such weapons impractical.[11] Since then violations of the convention by Russia, persistent allegations regarding Iraq's biological weapon activities, and a doubling of the number of states suspected of pursuing a biological weapons capability led most BWC members to the view that the treaty needed more teeth.[12] In recent years, European countries along with nongovernmental organizations (NGOs) have led the attempt to strengthen it, while U.S. support has been inconsistent and U.S. biotechnology companies have felt little governmental pressure to support the treaty efforts.

In 1994 member states established an Ad Hoc Group to draft a binding verification system for the convention. Debate focused on balancing intrusiveness with respect for sovereignty as well as the transfer of resources and assistance from rich countries to poor. During negotiations, the countries most interested in biological-genetic research (the United States, Japan, Germany) favored strong export control, strong protection for proprietary commercial and defense information, and nonintrusive verification visits. Governments of developing countries, in contrast, favored relaxation of export controls, generous conditions for sharing new drugs, and tougher inspections.

Although the United States was initially an active participant in the Ad Hoc Group, the Bush administration largely undercut the group's efforts. In July 2001 the United States angered Europe and much of the world by rejecting the draft protocol on enforcement mechanisms, primarily out of concern for U.S. biotechnology commercial interests. It also withdrew from the Ad Hoc Group, while at the same time stating that the delegation would remain at the negotiations in order to prevent agreement on a protocol without the United States, as had just happened at the Kyoto negotiations on global warming.[13]

At the review conference of the treaty in November–December 2001, the United States again opposed the protocol on verification and caused an uproar when it proposed disbanding the Ad Hoc Group. Most other BWC parties, including many U.S. allies, felt it was crucial to continue the talks. The review conference had to be adjourned, with no action taken, until November 2002 to prevent a breakdown.[14] In September 2002 U.S. Undersecretary of State John Bolton once again shocked allies by informing them that the United States opposed holding any multilateral meetings of BWC members whatsoever between the 2002 and 2006 review conferences. When the postponed second half of the review conference reconvened in November 2002, the United States again blocked discussion of any new treaty mechanisms. The conference saved face only by agreeing to a watered-down proposal that was eviscerated of most substantive achievements.[15]

Some pharmaceutical industry experts agreed with the U.S. decision to reject the draft protocol to the BWC but nevertheless criticized U.S. alternative proposals. In a report they expressed genuine puzzlement "that their government would advance such tepid proposals after the bioterrorist attacks of 2001 and in view of the continuing efforts of national and sub-national actors to acquire biowarfare capabilities."[16] The group called for the establishment of international standards, such as a criminalization treaty (proposed by Britain in June 2002).

U.S. officials continued to state their strong support of the BWC convention, while at the same time rejecting any means for demonstrating U.S. compliance with it. Once again, it was difficult not to notice the contradictions between U.S. officials' rhetoric about the BW threat, especially with regard to Iraq, and the weak steps the administration was taking to do something about it. As observers noted, if the narrow agenda of the BWC negotiations was not broadened, the Bush administration's argument that multilateral approaches are ineffective would become a self-fulfilling prophecy.[17]

COERCIVE DISARMAMENT: THE CASE OF IRAQ

The Security Council's efforts starting in 1991 to disarm Iraq using intrusive weapons inspections and sanctions represent the United Nations' most coercive attempts at disarmament. The Iraq case has prompted contentious debates over whether weapons inspections and sanctions can be successful disarmament tools as well as the appropriate role of military force in disarmament. If war proves to be necessary to control WMD, that will be a heavy blow to the strength and effectiveness of nonproliferation regimes. Although use of force in one or two cases might be necessary and could have a deterrent effect on other countries, it is unlikely that the international community, and especially the United States, will go to war with country after country to enforce disarmament.

Putting the Squeeze on Iraq

Following the Gulf War, Iraq was required under Security Council Resolution 687 (1991) to declare its WMD programs and facilities. Iraq initially denied that it had conducted any nuclear activities outside of those already under International Atomic Energy Agency (IAEA) safeguards and asserted that all its nuclear activities were in compliance with the NPT, of which it is a signatory. Inspections by UNSCOM, the commission mandated to carry out inspections, however, revealed a massive, covert nuclear weapons program, a more extensive ballistic missile system than had been previously known, and a large chemical weapons program. Subsequent discovery of Iraq's biological weapons program was one of the commission's greatest successes. Despite Iraq's long denial of the existence of this program, after the August 1995 defection of Hussein Kamel, who directed Iraq's WMD programs, Iraq acknowledged for the first time that it had produced biological weapons. UNSCOM oversaw the destruction of all declared CW munitions, manufacturing equipment, and facilities as well as Iraq's key biological weapons production facility and equipment, along with some 22 ton of growth media for BW.[18] Many experts argued that sustained inspections were far more effective in getting rid of hidden WMD than military might. The use of force destroyed only 15 to 25 percent of Iraq's WMD potential during the 1991 war,[19] whereas UN inspections eliminated "the bulk of Iraq's proscribed weapons programmes," although some suspected weapons remained unaccounted for.[20]

Putting the Squeeze on UNSCOM

Despite these seeming successes, UNSCOM had a difficult life and met a premature death. Iraqi concealment policies, coordinated by high-ranking officials and involving a number of Iraqi intelligence and security organizations, made UNSCOM's work extremely difficult. UNSCOM's effectiveness was also undermined by disagreement among the five permanent members of the Security Council over how vigorously to enforce the inspections regime and the continuation of sanctions. While the United States and Britain advocated strict enforcement, Russia, France, and China, motivated by bribery, economic interests, and concerns about sovereignty, were more sympathetic to Iraqi arguments about lifting the sanctions.

The most critical issue regarding UNSCOM, however, was the debate over the "politicization" of the inspectorate. Iraq charged that the United States was using UNSCOM as a vehicle for gathering intelligence on Iraq. After continuing tensions over the inspections, on August 5, 1998, Iraq banned

UNSCOM and IAEA weapons inspections, and on October 31 banned monitoring activities, resulting in the "Operation Desert Fox" airstrikes by the United States and Britain on December 16–19, which marked the end of UNSCOM's mission.

As it turned out, Iraq's accusations had been correct. Former UNSCOM inspector Scott Ritter admitted that the CIA had worked closely with UNSCOM as early as 1992, though the United States only passed on some of its information to UNSCOM; moreover, the United States had used inspections to gather data that eventually aided in targeting the "Desert Fox" airstrikes—a campaign with no Security Council authorization.[21]

Thus, as Susan Wright has argued, UNSCOM was hijacked by two games of deception—one played by Iraq and the other played by the United States. The use of UNSCOM's work to justify, without the support of the UN Security Council—and possibly to assist—the bombing of Iraq by the United States and Britain, discredited an international arms control system, compromised its effectiveness, and undermined trust in international cooperation.[22] UNSCOM had moved beyond simply being an assessor of intelligence to getting actively involved in the collection of intelligence using techniques and methods normally associated with national governments. These problems raised new debates over how a multilateral monitoring organization can function autonomously without its own intelligence-gathering capacity or whether the use of intelligence from governments inevitably compromises an international organization.

Iraq II: UNMOVIC 2002—The Problem of Proving a Negative

After a three-year hiatus UN weapons inspectors would return to Iraq in November 2002. In his January 2002 State of the Union address, President George W. Bush had labeled Iraq a member of an "axis of evil" along with North Korea and Iran. In subsequent months top U.S. officials repeatedly emphasized the dangers posed by Iraq, questioned the worth of arms inspections, and advocated the overthrow of Saddam Hussein as the only way to guarantee that Iraq would not develop WMD. On September 12, amid increasing speculation that the United States was preparing to invade Iraq to oust Saddam Hussein, President Bush delivered a speech to the UN calling on the organization to enforce its resolutions for disarming Iraq. Bush strongly implied that if the UN did not act, the United States would.[23]

Four days after Bush's speech Baghdad announced that it would allow arms inspectors to return "without conditions." The Bush administration continued to press the Security Council to approve a new toughly worded UN resolution labeling Iraq in "material breach" of its obligations, calling for Iraq to give weapons inspectors unfettered access, and authorizing the use of force if Iraq did not comply. Other countries, however, remained skeptical that the United States had provided any new information on Iraq's WMD that justified going to war. Russia and France in particular opposed any resolution that seemed to imply an automatic use of force. In late September the Bush administration seemed to signal a shift in its goals from "regime change" to changing Saddam's behavior on disarmament. In an October 20 interview Secretary of State Colin Powell stated, "If Saddam disarmed entirely and satisfied the international community, that would be a change in attitude, a change in the way the regime is looking at its situation in the world. . . . All we are interested in is getting rid of those weapons of mass destruction."[24]

But U.S. talk of war against Iraq continued to heat up, and on November 8, after eight weeks of contentious negotiations, France and the United States reached a compromise. The Security Council unanimously adopted Resolution 1441, requiring Iraq to provide "a currently accurate, full and complete declaration" of any weapons of mass destruction.[25] The resolution also authorized an unprecedented level of intrusiveness in inspections. Although many in the Bush administration clearly remained skeptical of the utility of inspections, the vote indicated widespread support in the international community for a multilateral process and for giving the inspections a chance to work. Resolution 1441 papered over significant disagreements, however, as most Security Council members, led by France, insisted that it must be followed by a second resolution authorizing war if Iraq refused to disarm. U.S. leaders, in contrast, held that the resolution provided a sufficient basis for military action if Iraq did not comply.

In setting up the new team of inspectors, UN chief inspector Hans Blix took significant steps to avoid any repetition of the spying that had plagued UNSCOM. Personnel from 44 countries amounted to a threefold increase in the pool of countries that made up UNSCOM, which had been heavily dependent on the United States. A crucial difference from UNSCOM was that all UNMOVIC staff were paid by the UN. One of the flaws in UNSCOM was that staff were mainly provided by governments who not only seconded their own people but paid them. They were open to the charge that their first loyalty was to their countries rather than to the UN.[26]

Iraq's 12,000-page declaration to the UN on its WMD on December 7 once again fell far short of the disclosure the UN required, and on December 19 Blix told the Council that the report was flawed and contained little new information. The United States declared Baghdad to be in "material breach" of its requirements because of the omissions, a phrase Washington could use to justify a war against Iraq. However, neither Blix nor any of the other Security Council members, including staunch ally Britain, supported that assessment. Multilateralism through the UN appeared to have forced the United States to back down, or at least hold off for the time being, as the Bush administration apparently considered and then rejected, forcing a confrontation with the UN over the use of force at that time.[27] Blix and other inspectors complained that the United States and Britain had failed to provide the inspection teams with intelligence to help them know where to look.

The Bush administration's arguments for military action against Iraq became more problematic when, in December 2002, North Korea suddenly emerged as a greater nuclear threat than Iraq. North Korea's announcement that it would restart its nuclear weapons production facilities created a new crisis for the international community and called into question the Bush administration's approach to Iraq. On December 20 North Korea kicked out IAEA inspectors while flouting international demands that it abandon its program for enriching uranium. In a stunning move, on January 10, 2003 North Korea announced that it would withdraw from the NPT. The Bush administration made clear that it would respond with diplomatic pressure rather than military force.[28]

The irony of the differing approaches to Iraq and North Korea was not lost on observers. Even though Iraq had resumed unfettered inspections, it was on the verge of being attacked militarily; North Korea had kicked out inspectors and was by its own admission pursuing nuclear weapons, yet would be subject only to diplomatic pressure. IAEA officials worried that inconsistent approaches to dealing with noncompliance with global nonproliferation norms would weaken the authority and integrity of international verification organizations and nonproliferation treaties.

By late January diplomacy was at an impasse as the United States sought to end inspections while France signaled it would veto a second Security Council resolution. A much-anticipated presentation by Powell to the Council on February 5 of U.S. intelligence information on Iraq's WMD failed to sway skeptical member states of the immediate need for war. As a U.S.-imposed March deadline for Iraqi compliance loomed, the United States and United Kingdom had committed votes for a second resolution only from Spain and Bulgaria, well short of the nine needed to pass a resolution. Without the votes, the Bush administration abandoned the UN effort. On March 17 Bush issued an ultimatum giving Saddam Hussein 48 hours to leave the country or war would begin.[29] As antiwar protests mounted in the United States and around the world, on March 19, U.S. forces began air strikes against government targets in Baghdad, and U.S. troops began moving into Iraq without UN authorization.

WHAT DIFFERENCE DID THE UN MAKE?

In less than a month the Iraqi regime was destroyed. However, the war's long-term consequences for disarmament and collective security through the UN remained to be seen. The angry debate over the legality of the U.S.-led war laid bare competing visions of the purpose of the Security Council—whether it is just to pass judgment on the use of force or rather to organize its collective use.[30] Many member states and others charged privately that U.S. leaders never intended anything but war, and that going to war without UN authorization gravely damaged the UN and international law. Further, after five months of searching WMD had yet to be found, casting severe doubts on the U.S.–U.K. portrayal of an imminent Iraqi threat. U.S. leaders' pleas for more time to find the WMD ironically echoed identical requests from UN inspectors only months earlier. Others charged that those who for years sought to weaken the sanctions and inspections efforts in Iraq—notably France, Russia, and China—and thereby eroded the Security Council's credibility, set the stage for the use of force.[31]

What difference did the UN make in the Iraq case? First, and perhaps iron-ically, it may have helped provide a reason for the Bush administration to go to war. In summer 2002 Bush administration hawks who had been dreaming since the early 1990s of a war to oust Saddam Hussein were casting about for a *causus belli*.[32] Enforcing UN disarmament resolutions on Iraq provided such a reason. The Bush administration's initial efforts to justify the war as "regime change" or "fighting terrorism" failed, and thus Bush ultimately had to turn to enforcement of UN resolutions as a way of framing his policy. Additionally, the Bush administration did attempt to gain a second Security Council resolution authorizing the use of force, even while reiterating its view that this was not legally required. Thus, while Bush may have sought to chal-lenge the very legitimacy of the UN (be relevant or die), UN mechanisms in fact provided him with a crucial lever to try to rally support for a war against Iraq. UK leader Tony Blair, however, was the only major leader to join Bush in committing a substantial military force to this end.

Second, this strategy of going to the UN provided avenues for other states to try to modify U.S. policy and empowered other actors to have an impor-tant say in the course of events. The latter included Blix and IAEA inspector Mohammed ElBaradei as well as UN Secretary-General Kofi Annan, who helped Iraq draft the letter that admitted inspectors. Finally, during the time that it operated UNMOVIC destroyed 72 Iraqi al-Samoud 2 missiles, whose range exceeded Security Council limits of 150 kilometers.[33]

Many observers argued that had U.S. diplomacy been less heavy-handed, including before September 11, the United States might have achieved Security Council support for a second resolution.[34] International anger over the Bush administration's opposition to the Kyoto global warming agree-ment, the International Criminal Court, and other mechanisms of interna-tional law appeared to have reduced the willingness of other nations to go along with the United States. U.S. mixed messages about its goals in Iraq—was it disarmament or regime change?—undercut the claim that the United States, too, wanted to avoid a war. Scant evidence of Saddam's WMD, along with revelations that U.S. and U.K. intelligence drew on forged documents and student papers, failed to convince most nations that Saddam posed an imminent threat.

It seems likely that U.S. policy on Iraq was dictated more by U.S. military timetables than by UN diplomatic constraints. The Bush administration may not have intended to go to war before spring 2003 anyway, so there was no harm in trying the UN first. Little evidence exists that either Bush or advi-sors other than Colin Powell were concerned about going it alone, either for reasons of having allies to pay the bills as in the 1990–1991 Gulf War or of domestic opinion.[35]

The Iraq case raises two larger issues for the future of coercive disarmament and collective security. The first is the role of force in making collective security work, that is, whether military preparations and diplomacy are mutually supportive or incompatible strategies. In the U.S. view it was only the threat of military force that enabled UN inspectors to return in the first place, and thus only military force could make the Security Council resolutions on Iraq work. The opposing view was that the military buildup—a buildup that some U.S. officials later argued could not be reversed without the U.S. losing face—undercut the process of trying to avert a war through inspections and diplomacy. It is significant that Chief inspector Blix testified that the U.S. military build up did help foster Iraqi cooperation with the inspections.[36]

The second issue is what constitutes success in an inspections process. U.S. leaders were expecting that either the UN inspectors would be rebuffed by Iraq or that they would find WMD, thereby justifying war. In contrast, others found the inspections evidence that, while Iraq was far from fully cooperative, the process itself was working and Iraq was effectively contained. These differing definitions of success contributed to a major clash of purposes at the UN and ultimately to the failure of diplomacy. Whereas the United States saw resolution 1441 as a way of rallying the world around its charge that Saddam Hussein was defying the inspections and demands to disarm, France and others saw it as a way of pressing the inspections forward as long as they were containing Iraq. After five months of scouring Iraq for WMD, with no success, the U.S. Iraq Survey Group concluded in an October 2003 report that the 1991 Iraq war, combined with UN inspections and sanctions, had effectively prevented Iraq from reconstituting its nuclear and chemical weapons programs, thus directly refuting Bush administration charges before the war that UN sanctions were not working.

The dilemma for the Security Council remains balancing how far it can go in accommodating the United States without being seen as a mere tool of U.S. hegemony with how far it can go in opposing the United States without condemning itself to irrelevance.[37]

ACCOMPLISHMENTS AND CONSTRAINTS

In its efforts to control WMD the UN has played a number of roles. As a negotiating forum, the UN serves at times mainly as an arena for the expression of the will of the member states or as a facilitator helping to coordinate states' positions, as in the case of treaty negotiations. At other times it acts as an agent in its own right, as seen in the actions of UNSCOM, chief weapons inspector Blix, or the chemical weapons monitoring agency. Finally, as an institutional and normative structure, it consists of the set of rules and norms embodied in UN disarmament treaties and resolutions that delegitimize weapons of mass destruction and set out standards of behavior for states.

It is in this latter area—norm creation—that the UN has made its clearest contribution to the control of WMD. It has assisted the negotiation of the major multilateral arms control and disarmament treaties, which provide the dominant framework for reducing the threat posed by WMD. Most importantly, it has helped to create a widespread normative opprobrium against WMD. The UN has carved out a niche for itself, especially in delegitimizing use of these weapons and banning their possession and testing. The strongest norm is against their use rather than against their possession, although the UN has developed a stronger legal framework regarding the latter. The NPT, for example, has prohibited the possession of nuclear weapons by most states of the world (horizontal proliferation), and the normative opprobrium against the spread of such weapons has been quite effective. It is extremely rare to see a state seeking to acquire such weapons—the overwhelming majority of the world community has rejected them.

The UN has also served as a continuing source of pressure for disarmament. Once the nonaligned states had a voting majority in the General Assembly starting in the early 1960s, the Assembly began to pass resolutions calling for a ban on the use of nuclear weapons and equating such use with crimes against humanity. The UN Department of Disarmament Affairs (DDA)—the hub of the Secretariat's efforts on disarmament—and the UN Institute for Disarmament Research (UNIDIR), based in Geneva, conduct a significant public education effort on disarmament. The DDA also works with the permanent missions in all the UN's disarmament-related meetings and facilitates the review conferences for key multilateral treaties such as the NPT. The numerous speeches and reports of both the Under Secretary-General for Disarmament Affairs and the UN Secretary-General on disarmament issues play an important role in calling attention to the need for norm development in various areas. The UN Disarmament Commission, a subsidiary of the General Assembly established in 1952, deliberates and makes recommendations to the GA, but has become a relatively marginal body.

The 1996 advisory opinion of the International Court of Justice on the legality of nuclear weapons marked the most significant UN intervention on the issues of use and disarmament. The court found that the use or threat of nuclear weapons is "generally" unlawful but said it could not "definitively" conclude whether it would be unlawful in the extreme circumstances of self-defense if the survival of the state were at stake.[38] Despite this uncertainty, the court's unanimous statement that the nuclear powers have an obligation to pursue nuclear disarmament was an important contribution to the normative architecture of disarmament and yet another step in the "agenda politics" of nuclear delegitimization. Overall, the UN's 57-year effort to delegitimize nuclear weapons and its continuing pressure for disarmament have contributed to making it impossible to think of nuclear weapons as "just another weapon."

While the UN can thus point to significant accomplishments in efforts to control WMD, it can also point to important failures. The UN has been largely unable to influence vertical proliferation (the acquisition of increasing numbers or types of nuclear weapons by the declared nuclear powers). The CTBT might do this if and when it enters into force. Further, with the major exception of the case of Iraq, one of the central aspirations of the UN— nuclear disarmament—has remained frustratingly elusive. The negotiations on disarmament that have taken place under UN auspices since the 1950s have been far more effective in contributing to the normative opprobrium than in reducing the numbers of nuclear weapons. Nonetheless, in the UN-negotiated bans on chemical and biological weapons, states agreed to disarm with respect to whole classes of weapons.

Further, the normative opprobrium against nuclear weapons is not yet total or universal. Existing stocks remain (there are still 30,000 nuclear weapons in the world today), and alliances such as NATO continue to tout the great value of such weapons as the basis for security. Recently the U.S. government has been implying that the very goal of nuclear disarmament might not even apply to the United States. The grave danger here is that continued possession of nuclear weapons by the declared nuclear states will in time erode the current global opprobrium against proliferation—as may be happening already, given the weak international responses to nuclear weapons developments in India, Pakistan, and North Korea. Greater attention to those states that continue to possess nuclear weapons may well be the real key to the effectiveness of future international disarmament. Additionally, since the five declared nuclear powers are also the five permanent members of the Security Council, putting a nonnuclear state (such as Germany or Japan) on the Security Council would help sever the link between nuclear weapons and great power status. However, the prospects of this happening any time soon look dim.

Finally, adding to the UN's problems, the body supposed to be dealing with WMD issues, the Conference on Disarmament (CD), has become moribund. The CD is the Geneva-based multilateral negotiating forum for disarmament and arms control issues. In principle the CD, which reports to the General Assembly, should be the most effective of the UN disarmament bodies and has some important treaties to its credit—the 1993 chemical weapons ban and the 1996 CTBT. Its precursor negotiated the 1968 NPT and the 1972 ban on biological weapons. The continuing scandal is that the CD has had no program of work for the last four years. During this period it has hardly been able to conduct discussions—let alone negotiations—on anything at all because of a deadlock between the United States and China over whether the CD should negotiate over the prevention of an arms race in outer space and also over a ban on the production of fissile materials. One problem is that the CD's consensus decision-making process gives a veto to any of the 66 members, which sovereignty-minded authoritarian countries have been loath to give up. But the real problem is the political agendas of a handful of key states. Unfortunately, a resolution of the CD's troubles is unlikely unless a crisis or overwhelming international demand propels negotiations.[39]

CONCLUSION: PROSPECTS FOR THE FUTURE

These problems raise the question of why the international community should continue dealing with the UN on WMD. Why not move outside the UN as the international community did in the Ottawa conference to ban landmines? This may, in fact, be a necessary strategy on occasion to sidestep states and procedures that obstruct progress. Still, the UN's long experience in dealing with the issue of WMD, both as a negotiating forum and as a source of technical expertise, make it an important resource. Making the UN more effective may require challenging the issue of consensus decision-making in the CD and elsewhere so that obstructionist states cannot block progress favored by large majorities.

The critical issue is how the UN will deal with U.S. power. The Bush administration posed a test of relevance for the UN, but the actual test is different than the one he posed. The real question is whether the UN can remain an arena for negotiated bargains over WMD or whether it will become—like the former Warsaw Pact—simply a handmaiden for the hegemon. The UN will need to find a way to deal constructively with the reality of U.S. hegemony without making itself irrelevant by simply succumbing to it. This may require a willingness at times to proceed without the United States.

"Muddling through," rather than strengthening current nonproliferation regimes, will likely result in a breakdown of current regimes (for example, a nuclear arms race in East Asia, the spread of WMD to terrorists, weapons in space) or in a failure to adequately control a future catastrophic risk posed by the development and spread of biological pathogens. Efforts to strengthen the nonproliferation regime will need to take account of the fact that the technological know-how for building nuclear weapons may now exist collectively among potential proliferators. That is, countries such as North Korea, Pakistan, and Iran can trade nuclear weapons technology and know-how among each other. This renders traditional style export-control regimes, such as the non-UN Nuclear Suppliers Group, which focuses on control of exports from established nuclear states, less effective. The UN could play an important role in any elaborated export control regime aimed at centralizing the somewhat disparate existing export regimes and at enshrining a new set of norms, with associated carrots and sticks, to deal with this problem.

Finally, and perhaps most importantly, the UN will need to delegitimize nuclear weapons for *all* states. The current asymmetrical system—where some countries are allowed to possess nuclear weapons while others are not—is probably unstable and unsustainable over the long haul. This bone in the throat of much of the world may well obstruct greater progress in reducing the risks of *all* weapons of mass destruction.

NOTES

* I would like to thank David Malone, Randy Rydell, and the editors of and participants in this project for helpful comments on earlier versions of this chapter.

1. United Nations General Assembly Resolution 1(1) (January 24, 1946).

2. Excerpts from the Nuclear Posture Review are available at www. globalsecurity.org.

3. Rebecca Johnson, "NPT Report: The 2002 Prepcom: Papering Over the Cracks?" *Disarmament Diplomacy* 64 (May–June 2002).

4. NPT/Conf.2005/P.C.1/WP.1.

5. The GA adopted it on September 10, 1996 by a vote of 158 to 3 (the negative votes were from India, Bhutan, and Libya). In total, 166 nations (including the five nuclear weapons states and Israel) had signed the CTBT, and 98 had ratified it by April 2003.

6. See George Perkovich, *India's Nuclear Bomb: Impact on Global Proliferation* (Berkeley: University of California Press, 1999).

7. Egypt, Iraq, Libya, Syria, and Lebanon have neither signed nor ratified the CWC. Israel has signed but not ratified.

8. Amy E. Smithson, *Rudderless: The Chemical Weapons Convention at $1\frac{1}{2}$*. Report No. 25 (Henry E. Stimson Center, September 1998), 66, at www.stimson.org/cbw.

9. Fiona Tregonning, "CWC Report: Emerging from a Trial By Fire?," *Disarmament Diplomacy* 67 (October–November 2002): 4.

10. Ibid., 5.

11. Jonathan Tucker, "Farewell to Germs: The U.S. Renunciation of Biological and Toxin Warfare, 1969–1970," *International Security* 27(1) (Summer 2002): 107–148.

12. Joseph Cirincione et al., *Deadly Arsenals: Tracking Weapons of Mass Destruction* (Washington, D.C.: Carnegie Endowment for International Peace, 2002), 31.

13. Barbara Hatch Rosenberg, "FAS Comments on U.S. Rejection of the Biological Weapons Protocol," comments at NGO Seminar for Ad Hoc Group (July 25, 2001), at www.fas.org/bwc/papers.htm.

14. "U.S. Reportedly Seeks Shutdown of BWC Debate," *Disarmament Diplomacy* 67 (October–November 2002).

15. Fifth Review Conference Final Report, BWC/Conf.V/17 (November 2002) at http://disarmament.un.org/wmd/bwc/pdf/bwccnfv17.PDF. Marie Chevrier, "Waiting for Godot or Saving the Show? The BWC Conference Reaches Modest Agreement," *Disarmament Diplomacy* 68 (December 2002–January 2003).

16. *Compliance Through Science: U.S. Pharmaceutical Industry Experts on a Strengthened Bioweapons Nonproliferation Regime* Stimson Center Report No. 48 (September 2002), 67.

17. Oliver Meier, "Bare-Bones Multilateralism at the BWC Review Conference," *Arms Control Today* (December 2002), 1.

18. "Iraq: A Chronology of UN Inspections and an Assessment of Their Accomplishments," an *Arms Control Association Special Report* (October 2002), 8, at www.armscontrol.org; and Stephen Black, "The UNSCOM Record," in *Iraq: A New Approach* ed. Jessica Matthews (Washington, D.C.: Carnegie Endowment for International Peace, 2002), at www.ceip.org/files/publications/iraq/mathews.htm.

19. See "Vexing Questions on Iraq's Arsenal," (March 18, 2003), at www.cbsnews.com/stories/2003/03/18/iraq/main544473.shtml.

20. "Iraq: A Chronology," 1.

21. Seymour Hersh, "Saddam's Best Friend: How the CIA Made it A Lot Easier for the Iraqi Leader to Rearm," *New Yorker* (April 5, 1999).

22. Susan Wright, "The Hijacking of UNSCOM," *Bulletin of the Atomic Scientists* (July/August 1999).

23. "President's Remarks at the United Nations General Assembly," (September 12, 2002), at www.whitehouse.gov/news/releases/2002/09/20020912-1.html.

24. Secretary of State Colin Powell on NBC's "Meet the Press," (October 20, 2002), at http://usinfo.state.gov/regional/nea/iraq/text/1020pwlnbc.htm.

25. S/Res/1441 (2002).

26. UNMOVIC, Eleventh Quarterly Report, S/2002/1303, (November 27, 2002), at www.un.org/Depts/unmovic.

27. Steven R. Weisman, "A Long, Winding Road to a Diplomatic Dead End," *New York Times* (March 17, 2003).

28. Seth Mydans, "North Korea Says it is Withdrawing from Nuclear Arms Treaty," *New York Times* (January 10, 2003); and Steven R. Weisman, "North Korea's Nuclear Plan Called 'Unacceptable;' Bush Seeks Diplomatic Solution," *New York Times* (December 14, 2002).

29. "The UN Security Council Has Not Lived Up to Its Responsibilities": President Bush Ultimatum to Iraq, Office of the Press Secretary, (March 17, 2003), at www.acronym.org.uk/docs/0303/doc17.htm.

30. See, for example, Edward C. Luck, "Making the World Safe for Hypocrisy," *New York Times* (March 22, 2003), A11; and Anne-Marie Slaughter, "Good Reasons for Going Around the UN," *New York Times* (March 18, 2003), A33.

31. Luck, "Making the World Safe for Hypocrisy."

32. Evan Thomas, "How We Got Here: The 12 Year Itch," *Newsweek* (March 31, 2003), 54–65.

33. UNMOVIC/ IAEA Press Statement on Inspection Activities in Iraq (March 17, 2003).

34. Glenn Kessler and Mike Allen, "U.S. Missteps Led to Failed Diplomacy," *Washington Post* (March 16, 2003), A15.

35. Nicholas Lemann, "How it Came to War," *The New Yorker* (March 31, 2003).

36. Oral Introduction of 12th Quarterly Report of UNMOVIC, Executive Chairman Dr. Hans Blix, Statement to the Security Council (March 7, 2003), at www.un.org/Depts/unmovic/recent%20items.html.

37. Simon Chesterman and David Malone, "The Fate of the Security Council," *International Herald Tribune* (January 27, 2003).

38. Ved Nanda and David Krieger, *Nuclear Weapons and the World Court* (Ardsley, NY: Transnational Publishers, 1999).

39. Rebecca Johnson, "CD Closes 2002 Still Deadlocked," *Disarmament Diplomacy* 67 (October–November 2002): 9.

CHAPTER 2

FACING THE CHALLENGE OF SMALL ARMS: THE UN AND GLOBAL SECURITY GOVERNANCE

Keith Krause

INTRODUCTION

Is the United Nations an important or marginal actor in international peace and security? The answer to this question depends, of course, on how one understands "security." There is little doubt that the drafters of the UN Charter imagined that the UN would play a central role in regulating, perhaps even reducing, violent conflicts between states—the traditional way of understanding "international security." There is also little doubt that this vision has not been realized. But in a world in which the concept of security has been broadened and deepened to include a wide array of threats to individual and collective well-being, does the UN system play perhaps a greater role than even its framers would have imagined?

Developments of the past decade point paradoxically in different directions. On the one hand, new or renewed instruments of "global security governance" have emerged to cope with an expanded range of global threats and insecurities as detailed in the other chapters of this volume—the ICC, sanctions, embargoes, peace-building, and other interventions. All of these rest upon a broadened understanding of security that includes not just interstate threats of violent conflict, but also regional, societal, and human security concerns. On the other hand, the extremely limited UN role in the American-led invasions of Afghanistan and Iraq underline the near-total irrelevance of the UN in the "high politics" of traditional interstate security relations. The overwhelmingly hegemonic position of the United States has also confirmed those (primarily realists) who believe that international institutions are empowered only insofar as they serve the interests of dominant powers and disregarded when they are an obstacle to the realization of narrow state interests.

The importance accorded to the United Nations in achieving global security thus depends in large part on how one conceptualizes world politics. This chapter focuses on one important case study—the emerging international response to the widespread proliferation and use of small arms and light weapons—to make a larger argument about the role of the UN in global security governance summarized as follows:

- many so-called "global" security challenges are being addressed at multiple levels of governance—from the local to the global—with domestic or locally oriented efforts often being more significant than externally oriented or interstate efforts;
- a narrow focus on the (limited) role of the UN in regulating conflict interactions between states ignores its much more important role at the local or national level in shaping or transforming state interests;
- a broader understanding of security that includes human and societal (or communal) security concerns must acknowledge that the sovereign state remains the primary institution for providing security for people and communities;
- in light of this, most "global" security policies and practices, such as those dealing with issues such as small arms, land mines, communal conflicts, postconflict peace-building, or international terrorism, do not regulate state interactions but reach deeply into the internal sovereignty and governance capacities of states and attempt to reshape the security relationship between states and their citizens; and
- a focus on states as the main actor in world politics is not helpful in understanding domains in which effective forms of influence (especially of individuals, grassroots organizations, transnational NGOs and "political or moral entrepreneurs") are wielded within or parallel to state-centered pathways of power.

The first part of the chapter introduces the issue of small arms, traces the role played by the UN and other actors in framing the issue and setting the international agenda, and analyzes outcomes of the 2001 UN conference on small arms. The second part examines more closely what we mean by "the UN system" in the context of international action to deal with small arms and raises some problems with the traditional hub-and-spoke or top-down conceptualizations. Part three un-bundles the concept of "actor" in this issue area, challenging not only the traditional hierarchy of state versus non-state actors but our more general understanding of how states, international organizations, and non-state actors shape and influence each other's interests and scope for action. Finally, the conclusion sketches a vision of the small arms problem as a "global or transnational public policy" issue.[1]

SMALL ARMS: WHAT PROBLEM? WHOSE SOLUTION?

There are at least 640 million small arms and light weapons in circulation worldwide. Each year they are implicated in several hundred thousand deaths and countless injuries in everything from homicides and suicides to large-scale criminality and warfare. The majority of direct victims in contemporary conflicts, in places such as Sierra Leone, Indonesia, the Democratic Republic of Congo, or Colombia, have been killed by small arms and light weapons, and they have been called the real "weapons of mass destruction" by more than one observer.[2]

There is, however, nothing new in all of this, and small arms have been a "problem" for decades. Yet in the 1990s the issue of small arms rose higher on the international security agenda, one result being that in July 2001 the UN convened a major international conference on "The Illicit Trade in Small Arms and Light Weapons in All its Aspects" (henceforth, UN 2001 conference). This conference, the fruit of more than five years of efforts from within the UN and by a loose coalition of states and nongovernmental actors, resulted in a *Programme of Action to Prevent, Combat, and Eradicate the Illicit Trade in Small Arms and Light Weapons in All Its Aspects.* Efforts to constrain the proliferation and use of small arms and light weapons have thus become framed as a problem on the multilateral peace and security agenda. How and why did this happen?

A purely realist/rationalist explanation could only account for this by identifying a change in the material circumstances faced by states, which is difficult since small arms and light weapons accounted for the overwhelming majority of conflict deaths since 1945 yet remained off the international security agenda until the mid-1990s. One can nevertheless identify three changes that might have increased states' interest in tackling the issue multilaterally:

- the increase in UN and multilateral peace keeping activity increased the dangers to states' forces of small arms proliferation;
- the end of the Cold War released a flood of surplus weapons onto the international market, arguably exacerbating regional conflicts; and
- civilians had increasingly become the new victims of these conflicts with increased costs for humanitarian relief operations and postconflict reconstruction efforts.

There is, however, no strong evidence to support the first two possibilities. In the mid-1990s, we simply did not know whether the magnitude of the problem (however defined) had increased, and whether any of the putative consequences of small arms and light weapons proliferation were real. The third factor was, however, explicitly invoked by UN Secretary-General Boutros Boutros-Ghali in 1995 when he encouraged the international community "to concentrate on what might be called 'micro-disarmament.' . . . practical disarmament in the context of the conflicts the United Nations is actually dealing with and of the weapons, most of them light weapons, that are actually killing people in the hundreds of thousands."[3] There are only two significant antecedents to this agenda-setting act. The first was a concrete postconflict weapons collection effort (started in August 1994) in Mali, spearheaded by Malian President Alpha Oumar Konaré. The second was the emergence of a body of "expert knowledge" (academic and NGO) on small arms beginning around 1993 and sponsored by major national and international NGOs such as the American Academy of Arts and Sciences, the British-American Security

Information Council (BASIC), Human Rights Watch, Pugwash, and the UN Institute for Disarmament Research.[4] Contributors included both arms control scholars and conflict researchers devoted to documenting the role of small arms and light weapons in conflict zones such as Northern Pakistan and Afghanistan, Somalia, Colombia, Rwanda, or Southern Africa.[5]

What must be noted is the total absence in the mid-1990s of efforts by any of the great powers or even middle powers to put the issue on the international security agenda. They either greeted the effort with indifference or attempted to limit the scope of international attention to illicit trafficking and postconflict situations. The initial framing of the problem of small arms and light weapons by the UN Secretary-General thus reflected a certain degree of institutional (or even perhaps individual) autonomy, since a power-centered analysis cannot really explain it.

How did actions within the UN system set the agenda subsequent to the UN Secretary-General's statement? Within a year a UN panel of governmental experts had been convened, which reported in 1997. One of its recommendations was that the UN should consider an international conference on the "illicit arms trade in all its aspects," which eventually was set for July 2001.[6] Most of the major policy initiatives that are currently being pursued are in the recommendations of the 1997 report. These include:

- enhancing postconflict disarmament and weapons collection efforts;
- strengthening cooperation among police and customs officials to stem illicit trafficking;
- destroying illegally held or surplus weapons;
- strengthening national control and regulatory systems;
- implementing stockpile security and safe weapons storage measures;
- adopting measures against illicit traffickers (including arms brokers);
- adopting (where appropriate) regional moratoriums on arms transfers and manufacture; and
- examining the feasibility of an international marking mechanism, and of restricting the manufacture and trade of weapons to authorized agents.

The 2001 UN conference produced a comprehensive *Programme of Action* that represents the only authoritative international consensus statement of the nature of the problem and the proposed solutions. Three overarching issues framed by the *Programme* were the focus on "illicit trade in small arms in all its aspects," the definition of small arms and light weapons, and the consequences that could be attributed to their "excessive accumulation and uncontrolled spread." While a narrow interpretation of "illicit trade" would have led to a focus exclusively on measures to curtail the illicit trade, the broad interpretation emphasized "in all its aspects" to establish that in order to curtail the illicit trade, measures would be required to address the legal trade, production, and possession of small arms. This opened the door to a wide-ranging examination of all aspects of the production, stockpiling, and trade in small arms. Similarly, the absence of a definition of small arms means that the policy debate is *not* restricted to military-style (fully automatic, designed to military specifications) weapons, leaving the interpretation of scope up to the different actors. In Brazil or South Africa, for example, the central concern is the widespread proliferation of handguns, not automatic weapons.

The *Programme of Action* commits states to adopting an array of national, regional, and global measures. These include:

- enhancing national legislation and regulation on production and transfer of small arms and light weapons;
- ensuring that manufacturers mark all weapons (and keep appropriate records) to allow identification and tracing of seized weapons;
- promoting (on a voluntary basis) increased transparency in small arms production and trade;
- improving the system of end-user certificates to reduce diversion and illicit trafficking;
- encouraging the destruction of weapons seized in criminal investigations, collected in postconflict disarmament programs, or deemed surplus to national requirements;
- increasing the physical security of stockpiles to prevent leakage from national holdings; and
- convening a review conference in 2006.

Several important issues were excluded in the negotiating process, and the document is nonconstraining (with language such as "where applicable, as appropriate," or "on a voluntary basis"). Two issues that were excluded because of American opposition were reference to the need to regulate civilian possession of weapons (a National Rifle Association red-line) and a prohibition on arms transfers to non-state actors. Reference to the desirability of increased transparency in production, stockpiling, and trade was opposed by many states generally against transparency, such as China or Arab League states, and no mandate to negotiate an instrument to regulate arms brokers was agreed upon, in part because the issue was considered not quite ripe (and perhaps too complex) for a legally-binding instrument. Finally, despite a concerted push by the European Union states, reference to specific export criteria did not win wide support, both among exporting and importing states.[7]

Overall though, two things are noteworthy about the *Programme*. First, the document presents a far-reaching set of normative standards for states, and compared to the multilateral state of play in the mid-1990s, it suggests that a relatively large consensus (geographically and politically) has emerged that small arms are a problem of international peace and security. The follow-up reporting process (at biennial conferences in 2003 and 2005 and at a review conference in 2006) ensure that continued attention will be placed on the issue. Second, the coalitions and groupings that emerged supporting or opposing various measures did not cleave along traditional North-South or "like-minded" lines, with only a few outlier states appearing on any given issue. Perhaps the most sustained and concerted opposition (which proved surmountable) emerged from the Arab League, which followed its traditional pattern of linking disarmament issues to the nuclear question and to the Middle East conflict.

If we consider the counterfactual, it is difficult to imagine reaching this point *without* the relatively high-level engagement of the UN system, from the Secretary-General on down. Although a fairly broad coalition of like-minded states (see Table 2.2) supported placing small arms and light weapons on the international security agenda, no one state took the lead on the issue, and they all agreed to work, at least partly, through the UN system (e.g.: First Committee resolutions, groups of governmental experts, UN conferences) in order to frame the issue and set the agenda. This in itself confirms that the UN can play an important agenda-setting role in some global security issues. But its importance actually goes beyond this.

COPING WITH SMALL ARMS: HUMAN SECURITY AND THE UN SYSTEM

Diplomatic declarations, however important they may be in setting the agenda, do not by themselves resolve security challenges. Certainly the diplomats involved in the political process prior and subsequent to the UN 2001 conference did not think so, as many of them (and most of the NGOs) cautioned before the conference not to put too much weight on the conference itself. So what role did the "UN" play in actually tackling the problem of small arms? There are two difficulties with answering this question: developing a benchmark for what counts as "actually tackling" and defining the scope of "UN action."

For many scholars the only evidence that the UN successfully tackled an issue would be binding treaty instruments with wide state compliance comparable to the Montreal Protocol on ozone-depleting substances or the Chemical Weapons Convention. From this standpoint nothing similar has been achieved to deal with small arms.[8] This vision of global security governance as global regimes or international law is, however, seriously myopic, resting as it does on a conception of global security governance that is state-centric and limited to the international level. As suggested above, most of the measures that have been proposed or that are being implemented to deal with different aspects of the small arms problem are national and regional in nature but have been catalyzed in part by the UN agenda-setting process. These range from simple awareness-raising to intergovernmental information exchanges, from the strengthening of national legislation to the development of comprehensive measures to remove weapons from postconflict zones.

Although only a short time has passed since the 2001 conference, it is possible to chart the development of national and local initiatives and overall progress in implementing the *Programme*. A database for this purpose has been created at the Small Arms Survey (http://www.smallarmssurvey.org/Database.html). Table 2.1 summarizes the main areas in which initiatives

Table 2.1 Distribution of recent initiatives to deal with small arms*

Small arms production	4
Regulating arms brokers	15
Measures dealing with transfers	25
Civilian possession	50
Stockpile management (including surplus destruction)	19
Practical disarmament measures	217
Transparency (including national reporting)	74
Efforts to combat crime and reduce gun violence	38

* Some double counting may occur. I am indebted to Silvia Cattaneo for these figures.

have been undertaken. The main emphasis has been in two areas: (1) practical disarmament measures that include weapons collection and destruction and postconflict disarmament, demobilization, and reintegration and (2) increased transparency through the publication of national reports or intergovernmental information exchanges.

While no effort has been made to assess the nature or importance of these initiatives, the sheer number in such a short time is impressive. Even in areas where many measures are largely declaratory (such as promising to tighten controls on arms brokers or civilian possession, for example, or emphasizing existing programs), it is clear that the reporting on implementation of the UN *Programme* has catalyzed a process of reflection within many governments. Sometimes such measures are triggered in the absence of any reference to the UN. The publication (and publicizing) of a report on small arms proliferation and use in the Pacific, for example, was directly responsible for eliciting a commitment from New Zealand to close apparent loopholes in national legislation.[9]

The second difficulty—defining the scope of "UN action"—is more complicated. "UN action" can be defined in terms of four concentric circles:

- direct actions undertaken by the primary UN agencies responsible for international peace and security—the Security Council, First Committee, Department for Disarmament Affairs (DDA), Conference for Disarmament (not technically a UN body), and direct institutional emanations (e.g.: groups of governmental experts);
- action undertaken, sponsored, or catalyzed by UN specialized agencies;
- actions in any global multilateral arena, including those of loosely connected regional organizations, specialized agencies, or extra-UN processes; and
- any actions (including those of states) whose origins or logic can be traced back to the agenda-setting of the UN.

In the area of small arms, I would argue that the further outward we move from the core, the more dense and significant the range of practical activities becomes and the more they begin to resemble a transnational public policy network. It is here that the idea that we can speak meaningfully of the "UN and global security" can be called into question.

Empirical evidence to support this claim is not difficult to produce. With respect to the first circle, practical activities have concentrated on the Department of Disarmament Affairs. Since the 2001 Conference the First Committee has passed an annual resolution, the Security Council has made a declaration, the Conference on Disarmament has done nothing, and a group of governmental experts on "marking and tracing" was established. DDA, on the other hand, has attempted to revive the Coordinating Action on Small Arms (CASA) and is promoting the establishment of a Small Arms Advisory Service (with voluntary extrabudgetary state contributions).[10] But with only a handful of staff, a budget devoted to small arms issues of less than one million U.S. dollars a year, and no operational or field activities (other than "visits"), the activities of DDA pale into insignificance next to those of other UN agencies, several states, and major NGO actors. With no ongoing negotiating processes, norm building, or development of international instruments, it is difficult to claim that the "core" of the UN system is acting at all. And many important actors in the small arms debate (including those promoting positive action) would like it to stay that way.

The picture shifts considerably when we move to the second circle. Here the most important specialized agency is the UN Development Program (UNDP), whose Bureau for Crisis Prevention and Recovery (BCPR) has a mandate to conduct what are called "weapons for development" weapons collection programs, and has conducted such activities on a large scale in places such as Albania, Mali, Kosovo, Congo-Brazzaville, the Solomon Islands, Haiti, and elsewhere. Its mission statement is clear:

> Where guns dominate, development suffers. Schools close, shops close, commerce stops, and the local economy grinds to a halt. Buildings are destroyed, bridges are blown up, and whatever development there has been, is gone. Private investment dries up and development organizations can't operate. Even after the shooting stops, there is no security. People can't return to their homes or a normal life. . . . UNDP's main mission is to promote development. Where small arms prevent development, UNDP's key concern is to provide programmes that reduce the demand for guns, and offer other avenues toward security, sustainable livelihoods, and development opportunities.[11]

The BCPR has a staff of about ten, a trust fund (established in 1998), and a current three-year budget (until 2004) of around 20 million dollars from donors that include Great Britain, Belgium, Canada, the Netherlands, Norway, and Switzerland. Other specialized agencies with specific small arms programs (on a much smaller scale than UNDP but comparable to DDA) would include the World Health Organization (WHO), UNICEF, and the Center for International Crime Prevention (CICP), whose main role is to promote ratification (and eventual implementation) of the UN *Firearms Protocol*.

Beyond the direct UN orbit lie a host of regional organizations and other multilateral processes that have also developed wide-ranging practical measures to tackle small arms and light weapons proliferation and use. A comprehensive catalogue is beyond the scope of this chapter, but two examples from the Euro-Atlantic region and from Southern Africa illustrate well the scope and range of activities.[12] Within the Euro-Atlantic area, small arms have become a regular part of the work of the Organization for Security and Cooperation in Europe (OSCE) and the Euro-Atlantic Partnership Council (EAPC). Within the OSCE alone, beginning with a workshop in 1998 to deliberations in the Forum for Security Cooperation in 1999 up to a Ministerial document in November 2000, the issue of small arms was brought within the traditional framework of OSCE activities, concentrating on information exchanges, confidence building, mutual assistance, and norm building. Subsequent activities have included two information exchanges in 2001 and 2002 and a series of workshops in Vienna, Central Asia, East-Central Europe, and the Caucasus.[13] Current work is focused on the development of a "best practices guide" in such areas as brokering legislation, export controls, safe storage techniques, and weapons collection and destruction, which will likely form the foundation for a series of activities designed to "cascade" these multilateral norms down to the national level for implementation.

Within Southern Africa the focus has been rather on the development of regional practices and norms within the framework of the Southern Africa Development Community (SADC).[14] Two specific legal instruments have been launched: the SADC *Protocol on the Control of Firearms, Ammunition and Other Related Materials* (signed in August 2001, not yet entered into force) and a cooperation agreement between police and customs officials.[15] Although not yet fully implemented, the Protocol commits states to undertaking a whole host of measures dealing with civilian possession, marking and record keeping, arms brokers, mutual legal assistance, and so forth. It takes its inspiration from the UN *Programme of Action* but goes beyond it in several areas. Although effective compliance is patchy, it is clear that the future efforts to tackle the problem of small arms and light weapons will be concentrated, here as in the OSCE, at the regional or subregional level and will imply mostly changes in domestic legal/regulatory frameworks and practices. Similar examples could be adduced for South America and the European Union, although in other regions the level of activity is considerably less.

Finally, there are the countless activities that take place at the national and local level, the volume and scope of which has exploded since the UN 2001 conference. Indicative of the levels of activity, an ongoing compendium of national, international, and NGO activities had grown to more than 100 pages by early 2003.[16] Although money does not tell the whole story, it is important to note that the major donors (including the United Kingdom, Germany, Switzerland, Norway, the Netherlands, the United States, Japan, and Canada) each spend several million U.S. dollars per year on small arms activities, with many smaller donors (including Sweden, Belgium, Denmark, and Finland) spending at least tens or hundreds of thousands of dollars.[17] The bulk of the money is spent on weapons collection and destruction, sponsoring NGO work (research and activism), organizing workshops and conferences, and implementing regional agreements. The number of NGOs active in this area has grown from 13 in 1998 to more than 400 by the end of 2002.

How, then, can the UN be said to be promoting "global security" in a world in which states have primary responsibility for ensuring the security of their citizens and in which most of the practical measures to deal with small arms take place at the local or national level? The most common response beyond those issue areas in which the UN does actually play a strong role in "circle one," is to highlight the UN's role as a standard-setting or norm-building institution. While this captures part of the picture, understanding fully the role played by the UN requires focusing on (1) the production and diffusion of the ideas and institutions that inform practical security-building measures and (2) the changed understandings of domestic governance states are expected to adopt. In other words, what is the role of the UN in framing the desirable scope of state-society relations, in empowering (or disempowering) social actors, and in shaping the terrain for microlevel security building? Small arms do not represent a classic interstate arms control and disarmament issue to be regulated by international treaty or regimes. Rather the causes, consequences, and solutions to the proliferation and misuse of small arms are to be found at all levels of "governance," from local communities to states, regions, and up to international society.

WHO ARE THE KEY ACTORS, HOW DO THEY ACT?

Evaluating the role of the UN in shaping state-society relations requires that we abandon the top-down vision of how the relevant actors are constituted and interact within global security arenas.[18] A simplified top-down diagram would be as follows:

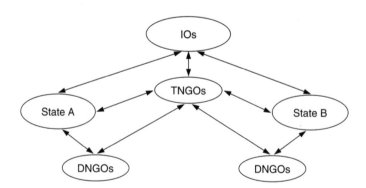

IOs: International Organizations
TNGOs: Transnational NGOs
DNGOs: Domestic NGOs

Figure 2.1 A Simplistic Vision of "Global Governance"

Exactly which way the influence pathways run depends on one's assumptions about the nature of power. For a realist, for example, the diagram would emphasize the influence exercised by states, both on international organizations and on transnational or domestic NGOs. For a scholar of transnational NGOs, by contrast, emphasis would be placed on the role of the TNGOs and on the complex feedback loops associated with interest and identity formation. But all of these visions, helpful though they might be heuristically, are inadequate for understanding actual processes of influence, norm diffusion, and, most importantly, policy change. They lead us to ask "who influences whom" in a somewhat mechanistic quest to identify the direction (and intensity) of the arrows and then to develop a picture of the relevance or influence of different institutional actors, ranging from states to international organizations to NGOs, or corporate actors.

In the area of small arms (as in many other issues), we need instead to regard the UN system as part of a complex transnational governance network, within which a wide range of "sites of potential power" (mainly nonmaterial) can be identified. Many people have invoked the metaphor of a network; few have gone so far as to un-bundle the concept of "actor" that is implied by the network metaphor. To do so challenges not only the traditional classification (and hierarchy) of states versus international organizations or non-state actors, but our whole understanding of how these sites of potential power are used by actors (often individuals or specific organizations) to shape and influence individual, institutional, and state interests and scope for action. Instead of just treating the traditional "actors" as the nodes of the network (as in the above diagram), we need to insert political analogs to networks' physical hardware (such as routers, switches, gateways, bridges, and hubs) within and between the nodes, treating these as the microlevel sources of influence and change.[19] One useful way to do this is with the notion of a "boundary role" occupant.

With respect to small arms, three types of actors—like-minded states, a small set of relatively large transnational NGOs, and several key individuals (within IOs, states, NGOs, or as independent experts)—played important roles as boundary role occupants, playing the roles of "bridges, gateways, and routers" within the broad multilateral constellation of efforts to tackle the problem of small arms. The main actors are identified in Table 2.2.

These key individuals, or other individuals empowered by activist "like-minded" states, exercise influence within the overall transnational public policy network by acting as "boundary role occupants." They are "agents for purposes of bargaining and negotiation; that is, they attempt to influence the behavior of other persons and organizations whose priorities may differ from the priorities of their own organization."[20] Here I can only offer three examples, one drawn from each category, to illustrate how this works, but these examples are representative. In all of these cases, these entrepreneurial actors are aware of the constraints they face, have limited and realistic expectations

Table 2.2 Major "Boundary Role Occupants"

Like-minded states	Transnational NGOs or related actors	Key individuals
Belgium	Bonn International Center for	Peter Batchelor (SAS)
Canada	Conversion	Paul Eavis (Saferworld)
Colombia	IANSA	Rubem Fernandes (Viva Rio)
Denmark	Institute for Security Studies	Virginia Gamba (ISS/SaferAfrica)
Germany	International Alert	Owen Greene (Bradford)
Japan	SaferAfrica	Joao Honwana (UN DDA)
Netherlands	Saferworld	Kate Joseph (OSCE)
Norway	Small Arms Surveys	Edward Laurance (Monterey)
South Africa	UNIDIR*	Geraldine O'Callaghan (DFID)
Sweden	Viva Rio	Johan Peleman (IPIS Belgium)
Switzerland		Camilo Reyes (Colombia)
United Kingdom		Carlos dos Santos (Mozambique)
		Robert Scharf (UNDP BCPR)

* UNIDIR is technically not an NGO, but for my purposes it can be treated as such here.

or ambitions for the influence they can exercise, and strive to "push the envelope" given those limits.

With respect to individuals, an ideal type-case would be Professor Edward Laurance from the Monterey Institute (and formerly the U.S. Arms Control and Disarmament Agency). Laurance wrote some of the earliest reports on small arms (1996), was the expert consultant to the first UN Group of Governmental Experts on small arms in 1996–97, and subsequent to that was the administrator in 1998–99 of the Preparatory Committee for a Global Campaign on Small Arms and Light Weapons, an Internet community of NGOs that later evolved into the umbrella NGO organization, the International Action Network on Small Arms (IANSA). He also was the expert consultant who prepared the first draft of the UN 2001 Conference Program of Action. He is a typical boundary role occupant, working on different sides of the fence and attempting to introduce perspectives and "interests" from the various conventionally understood actors directly into the policy and interest-formation processes of other actors. Noteworthy also is that he does *not* have close ties to his own (U.S.) government. Owen Greene (Bradford University, consultant to the Swiss and Norwegian governments and the UN), Geraldine O'Callaghan (formerly with the NGO BASIC, now working for DFID), Kate Joseph (formerly with the NGO BASIC, now working for the OSCE), and Virginia Gamba (ISS/SaferAfrica) all occupy similar roles.

With respect to NGOs the types of partnerships that are being developed go beyond traditional oppositional (or co-opted) NGO activism. Instead NGOs are often themselves directly inserted into the policy process. The Small Arms Survey, for example, conducted (under an "expert secondment") the assessment of the 2001 OSCE information exchange within an organization that has been historically resistant to involving NGOs in its activities in any way. Similarly it drafted (based on its own research) one state's contribution to the 2003 OSCE "best practices" guide for national policies and took the lead (with ISS in South Africa) in drafting a set of reporting guidelines for implementation of the 2001 *Programme of Action*, promoted (with little success) by the UN Department of Disarmament Affairs and now being used within an informal group of like-minded states to "lead by doing" in implementing comprehensive and effective national reporting on the UN *Programme of Action*. The Institute for Security Studies (Pretoria) played a similar role in drafting the Bamako Declaration—the ministerial-level document produced by the Organization of African Unity leading up to the 2001 UN Conference, and SaferAfrica fulfilled the same function with the Nairobi Declaration, which combated the proliferation and availability of small arms and light weapons in East Africa and the Great Lakes region. It also established (in 2000) the Nairobi Secretariat to coordinate its implementation. In all of these cases, close (but not conflict-free) personal ties between individuals from the relevant NGO and different states or international organizations were crucial to this "bridge-building" exercise.[21]

Finally, with respect to states there has not been a formal process of establishing a group of like-minded states, but in at least two cases states (Switzerland and Colombia) have taken the lead in convening consultations in support of policy initiatives (concerning marking and tracing and the monitoring of the implementation of the UN 2001 *Programme of Action* in advance of the 2003 review conference, respectively). The aim in both cases has been to build a cross-cutting minilateral coalition that will serve as a platform for further development of these initiatives. The participating states in the Human Security Network have also taken up the issue of small arms, and although the network itself has not launched any concrete initiatives, there appears to be an informal "support network for small arms" developing among some of the key members of the network, operating in a variety of multilateral forums.

This analysis supplements that of Margaret Keck and Kathryn Sikkink, who focus on the way "transnational advocacy networks" operate (almost treating them as "actors") to influence the interests and practices of governments. Although they acknowledge that "networks often have their greatest impact by working through governments and other powerful actors," they in general keep these two actors (and IOs) distinct and focus on the claim that government policies often "have emerged as a response to pressure from organizations in the . . . network."[22]

This model does not fit well the case of small arms for three reasons. First, policy innovation and promotion appears to occur equally within different "types" of actors—states, NGOs, or IOs. Second, the most important initiatives have often been developed or emerged in a way that cannot be described either in terms of "pressure" or influence of one actor on another but rather in a process that implicates boundary-role occupants most directly. Finally, Keck and Sikkink ultimately privilege the role of NGOs (or transnational networks) as the *source* of policy innovation; in the case of small arms, given the nature of NGO funding (almost entirely dependent on states), it is difficult to argue that NGOs develop and pursue an agenda distinct from the interests of key state actors, especially the like-minded states identified above.[23]

CONCLUSION: THE UN AND TRANSNATIONAL PUBLIC POLICY NETWORKS

How should we conceptualize the role of the UN in promoting global security governance? The case of small arms and light weapons may not be representative of all international peace and security issues, but neither is it unique. In several important respects, it is what has been called a "global public policy" issue. Central characteristics of global (or transnational) public policy issues include:

- the issue is complex, multidimensional, and often transdisciplinary;
- the actors are multiple and diverse;
- complex collaborative relationships emerge between the actors;
- agenda-setting and framing are central strategies;
- policies and practical measures are pursued simultaneously at all—but often most intensively at lower—levels of governance;
- norm creation and diffusion is important;
- compliance monitoring requires high levels of transparency concerning issues normally regarded as within the domestic sovereign domain of states.[24]

Adopting a "public policy" approach is anathema to many international relations scholars. To some "policy analysis" smacks of an a-theoretical and problem-solving approach to political science. To others policy analysis revolves around domestic governance arrangements—policies pursued domestically—and is not relevant to interstate relations. What I have argued here, however, is that the literature on multilateralism and global governance has in general remained stuck in a state-centric vision. As Wolfgang Reinicke put it, "given their focus on external sovereignty, neither realism nor liberalism was helpful in rationalizing this type of cooperation, as states' interests and identities in the international system now go beyond the mere defense of external sovereignty."[25]

Without adopting some elements of a "public policy" perspective, those approaches that claim to be more sociological (constructivist) in orientation cannot realize their true theoretical or empirical potential. By taking a public policy approach on board, the literature on global governance could go beyond the assertions that international organizations set norms and frame problems to examine the way in which many of the practical activities of the UN system are deeply "interventionist" and are intended to reshape in fundamental ways the scope of state action, state-society relations, and the overall understanding of sovereignty.

John Ruggie and Anne-Marie Burley (Slaughter) argued convincingly that the post-1945 constellation of international institutions should be understood as the outward projection of the American New Deal state.[26] The case of small arms and light weapons both challenges and deepens this analysis. On the one hand it is impossible to argue that the current efforts of the international community to deal with this threat to security either mirror closely the interests of the global hegemony (or even really of a small group of Western states) or reflect the externalization of its/their domestic practices. The reasons for this are not difficult to discern. Policy making in the global arena is not conducted in the same fashion as it was in the mid-1940s, when a group of mainly white, middle-aged Western men could assemble around a table and negotiate away any major differences between them. The cleavages are deeper, the consensus harder to find and more minimalist, the actors more numerous and more diverse, and the issues more complex. This situation is not unique to the problem of small arms.

But on a deeper level many of the most important and innovative peace and security activities of the UN system, including small arms initiatives, can be seen as the outward projection of a particular conception of the state and of state–society relations. The increasing importance of transnational nongovernmental advocacy networks and of informal "like-minded" groupings of states is a fundamentally liberal (even perhaps Anglo-Saxon) institutional expression. Similarly, the emphasis on "good governance," "human security," "security sector reform," and "democratization" all underscore the fundamentally *internal* or domestic orientation of many multilateral initiatives, which while they may be framed or promoted at the global or multilateral level, rest crucially on a specific (liberal) understanding of state–society relations. In the case of small arms, most of the concrete initiatives—to constrain civilian possession of weapons, to reduce their availability for non-state actors, to restrict exports to states with a good record on conflict and human rights issues, and so forth—rest on a vision of the state as the primary *provider* of (and certainly not a threat to) security for people and groups. It therefore behoves us to understand the normative underpinnings of this vision of multilateral action and global governance.

NOTES

1. See Wolfgang Reinicke, *Global Public Policy: Governing without Government* (Washington: The Brookings Institution, 1998); P.J. Simmons and Chantal de Jonge Oudraat, *Managing Global Issues* (Washington: Carnegie Endowment for International Peace, 2001). I prefer the term "transnational" since it invokes more directly the multiple levels at which public policy is developed in world politics.

2. See *Small Arms Survey 2001: Profiling the Problem* (Oxford: Oxford University Press, 2001); *Small Arms Survey 2002: Counting the Human Cost*

(Oxford: Oxford University Press, 2002); *Small Arms Survey 2003: Development Denied* (Oxford: Oxford University Press, 2003).

3. United Nations General Assembly, *Supplement to the Agenda for Peace* A/50/60-S/1995/1 (January 3, 1995): paras. 60–61.

4. Key contributions would include: Jeffrey Boutwell et al., *Lethal Commerce* (Cambridge, Mass.: American Academy of Arts and Sciences, 1995); Jasjit Singh, ed., *Light Weapons and International Security* (Indian Pugwash Society and British American Security Information Council, 1995); Christopher Louise, "The Social Impacts of Light Weapons Availability and Proliferation," Discussion Paper 59, (United Nations Research Institute for Social Development, March 1995); the series of studies in the UN Institute for Disarmament Research project, "Managing Arms in Peace Processes"; and the various BASIC occasional papers on light weapons issues.

5. Significant contributors to these would include: Aaron Karp, Michael Klare, Edward Laurance, Nathalie Goldring (arms controllers) and Chris Smith, Tara Kartha, Jacklyn Cock, Clement Adibe, Jakkie Potgeiter, Alex Vines, Virginia Gamba, Kathi Austin, and Steve Goose (conflict researchers).

6. United Nations, *Report of the UN Panel of Governmental Experts on Small Arms*, A/52/298 (August 27, 1997); *Report of the UN Group of Governmental Experts on Small Arms,* A/54/258 (August 19, 1999).

7. See Keith Krause, "Multilateral Diplomacy, Norm Building and UN Conferences: The Case of Small Arms and Light Weapons," *Global Governance* 8 (2002): 247–263.

8. Although a legally-binding instrument does exist (but has not entered into force) dealing with one dimension of the problem: the UN Firearms Protocol, which forms part of the United Nations Convention against Transnational Organized Crime (opened for signature in May 2001, signed by the end of 2002 by 52 states and ratified by 3).

9. Philip Alpers and Conor Twyford, "Small Arms in the Pacific" *Small Arms Survey Occasional Paper* 8 (March 2003). Available at http://www.smallarmssurvey.org/OPapers/OPaper8Pacifics.pdf See Theresa Garner, "Illegal Guns Threaten Pacific Peace," *New Zealand Herald* (April 3, 2003).

10. Details drawn from Laurance and Stohl, *Making Global Public Policy,* 12–14. As of mid-2003 the prospects for the SAAS were slim, given the funding priorities of donor states.

11. "UNDP's Role in Small Arms Reduction: A Primer." Available at: http://www.undp.org/erd/smallarms/undp.htm

12. Information here and below is drawn from personal involvement, from *Small Arms Survey 2001: Profiling the Problem* (Graduate School of International Studies, Geneva; Oxford: Oxford University Press, 2001), 251–291 and *Small Arms Survey 2002* (Graduate School of International Studies, Geneva; Oxford: Oxford University Press, 2002), 235–278, and from the comprehensive document of the Geneva Process, *The UN Programme of Action to Prevent, Combat and Eradicate the Illicit Trade in Small Arms and Light Weapons in All Its Aspects: Follow-up Actions since July 2001.*

13. See Kate Joseph and Taina Susiluoto, "Tackling Small Arms Trafficking in the OSCE," *Helsinki Monitor* 2 (2002): 11–24. I was also a "governmental expert" seconded to the FSC as a support officer to prepare the assessment of the 2001 information exchange.

14. The 14 member countries of SADC are: Angola, Botswana, Democratic Republic of Congo, Lesotho, Malawi, Mauritius, Mozambique, Namibia, Seychelles, South Africa, Swaziland, Tanzania, Zambia, and Zimbabwe.

15. *Small Arms Survey 2003: Development Denied* (Oxford: Oxford University Press, 2003), 237–246.

16. *The UN Programme of Action to Prevent, Combat and Eradicate the Illicit Trade in Small Arms and Light Weapons in All Its Aspects: Follow-up Actions since July 2001.*

17. Exact figures are notoriously difficult to come by, but available information supports this rough estimate and categorization.

18. See Keith Krause and W. Andy Knight, eds., *State, Society and the UN System* (Tokyo: United Nations University Press, 1995).

19. See http://networking.ittoolbox.com/nav/t.asp?t=365&p=365&h1=365

20. See   http://www.hq.nasa.gov/office/pao/History/SP-483/ch8-4.htm The crucial role of individuals in "boundary roles" has been explored in fields such as organizational theory and management/ business studies. See Steven Currall and Timothy Judge, "Measuring Trust Between Organizational Boundary Role Persons," *Organizational Behavior and Human Decision Processes* 64 (1995): 151–170.

21. There is, of course, also a host of more traditional activities, for example, the promotion by the Fund for Peace of a *Model Convention on the Registration of Arms Brokers and the Suppression of Unlicensed Arms Brokering*, or the Arias Foundation-sponsored (with other NGOs) *Framework Convention on International Arms Transfers.* See http://www.fundforpeace.org/publications/reports/model_convention.pdf; http://arias.or.cr/fundarias/cpr/armslaw/fccomment.html.

22. Keck and Sikkink, *Activists beyond Border: Advocacy Networks in International Politics* (Ithaca, N.Y.: Cornell University Press, 1998), 102, and especially 8–10, 16–25, and Figure 1(13).

23. Virtually *none* of the main NGO actors have independent sources of revenue, with the exception of Amnesty International, and to a lesser extent, Oxfam. All of those mentioned in Table 2.2 depend on government funding for their small arms work.

24. Loosely modeled on Edward Laurance and Rachel Stohl, *Making Global Public Policy: The Case of Small Arms and Light Weapons, Occasional Paper no. 7* (Geneva: Small Arms Survey, 2002). Also available at http://www.smallarmssurvey.org/OccasionalPapers.html; P.J. Simmons and de Chantal de Jonge Oudraat, *Managing Global Issues: Lessons Learned* (Washington, D.C.: Carnegie Endowment for International Peace, 2001), 3–17.

25. Wolfgang Reinicke, *Global Public Policy* (Washington, D.C.: Brookings Institution Press, 1998), 85–86.

26. John Ruggie, "International Regimes, Transactions and Change: Embedded Liberalism in the Postwar Economic Order," *International Organization* 36(2) (Spring 1982): 379–416; Anne-Marie Burley, "Regulating the World: Multilateralism, International Law, and the Projection of the New Deal Regulatory State," in *Multilateralism Matters,* ed., John Ruggie (New York, N.Y.: Columbia University Press, 1993), 125–156.

Chapter 3

Improving the Effectiveness of UN Arms Embargoes

W. Andy Knight

Introduction

The recent splintering of the UN Security Council over the illegal U.S. military action in Iraq demonstrates the problem associated with not having an effective coercive diplomatic option, short of war, available to the international community to signal displeasure to a deviant state. The UN Charter does make provision for such an option through sanctions, which are intended to compel deviant parties to comply with the will of the international community—as represented in the UN. In effect, sanctions can be considered one of the arms of coercive diplomacy in that they employ threats or limited coercion "to persuade an opponent to call off or undo an encroachment."[1]

International sanctions are, however, blunt instruments when applied to a target state, as the experience in Iraq between 1991 and 2003 clearly shows. They are decidedly punitive in intent,[2] and one recurrent problem with their use has been unintended collateral damage.[3] Compounding this problem, particularly since the end of the Cold War, is the fact that international sanctions are now imposed often on rebel movements (e.g., in Angola, Rwanda, and Sierra Leone). It has been difficult, if not impossible, to prevent damage to civilian populations that have nothing to do with the behavior of targeted non-state actors.

To minimize this collateral damage, much emphasis has been placed recently within diplomatic and academic circles on developing "smart sanctions"—a concept that involves directing sanctions at specific individuals or governing elites responsible for violating international norms. One such examination, labeled the *Interlaken process* and initiated in 1988 by Switzerland, dealt with the imposition of financial sanctions. Another initiative, by Germany, resulted in the *Bonn-Berlin process* that focused on aviation and travel sanctions and arms embargoes.[4] Sweden announced a third—the *Stockholm Process*—focusing on ways of making sanctions smarter.[5]

ARMS EMBARGOES AS TARGETED SANCTIONS

While discussions about targeting economic sanctions are recent, "targeted" arms embargoes have been used by the UN since 1948.[6] This chapter examines the use of these sanctions during the Cold War and post–Cold War periods, their variable impacts, and the reasons for their success or failure. At the heart of the analysis is the question of whether or not UN arms embargoes have made any difference in inducing compliance with Security Council resolutions. The conclusion of this chapter offers recommendations for strengthening UN arms embargoes.

HISTORY OF UN ARMS EMBARGOES

An arms embargo is a specific genre of sanction that takes the form of a restriction, ban, prohibition, interdiction, or quarantine of arms or arms-related *materiel*, as well as military advice and training. The term "arms embargo" is not used in the UN Charter, but Articles 40 and 41 of that document provide the legal framework for the multilateral imposition of this form of sanction. UN arms embargoes are used to communicate authoritatively the international community's displeasure with deviant states and to reinforce international norms.[7]

As Cortright and Lopez put it, "By denying aggressors and human rights abusers the implements of war and repression, arms embargoes contribute directly to preventing and reducing the level of armed conflict."[8] So evaluation of the success or failure of these UN instruments depends on the extent to which they are able to compel target states to comply with the wishes of the UN Security Council and to follow specified international norms.

This section of the chapter unveils the UN's record with these targeted instruments of coercive diplomacy, beginning first with the Cold War era (1945–1989) and then moving on to the post–Cold War period (1990 to the present). Dividing the analysis this way allows one to see the extent to which the political environments of these two periods had impacts on arms embargoes. During the Cold War, the possibility of conventional regional conflicts escalating into global nuclear war was very real. It therefore made sense for UN member governments to favor the use of sanctions over military force. Yet, because of the use of the veto by the great powers, sanctions were rare. With the end of the Cold War, intrastate conflicts threatened to usher in a new era of global disorder, and this led to a marked increase in the utilization of UN arms embargoes.

The Cold War Era

The imposition of UN sanctions was a rare occurrence during the Cold War. Indeed, there were only two cases of UN economic sanctions and five cases of UN arms embargoes.[9] The first UN arms embargo was imposed on Egypt, Iraq, Lebanon, Palestine, Saudi Arabia, Syria, Transjordan, and

Yemen in 1948 after the outbreak of the first Arab-Israeli war.[10] The Arab states intervened to establish Palestinian rule over all of Palestine, and in response the Security Council asked all states to refrain from exporting war *materiel* to the eight Arab countries in the hopes of forcing their withdrawal.[11] This arms embargo was not very effective for at least three reasons. First, the language of the Council resolution did not imply legal obligation. Second, the monitoring of this embargo was assigned to the UN Truce Supervision Organization (UNTSO), which already had its plate full monitoring a cease-fire and separating hostile factions. Third, while the Council asked governments "to take all possible steps to implement" the embargo, not all states had the resources to implement this task. These basic problems were repeated in subsequent UN efforts to impose arms embargoes during the Cold War.

The Security Council imposed a second arms embargo in 1961 when it asked all UN members to refrain from supplying the new state of Congo with military personnel and arms.[12] Unlike the previous case, this resolution specifically asked states to stop their nationals from selling arms to the embargoed state. It also requested that member governments deny transportation and transit facilities used for the supply of armaments destined to the Congo. However, the command issued to UN member governments was not as decisive and firm as it could have been. In addition, many states did not have legislative and administrative procedures in place to constrain their nationals who were involved in the arms trade. The UN peacekeeping force in the Congo (ONUC) was also mandated to monitor and stop the flow of arms, but it did little because it was busy with a large number of undertakings.

The third UN arms embargo was imposed on Portugal and its Territories in 1963.[13] All UN member states were asked to refrain from offering any assistance to the Portuguese government that would facilitate repression of people in the Portuguese territories. The Council's resolution specifically called for measures to prevent the sale and supply of arms and military equipment to the Portuguese government. It also asked Portugal to withdraw its military troops from the Territories and asked member states to assure compliance—a task at which they failed miserably.

Three years later, after illegal authorities in Southern Rhodesia unilaterally declared independence from Great Britain, the Security Council passed resolution 217 condemning the usurpation of power and calling on all UN members "to desist from providing" the racist Southern Rhodesian regime with arms, equipment, and military material. This fourth arms embargo was supported by mandatory economic sanctions imposed on oil and petroleum products. This was the first instance in which Chapter VII of the UN Charter was used explicitly to support an arms embargo. Realizing the importance of monitoring the implementation of sanctions, the Security Council created a new mechanism known as the Sanctions Committee to monitor the embargo.[14] However, according to Kirgis, the procedures followed by the Sanctions Committee in this case were ineffective in tracking suspect transactions

between Rhodesia and South Africa (or Mozambique). Neither did the
Sanctions Committee enjoy full cooperation from all UN member states.[15]
Countries like the United States continued to trade with Rhodesia in violation
of the arms embargo and arms entered that country through South Africa and
Mozambique. Margaret Doxey points out that those violations were uncov-
ered not by the Committee but "through the detective work of investigative
journalists."[16]

The fifth case, involving challenges to white minority rule in South Africa,
spanned the latter years of the Cold War and the beginning of the post–Cold
War period. In response to the 1960 Sharpeville massacre in South Africa,
the Security Council passed a resolution solemnly asking all states "to cease
forthwith the sale and shipment of arms, ammunition of all types, and military vehicles to South Africa."[17] Initially, this voluntary arms embargo did
not have much "teeth" and was ignored by several states, including the
United States. When it was clear that the embargo was not working, the
Council passed Resolution 421 creating a Sanctions Committee to study
ways and means of making the embargo more effective. However, without a
monitoring body verification of compliance was next to impossible.[18]

Additional resolutions were adopted by the Council to strengthen an
absolute ban on shipments of arms and military equipment to South Africa.[19]
Yet the embargo continued to be violated. The significant leaks of arms into
South Africa stemmed from two major weaknesses. The first was the refusal
of most Western countries, particularly the United States, to comply. So-
called "gray area" items were consistently allowed to enter South Africa. The
second was the exclusion from the embargoed list of far too many elements
with clear military applications, the most obvious being oil, nuclear technology, and computer equipment.[20] Additionally, the Reagan administration's
policy of constructive engagement with the apartheid regime resulted in a
significant relaxation and undermining of the arms embargo. Indeed, the
United States was accused of turning a blind eye to violations by American
companies. Although eventually some U.S. companies were investigated
and charged, it is evident that enforcement of the embargo by the U.S.
government was lax.[21]

Despite the seemingly *sui generis* nature of UN arms embargoes, some
common threads were present in the five Cold War cases. In all cases the
UN had no independent information gathering and intelligence capability
upon which the Council could base its judgments. As a result it depended on
incomplete information gleaned from media reports, its information offices,
and various states and NGO sources.

Most of the Council's resolutions on arms embargoes during this period
tended to lack strong backing from the members. Asking states "to refrain
from" doing something (as was the case with the embargoes imposed
on Arab states, the Congo, and Portugal) is not nearly as resolute as issuing
a command. Calling on states "to desist from providing" arms to a regime
(as happened in the Southern Rhodesian case) is not assertive enough to

induce compliance. It was not until the late 1970s that the Council finally began to strengthen the directives issued to member states in UN arms embargoes resolutions when, in the South African case, the voluntary arms embargo became mandatory.

The major problem with the way UN arms embargoes were imposed was the absence of a dedicated body to monitor compliance. The creation of Sanctions Committees was intended to bridge that gap. However, what we learn from the use of Sanctions Committees in the South African and Southern Rhodesian cases is that they were not very effective. They did not receive thorough information on relevant developments from state and non-state actors. Even with the adoption of the Sanctions Committee for South Africa, there were continued violations as arms and military-related equipments were smuggled into South Africa by some companies.[22] In essence, during the Cold War UN arms embargoes were not generally effectively applied. But several important lessons were learned from those experiences. As is shown below, many of the lessons helped improve the future application of arms embargoes.

The Experience of the Post–Cold War Period

John Stremlau observed that the "coincidental end of the Cold War and Iraq's aggression against Kuwait opened the way for experimenting with multilateral policy instruments . . ."[23] This included experimentation with voluntary and mandatory arms embargoes in response to aggression, civil war, state collapse, breaches of peace accords, humanitarian emergencies, human rights violations, genocide, ethnic cleansing, military coups, the harboring of terrorists, and interstate conflict. Since the end of the Cold War, there has been a noticeable increase in the UN's resort to imposing arms embargoes. Not well equipped to address the increasing number of civil conflicts, the UN has had to find innovative ways of dealing with violent conflicts within states that could pose threats to regional and international peace.

The twelve cases of arms embargoes imposed by the UN Security Council since the end of the Cold War have concerned Iraq, the Former Yugoslavia, the Federal Republic of Yugoslavia (including Kosovo), Libyan Arab Jamahiriya, Haiti, Afghanistan under Taliban control, Somalia, Liberia, the UNITA rebellion in Angola, Rwanda, Sierra Leone and the RUF, and Ethiopia/ Eritrea. In all of the above cases, proliferation of small arms and light weapons exacerbated the conflicts, increased the threats to civilians, undermined political and economic development, and destabilized communities. It is no wonder, therefore, that one of the UN Security Council's primary concerns in the post–Cold War period has been to find ways of strengthening "the effectiveness of arms embargoes as a means to diminish the availability of arms with which to pursue armed conflict."[24] It is notable that arms embargoes during the Cold War era were directed at governments, while in the post–Cold War period, non-state actors have also become important targets.[25] In light of growing concerns that sanctions were having devastating impacts on private groups, the UN tried to find ways of minimizing their negative impacts by targeting the sanctions.[26]

The focus of this next section of the chapter is on how the UN Security Council tried to adapt embargoes during the post–Cold War period to make them more effective. It looks specifically at six ways in which the UN tried to improve these tools of coercive diplomacy: (1) clarifying objectives of UN Security Council resolutions; (2) firming up the wording of action clauses of the Council's resolutions; (3) expanding the list of embargoed items; (4) calling on states to build their capacity to monitor and enforce embargoes; (5) developing what can be called a subsidiarity approach to implementing embargoes; and (6) improving the UN's ability to monitor and enforce arms embargoes.

Clarifying Objectives

The objectives of UN arms embargoes are found in Security Council resolutions. One lesson the UN seems to have learned from its Cold War experience is that objectives of Council resolutions must be clearly stated and circumscribed. However, there are usually a wide variety of implied and explicit objectives in the resolutions, for example, upholding an international norm (in the Iraqi case); stopping blatant human rights abuses, ethnic cleansing, and indiscriminate killing (in the cases of Angola, the former Yugoslavia, Liberia, Rwanda, Sierra Leone, and Somalia); forcing a regime to hand over terrorists (in the cases of Libya and Afghanistan); restoring a legitimately elected leader to his rightful position (as in the Haitian and Sierra Leonean cases); trying to end a civil war (as in most of the African cases); and bringing an end to interstate conflict (as in the Ethiopia/ Eritrea case). Assessing arms embargoes' effectiveness depends largely on understanding these goals and subgoals in the resolutions.

To some extent post–Cold War UN Security Council resolutions imposing arms embargoes have been clearer than those of the Cold War period. Over this period of experimentation with arms embargoes, the Security Council has become more adept at stating the objectives of these instruments and pinpointing specific targets of the embargoes. In some cases the Council has imposed embargoes specifically targeted at rebel groups or individuals who seek to undermine "legitimate" governments. Examples include the arms embargoes imposed on UNITA in Angola, on the nongovernmental forces trying to undermine the Rwandan government, and on the RUF in Sierra Leone. These examples illustrate the care and attention now being given by the UN to stating the specific aims of arms embargoes.[27] The resolutions provide an indication of what is required to end an embargo. Yet some observers are still critical of the UN's actions in this area. They argue that the effectiveness of arms embargoes could be further improved if the Council resolutions were more specific about how an embargo was expected to contribute to the objectives and subgoals of the international community.

Firming up the Wording of Action Clauses

Related to the objectives of arms embargoes is the wording of action clauses in UN Security Council resolutions calling for these sanctions. Such wording during the Cold War period tended not to be very resolute. However, the Security Council did demonstrate some learning in this area by the time it imposed the arms embargo on South Africa. For instance, the Council adopted resolution 660 (1990) that demanded that Iraq withdraw "immediately and unconditionally" its troops from Kuwait. This was followed by another resolution demanding that all states prevent "the sale or supply by their nationals" of weapons to Iraq.[28] The arms embargo imposed on Libyan Arab Jamahiriya for failing to cooperate with the UN in establishing culpability for two terrorist incidents[29] stemmed from a Security Council resolution prohibiting states and their nationals from supplying Libya with arms. Similarly, the Council resolution imposed an arms embargo on Haiti prohibiting the sale or supply of arms and related *materiel*. The arms embargo imposed in 1992 on Taliban-ruled Afghanistan for harboring terrorists demanded that Osama bin Laden, head of the al-Qaeda terrorist network, be turned over to appropriate authorities.[30] In response to the heavy loss of life and widespread material damage in Somalia, the Security Council issued a resolution in 1992 calling for the immediate implementation of "a general and complete embargo on all deliveries of weapons and military equipment to Somalia" until the Council decided otherwise.[31] And in yet another case of senseless, widespread killing of innocent civilians, this time in Liberia during that same year, the Council, deeply troubled that the conflict could spill over into the region and threaten international peace and security, passed resolution 788, aimed at stopping immediately all weapons and military equipment from entering Liberia until the Council decided otherwise.

However, not all Council resolutions during the post–Cold War era have been that decisive in their wording. When the Council called an emergency session in September 1991 to consider the impact of Yugoslavia's violence, ethnic cleansing, and gross human rights violations, it reverted to the old irresolute language by simply asking states "to refrain from" taking any action that might increase regional tensions.[32] Similarly, the arms embargo against the National Union for the Total Independence of Angola (UNITA) was indecisive in its command that states "refrain from providing any form of direct or indirect military assistance to UNITA," although a later resolution was firmer.[33] In any event, decisiveness in resolution wording is not sufficient to induce compliance with those commands. Demanding that the Taliban hand over bin Laden, for instance, did not produce the desired result.

Expanding the List of Embargoed Items

The list of embargoed items in post–Cold War resolutions changed as states learned from previous embargoes. In Cold War cases the Security Council usually called for general bans on arms and war materials. After the end of the Cold War, the UN developed a more systematic and purposeful approach to closing loopholes in the Council's arms embargoes resolutions.

The Iraqi government, for instance, initially used such loopholes to get around the embargo imposed on that country. According to U.S. intelligence, Iraq imported trucks for civilian use and then converted them into mobile missile launchers.[34] This is why, over time, the Council expanded the list of embargoed items to include all types of military-related materials. For instance, the arms embargo placed on Libya prohibited states and their nationals from supplying that country with aircraft, aircraft components, engineering or maintenance services, "arms and related *materiel* of all types, including the sale and transfer of weapons and ammunition, military vehicles and equipment, paramilitary police equipment and spare parts for the aforementioned, as well as provision for any type of equipment, supplies, and grants of licensing arrangements for the manufacture and maintenance" of the above items. It also prohibited any technical advice, assistance, and training related to the manufacture, maintenance, and use of military equipment to Libya.[35] In the Haitian case petroleum and petroleum products were prohibited along with arms and related *materiel* of all types, while in the Afghanistan case "technical advice and assistance or training related to the military activities of the armed personnel under the control of the Taliban" was forbidden by the Council.

The report from the *Bonn-Berlin process*, mentioned earlier, suggested that expansion in the list of embargoed items "may increase embargo effectiveness" and also "help to enforce provisions of international law against the activity of mercenaries . . . and private security firms." However, this report was quick to add that one of the "principal shortcomings" of UN arms embargoes "is the lack of internationally agreed upon lists of terms or goods," and it recommended that the Arms Trade Registry, the Small Arms Registry and the Munitions List, and the Dual-Use Lists used in the Wassenaar Arrangement might be a good starting point for developing such a list.[36]

Building State Capacity

Broadening embargoed items, however, is not enough for ensuring effective implementation of arms embargoes. Many states, particularly in the developing world, lack the technical and material means to carry out the tasks involved in complying with arms embargoes. Furthermore, many of these states do not have adequate domestic legislation that would empower them to seize embargoed goods, freeze assets of arms violators who operate in their countries, impound vehicles and vessels, deal with transshipment loopholes, and bring criminal charges against sanction busters. In the UNITA case, a UN Panel of Experts found that national governments "are often constrained by inadequate domestic legislation that hinders effective action" in terms of complying with UN arms embargoes.[37]

It would help the organization's cause significantly if it were in a position to take action against leaders of states that facilitate the illicit dealings of arms dealers and brokers. So far the UN does not seem to possess that capability. It has not taken actions against countries like Bourkina Faso, Kenya, Tanzania, and Uganda—all major transshipment points for arms shipments to the states of Western, Central, and Eastern Africa. Similarly, very little has been done to address the problem of Cold War stockpiles of weapons in Eastern Europe that are finding their way into African conflicts. The problem is that arms trafficking is a very complex and convoluted business. A single sale of weapons could involve brokers, banks, transportation companies, and various transshipment points. False end-user certification can enable traffickers and their clients to circumvent UN arms embargoes while keeping states in the dark. Victor Butt, an arms dealer operating in Africa, has reportedly been able to do this with impunity. He has been able to get weapons into Angola, Cameroon, Kenya, Libya, the Democratic Republic of the Congo, Rwanda, Sierra Leone, Sudan, and Uganda in violation of UN embargoes.[38]

Also, it appears from the report of one UN panel of experts that several Eastern European governments have little control over arms dealers operating in their territories. Certainly this points to the need for greater international efforts to license and control private arms brokers and for states to begin to align their domestic legislation with the international norms upon which the imposition of UN arms embargoes is based. As Ken Epps puts it, the "variation in member [states] legislative capacity is a fundamental weakness of the existing UN embargo system which those seeking to circumvent arms embargoes have manipulated to their advantage."[39]

Developing a Subsidiarity Approach to Counter Arms Embargoes Violations

The UN has tried various ways of monitoring embargoes. One method has been to utilize regular UN peacekeeping forces to monitor implementation of arms embargoes. Another has been to draw on regional bodies' assistance. The Security Council has utilized Chapter VIII of the UN Charter concerning regional organizations to develop what can be called a subsidiarity approach to arms embargo monitoring.[40] Through cooperation and coordination with regional organizations like the European Community, the CSCE / OSCE, the SAMs, NATO, the WEU, the OAS, the OIC, the League of Arab States, the OAU and ECOWAS, the UN has tried to shore up the monitoring and enforcement aspects of arms embargoes.

An interesting case of UN-regional organization collaboration concerned the Yugoslav wars of 1992–1995. When it became clear in 1992 that not all UN member states were adhering to the provisions of the embargo imposed on Yugoslavia,[41] the Security Council passed resolution 820 (April 17, 1993) as a means of dealing with transshipment loopholes. In addition to implementing a naval blockade, the UN Protection Force (UNPROFOR) was given specific customs control functions. The arms embargo was strengthened further with the presence of international Sanction Assistance Missions (SAMs) in the area, the appointment of a Sanctions Coordinator by the

OSCE, and collaboration between the European Community Monitoring Missions and the UN Sanctions Committee on an inspections system. The Sanctions Committee frequently dealt with alleged and actual violations of the embargo brought to its attention by NATO and WEU naval forces in the Adriatic Sea. While all of these efforts improved the chances of state compliance with the Council's resolution, by 1995 the Sanctions Committee became aware of further violations of the embargo involving arms smuggling using clandestine and very sophisticated techniques.[42]

The UN Sanctions Committee blamed this ineffectiveness also on the absence of "a system for monitoring the air and land freight traffic parallel to the existing NATO/ WEU arrangements in the Adriatic Sea" and those of the SAMs at land entry points along the Danube.[43] To improve this situation regional states were urged by the Council to make personnel available for effective monitoring, particularly in Kosovo, and to act promptly to stem embargo violations.[44]

The main problem with a subsidiarity approach to monitoring and enforcing UN arms embargoes, though, is that most regional bodies lack the capability to do the job required. The OAU and ECOWAS have had a difficult time tracking the movements of illicit arms brokers in the Great Lakes region and specifically in Liberia and Rwanda. The OAU experienced similar difficulty in the horn of Africa in its attempt to stem the flow of weapons into Somalia, Ethiopia, and Eritrea. On the other side of the coin, some regional and subregional bodies are beginning to develop methods that could supplement UN efforts. For instance, in June 1998, the EU adopted a code of conduct on arms exports that obliges its member states to refrain from shipping military equipment that could in any way be used for internal repression or international aggression.[45] The Southern African Development Community (SADC) drafted a protocol on the control of small arms that helped to enforce the arms embargo imposed on UNITA. One should note as well that had it not been for the credible monitoring and enforcement capabilities of the United States and Canada, the OAS's efforts to implement the arms embargo on Haiti might not have been as successful as it turned out to be. While the regional bodies have been increasingly helpful, some need additional resources to be able to meet the UN's expectation of them as reliable partners in monitoring and enforcing arms embargoes.

Improving Monitoring and Enforcement
Since the effectiveness of UN arms embargoes is so heavily dependent on a system of surveillance and enforcement, it is surprising that the UN does not have a dedicated body to perform these tasks. An innovation of the Cold War period was the creation of UN sanctions committees that certainly enhance the effectiveness of embargoes. Sanctions committees have performed a variety of tasks, ranging from drawing up guidelines for strengthening embargoes to soliciting information on violations of embargoes, recommending measures for dealing with such violations, and approving exceptions to arms

embargoes. From time to time Sanctions committees are asked to examine the UN Secretary-General's progress reports on embargoes' implementation and on ways to sharpen these tools. These committees are expected to identify individual violators and recommend specific action against them. In recent cases, such as those of Rwanda and Liberia, UN sanctions committees have appointed panels of experts to investigate specific allegations of sanctions busting and recommend appropriate punishment.

However, analysis of their performance reveals the heavy dependence that sanctions committees have on UN member states and their national technical means (NTM),[46] other UN agencies, regional organizations, UN peacekeeping missions, NGOs, academics, and journalists.[47] In assessing the performance of the Sanctions Committee for Iraq, the UN Sanctions Secretariat acknowledged that although the embargo was "effectively enforced in general terms," there were only a few reports of alleged violations brought to the attention of the Committee. Indeed, it took Israeli sources to reveal that Syria, while it was President of the UN Security Council, colluded with Iraq to violate the arms embargo by acting as a middleman for military equipment from Eastern Europe.[48]

Clearly sanctions committees need to have better and more independent intelligence means at their disposal and under their direct control if they are to be meaningful monitoring and enforcement bodies. The UN Sanctions Secretariat acknowledged this fact when it concluded that the arms embargo placed on Iraq could have been "more effective if the Committee, with the necessary mandate from the Council, had more means under its direct control to monitor and enforce the sanctions."[49]

CONCLUSION

Since 1948 the UN has imposed arms embargoes as a means of inducing compliance with particular UN Security Council resolutions. It has become evident that when properly targeted, arms embargoes play a major role as instruments of conflict prevention through limiting access to weapons and deterring states from acquiring and using those weapons.

UN arms embargoes are one genre of international sanctions, and they have become a regularly used instrument of coercive diplomacy, particularly since the end of the Cold War. The UN and its member states have found arms embargoes to be a desirable alternative to military force when faced with threats to the peace—either international or regional. Arms embargoes allow the UN to target those groups and devices that injure, maim, and kill civilians in interstate and intrastate conflicts. In that sense they are considered "smart sanctions." However, the UN has been trying to make them smarter by refining how they are crafted, monitored, and implemented.

The UN's experience with arms embargoes is instructive for a couple of reasons. First, it demonstrated that a cybernetic form of institutional learning is possible within the UN system, although the basic mode of change utilized has been predominantly that of reflexive adaptation.[50] Second, it has shown that while slow to learn, UN bodies are capable of using past experience to improve incrementally their functioning and effectiveness. There were incremental adaptations to the manner in which arms embargoes were imposed and administered by the UN over the period analyzed in this chapter.

The tasks involved in monitoring and implementing arms embargoes are varied. These tasks are being done, in some cases poorly, by a variety of agents and bodies. Below are five specific recommendations that flow from the above analysis, which could improve the effectiveness of UN arms embargoes.

First, it would seem that, if the international community is truly serious about making arms embargoes effective, the time has come for the UN to establish a comprehensive mechanism dedicated to monitoring, implementing, and enforcing these sanctions. This body would have a norm-building function in that it would help to develop norms for controlling the sale of weapons and related *materiel* to countries. It would also be responsible for drafting codes of conduct on arms transfers, the establishment of transparency mechanisms, and the methods used by states and international organizations in enforcing embargoes. It will be important to provide secure funding and appropriate expertise to this body so that it can properly carry out its functions, including developing a database and maintaining a ready inventory of experts who could be called on at a moment's notice to verify the application of arms embargoes or search out violators. Sanctions committees and expert panels would operate under this new UN Unit.

Second, it seems prudent for the UN to develop a more systematic plan for assisting member states in adopting legislative, administrative, and technical apparatuses to facilitate compliance with arms embargoes. National legislation ought to be put in place in every UN member country to ensure that governments criminalize UN arms embargo violations. Governments should then be in a position to prosecute violators who supply or aid in supplying embargoed weapons to targeted states and non-state actors. Such legislation should also give governments the ability to prosecute their nationals who violate embargoes even if the offenders have committed the deed on foreign soil. Each UN member government should also specify a particular domestic department to oversee the government's compliance with UN arms embargoes.

Third, the UN needs to send a clear signal to all member states that "mandatory sanctions" are indeed "mandatory." Those states that flagrantly disregard the UN Security Council's wishes with respect to arms embargoes ought to be penalized severely. This can be done effectively by applying targeted financial, travel, and other sanctions to their leadership and their families, as was done to Liberia when it flagrantly violated UN arms embargoes imposed on the RUF in Sierra Leone. In the absence of an international body that could effectively monitor and enforce arms embargoes, the international community has to hope that major powers commit funds and forces to help police areas close to the targeted state. It is no secret that the success of the

UN arms embargo on Iraq is linked to the fact that the United States and its allies have made substantial commitments to monitoring and interdicting shipments to Iraq, especially by sea. The U.S. Maritime Interception Force (MIF), in particular, has been responsible for monitoring naval traffic in the Northern Gulf.[51]

Fourth, the UN needs to find a better method of dealing with NSAs, particularly illicit arms brokers and arms traffickers. These "merchants of death" include financiers, exporters, importers, transport agents, negotiators/ middlemen, and common criminals and are generally unregulated.[52] In fact, only 12 countries in the world have legislation to regulate arms brokers. But most arms dealers circumvent even these countries' laws by operating in countries that do not have such laws. And according to Kathi Austin, the few governments that have this legislation "rarely scrutinize or prosecute traffickers' activities under their own laws."[53] Why? Because in doing so, arms brokers might reveal the extent to which some of these governments have used them as middlemen to purchase or sell illicit arms covertly. Some governments, like the United Kingdom, are beginning to adopt new arms export controls that, among other things, require the registration and licensing of arms brokers.[54] The U.S. Congress passed an amendment in 1996 to the Arms Export Control Act (AECA) that now requires all arms brokers residing in the United States, whether they are citizens or not, to register and obtain licenses for all arms deals transaction whether on U.S. soil or not.[55] It would be a significant first step in the attempt to control the flow of weapons if all states were to follow suit, or better yet, if there were a global convention to regulate all arms brokering and trafficking.

If arms dealers who violate UN arms embargoes are subjected to major fines or long-term imprisonment when caught, this could significantly increase the cost of violating sanctions and cause those individuals to think twice before engaging in another violation. Perhaps another way of deterring these individuals is to treat them as international criminals and have them brought before the International Criminal Court and charged with crimes against humanity. The violation of arms embargoes ought to be made an international criminal offence. After all, traffickers are the vendors of instruments of death that are decimating large populations, particularly on the African continent.

Fifth, states that produce arms must bear the brunt of the responsibility for ensuring that individual arms dealers or military firms operating in their private sectors are monitored closely with respect to arms exports and sales. This means putting in place the required legal, administrative, and technical mechanisms to carry out this function. No UN arms embargo can be implemented successfully without the cooperation of states that produce and sell arms—whether this comes in the form of assistance with patrolling the high seas or the air to ensure that arms do not get into a target state, or in the form of enforcing restrictions on the export of military goods, or in the form of setting up a monitoring and verification mission to ensure that embargoed arms do not enter target states. Any discussion of the use and targeting of arms embargoes should keep in mind that the activities of both the "source" and "target" states should be scrutinized.

The "name and shame" policy adopted by countries like Canada and the United Kingdom, and by the UN itself may be marginally effective, in some cases, as a deterrent to violations. The intense discussion and debate that accompanied the release of the Angola and Sierra Leone reports on sanctions busting indicate the impact that merely exposing violations can have.[56] In response to these reports, some governments have taken steps to improve their export control laws and to eliminate loopholes in domestic law that allowed arms dealers to circumvent the intent of UN arms embargo resolutions. Kofi Annan has noted that the public identification of international arms merchants has been one of the single most important tools in combating the arms trafficking problem. Yet this has not been all that effective against certain arms traffickers like the De Decker brothers and Victor Butt.

The UN ought to consider more drastic measures for dealing with these merchants of death. It is equally important to the success of an arms embargo that those states proximate to the target state, transit states, as well as those in some form of interdependent relationship with the target state agree to cooperate in monitoring and enforcing the embargo. This might require providing these states with special financial and technical assistance to help them implement embargoes.

In closing, the UN is generally applauded as a norm-creating and norm-building body, but it is concurrently criticized for its failure to enforce the norms it develops. Making arms embargoes more effective would strengthen the UN's enforcement capability. Targeted sanctions, among which arms embargoes are the most fully developed, combined with an effective international agency to monitor and enforce them can go a long way in improving the image of the UN as a relevant and effective instrument of global governance.

NOTES

1. Gordon Craig and Alexander George, *Force and Statecraft: Diplomatic Problems of our Time*, 3rd ed. (New York: Oxford University Press, 1995), 196.
2. Patrick Clawson, "Sanctions as Punishment, Enforcement and Prelude to Further Action," *Ethics and International Affairs* 7 (1993): 17–37.
3. Lori Damrosch, "The Civilian Impact of Economic Sanctions," in *Enforcing Restraint: Collective Intervention in International Conflicts* ed. Lori Damrosch (New York: Council on Foreign Relations, 1993), 274–315.
4. *Targeted Financial Sanctions. A Manual for the Design and Implementation. Contributions from the Interlaken Process* (Providence, RI: Thomas J. Watson, Jr. Institute for International Studies, Brown University 2001, coordinated by Prof. Thomas Biersteker), and *Design and Implementation of Arms Embargoes and Travel and Aviation Related Sanctions: Results of the "Bonn-Berlin" Process* ed. Michael Brzoska (Bonn: Bonn International Center for Conversion, 2001).

5. The results of this analysis were presented to the UN Security Council in February 2003. This work can be followed on the website: www.smartsanctions.se.

6. W. Andy Knight, *The United Nations and Arms Embargoes Verification* (New York: Mellen Press, 1998), 3.

7. They are also used as a form of deterrence, retribution, and international symbolism. W. Andy Knight, *The United Nations and Arms Embargoes Verification*, 21–22.

8. David Cortright and George Lopez with Linda Gerber, "Sanctions *Sans* Commitment: An Assessment of UN Arms Embargoes," *Project Ploughshares*, Working Paper 02-2.

9. The two multilateral economic sanctions were imposed on Rhodesia (1966–1979) and South Africa (1979–1994).

10. Itamar Rabinovich, "Seven Wars and One Peace Treaty," in *The Arab–Israeli Conflict: Perspectives* 2nd edition ed. Alvin Z. Rubinstein (New York: Harper Collins Publishers, 1991), 35–38.

11. UNSC Resolution 50 (May 29, 1948).

12. UNSC Resolution 169 (1961).

13. UNSC Resolution 180 (1963).

14. UNSC Resolution 253 (1968).

15. Frederic L. Kirgis, Jr., *International Organizations in their Legal Settings*, 630.

16. Margaret Doxey, *International Sanctions in Contemporary Perspective* (New York: St. Martin's Press, 1987), 108.

17. UNSC Resolution 181 (August 7, 1963).

18. "Smart Sanctions, the Next Step: Arms Embargoes and Travel Sanctions," *The Experience of the United Nations in Administering Arms Embargoes and Travel Sanctions,* for the Second Expert Seminar, Berlin, December 3–5, 2000–an informal background paper prepared by the United Nations Sanctions Secretariat, Department of Political Affairs (United Nations, New York, January 25, 2001), 6.

19. UNSC Resolutions 558 (1984) and 591 (1986).

20. Caryle Murphy, "Embargo spurs S. Africa to build weapons Industry," The Washington Post, July 7, 1981, p. A12.

21. See Richard Knight, "Shotguns and Ammunition Sold to Apartheid South Africa in Violation of the United Nations Embargo," http://richardknight.homestead.com/files/shotguns.htm.

22. See Michael T. Klare, "Evading the Embargo: Illicit U.S. Arms Transfers to South Africa," *Journal of International Affairs,* 35(1) (Spring/Summer 1981): 25–28.

23. John Stremlau, *Sharpening International Sanctions: Towards a Stronger Role for the United Nations,* A Report to the Carnegie Commission on Preventing Deadly Conflict (New York: Carnegie Corporation, November 1996), 21.

24. UN Doc. SC/6574, 3927th Meeting (Night) (September 16, 1998).

25. For instance, an arms embargo was imposed on the National Union for the Total Independence of Angola (UNITA), a rebel faction in Angola.

26. Boutros-Ghali, *An Agenda for Peace*, A/47/277-S/24111; his *Supplement to An Agenda for Peace*, A/50/60-S/1995/1; and UN General Assembly resolution 51/242, Annex II.

27. Boutros-Ghali, *An Agenda for Peace*, A/47/277-S/24111; his *Supplement to An Agenda for Peace*, A/50/60-S/1995/1; and UN General Assembly resolution 51/242, Annex II.
28. UNSC Resolution 661 (August 6, 1991).
29. UNSC Resolution 731 (1992) for the terms of the embargo.
30. UNSC Resolution 1267 (October 15, 1999).
31. UNSC Resolution 733 (January 23, 1992).
32. UNSC Resolution 713 (1991).
33. UNSC Resolution 864 (1993).
34. "U.S. Accuses Iraq of Arms Violations," BBC News, http://news.bbc.co.uk/1/hi/world/middle_east/1858942.stm, March 6, 2002.
35. UNSC Resolution 748 (March 31, 1992).
36. BICC, *Design and Implementation of Arms Embargoes and Travel and Aviation Related Sanctions*, 29.
37. *Smart Sanctions, The Next Step*, 9–10.
38. U.S. Department of State, "Arms and Conflict in Africa," http://www.state.gov/s/inr/rls/fs/2001/4004.htm, July 1, 2001.
39. Ken Epps, "International Arms Embargoes," *Ploughshares Working Paper* 02-4, at http://www.ploughshares.ca/content/WORKING%20PAPERS/wp02 5 (accessed March 27, 2003).
40. W. Andy Knight, "Towards a Subsidiarity Model for Peacemaking and Preventive Diplomacy: Making Chapter VIII of the UN Charter Operational," *Third World Quarterly*, 17(1) (March 1996): 31–52.
41. See UNSC Resolution 787 (November 16, 1992).
42. This information was provided by the EU/ OSCE Sanctions Coordinator.
43. *Smart Sanctions, the Next Step*, 14.
44. UNSC Resolution 1199 (1998).
45. Kathleen Miller and Caroline Brooks, *Export Controls in the Framework Agreement Countries*, BASIC Research Report (British American Security Information Council, July 2001.). Available from http://www.basicint.org.
46. These NTMs may include: reconnaissance satellite systems, aerial photographs, radar and electronic sensors, and communications collection stations.
47. On interagency cooperation see W. Andy Knight, *The United Nations and Arms Embargoes Verification*, 107–118.
48. http://www.factsofisrael.com/load.php?p=http://www.factsofisrael.com/blog/archives/000194.html.
49. *Smart Sanctions, the Next Step: Arms Embargoes and Travel Sanctions*, 2nd Expert Seminar, Berlin (December 3–5, 2000), 7.
50. W. Andy Knight, "Learning in the United Nations," in *Adapting the United Nations to a Postmodern Era: Lessons Learned* ed. W. Andy Knight (Houndmills: Palgrave, 2001), 28–38.
51. Cortright and Lopez, "Sanctions Sans Commitment: an Assessment of UN Arms Embargoes," 10.
52. Loretta Bondi, *Expanding the Net: A Model Convention on Arms Brokering* (Washington, DC: The Fund for Peace, June 29, 2001), 10.
53. Kathi Austin, "Illicit Arms Brokers: Aiding and Abetting Atrocities," *The Brown Journal of World Affairs*, 9(1) (Spring 2002): 205.

54. Letter (from the Director of Saferworld), "Arms Export Controls," *The Times* (London) (June 25, 2001), 13.
55. U.S. Congress, Public Law 164, 104th Congress, 2nd Session (July 21, 1996), section 151, and *The Arms Export Control Act,* U.S. Code (U.S.C), volume 22, Section 2778(b), 1976.
56. Michael Brzoska, "From Dumb to Smart? Recent Reform of UN Sanctions," *Global Governance,* 9(4) (October/December 2003).

PART II

CONFLICT PREVENTION AND RESOLUTION

CHAPTER 4

WHEN ASPIRATION EXCEEDS CAPABILITY: THE UN AND CONFLICT PREVENTION

Andrew Mack and Kathryn Furlong

For the United Nations but also for me, personally, as Secretary-General there is no higher goal, no deeper commitment, and no greater ambition than preventing armed conflict . . .

—Kofi Annan, 1998[1]

INTRODUCTION

Conflict prevention is enshrined in Paragraph 1, Article 1 of the UN Charter, which refers to the need for "effective collective measures for the prevention and removal of threats to the peace and for the suppression of acts of aggression or other breaches of the peace." Article 1 says nothing about how prevention might be achieved, and in practice preventive policy can take many forms. While most commonly associated with the relatively traditional idea of "preventive diplomacy," threats of physical or economic coercion may also be preventive instruments. Finally, there is what is sometimes called "early" or "structural" prevention—strategies that address the so-called "root causes" of armed conflicts. The latter is the focus of this chapter.

During the Cold War the East-West divide ensured that the Security Council, the UN body charged with the responsibility for maintaining the peace, paid little attention to conflict prevention. Throughout this period the rival superpowers and their allies sought security from each other primarily via deterrence and diplomacy. Conflict was seen as endemic in an international system riven by deep ideological difference. The veto system in the Council kept most conflicts off the UN's agenda. Collective security, with its stress on the indivisibility of peace, was unthinkable during the Cold War years despite being the core principle of the UN Charter. During this period the Council operated as little more than an arena of superpower competition.

Even in those civil wars in the developing world where superpower rivalry was not an issue, the UN showed no real interest in conflict prevention. The ostensible reason for this inaction was that the organization's security mandate dealt only with threats to international peace and security. Civil wars that did not threaten international peace were thus off limits to the UN. This legal proscription was not, however, a real barrier to pursuit of preventive policies—when it wanted to, the Council never had a problem constructing a rationale to legitimize intervention. The Permanent Five members of the Council simply did not care about small wars on the world's periphery unless their interests were engaged—and usually they were not. Little has changed in this respect.

Not until the end of the Cold War and the UN's liberation from the debilitating ideological constraints of superpower rivalry did other security issues become more salient. Only then did the concept of conflict prevention begin to be taken seriously.

THE EMERGENCE OF CONFLICT PREVENTION

As the UN emerged from the stifling ideological glacis of the Cold War, its involvement in global security issues increased exponentially. The number of resolutions passed in the Council rose from an average of 15 a year from 1946 to 1989 to more than 60 a year during the 1990s. The number of resolutions authorizing the use of force also increased dramatically.[2] Peacekeeping operations grew rapidly in number and became far more complex and expensive. With the publication of Secretary-General Boutros Boutros-Ghali's *Agenda for Peace* in 1992, the idea of preventing—as against simply reacting to—conflicts became the focus of serious high-level official reflection for the first time. But Boutros-Ghali's approach to prevention was far more limited than that of today. *Agenda for Peace* presented prevention as a policy largely restricted to preventive diplomacy—a package of measures "to create confidence" that required "early warning based on information gathering and informal or formal fact-finding." In practice preventive diplomacy involved traditional diplomatic instruments like mediation, conciliation, and good offices but could also include more intrusive and novel policy options such as "preventive deployments and, in some situations, demilitarized zones."[3]

The "root causes" approach to prevention that was to become increasingly salient in the late 1990s was barely mentioned in *Agenda for Peace*. The importance of "economic despair, social injustice, and political oppression" as causes of armed conflict were noted but not discussed in any detail.[4] The Secretariat had long been reluctant to address these issues for fear of being accused of interfering in the internal affairs of member states. Postconflict peace-building practices, which were associated with the new comprehensive UN peace operations of the 1990s, were seen as a way of preventing the recurrence of warfare. However, preventing wars from arising in the first place by addressing their root causes was not yet on the UN's political agenda—and was only just beginning to be discussed within the Secretariat.

In 1995 Boutros-Ghali published the supplement to an *Agenda for Peace*, which used the term "peace-building" to refer to both pre- and postconflict measures. Like *Agenda for Peace*, the supplement focused overwhelmingly on preventive diplomacy on the one hand and postconflict peace-building on the other. The longer-term prevention mission was described in passing as the "creation of structures for the institutionalization of peace." What this might mean in practice was not addressed. There were, as we will see, political reasons for the Secretariat's hesitancy to embrace prevention approaches focusing on "root causes."

"Structural" Prevention Makes its First Appearance

In 1995 the UN's Geneva-based Joint Inspection Unit (JIU) published a provocative report entitled *Strengthening of the United Nations System Capacity for Conflict Prevention.*[5] The JIU report picked up where *Agenda for Peace* left off, arguing not only for an enhancement of the UN's preventive diplomacy capacity but also for what it called a "comprehensive conflict prevention strategy," which foreshadowed many of the ideas that were to become official conventional wisdom by the end of the decade. What made the "comprehensive strategy" a radical departure from past practice was the JIU's embrace of "preventive peace-building" or "structural prevention"— an umbrella term for policies that addressed the so-called "root causes" of armed conflict. The "comprehensive strategy" integrated preventive peace-building with preventive diplomacy and postconflict peace-building policies.

The JIU inspectors identified poverty and underdevelopment as key "root causes." The key to averting conflicts, they argued, was "a long, quiet process of sustainable human development . . . an integrated approach to human security."[6] This would require the UN to play a more active role in helping countries choose "appropriate development strategies."[7] The report went on to argue that many UN agencies—UNCTAD, UNDP, UNEP, WFP, and UNESCO—as well as the World Bank and regional organizations were already addressing the "root causes" of conflict. What was needed was better coordination between them—a recurrent theme in UN reports. In today's UN the JIU's report would appear unremarkable; in the mid-1990s it was quite controversial.

In June 1997 Secretary-General Kofi Annan sent detailed comments on the report to the General Assembly. Annan's comments derived from a discussion of the report by members of the high-level interagency Administrative Committee on Coordination (ACC), which had been wrestling with the often-confused concept of peace-building at its June meeting in Geneva. The ACC's cumbersome definition of peace-building was not dissimilar to that of the JIU Report. "Peace-building," according to the ACC, is "a broad-based approach to crisis prevention and resolution [that] should comprise integrated and coordinated actions aimed at addressing any combination of political, military, humanitarian, human rights, environmental, economic, social, cultural, and demographic factors so as to ensure that conflict was prevented or resolved . . ."[8]

While the ACC endorsed the idea of a comprehensive approach to peace-building in principle, Annan's note to the Assembly had some pointed criticisms of the JIU Report. There was, he argued, a fundamental difference between preventive development which is not directed specifically at the prevention of conflict, and "peace-building," which is carried out under a political mandate specifically to prevent the eruption or resumption of conflict.[9] At first glance this argument makes little sense. If development programs are designed to reduce the risk of conflict, why should they not be described as "peace-building" as the ACC defines it? The answer has more to do with UN politics than logic.

A "political mandate" could mean one of two things. Either the Secretariat had authorization from the Council (or possibly just the Assembly) to pursue preventive measures, or preventive measures had been authorized by the Secretary-General "with, of course, the agreement of the government concerned."[10] Absent such authorization the pursuit of prevention strategies by the Secretariat could be seen as political interference in the internal affairs of member states—an issue of major concern among members of the G-77. The tension between the need to act effectively on the prevention front and the need to respect sovereignty has long bedeviled UN policymakers. As early as 1992 Boutros-Ghali argued in *Agenda for Peace* that the "time of absolute and exclusive sovereignty . . . has passed." Yet in the same report he also argued that in "situations of internal crisis the United Nations will need to respect the sovereignty of the State; to do otherwise would not be in accordance with the understandings of Member States in accepting the principles of the Charter." The latter statement completely negates the former but such contradiction is unsurprising. It is typical of UN reports to try to speak to as many constituencies as possible—often sacrificing consistency and logic in so doing.

SOVEREIGNTY AND POLITICS

One of Annan's main criticisms of the JIU's proposals for improving prevention policy was that they had underestimated member state concerns about sovereignty. In support of his case he pointed to the resistance by a majority of states to Boutros-Ghali's proposal to create integrated UN offices in some developing countries on the grounds that such a move was intended to "obtain political reporting on Member States' internal affairs."[11] Few outside the UN system realize that UN agencies are "precluded by their mandates from reporting on political matters."[12] This proscription has little basis in logic given that politics are an integral part of the development, health, environment, and other issues that these agencies address and given the reality that they do report on political matters—albeit circumspectly.

However, this proscription is yet another indicator of the deep-seated resistance to what many developing countries see as spying on their internal affairs. This developing-country concern even applies to preventive diplomacy. A case in point noted by Annan is the ridiculous demand by the Assembly that preventive diplomacy missions be "transparent" as well as "confidential"—a practical as well as logical nonsense. G-77 objections have long prevented the Secretariat from creating any serious intelligence and analytic capacity that could be used for early-warning purposes and to create more effective prevention policies.

Annan also criticized the JIU stress on the importance of development policies in preventive peace-building. Such policies, he said, could only be described as preventive development "if they had a specific political purpose, also agreed by the government [of the country in question], of contributing to the prevention of the outbreak of a new conflict or the recrudescence of an old one."[13] The assertion that conflict prevention was an "essentially political" activity suited the Department of Political Affairs (DPA), whose mandate was political and whose officials knew very little about economic development. (Annan's comment was almost certainly written by DPA officials.)

The UN Development Program, unsurprisingly, preferred to conceive prevention in more developmental terms. In 2000 UNDP Administrator Mark Malloch Brown said, "When we talk prevention we mean using existing, acknowledged tools [of development policy] in transparent, accepted ways: for example, helping developing countries make use of . . . poverty action plans to identify and respond to potential social problems such as growing inequality."[14] Malloch Brown's position was the obverse of the Annan/DPA line. For UNDP prevention does not have to be "essentially political." It is a natural outgrowth of good development policy, but the difference between UNDP's position and that of DPA has less to do with analytic conviction than bureaucratic "turf" interests.

While the political concerns that lie behind this argument are obvious enough, it makes little substantive sense. We know that in most societies as the level of development rises, the risk of political violence declines—though why this should be the case remains a contested issue. Countries with a per capita income of U.S.$600 have half the risk of being involved in an armed conflict within five years of countries with a per capita income of U.S.$250. When incomes rise to U.S.$1200, the risk halves again. Policies that promote equitable development are conflict prevention policies regardless of whether or not they have a "specific political purpose."

"STRUCTURAL" PREVENTION BECOMES POLICY—AT LEAST RHETORICALLY

Despite the concerns that Annan had expressed in 1997 and that reflected the views of many in the Department of Political Affairs, support for "root causes" approaches to prevention continued to broaden in the Secretariat as the decade moved to a close. This shift in mood was due less to increased confidence in the viability of prevention policies than to growing pessimism within the Secretariat about the viability of some of the UN's peace operations as they were then constituted and run.

In 1998 two major reports had documented the organization's catastrophic failures in Rwanda (where the genocide had followed shortly after the UN's debacle in Somalia) and Srebrenica. As the Brahimi Report on peace-keeping was to point out in 2001, many of the problems that had caused these failures were endemic to the UN system.[15] Security Council mission mandates were often inappropriate with lightly armed peace-keepers being sent into war zones, and with many peace operations being woefully underfunded. Most of the responsibility for this could be attributed to the Council and to member states, more generally. As Secretary-General Annan's own devastating 1998 report on the massacre at Srebrenica noted concerning the Council's responsibility: "None of the conditions for the deployment of peace-keepers had been met: there was no peace agreement—not even a functioning cease-fire—there was no clear will to peace and there was no clear consent by the belligerents. Nevertheless, faute de mieux, the Security Council decided that a UN's peace-keeping force would be deployed. Lightly armed, highly visible in their white vehicles, scattered across the country in numerous indefensible observation posts, they were able to confirm the obvious: there was no peace to keep."[16]

The central difficulty with the Council's approach to intervention can be stated simply enough. It is extraordinarily difficult to persuade the key Council members to commit major resources—human as well as political and economic—to issues in which they perceive no major interests to be at stake. This was most tragically obvious in the case of Rwanda but remains a continuing and pervasive source of concern.[17]

In such a context it was not surprising that arguments in favor of prevention should have come to resonate more strongly in the Secretariat and even in the Council. Prevention, as was increasingly being pointed out, was cheaper than cure—in lives as well as money. Interest in embracing prevention within the system was complemented and reinforced by pressure from civil society groups—not least by the many NGOs accredited to the UN and the umbrella European Platform for Conflict Prevention, a 200-strong NGO consortium. The increased interest in "structural prevention" within the Secretariat was paralleled by growing pressure to address "root causes" from influential member states. Notable among the latter was Britain, where the Department for International Development led by Claire Short was pouring millions into prevention policy. Prevention had also been taken up by the OECD's Development Assistance Commission and—with less and less diffidence—by the World Bank. By 1999 the G-8 were taking an increasing interest in the issue. In their communiqué from the July 2000 summit meeting, G-8 ministers indicated that they were firmly in the prevention camp—rhetorically at least.

In the publication of the 1999 Secretary-General's Report on the Work of the Organization,[18] the idea of a comprehensive approach to prevention was embraced without reservation—at least within the Secretariat. The key question was—and remains—how to turn rhetorical commitment into effective policy. The 1999 report noted that: "Today no one disputes that prevention is better, and cheaper, than reacting to crises after the fact. Yet our political and organizational cultures and practices remain oriented far more towards reaction than prevention."[19] In March 2000 the well-received Secretary-General's *Millennium Report* noted: "There is near-universal agreement that prevention is preferable to cure, and that strategies of prevention must address the root causes of conflicts, not simply their violent symptoms."[20]

With respect to security the Secretariat now agreed that what was needed was a shift from a "culture of reaction" to a "culture of prevention." There was also increased emphasis on the security/ development nexus at the very heart of "structural prevention." The "Freedom From Fear" chapter of the *Millennium Report* argued that "... every step taken towards reducing poverty and achieving broad-based economic growth is a step towards conflict prevention."[21] In July 2001 *Prevention of Armed Conflict: Report of the Secretary-General* was presented to (and later endorsed by) the Security Council.[22] The report's endorsement by the Council added authority to the prevention/ peace-building cause. Like the *Brahimi* and *Millennium* reports, *Prevention of Armed Conflict* has become a much-cited source.

Much of the report was devoted to a survey of what various UN agencies contributed to prevention. This was more detailed than, but otherwise very similar to, the survey undertaken by the JIU for its 1995 prevention report. The contents of *Prevention of Armed Conflict* are long on description and relatively short on analysis. It was and remains a highly political document designed not least to assuage the concerns of member states from the developing world about possible interference in their internal affairs. Its introduction, for example, stresses that: "... the primary responsibility for conflict prevention rests with national Governments. ... The main role of the UN and the international community is to support national efforts for conflict prevention and assist in building national capacity in this field."[23] The message here—that successful prevention does not undermine state sovereignty but enhances it—was clearly directed at G-77 prevention skeptics.

The fact that development, always the primary concern of the G-77, is critical to prevention was also strongly reiterated: "Conflict prevention and sustainable and equitable development are mutually reinforcing activities. An investment in national and international efforts for conflict prevention must be seen as a simultaneous investment in sustainable development since the latter can best take place in an environment of sustainable peace."[24] G-77 states are far more comfortable with a stress on development-as-prevention than prevention policies that emphasize good governance, democratization, security sector reform, and respect for human rights, which some key donor states promote. This is a source of tension between some developing states and donor agencies—especially when the former are led by undemocratic, corrupt, and repressive regimes.

The Secretary-General's report made the by-now-familiar argument that security and equitable development are two sides of the same coin—each

necessary for the achievement of the other. It contained much that was
sensible but little that was new. There were, however, some pointed criticisms
buried in the long text to which we will return later. Within the system real
efforts are now being made to enhance prevention policy, but these mostly
involve an increased effort towards enhancing intrasystem coordination.[25]
This is further evidence for the growing acceptance of "structural prevention"
by those parts of the broader UN system—like the World Bank—that had
previously been reluctant to embrace such policies. How effective such
efforts will be in actually reducing conflicts given resource constraints
remains to be seen.

Decoding the UN's Prevention Discourse

Outsiders trying to follow a paper trail of the emerging consensus on prevention within the UN have often been surprised by the inconsistency of various
reports and extraordinary confusion of terms used to describe the organization's prevention policies. The latter include "peace-building," "pre-conflict
peace-building," "preventive development," "preventive deployment," "preventive disarmament," "preventive peace-building," "structural prevention,"
and "operational prevention"—and there are almost certainly other terms as
well. How can such confusion persist? The answer lies in part in the fragmented nature of the UN system and in the lack of communication between
its constituent parts. But the inconsistencies in definition and policy approaches
also reflect the intense bureaucratic politics that are a defining characteristic of
the internal operations of the UN.

There are even major inconsistencies between the Secretary-General's
own reports. This is difficult for outsiders to comprehend, but in fact the
Secretary-General does not write these reports himself—"his" reports reflect
differences in assumptions between both individual authors and the bureaucratic interests they represent. If DPA is writing a Secretary-General's report,
one can be sure that the stress will be on the "essentially political" nature of
prevention. Contributions from UNDP, by contrast, will tend to stress the
preventive role of economic and social development.

All major reports that go out under the Secretary-General's name are
reviewed by senior officials in his executive office. But these officials do not
ensure consistency between different reports, and they may know little about
the substance of the issue in question. They are, however, skilled at detect-
ing material that might be controversial. Given a natural inclination to avoid
any sort of controversy that might embarrass the Secretary-General, the
executive office will often require potentially controversial material to be
removed from the report in question. Recognizing this, report writers tend
to self-censor their reports. Not surprisingly then, the Secretary-General's
reports are often anodyne and sometimes excruciatingly boring. If the
Secretary-General personally intervenes—as Kofi Annan did with the young
authors of his Srebrenica report—and instructs them to "tell it as it is," the

result can be startlingly frank and hard-hitting. But this is the exception and not the rule.

Report writers often have little familiarity with what was written five or more years earlier in their own departments—when they may have been pursuing tasks wholly unrelated to prevention issues. And the search function of the UN's website is so awful that tracking down in-house material on prevention produced by different departments can be extraordinarily difficult. Often reports seek to fudge what are essentially irreconcilable differences. This does not necessarily signal that an author lacks competence—though it may. It is far more likely to mean that she/ he is trying to embrace contradictory political positions in response to the imperatives of bureaucratic politics. Statements that speak to different constituencies, but which are contradictory, may appear in different parts of a report, the author hoping that no one notices the contradiction. Boutros-Ghali's insistence in *Agenda for Peace* that sovereignty is "no longer absolute" and that "in situations of internal crisis the United Nations will need to respect the sovereignty of the State" is a case in point.

Students of UN affairs who seek to track the evolution of policy by decoding UN reports also need to understand that many UN reports have little or no impact on policy. Many of them are mechanically produced by overworked staff without much substantive expertise in the subject matter. They are frequently produced in response to requests by member states and often reflect bureaucratic or political imperatives rather than substantive analytic contributions to evolving policy debates. Some—like an ill-fated report on peacebuilding that was produced at the same time as the Secretary-General's report to the Council on conflict prevention—are never released or even finished. Obviously a Secretary-General's report may have greater impact when endorsed by the Council than if it is simply produced as an in-house document, but Council endorsement does not necessarily mean that action will follow. Rhetorical affirmation and exhortation are as characteristic of the Council's deliberations as substantive commitment to policy.

Finally, it is important to realize that report writers dealing with prevention issues have a delicate balancing act to maintain. On the one hand they need to convince their intended constituency of the direness of the risks that need to be addressed—and hence the urgent need for more effective action and resources. On the other hand they have to avoid presenting too dire a picture in case donors come to believe that problems are insurmountable and not worth wasting resources. The UN has to be presented as capable—but under-resourced.

BARRIERS TO CREATING AN EFFECTIVE UN PREVENTION POLICY

Buried in the careful and bland language of the Secretary-General's *Prevention Report* are some oblique but telling criticisms. In the introduction to the report the Secretary-General suggests that—notwithstanding the long list of initiatives that follow—the UN has yet to "translate the rhetoric of conflict prevention into concrete action." Later (in paragraph 154) he argues that "adequate capacity for conflict prevention is still lacking" in the Secretariat. In paragraph 64 he notes that the UN has yet to develop an enabling environment "in which United Nations staff are encouraged to develop a proactive, preventive mind set and in which incentives and accounta bility for preventive measures are put in place." Member states are openly crit-icized in paragraph 72 for failing to deliver the prevention resources they have promised. "Too often departments, agencies, and programs have found that proposals, having received political endorsements from member states in one forum, fail to win support from the same states in other—particularly financial—forums."

Elsewhere in the report are veiled criticisms of the operations of the inter-agency framework team that deals with prevention and of the failure of the new executive committees to deal with prevention issues. But the Secretary-General does not deal in any real detail with what are arguably the four most important barriers to creating an effective structural prevention policy within the UN. These are the lack of analytic capacity within the system, interde-partmental "turf wars," the so-called political will issue, and the UN's lack of comparative advantage in dealing with security/development issues.

The Analysis Gap

The Secretariat has only minimal research capacity and lacks both the research culture and research resources that exist in the World Bank. Policy is often driven more by precedent, mandates, and politics than by data and analysis. One consequence is that in-house analysis of the generic causes of violent conflict is rarely evidence-based—without proper resources the situation could not be otherwise. UN prevention practice is rather like medical practice without the benefit of epidemiology. Effective structural prevention policy requires knowledge of the factors that—in general—predispose countries to violent conflict as well as particular knowledge of individual countries. Econometricians at the World Bank and elsewhere have provided a wealth of information on the former. But their findings are largely inaccessible to the innumerate, and little effort has been made by their authors to translate them for the policy community. This literature—and the data on which it depends—has had little impact on the UN system. The consequence is obvi-ous. Prescriptions for addressing the root causes of violence are unlikely to succeed if those causes are not understood.

While there have been repeated demands from the Secretariat for more resources to improve in-house analytic capacities, these demands are unlikely to be met—at least to the degree needed. In many cases it may well be prefer-able to have most research contracted out to independent researchers, perhaps working with in-house officials. The International Peace Academy (IPA)

often plays this role for the UN, but IPA's limited resources are not commensurate with the system's needs. Involving independent researchers to a
much greater degree would help avoid the politicization that affects some
reports. Such an involvement would also mean that researchers with specific
expertise could be engaged for specific purposes. The research process that
created the Brahimi Report on peace-keeping provides a good example of
how inside/outside collaboration can work effectively in practice. The work
of the expert panels on "blood diamonds" and related issues in sub-Saharan
Africa also reminds us that independent outsiders can provide far more forth-
right and critical reporting than is usually possible from politically restrained
Secretariat officials.

There is another analytic issue here. The need for conflict prevention has
become widely accepted—at least at the rhetorical level—not only in the UN
system but also in the World Bank, the G-8, and the OECD. The idea that
development policy should be "informed by a concern for conflict prevention" or "viewed through the conflict prevention lens" has become a verita-
ble mantra within the system. This is perfectly sensible at one level—but
what it means in practice is by no means clear. Would development policy be
any different if viewed through the "prevention lens"—and, if so, how?
These and other critical questions have barely begun to be answered in the
Secretariat.

Turf Wars

Interdepartmental rivalries and differing agendas have made creating cohesive
structural prevention policy within the UN extraordinarily difficult. Almost
everyone agrees that the "root causes" of violent conflict are to be found in the
nexus between security and development. But over-worked officials in DPA—
the department designated as the "focal point" for peace-building prevention—
know little about development issues. They have traditionally viewed
prevention primarily in terms of preventive diplomacy—a quintessentially
political endeavor. The parts of the UN house that deal with development have
not, until recently at least, conceived of development as a conflict prevention
tool. The result has been that long-term prevention has tended to fall between
the institutional cracks. It was not until 2002 that an informal working group
of DPA and UNDP officials was created to discuss "structural prevention."

Annan's creation of four executive committees as part of his 1997 reform
package was supposed to enhance interdepartmental understanding and
cooperation. The committees should act as instruments for those seeking to
bring real coherence to cross-system prevention policy. But they have yet to
do this. Paragraph 66 of the Secretary-General's Prevention Report argues
that preventive actions of a developmental nature are "the natural purview"
of one of the four executive committees—the system-wide UN Development
Group (UNDG). This may be true. But UNDG has been deeply involved
with the Millennium Development Goals (MDGs) reporting process, and

while its members were tasked with creating a guidance note on prevention, UNDG simply doesn't have the resources to do more than skim the surface of this issue. The Secretary-General notes in his report that most of the work of the executive committees to date "has addressed issues other than conflict prevention" and that he intends "to promote their more proactive use for that purpose in future." This has yet to happen.

The Security Council, a preeminently political body, has embraced the idea of addressing the root causes of conflict, but the permanent representatives of Council member states and their staffers rarely understand much about those socio-economic factors that are the root causes of violence. Their expertise is diplomacy, not economics. The Economic and Social Council might seem a more appropriate venue for dealing with structural prevention—but it lacks the authority of the Council and is not taken very seriously within the UN system.

The "Political Will" Question

Effective preventive action by the UN's requires sustained political will on the part of member states. First and foremost, this includes a readiness by the membership as a whole to provide the UN with the necessary political support and resources for undertaking effective preventive action in specific situations.[26] The failure of member states to provide the resources necessary for the UN to mount effective prevention operations is a constant refrain in almost all UN reports and is invariably attributed to "lack of political will."

What "lack of political will" means in practice is rarely spelled out but is fairly obvious in this case. "Political will" is a reflection of the pattern of the perceived interests of the major players on the Council. Despite their rhetorical commitment to prevention, these players rarely see their vital interests being served by providing the resources necessary to promote it. This is not surprising. First, the Secretariat is not clear what preventive policies to "address root causes" of conflict would mean in practice. Second, member states are being called on to provide resources now in order to (possibly) prevent conflicts five, ten, or fifteen years into the future. Success in the future means that nothing happens. There will be nothing to show for the expenditure but the absence of a war that might not have happened anyway. This is not an easy proposition to sell to politicians who are unlikely to be in office even if the investments eventually have their desired effect.

Contrast this with the imperative to act when there is a major humanitarian tragedy. Here there are immediate urgent needs and—as the aid flows in and the hungry are fed—a clear and desirable result. Kofi Annan likes to quote an old Chinese proverb to the effect that "it is difficult to find money for medicine, but easy to find it for a coffin." He has a point.

A second problem with the approach taken by many member states to UN policy has been well summed up by long-time UN observer, Edward Luck, who notes the following in a powerful recent critique of UN prevention policy: "In one issue after another, UN member states have adopted laundry-list action plans, based on comprehensive, undifferentiated strategies that have not required setting priorities or making choices that might offend one group of member states, agencies, domestic constituencies, or other. The expanded concept of prevention, it seems, is in danger of following this well-worn path towards rhetorical glory and programmatic irrelevance."[27] Luck also notes that, in sharp contrast to their rhetorical enthusiasm for prevention, member states have been strikingly resistant to funding prevention policies in practice.[28] Thinking about how such behavior might be categorized, hypocrisy is a word that comes to mind.

The UN's Lack of Comparative Advantage with Respect to Structural Prevention

If, as most analysts agree, structural prevention policies lie in the realm of development policy, then it follows that—in terms of development funding and expertise—the UN is at a comparative disadvantage compared with the World Bank and the major donor states. Its development assistance resources are simply too small. UNDP's core budget is less than ten percent of that of the World Bank and less than the combined budgets of the donor states. To put it bluntly, if the UN is not a major development actor, it cannot be a major structural prevention actor in the field. This is not to say that UNDP and DPA cannot make a difference on the ground—simply the value they can add is restrained by the very limited resources at their disposal.

CONCLUSION

Effectively promoting structural prevention is not easy. For international organizations like the UN, the EU, and the World Bank, as well as for individual donor states, prevention is a form of long distance social engineering practiced over vast distances with inadequate information and insufficient resources. It often seeks to change the behavior of governments that either lack the capacity to achieve needed reforms that will reduce the risks of violence or that are deeply resistant to implementing them. The UN simply does not have the resources to be a major player in the provision of on-the-ground prevention programs. The most cost-effective way for the organization to assist the cause of prevention would be to focus more attention on its traditional and still critical preventive diplomacy role—a realm in which it does have a comparative advantage and where the financial costs are relatively modest.

The UN can also promote prevention via its often-overlooked ability to help create, sustain, and enhance global norms. The organization's major asset here is its credibility. Unlike the Bank, the IMF, and the WTO, the UN has not been a target of violent demonstrations. Its credibility, especially in the developing world, remains high as countless polls attest. Key UNDP and

Secretariat officials—in particular UNDP's administrator and the Secretary-General—could play a much greater role as "norm entrepreneurs" and sustainers—making the case for prevention clearly and compellingly. There are two important audiences for such a policy—the donor community, many of whose members are suffering from "aid fatigue," and those G-77 states who still view prevention policies as unwarranted interference in their internal affairs. There is an interesting precedent for such an approach—the UN's strategy for promoting the MDGs that emerged from the Millennium Declaration.

This strategy has four elements:

- The Millennium Project, which analyzes policy options and will develop a plan of implementation for achieving the MDGs. This is a public-private cooperative endeavor directed by Columbia University's Jeffrey Sachs.
- The Millennium Campaign, which mobilizes political support for the Millennium Declaration among developed and developing countries. This is led by Evelyn Herfkens, the Secretary-General's executive coordinator for the MDG Campaign.
- Country-level monitoring of progress towards achieving the MDGs, led by the UN Development Group.
- Operational country-level activities, coordinated across agencies through the UN Development Group, which help individual countries implement policies necessary for achieving the MDGs.[29]

One of the ironies of the MDGs is that—though no one disputes the interdependence of security and development—not one of the 48 indicators that are used to monitor progress towards the various development goals relates to security. The MDGs call for a halving of world poverty by 2002—yet there has been no call for halving the numbers of wars or refugees. A UN-led strategy to promote coordinated structural prevention in conjunction with other international agencies and donor governments could complement the Millennium Development campaign and monitoring process. Combining the sorts of analytic capabilities that the Sachs team is bringing to the Millennium Project with a powerful advocacy campaign and effective country-level monitoring would be a relatively low-cost, potentially high-return strategy for the UN. Norm-building, -sustaining, and -enhancing are not sufficient for successful conflict prevention, but these are roles where the UN can play to its strengths—not its weaknesses.

NOTES

1. United Nations, "Secretary-General Says Proposals in His Report on Africa Require New Ways of Thinking, of Acting," (1998), para. 5.
2. Peter Wallesteen and Patrik Johansson, *The New Security Council: UN Decision-Making in Perspective*, (forthcoming 2004), 1.

3. United Nations, *An Agenda for Peace: Preventive Diplomacy, Peacemaking and Peace-Keeping* (New York: United Nations, 1992). para. 23.
4. Ibid. para. 15.
5. H. L. Hernandez and S. Kuryama, *Strengthening of the United Nations System Capacity for Conflict Prevention* (Geneva: Joint Inspection Unit, United Nations, 1995).
6. Ibid, 32.
7. Ibid, 32.
8. Administrative Committee on Coordination, "Summary of Conclusions of the Administrative Committee on Coordination at Its First Regular Session of 1997," (Geneva: United Nations, 1997), 7.
9. United Nations General Assembly, "Report of the Secretary-General on the Work of the Organization Joint Inspection Unit: Strengthening of the United Nations System Capacity for Conflict Prevention," (1997), para. 7.
10. Ibid, para. 26.
11. Ibid, para. 19.
12. Ibid, para. 45.
13. Ibid, para. 26.
14. Mark Malloch Brown, *Administrator's Statement on UNDP's Role in Crisis and Post-Conflict Situations before the UNDP/UNFPA Executive Board 2nd Regular Session* (New York: UNDP, 2000), 17.
15. United Nations, *Report of the Panel on United Nations Peace Operations* (2000).
16. United Nations General Assembly, *Report of the Secretary-General Pursuant to General Assembly Resolution 53/35: The Fall of Srebrenica* (1999), para. 492.
17. The neglect of humanitarian/security issues in which the interests of major powers are not engaged is not restricted to the Council. In 1999, for example, more than 60 percent of UNHCR's requests for assistance were for aid to the Balkans. This was despite the fact that the war in Kosovo had generated fewer than 10 percent of the world's refugees for less than 6 months. Africans unsurprisingly saw UNHCR's requests as reflecting European racism.
18. Andrew Mack was the main author of this report.
19. Kofi Annan, *Preventing War and Disaster: A Growing Global Challenge* (United Nations General Assembly, 1999), para. 60.
20. Kofi Annan, *We the Peoples: The Role of the United Nations in the 21st Century* (United Nations: 2000), 44. Andrew Mack drafted the security chapter of the Millennium Report.
21. Ibid, 45.
22. United Nations, *Prevention of Armed Conflict: Report of the Secretary-General* (New York: 2001).
23. Ibid, 2.
24. Ibid.
25. See Tapio Kanninen and Jochen Prantl, *Conflict Prevention as Concept and Policy at the United Nations: A Policy Planning Perspective*, (forthcoming, 2002) for a useful insiders' review of UN prevention policies.
26. United Nations, *Prevention of Armed Conflict: Report of the Secretary-General*, para. 169.

27. Edward C. Luck, "Prevention: Theory and Practice" in *From Reaction to Prevention: Opportunities for the UN System* eds. Fen Osler Hampson and David M. Malone (Lynne Rienner, Boulder, 2002), 257.
28. Ibid, 258.
29. See Millennium Project, http://www.unmillenniumproject.org/html/about.htm.

CHAPTER 5

CAN THE UN STILL MEDIATE?

Fen Osler Hampson

The 1990s marked the heyday of UN involvement and success in the peaceful settlement of international disputes. Not only did the UN have more peace-keepers in the field than ever before, but it also played a major role in helping to negotiate and implement many settlements that ended some of the world's bloodiest and protracted civil conflicts.[1] By the time the decade ended, the Secretary-General had fielded more than 20 special/ personal representatives or envoys into conflict zones, most of whom were involved in some form of international mediation or ongoing negotiation activity.[2] Today the world looks rather different. There are fewer UN peace-keepers in the field, and although the Secretary-General continues to field a large number of his special representatives in zones of conflict, efforts to reach a negotiated settlement in many hot conflict zones like Burundi and the Democratic Republic of the Congo (or "frozen" conflict zones, like Cyprus) have eluded repeated attempts at mediation. Why is this so? In what sense has the world of international negotiation and mediation changed? And what can we say about the actual track record of UN-led (or assisted) mediation efforts in ending violent, international disputes?

In addressing these two questions, this paper argues that not only has the general, strategic, international context of mediation changed, but that the feasibility of UN mediation is largely shaped by the ties of the conflicting parties with major powers and the predispositions of those powers to seek a negotiated resolution to the conflict in question. However, this apparent affirmation of what could be characterized as a *realist* position that geopolitical considerations fundamentally shape the prospects of reaching a negotiated settlement must be qualified by three key caveats. The first is that the military balance between two or more warring parties is a major facilitator of accord. The second is that there is an important spillover effect from past UN involvement, which defines and shapes the opportunities for successful UN mediation. The third is that many of today's conflicts are relatively impermeable to mediation by any third party, including the UN, because the parties themselves have not only learned to "live" with the conflict, but their threshold for pain is sufficiently high and their own psychological, cultural, religious, and political identities are so wedded to the conflict that even when there is a military stalemate, it is very difficult to engage them in a search for negotiated options.

Assessing the opportunities for UN-led mediation, we must first acknowledge how the world of conflict management has changed since the end of 1980s and beginning of the 1990s. As Monty Marshall and Ted Robert Gurr have both noted, international conflict reached its peak during this period (as measured by both the number of international conflicts and the number of fatalities or war-related deaths in those conflicts).[3] Both sets of numbers witnessed a decline towards the end of the decade, and the world is, in some ways, a less violent place than it was a decade ago. The decline in the number of conflict zones therefore has, in a real sense, reduced the demand for international (including UN) peacemakers and peace-keepers. Even so, there remains a relatively large number of conflicts in the Middle East, Africa, Southeast and Northeast Asia, the Pacific, and much of Eurasia that have persisted or endured into the twenty-first century.

UN-LED MEDIATION IN THE 1980S AND 1990S

In a seminal article entitled, "Why the UN Fails," published in *Foreign Affairs* in 1994, Saadia Touval argued that the UN had a poor track record in trying to resolve conflicts. Examining the record of UN intervention in Afghanistan, Angola, Haiti, Somalia, and the former Yugoslavia, Touval offered a number of reasons why the UN record was so poor and why, in his words, "UN mediation . . . [had] extended or aggravated many of those disputes."[4] Key among them were the following: (1) the UN lacks the leverage of great powers to force the parties to the negotiating table; (2) the UN is insufficiently flexible and dynamic in an organizational context to pursue a coherent and effective negotiating strategy; (3) the UN is the mediator of "last resort" and usually has to deal with the most intractable disputes where others have tried and failed; and (4) the UN lacks a sufficient "aura of legitimacy" because of its inability to pursue coherent policies and its allegedly poor track record of conflict management.

Touval's assessment was heavily influenced by the failure of the Vance-Owen mediation mission in Bosnia. It was also to some extent skewed by his selection of cases. By the end of the 1990s, however, the UN could point to some mediation successes, although the record of intervention was still a mixed one.[5] Touval may have also overstated his argument about the UN's structural deficiencies in mediation. As the record shows, the UN does have important sources of leverage in mediation and can pursue flexible and dynamic negotiating strategies under the right set of circumstances.[6] Although a detailed assessment of the UN's mediated interventions in the 1980s and 1990s is well outside the scope of this paper, and there is an obvious temptation to focus on the UN's negotiation failures, we can point to a number of cases where the UN did succeed through its mediated interventions in promoting a peaceful settlement of major conflicts. The conditions underlying these successful cases are also instructive about the potential strengths that the UN can bring to a negotiation process.

Iran–Iraq War

The UN played a significant role in mediating an end to the Iran-Iraq war and assisting with the implementation of Resolution 598 in 1988, which provided for a cease-fire and the deployment of an unarmed UN military observer force (UNIIMOG).[7] As soon as the war broke out in 1980, the UN moved quickly to try to broker a negotiated end to hostilities. The UN Secretary-General, Kurt Waldheim, provided good offices to the parties, and the Security Council adopted Resolution 479 that called for an immediate end to the conflict and a negotiated resolution. In spite of repeated efforts to get the parties to enter into negotiations, the UN's special representative had difficulty gaining traction. And it was only when the parties reached a point of military and financial exhaustion following Iraq's brutal missile and chemical weapons attacks on Iran in the late 1980s that a cease-fire agreement was concluded.

A clear source of the UN's difficulties in negotiating with the parties in the earlier phases of the conflict was that it was seen to be biased as result of great power leanings toward Iraq. Iran was unhappy about the fact the UN Security Council failed in its early resolutions to declare Iraq the aggressor in the conflict, and to call for a return of captured territory. One of the consequences of the U.S. embassy hostage crisis in Iran was that the United States viewed Iran as a pariah in international affairs. Washington's efforts to curry favor with Iraqi president Saddam Hussein and its jockeying for influence in the Middle East with Moscow also compromised the Security Council's neutrality and the efforts by the UN mediator to broker a cease-fire. One of the reasons why Iran agreed to accept Resolution 598 was that it contained a key provision to establish a board that would assess which party was the aggressor in the conflict—a provision that was introduced by the Federal Republic of Germany to strike a more balanced note in the Council's deliberations.

El Salvador

The resolution of the Salvadoran conflict stands out as one of the clearest examples of successful UN mediation in the 1990s. The special representative of the Secretary-General, Alvaro de Soto, played a key role in leading the parties to a negotiated settlement.[8] Although a military stalemate helped propel the parties to the negotiating table, the parties' fundamentally conflicting political objectives meant that a political settlement was not preordained. The government's main goal was to end the war, whereas the goal of the Farabando Marti National Liberation (FMLN) was to change Salvadoran society, initially by demobilizing the armed forces. Because there was no straight or easy quid pro quo, it took an outside mediator to help the parties reach a negotiated settlement.

The United Nations was the mediator of choice in El Salvador because it was able to "neutralize" outside parties and build on the new U.S. and Soviet interest in backing an end to old Cold War conflicts and defusing regional conflicts. Through the United Nations, the two superpowers had an indirect seat at the table and therefore were able to lend their support to the negotiations. The UN special representative helped to overcome some of the key barriers in the negotiation by being a source of proposals, reframing the meaning of concessions, creating a sense of urgency, imposing deadlines, and offering side payments, assurances, and the threat of sanctions if progress were not forthcoming. In undertaking these tasks, it enjoyed the support of the "four friends"—Spain, Venezuela, Colombia, and Mexico—who lent their encouragement and political support when negotiations appeared to be floundering.

Cambodia

The Paris Peace Accords of 1991, which brought an end to the long-standing conflict in Cambodia, were also successfully negotiated under UN auspices. However, it is important to acknowledge that a number of other third parties played a key role in the prelude to reaching a negotiated settlement. Initially, negotiations were directed by ASEAN, which succeeded in bringing the interested parties together for discussion. ASEAN's initial mediation efforts were followed by those of Indonesia, Australia, France, and subsequently the five permanent members of the Security Council. France worked with Indonesia to convene the first Paris conference on Cambodia. Those talks failed. The United States then led eight months of negotiations among the Permanent Five, which culminated in August 1990 in agreement on a framework that provided for the second (and successful) Paris conference in October 1991.[9] In this case, the key supportive condition was the end of the intense great power rivalry in Southeast Asia and the decline in great power partiality with respect to local combatants.

The negotiated agreements were subsequently implemented by the United Nations through UNAMIC and UNTAC, which performed a wide range of roles and functions, including fact finding, mediation, verification, monitoring, humanitarian assistance, refugee relocation and assistance, electoral preparation, electoral supervision and monitoring, civil administration, rehabilitation, engineering and infrastructure reconstruction, cantonment, disarmament, and demobilization.

Mozambique

Although the Mozambican peace accords were negotiated between the Marxist-led government party, FRELIMO, and the opposition, guerrilla movement, RENAMO, with the assistance of Sant'Egidio, a Catholic lay organization, and the direct support of the Italian government, implementation of the General Peace Agreement, which was signed in 1992, was undertaken by the

United Nations.[10] Once again, it is important to situate the end to this conflict in a wider, strategic context, which had seen the end of the superpower rivalry in Southern Africa with the negotiation of the Angola-Namibia peace accords in the late 1980s.

The special representative of the Secretary-General, Aldo Ajello, who was responsible for overseeing the implementation of the agreement, played a critical role in mediating between the parties when one of the parties threatened not to honor its negotiated commitments.[11] In the run-up to the UN supervised elections in Mozambique, the leader of RENAMO, Afonso Dhlakama, announced that he was pulling out because he feared that the elections were rigged by the government. The fate of the entire peace process hung in the balance. When Dhlakama indicated that "the international community [would] understand his decision" to pull the plug on the peace process, Ajello intervened. He was able to bring enough external pressure on Dhlakama to make him reverse his decision and participate in the elections in exchange for written guarantees that every complaint pressed by RENAMO would be investigated by the UN's Supervision and Monitoring Commission.

Guatemala

A UN mediator, Jean Arnault, also helped secure a settlement in 1996 to the long-standing civil war in Guatemala—a conflict which cost some 150,000 lives and 50,000 "disappeared" persons. This conflict pitted central authorities in the "core" against indigenous communities in the "periphery." The settlement was negotiated between the government of Guatemala, led by the National Advancement Party (PAN), and the Guatemalan National Revolutionary Unity (URNG) guerrillas. The UN mediator played a critical role in establishing sufficient trust between the parties so as to allow direct, face-to-face negotiations to take place and helped thrash out the key details of a political settlement. These contacts were also crucial in allowing cantonment and demobilization of forces to take place once the settlement was signed. The UN mediator's task was aided by six friends of the peace process—Norway, the United States, Mexico, Venezuela, Spain, and Colombia. In some ways, the peace process in Guatemala marked an important innovation in peacemaking through its involvement of civil society actors in the peace process. The peace accords also set in motion some ambitious targets for democratization and the promotion of greater levels of equity in Guatemalan society, which were only partially met during their implementation. As Stanley and Holiday report: "Negotiations under UN 'moderation' proved more fruitful than earlier talks, in part because the Guatemalan parties were better prepared to make progress, in part because the UN focused more international attention on the process, and in part because UN moderator Jean Arnault gained the confidence of the two sides. The UN's strategy during the talks, particularly the last phase, was to help the government translate its proposals into terms acceptable to the UNRG."[12]

Tajikistan

The United Nations helped to facilitate negotiations between the Tajikistan government and Islamic rebel groups in a war that displaced one-sixth of the country's total population of six million following the breakup of the Soviet Union. The December 1996 peace agreement, which was signed between Tajik President Imamali Rakhmonov and the Islamic leader Siad Abdullo Nuri, saw a reduction in the level of armed violence. In 1997 the two sides agreed to the terms of a final peace, involving a power-sharing arrangement in the Commission for National Reconciliation, prisoner exchanges, amnesty laws, and the integration of armed forces of both sides into a new military structure. Although the implementation of the settlement has been marred by continued outbreaks of violence and resurgent Islamic fundamentalism, a variety of nongovernmental organizations have been hard at work promoting intercommunal reconciliation.[13]

LESSONS FROM UN PEACEMAKING

Some clear lessons spring from these more successful episodes of UN mediation and peacemaking in the final decade and a half of the twentieth century.

The first lesson is that no matter who is the mediator, the parties to the dispute have to be ready to consider seriously the negotiated option as a way out of the conflict. In other words, conflicts must be "ripe for resolution" before a durable peace settlement can be negotiated and implemented. Although the concept of ripeness is somewhat problematic and difficult to operationalize without being tautological, it is nonetheless widely recognized as critical to understanding why warring parties may be interested in reaching a negotiated settlement.[14] Of the various factors that may make resolution more attractive, thereby enhancing the prospects for successful third-party intervention, Zartman suggests that the prime conditions are that neither side in a conflict feels it can win the conflict, and the parties perceive the costs and prospects of continuing war to be more burdensome than the costs and prospects of settlement. The prospects for a negotiated settlement to a dispute are thus greater when war weariness has set in among the parties and a conflict has reached a plateau or "hurting stalemate" in which unilateral (military) solutions are no longer believed to be viable or achievable. One of the reasons why Iran and Iraq were prepared to consider a negotiated cease-fire as the first step to ending the war was that neither side was able to win the war after almost eight years of fighting. The same is true in El Salvador and Guatemala. Close observers of these two conflicts have also noted that they were characterized by a military stalemate after many years of protracted violence in which neither government nor guerrilla opposition forces were able to secure a decisive victory over their opponents. As different Cambodian factions lost their principal external sources of support in a civil war that had exacted an enormous price on the Cambodian people, there was clearly enough "ripeness" to pursue negotiations and reach a political settlement. War weariness among the parties also created strong incentives for negotiations in Mozambique.

A second lesson is that successful UN mediation requires the clear and unambiguous support of the Security Council and Council mandates that do not compromise the mission of the UN mediator.[15] If Security Council members—especially the Permanent Five—are divided or are perceived by the parties to a dispute as trying to manipulate mandates to serve their own partisan interests (as they were during much of the Cold War), it is difficult for mediators to gain the necessary traction to move negotiations forward. Quite clearly, one of the main obstacles to successful UN mediation in the early years of the Iran-Iraq conflict was the fact that the UN Security Council was not true to its own principles. This was so because it failed to condemn Iraqi aggression and call for a restoration of the territorial status quo ante. This made it difficult for the UN mediator to secure Iranian cooperation in the negotiations. Similarly, early UN efforts to become involved in the peace process in Central America in the early 1980s were stymied by U.S. opposition in the Security Council.[16]

A third lesson is that it is a mistake to think that the UN's only mediation assets are neutrality and impartiality and that the UN is not a "mediator with muscle." In those situations where coercive intervention is desirable, as in the case of Mozambique or Tajikistan, UN mediators can sometimes bring the full weight and pressure of Security Council members to bear on the parties. However, such pressure can only be exerted if (1) there are clear lines of authority between the mediator, the Secretary-General, and the Security Council, and (2) if the Council itself is prepared to deploy force or carry through on threats and offers made by the mediator. A mediator's leverage is obviously undermined if parties feel that the mediator is an independent actor who has little capacity to make good on promises or threats.

Likewise, coordination in a mediation should involve the careful crafting of a coherent political strategy that diminishes the possibility that outsiders will undermine the peace process. For example, the Cambodian peace process in the later 1980s and early 1990s was related to the understandings leading up to the Paris peace accords. China, Russia, Vietnam, and the United States were keen to reduce their regional rivalries, exit from military commitments that were increasingly costly, and bring about a withdrawal of Vietnamese troops from Cambodia. The success of the peace process and the political settlement in Cambodia were intimately related to the *shared* policies of entente and a systemic realignment of U.S.–Soviet and Soviet–Chinese relations with the end of the Cold War, all of which made cooperation and support for the United Nations' peace plan and Permanent Five-led negotiations possible.[17]

A fourth lesson is that sometimes the UN has the right personnel for a mediatory mission. For example, to understand why the United Nations ended up being the "mediator of choice" in El Salvador, one has to look beyond its perceived "neutrality" by the various parties, beyond the fact that the United Nations represented "great-power" interests through the Security Council, to the fact that the Secretary-General himself at that time, Javier Perez de Cuellar, and his special representative came from the region and were willing to give the negotiations the political commitment they required.[18] With a different cast of personalities, the United Nations may not have been able to play such an effective role. Recall that concerns about Perez de Cuellar's impending departure from his post helped propel the negotiations to closure.

A fifth lesson is that mediated interventions generate their own psychological and political momentum. Success breeds success, and failure breeds failure. The UN's obvious success in mediation in El Salvador paved the way for its subsequent success in helping to negotiate an end to the civil war in Guatemala. The successful UN peacekeeping operation in Namibia helped raise the enthusiasm level for UN peacekeeping operations elsewhere in southern Africa, including Mozambique. UN mediators also clearly had both the trust and confidence of the parties. In both sets of conflicts, the UN's reputation as the "mediator of choice" was clearly well deserved.

MEDIATING CONFLICTS IN THE TWENTY-FIRST CENTURY

As alluded to above, the UN's more recent track record in mediation to some extent compares unfavorably with its record a decade earlier because there are fewer conflicts to mediate. However, there are a number of important reasons why the UN may experience difficulties being a successful mediator in this decade. The first is that many of today's conflicts are based on deeply entrenched differences and, therefore, are immune to any kind of peaceful third party intervention. The second is that in many—though obviously not all—of these conflicts there are formidable barriers to intervention by *any* third party, including the UN. The third reason is that the UN, in spite of its considerable mediation assets, is not always the mediator of choice. This is because nongovernmental organizations or small states, which have different political assets, are preferred for mediating certain kinds of conflict. In other types of conflict, the parties continue to look to great powers as mediators for the same reasons identified by Touval almost a decade ago.

The Intractability Problem

Many of today's conflicts are intractable. In spite of the fact that some of them have been the subject of prolonged and sustained international efforts to end them, including mediation, military intervention, peacekeeping, and/or humanitarian and development assistance, they have proven to be extraordinarily resilient to any kind of settlement or resolution.[19] Their resistance to a settlement may appear to derive from a single cause or principal ingredient, but closer examination usually points to multiple causes.

For the UN or any other third party, mediating an intractable conflict is an exercise in frustration. Violence is a more or less permanent feature of these conflicts even though the actual level of violence may be intermittent, sporadic, or even seasonal. Such conflicts may be stalemated because they have not reached that plateau—what William Zartman calls a mutually "hurting stalemate"—where the costs of a political settlement are appreciably lower (and recognized to be so) than the military and political costs of continued fighting.[20] They do not reach that "ripeness" until all of the parties are seriously open to resolving their differences through negotiation.

The Israeli–Palestinian conflict is a classic example of an active intractable conflict: it has persisted for almost five decades; violence is episodic but recurrent; and the conflict has refused to yield to the persistent efforts of various third parties, including small countries like Norway and a superpower like the United States. In addition, it is one conflict where the UN is not wanted by one of the key parties to the conflict, Israel. Most importantly, though, the conflict falls into the intractable category because none of the parties to the conflict is prepared to renounce completely the use of force and violence to achieve its political objectives.[21]

Another example of an intractable conflict is the war in the Sudan (where the UN has been a non-player). Some two million people have died in the conflict that has gone on for some 19 years between the Sudanese government dominated by Arabic-speaking Muslims and the SPLA and other rebel groups in the south who have been fighting for greater autonomy for Christian and animist groups. The United States government has hosted talks between the two sides in the Kenyan capital, Nairobi. Although the two sides have not been able to resolve their differences, they have agreed to extend their truce until the end of March 2003. The key points of contention are the details about sharing power and wealth between northern and southern Sudan.

Conflicts in Kashmir, Afghanistan, Democratic Republic of Congo, and Colombia also fall into the active intractable category because the parties to these disputes have not completely renounced violence.

High (or Insurmountable) Barriers to Entry

Third parties, including the UN, that seek a peaceful resolution to a dispute may not be able to make progress as mediators when faced with "denial" by a relatively powerful state. For example, the division of Kashmir into Indian and Pakistan-held sectors has witnessed repeated outbreaks of violent armed conflict between the two countries, the most serious of which occurred in 1965. The only instance of outside mediation in the conflict took place in 1966 when the Soviet Union tried unsuccessfully to broker a settlement between the two countries for largely self-interested reasons. Since that ill-fated attempt, India has actively resisted any kind of external mediation, fearing that any sort of third party intervention would lend legitimacy to Pakistani claims to Kashmir.

Key actors in a conflict may also perceive a higher interest—as well as lower risk—in managing the conflict themselves than in attempts to resolve it. That is, they may prefer to freeze the conflict in order to contain its spread, deter an adversary or rogue power, and limit the potential regional damage. For many years the United States has stationed its troops in South Korea because deterrence is seen as the best conflict management strategy for the Korean peninsula. The point is that third parties, especially powerful ones, have strategic options and wide-ranging interests. A mediated settlement that entails negotiation with the enemy of a regional ally involves real risks—not least in terms of relations with the affected ally and other allies. Some third parties have such strong geopolitical or strategic interests in a region where an intractable conflict exists that it becomes off limits for mediation until their interests shift. Korea may be such a case. Others, historically, might include Cuba's role in southern Africa until the late 1980s and the roles that Vietnam and China played in Cambodia until the early 1990s. Today, this analysis would apply to Russia's role in the Caucasus conflicts. On the other hand, experience suggests that a dogmatic adherence to deterrence and tit-for-tat power balancing or damage limiting strategies may blind states to opportunities for successful mediation efforts; such opportunities can emerge from changing circumstances, crises, leadership changes, and other factors.

Proliferation of Other Mediators

During the Cold War period, the superpower conflict tended to prevent third party mediation in different regional conflict zones, for example, the Middle East, Africa, and Asia. Now new actors, including governments, nongovernmental organizations, and regional organizations, are involved.[22] Different actors have different mediation strengths and weaknesses. As Jeffrey Rubin (1992) has suggested, there are different kinds of resources and influences that mediators can bring to the negotiating table, and these are related to different bases of power, including reward power, coercive power, expertise, legitimacy, and informational power. Whereas nongovernmental organizations and private, individual mediators are low in reward and coercive power capabilities, they may be strong in expert power capabilities.[23] Regional organizations may have special strengths, such as being closer to the problem and consequently having a better understanding of the sources, dynamics, and alternative points of intervention in a conflict. NGOs may lack leverage in a conflict as their relationship to power holders is more removed than intergovernmental organizations, but they may have other assets, including special relationships with governments and intergovernmental players from which they can borrow leverage.

In Mozambique, Sant'Egidio became part of the political landscape and was able to play an important role by offering negotiating space to the parties, which allowed the parties to conceive and accept alternatives to their otherwise hardened positions. More recently, in the civil war in Sri Lanka—one of the world's more intractable conflicts—the parties turned to Norway to serve as facilitator in negotiating a cease-fire and the broad outlines of political settlement. Norway was an acceptable mediator to the Singhalese-dominated government and to the northern Tamil "Tiger" insurgency movement partly because it was one of the country's major development assistance donors and had a strong reputation for competence and impartiality. The peace talks, brokered by the Norwegian government, have been taking place in Nakhon Pathom in Thailand. Although the talks were originally expected to focus mostly on humanitarian issues such as de-mining and refugees, the parties have gone further and agreed to the establishment of three committees to examine rehabilitation needs in war-torn areas, to promote military de-escalation, and to look at political questions at the heart of the 19-year civil war.

As a consequence of the proliferation of mediators on the international stage, the UN finds itself operating on a more crowded playing field, where other mediators are competing for the attention of the warring parties. This does not necessarily mean that the UN is relegated to the sidelines, but it does mean that it has to choose its negotiating opportunities with care.

RECENT UN MEDIATION INITIATIVES

It is difficult to draw any hard-and-fast generalizations about when and where the UN has an effective mediation role to play in today's conflicts. In some cases, it is quite clear that the UN is essentially "grandfathered" as the mediator of choice as a direct consequence of its previous mediated interventions. In other cases, the UN has emerged as a mediator during the peace-building phase of peace operations because the UN is responsible for implementing a settlement that has been negotiated by other third parties. Cyprus and the Western Sahara are the most obvious grandfathered cases of UN mediation.

Cyprus

Cyprus provides a classic example of an intractable conflict that, at least until recently, appears to have been frozen. In spite of almost 40 years of ongoing mediation, the UN (along with various other third parties like the United States and NATO) has been unable to bring about a negotiated settlement. Although the absence of a hurting stalemate is one possible impediment to resolution, the UN's problems in reaching a negotiated settlement historically have been compounded by the "hands off" attitude by the United States and other permanent members of the Security Council towards the self-determination and territorial claims of the parties. In addition, there is the fact that none of Turkey's key allies in NATO, especially the United States, is willing to force Turkey to compromise. The Security Council mandate, which established UNFICYP in 1964, advised the peacekeeping force "to use its best efforts to prevent a recurrence of fighting, as necessary, to contribute to the maintenance and restoration of law and order and a return to normal conditions." Following Turkey's invasion of the island in 1974, the mandate was changed to include humanitarian functions. The "restoration of law and order" was never defined in spite of the dramatic change in political circumstances.

Although the mandate gave the UN the necessary flexibility to deal with the situation, the lack of political direction hampered its ability to affect a change in the political environment in which it has operated, at least until relatively recently.[24] Turkey's desire to gain admission to the European Union, coupled with Greece's own desire to see Cyprus enter into the union, has been simultaneously a complicating element in the UN-led negotiations, and also a source of some leverage. The United States' own interest in supporting Turkey's entry into the European Union in order to promote political and regional stability has also renewed its own interest and involvement in reaching a political settlement to the dispute over Cyprus.

Western Sahara

The Western Sahara is another "grandfathered" case of UN mediation and involvement in peacekeeping. UN engagement in the conflict dates to Spain's withdrawal from the Western Sahara in 1976 and the conflict over territorial jurisdiction between Morocco and the independence movement led by the Frente Popular para la Liberacion de Saguia el-Hamra y de Rio del Oro (Frente POLISARIO).[25] The UN and the OAU brokered a set of "settlement proposals" that were accepted in 1988 by the Moroccan government, which had taken control of the territory, and the Frente POLISARIO, which was supported by Algeria. Under the provisions of the agreement, the United Nations would sponsor a referendum on Western Saharan independence to be managed by the United Nations Mission for the Referendum in Western Sahara (MINURSO). The referendum was to have taken place in 1992 following a negotiated cease-fire, but it never took place. Although both sides have indicated their commitment to implementing the settlement proposals, they have not been able to agree on the modalities for a referendum. In spite of repeated efforts by the Secretary-General through his personal representatives to mediate a resolution to the outstanding issues that stand in the way of an agreement, divisions remain over a number of key issues, including the repatriation of refugees and the appeals process associated with voter eligibility in the referendum. Arguably, another frustrating factor is the unwillingness of France and the United States to pressure Morocco because of the strategic importance they place on the stability of King Hassan II's regime.

In other cases, the UN finds itself driven into a mediation role as a result of responsibilities it has acquired for peace-building, as in the case of Afghanistan or East Timor (where it also helped to mediate East Timor's independence from Indonesia). Mediation among previously warring parties has become part and parcel of peace-building challenges.[26] This is not necessarily a new trend. Those responsible for managing peacekeeping and peace-building operations often find themselves cast in the role of mediator among previously warring parties.[27] The terms of a peace settlement often set strict limits on the mandates of third parties responsible for assisting with the implementation of the settlement in question. The terms can therefore create their own set of constraints, not all of which are conducive to peace-building. Military, humanitarian, and development objectives are frequently at odds. As Aldo Ajello observes, the implementation phase of a settlement changes the balance of forces between government and opposition, tending to favor the ruling party that is running the country.[28] This creates strong incentives for the opposition to defect from the peace process. In this strained environment it is all too easy for those responsible for implementation to lose sight of the "big picture" and their broader political objectives. There is obviously no substitute for carefully mediated and planned peace agreements that are not just driven by a sense of urgency for the quick fix but by a clear strategic vision.

Afghanistan

The UN's most recent role in Afghanistan follows the U.S.-led military intervention to overthrow the Taliban regime and rout the terrorist group al-Qaeda following the events of September 11, 2001. For many years, prior to the consolidation of Taliban rule in the country, the UN was involved in trying to mediate a political settlement among the country's different warring factions. At the Bonn Conference, which was convened in November 2001 following the collapse of the Taliban regime, the United Nations Special Mission for Afghanistan (UNSMA) played a key role in mediating among Afghanistan's different factions to establish an interim authority that would be replaced after six months by a transitional authority selected by the *loya jirga*, a body representing different Afghani groups. Under the agreement, popular elections would eventually be held for a new government. One of the main difficulties at the Bonn meeting was the issue of adequate representation of the Afghani people, especially in the interim authority. The Secretary-General's special representative, Lakhdar Brahimi, played a critical role in getting the different factions to reach an agreement, which saw Hamid Karzai sworn in as chairman of the interim administration.

East Timor

The UN's involvement in East Timor dates to the UN General Assembly Resolution of 1960, when East Timor was added to the UN's list of non-self-governing territories.[29] When Portugal, which administered the territory, finally sought to establish a provisional government in 1974, a civil war broke out between those who wanted outright independence and those who wanted to unite the territory with Indonesia. Indonesia subsequently intervened and forcibly annexed East Timor in 1976. From 1982 on, the UN conducted negotiations with Indonesia and Portugal to resolve the status of East Timor. A set of agreements was finally concluded in 1999 under which the UN would consult with the people of East Timor concerning their views on a "special autonomy status" for the territory within Indonesia. There was considerable violence, much of which was instigated by Indonesian security forces, who opposed East Timorese independence. In September 1999, a multinational force led by Australia was deployed to East Timor to quell the violence and help the United Nations Mission in East Timor (UNAMET) restore civil authority and facilitate humanitarian assistance. Voters finally went to the polls in August 2001 to elect a constituent assembly tasked with the responsibility of writing and adopting a new constitution for the country and helping a new East Timorese government run the territory before it received its independence on May 20, 2002. In the post-independence period, the United Nations has continued to maintain its presence with a successor mission known as the United Nations Mission of Support in East Timor. It is responsible for helping maintain security in the country and providing core administrative assistance to the new government.[30]

Mediation Back-Up in Other Conflict Zones

In Sri Lanka, Burundi, the Congo, and other zones of conflict, the United Nations has not always been at the center of mediation efforts. However, it is not necessarily a spectator either. In Burundi, for example, the United Nations Office has supported key initiatives aimed at promoting peace in that country. The United Nations was extremely supportive of the efforts of former South African President Nelson Mandela, who was designated by the African heads of state to serve as a facilitator in the conflict. That support extended to allowing Mr. Mandela to address the members of the Security Council in order to raise the profile of the conflict. The Secretary-General's own special representative, Jean Arnault, was tasked to head the United Nations Office in Burundi and to work with the parties to build a consensus around peace talks.

The civil war in the Congo provides another example of an intractable conflict where the United Nations has been unable to make significant headway in bringing about a negotiated resolution. The complexity and deeply entrenched nature of Congo's civil war and the large number of actors and interests involved have made the conflict a particularly difficult one to resolve.

The origins of the war can be traced to the period following Rwanda's genocide in 1994, when Laurent Kabila rose to power in Congo (formerly Zaire), overthrowing Mobutu Sese Seko in 1997. In 1998 Rwanda and Uganda, supported by Congolese rebels, attempted to overthrow President Kabila, while Angola, Zimbabwe, Namibia, Sudan, and Chad sent troops to defend him. The situation in the Congo soon deteriorated into chaos, characterized by widespread looting, disease, and famine that has claimed the lives of millions over the course of four years. Fighting over the Congo's vast mineral resources is one of the main factors that perpetuate the conflict.

Since 1999 a series of pacts, cease-fires, and peace agreements have been reached, and foreign troops have agreed to withdraw, but promises have been broken on all sides and violence has continued. Although the UN has not always been at the center of negotiations among the warring parties (South Africa, for instance, has played a major role), it has supported peace talks and has been active in terms of sending delegations to help mediate the ongoing dispute. More recently, the UN has been increasing the numbers of peacekeepers sent to the region in an effort to advance the fragile peace process. Despite the signing of a recent UN–South Africa–brokered peace deal among the parties, internal fighting persists among rebel groups and promises continue to be broken.

CONCLUSION

In the twenty-first century, the UN is still an important mediator of international disputes. But it also finds itself playing on a more crowded stage as there are other mediators who are more than willing to parachute into conflict zones with offers of good offices. Whereas the UN's principal strengths are its ability to focus international pressure and attention on a problem—though not always with unqualified, positive results—this is not necessarily what the parties want. Sometimes they prefer to work with small powers or nongovernmental organizations because this allows them to take the conflict out of the political spotlight, as in the case of Norway's intermediary roles in the Oslo peace process or currently in Sri Lanka. It is also arguably the case that today's conflicts are more intractable, and therefore less amenable, to the mediated interventions of any third party, including the UN. The UN may find itself the mediator of choice because of its previous involvement in these protracted conflict cases, as has happened in Cyprus. It may also find itself playing the role of mediator of last resort because others have tried and failed, as was the case in Burundi. In these situations, its intermediary efforts may be compromised by poorly timed take-overs by those who intervened before. In other cases, like Afghanistan, the UN may be driven into an intermediary role as a result of the U.S. war against terrorism and the U.S. proclivity to allow the UN to pick up the pieces after the withdrawal of U.S. forces. In these cases, mediation merges with the tasks of peace-building and efforts to bring political, social, and economic order to societies that have been torn apart by repeated interventions by outsiders.

Getting the parties back to the negotiating table and resurrecting old formulas (or devising new ones) are formidable challenges and ones that the UN may be ill-equipped to handle. In spite of these hurdles, it is still too early to write off the UN as a mediator given its past track record of success and its obvious staying power in difficult situations. It is also true that when a negotiated settlement is reached, there will continue to be demands of effective mediation during the settlement's implementation—the so-called peace-building phase of peacemaking. More often than not, the UN will be cast in this role because it will be given the responsibility for implementing a settlement.

NOTES

1. Yasushi Akashi, "The Limits of UN Diplomacy and the Future of Conflict Mediation," *Survival* 37 (Winter 1995–6): 83–98 and Kjell Skjelsbaek, "The UN Secretary-General and the Mediation of International Disputes," *Journal of Peace Research* 28(1) (1991): 99–115.
2. Cyrus R.Vance and David A. Hamburg, *Pathfinders for Peace: a Report to the UN Secretary-General on the Role of Special Representatives and Personal Envoys* (New York: Carnegie Commission of New York, 1999).
3. Ted Robert Gurr, "Containing Internal War in the Twenty-First Century," in *From Reaction to Conflict Prevention: Opportunities for the UN System* eds. Fen Osler Hampson and David Malone (Boulder, Colo.: Lynne Reinner, 2002), 41–62; and Monty G. Marshall, "Measuring the Societal Impact of War," in *From Reaction to Conflict Prevention* eds. Fen Osler Hampson and David Malone, 63–104.
4. Saadia Touval, "Why the UN Fails," *Foreign Affairs* 73(5) (September/ October, 1994): 44–57.
5. Edward A. Amley, Jr. "Peace by Other Means: Using Rewards in UN Efforts to End Conflicts," *Denver Journal of International Law and Policy* 26 (Winter, 1998): 235–297. Fen Osler Hampson, *Nurturing Peace: Why Peace Settlements Succeed or Fail* (Washington, D.C.: United States Institute of Peace, 1996).
6. Wolfgang Biermann and Martin Vadset *UN Peacekeeping in Trouble: Lessons Learned from the Former Yugoslavia; Peacekeepers' Views on the Limits and Possibilities on the United Nations in a Civil War-Like Conflict* (Aldershot, UK: Ashgate, 1998). Jan Eliasson, "Establishing Trust in the Healer: Preventive Diplomacy and the Future of the United Nations," in *Preventive Diplomacy: Stopping Wars Before They Start* ed. Kevin M. Cahill (New York: Basic Books and the Center for International Health and Cooperation, 1996). Thomas F. Marsteller Jr. and Paul E. Mason "UN Mediation: More Effective Options," *SAIS Review* 5(2) (1985): 271–284.
7. Cameron R. Hume, *The United Nations, Iran, and Iraq: How Peacemaking Changed* (Bloomington: Indiana University Press, 1994).
8. Alvaro De Soto, "Ending Violent Conflict in El Salvador" in *Herding Cats: Multiparty Mediation in a Complex World* eds. Chester A. Crocker, Fen Osler Hampson, and Pamela Aall (Washington, D.C. United States Institute of Peace Press, 1999), 345–386. Gerardo L. Munck and Chetan Kumar, "Civil Conflicts and the Conditions for Successful International Intervention: a Comparative Study of Cambodia and El Salvador," *Review of International Studies* 21 (April 1995): 159–181.

9. Richard H. Solomon, "Bringing Peace to Cambodia" in *Herding Cats* eds. Chester A. Crocker, Fen Osler Hampson, and Pamela Aall, 325–344. Richard H. Solomon, *Exiting Indochina: U.S. Leadership of the Cambodia Settlement and Normalization with Vietnam* (Washington, D.C.: United States Institute of Peace Press, 2000).

10. Andrea Bartoli, "Mediating Peace in Mozambique: The Role of the Community of Sant'Egidi," in *Herding Cats* eds. Chester A. Crocker, Fen Osler Hampson, and Pamela Aall (Washington, D.C.: Institute of Peace Press, 1999), 245–274.

11. Aldo Ajello, "Mozambique: Implementation of the 1992 Peace Agreement," in *Herding Cats,* 1999.

12. David Holiday and William Stanley, "Everyone Participates, No One is Responsible: Peace Implementation in Guatemala," in *Ending Civil Wars: The Implementation of Peace Agreements* eds. Stephen John Stedman, Donald Rothchild, and Elizabeth M. Cousens (Boulder, Colo.: Lynne Reinner, 2003), 429

13. Harold H. Saunders, "Prenegotiation and Circumnegotiation: Arenas of the Peace Process," in *Managing Global Chaos* eds. Chester A. Crocker, Fen Osler Hampson, and Pamela Aall (Washington, D.C.: United States Institute of Peace, 1996), 419–432. Harold H. Saunders, "The Multilevel Peace Process in Tajikistan," in *Herding Cats* eds. Chester A. Crocker, Fen Osler Hampson, and Pamela Aall, 159–180.

14. William I. Zartman, *Ripe for Resolution: Conflict and Intervention in Africa* (New York: Oxford University Press, 1989). Willaim I. Zartman, "The Timing of Peace Initiatives: Hurting Stalemates and Ripe Moments," *The Global Review of Ethnopolitics* 1(1) (2001): 8–18.

15. Boutros Boutros-Ghali, "Challenges of Preventive Diplomacy: The Role of United Nations and its Secretary General," in *Preventive Diplomacy: Stopping Wars Before They Start* ed. Kevin M. Cahill (New York: Basic Books and the Center for International Health and Cooperation, 1996). Anthony Parsons, *The Security Council. An Uncertain Future* (London: David Davies Memorial Institute Occasional Paper, 1994).

16. Alvaro De Soto, "Ending Violent Conflict in El Salvador," in *Herding Cats* eds. Chester A. Crocker, Fen Osler Hampson, and Pamela Aalls. Fen Osler Hampson, *Nurturing Peace.*

17. Richard H. Solomon, "Bringing Peace to Cambodia," in *Herding Cats* eds. Chester A. Crocker, Fen Osler Hampson, and Pamela Aall, 325–344. Richard H. Solomon, *Exiting Indochina.*

18. Alvaro De Soto, "Ending Violent Conflict in El Salvador," in *Herding Cats* eds. Chester A. Crocker, Fen Osler Hampson, and Pamela Aalls. Fen Osler Hampson, *Nurturing Peace.*

19. Oliver P. Richmond, "Mediating Ethnic Conflict: a Task for Sisyphus?" *Global Society* 13(2) (April, 1999): 181–205. Donald Rothchild, "Ethnic Bargaining and the Management of Intense Conflict," *International Negotiation Journal* 2(1) (1997).

20. William I. Zartman, *Ripe for Resolution.*

21. Louis Kriseberg, *International Conflict Resolution: The U.S.–USSR and Middle East Cases* (New Haven: Yale University Press, 1992).
22. Chester A. Crocker, Fen Osler Hampson, and Pamela Aall, *Herding Cats.*
23. Herbert C. Kelman, "The Interactive Problem-Solving Approach," in *Managing Global Chaos* eds. Chester A. Crocker, Fen Osler Hampson, and Pamela Aall, 501–520. Herbert C. Kelman, "Social-Psychological Dimensions of International Conflict," in *Peacemaking in International Conflict: Methods and Techniques* eds. I. William Zartman and J. Lewis Rasmussen (Washington, D.C.: United States Institute of Peace, 1997), 191–238.
24. Karl Th. Birgisson, "UN Peacekeeping Force in Cyprus" in *The Evolution of UN Peacekeeping: Case Studies and Comparative Analysis* ed. William J. Durch (New York: St. Martin's, 1993), 219–236. Fen Osler Hampson, "The Pursuit of Human Rights: The UN in El Salvador," in *UN Peacekeeping, American Policy, and the Uncivil Wars of the 1990s* ed. William J. Durch (New York: St. Martin's, 1996), 69–102.
25. Salim Fakirani, "The Role of International Law in the Negotiation and Implementation of Peace Agreements: The Case of Western Sahara," Research Essay Submitted to the Norman Paterson School of International Affairs, Carleton University (Ottawa, Canada, 2002).
26. Michele Griffin and Bruce Jones, "Building Peace Through Transitional Authority: New Directions, Major Challenges," *International Peacekeeping* 7(4) (Winter, 2000): 75–90. Astri Suhrke, "Peacekeepers as Nation-Builders: Dilemmas of the UN in East Timor," *International Peacekeeping* 8(4) (Winter, 2001): 1–20.
27. Fen Osler Hampson, *Nurturing Peace.*
28. Aldo Ajello, "Mozambique: Implementation of the 1992 Peace Agreement," in *Herding Cats.*
29. Joel C. Beauvais, "Benevolent Despotism: A Critique of UN State Building in East Timor," *New York Journal of International Law and Politics* 33(4) (Summer, 2001): 1101–1178. Jarat Chopra, "The UN's Kingdom of East Timor," *Survival* 42(3) (Autumn, 2000): 27–39. James Cotton, "Against the Grain: The East Timor Intervention," *Survival* 43(1) (Spring, 2001): 127–142.
30. Ramesh Thakur, "Cambodia, East Timor and the Brahimi Report," *International Peacekeeping* 8(3) (Autumn, 2001): 115–124.

PART III
REVERSING, DETERRING, AND PUNISHING AGGRESSIONS

CHAPTER 6

ANOTHER RELUCTANT BELLIGERENT: THE UNITED NATIONS AND THE WAR ON TERRORISM

Edward C. Luck

INTRODUCTION TO A DILEMMA

Terrorism is only marginally more welcome on the agenda of the United Nations than it is in our cities and neighborhoods. Diplomats and international civil servants, much like the rest of us, understand that they must address terrorism. But they, too, wish it would go away or that someone else would take care of it. No one really knows what motivates others to undertake vicious and seemingly random attacks on innocent civilians, nor have any particularly novel or effective means of deterring or preventing such acts appeared. Though the world body took steps to ratchet up both its normative and operational opposition to terrorism in the 1990s and again after the attacks on the United States of 9/11, it remains much more of a bit player on the former than the latter. This paper asks why this is so, and whether there are grounds to expect the UN to evolve into a more enthusiastic, well-rounded, and central participant in counterterrorism efforts in the future.

In some ways, the UN's persistent ambivalence about tackling terrorism seems counterintuitive. Surely there are few issues that have so preoccupied public, parliamentary, and media attention in recent years, especially, but hardly exclusively, in the United States and other influential member states. Nor have many issues simultaneously affected life on so many continents and in such diverse countries. For an organization such as the UN, which constantly frets about its public image, the chance to demonstrate leadership on such a global, hot, and cutting-edge problem should be attractive, even irresistible. If the UN is to reassert its core purpose of maintaining international peace and security, what better way than by joining, without hesitation or reservation, the fight against terrorism, arguably the most acute threat to peace and security of the early twenty-first century?

Counterterrorism, moreover, would offer the opportunity of giving operational and substantive content to three of the Secretary-General's favorite themes: conflict prevention, human security, and the growing role of non-state actors. Preventing assaults on civilians by terrorist groups would seem to be one policy goal that could draw all three themes together in a powerful and mutually reinforcing message. True, prevention has been a rather uneven and uncertain pursuit even in more conventional forms of conflict, but the notion is not going to gain traction by skipping the hard cases. As the Secretary-General has underlined, the UN needs to be as concerned about dealing with uncivil as civil society. In the perverted logic of terrorism, uncivil society can affect the behavior of states by attacking the most civil and vulnerable elements of society. How can the UN be a credible voice for human security if it shirks the responsibility of giving practical content to the goals of "protecting the vulnerable," "preventing deadly conflict," developing "a more human-centered approach to security," and reinforcing "freedom from fear" trumpeted in the Secretary-General's Millennium Report?[1]

Like it or not, the UN will have a hard time walking away from this challenge when, as the Secretary-General's Policy Working Group on the United Nations and Terrorism put it, "terrorism is, and is intended to be, an assault on the principles of law, order, human rights and peaceful settlement of disputes on which the world body was founded."[2] The UN, in other words, stands for everything that terrorists oppose. So it is no coincidence that, despite the reluctance of the UN's embrace of the antiterrorist cause, Osama bin Laden and his colleagues in al-Qaeda have placed the world organization in a prominent position on their list of possible targets. Even in the unlikely scenario that the perpetrators of terrorism permit the UN to turn its collective back on their destructive vocation, it is doubtful that the member states would allow it. Though most are reluctant to bring their complaints about terrorist or counterterrorist acts to the Security Council, when they do it tends to be with great feeling. Whether the subject is terrorism or counterterrorism, the legitimating decisions and pronouncements of the world body matter to capitals, including to the most influential ones.

Here lies the dilemma. For political reasons, the UN—despite its ambivalence—is drawn to cases of terrorism like a moth to a flame. Yet a host of historical, conceptual, structural, and political forces keep the organization from going much beyond its distinctive and valuable normative role. Its programmatic initiatives, while innovative, remain modest. The remainder of this paper describes each of these four forces in turn and then draws some broad conclusions about the future prospects for the UN's involvement in taming terrorism.

History, Context, and Standards

Before turning to what the future might hold, or even to an assessment of present efforts, it would help to get a feel for what has been attempted in the past and how these earlier initiatives fared. After all, international efforts to curb terrorism are hardly of recent vintage. Spurred primarily by worries about the international implications of political assassinations, in the mid-1930s the League of Nations drafted a Convention for Prevention and Punishment of

Terrorism as well as a companion Convention for the Creation of an International Criminal Court to try those accused of offenses under the terrorism convention.[3] Several delegations urged the adoption of the court to prevent impunity for terrorist crimes, while others, including the United States, of course, saw such a step as premature. Though these conventions never received enough ratifications to take effect, much of the rhetoric of alarm that propelled them would sound familiar to contemporary readers. The Soviet representative on the Committee for the International Repression of Terrorism, for instance, stressed "the exceptional gravity of terrorist activities and the danger which they present to international relations."[4] Presaging worries about the effects of globalization, Count Carton de Wiart of Belgium, president of the 1937 negotiating conference, warned that "[w]e cannot but realise with shame and disquiet how advancing knowledge and improved communications have served in their turn to menace the security of persons and property and helped to promote acts designated by that new term 'terrorism'—acts which, by reason of their gravity and contagious nature, are prejudiced not only to the interests of individuals as such or of one or more specific States, but may affect mankind as a whole."[5] The drafters foresaw that terrorist violence not only threatened individuals, it also could complicate relations among states. In some cases, this may be precisely what the perpetrators intend.

The prescient convention, moreover, sought to limit the transfer of small arms that might be used in terrorist acts and to require arms manufacturers to register purchases of such weapons and to mark each arm with a serial number or other distinctive marking (Article 13). Foreshadowing current efforts by the UN, the Czech government underlined the possibility "by bringing national laws into unison . . . of obtaining an effective means of coping with the use of criminal violence for political ends."[6] It noted the complementarity, in that regard, of the 1929 Convention for the Suppression of Counterfeiting Currency and the 1936 Convention for the Suppression of the Illicit Traffic in Dangerous Drugs. The Terrorism Convention also managed something that has proven elusive for the UN: to articulate a straightforward definition. "Acts of terrorism," according to Article 1, "means criminal acts directed against a State and intended or calculated to create a state of terror in the minds of particular persons, or a group of persons, or the general public."

Despite these early roots, efforts to promote international cooperation against terrorism did *not* receive a boost with the creation of the United Nations in 1945. The new organization's Charter, shaped by the all-consuming task of trying to forestall another round of massive interstate violence, failed to mention terrorism either as one of its many diverse concerns or as a threat to international peace and security, whose maintenance was to be the purpose of the Security Council. Nevertheless, the UN's involvement with stemming terrorism has evolved and grown. Generally, the trend has been toward deeper, more sustained, and more substantive engagement.[7]

During the organization's first quarter century, neither the Security Council nor the General Assembly addressed terrorism directly. In 1968 and

1969, Secretary-General U Thant first used his good offices in situations of airline hijackings.[8] By and large, however, terrorism—though hardly rare—was viewed as a local, not global, phenomenon, something for states to deal with individually or bilaterally. With Cold War tensions and the threat of nuclear armageddon permeating the international atmosphere, terrorists were clearly not the world's first concern.

By the early 1970s, several developments began to change this stagnant picture. The frequency, violence, and reach of terrorist incidents started to expand noticeably, and media attention grew apace.[9] The Council passed its first anti-hijacking resolution (256) in 1970, but largely East-West and North-South splits among the members about how to handle terrorism seemed only to deepen and sharpen as the number of cases referred to the Council grew. The Assembly seemed to be as interested in understanding and rationalizing terrorism as in suppressing it, while the majority of members of the Council got more exercised about the evils of counterterrorism tactics—especially those employed by Israel and the United States—than of the terrorist acts that sparked them. The first lonely veto by the United States was cast by George H.W. Bush in response to a draft resolution that failed to mention the slaughter of Israeli athletes at the 1972 Munich Olympics. Many more U.S. vetoes followed over the next two decades on drafts concerning terrorism and counterterrorism, mostly related to the Middle East. Not until the Cold War began to thaw in the late 1980s and even former state sponsors of terrorism came to have second thoughts, did international politics permit the UN to take on an active operational role in aspects of the antiterrorist campaign.

With the 1990s the UN rediscovered the long-neglected enforcement provisions of Chapter VII. In three cases—Libya, Sudan, and Afghanistan—mandatory economic, travel, arms, and diplomatic sanctions were invoked by the Council in an effort to persuade the target states to forsake their apparent support of terrorist actions and groups.[10] The sanctions may well have helped persuade Libya eventually to give up the two suspects in the bombing of Pan Am 103 and UTA 772 and Sudan to ask Osama bin Laden to shift his base of operations to Afghanistan, but the Taliban was unmoved. Whatever their effectiveness, the reputation of sanctions in general began to suffer around Turtle Bay as concern rose for their humanitarian costs, particularly in Iraq. Nevertheless, the Security Council had finally demonstrated—after 47 years—a willingness not only to label terrorism a threat to international peace and security, but also to undertake collective enforcement measures aimed at its suppression.

Despite the vagaries of international politics, moreover, the UN has managed to make seminal contributions to the expansion of international norms against terrorism over the last 40 years. Specifically, the UN and related agencies have helped develop ten conventions and two protocols outlawing various terrorist acts (attacks on aircraft, airports, diplomats, maritime navigation and fixed platforms, and nuclear material and the taking of hostages) or requiring states to mark plastic explosives, suppress terrorist bombings, and curb terrorist financing. Only the latter two conventions, adopted by the Assembly in 1997 and 1999, respectively, however, refer to terrorism in their titles. In contrast, less burdened by the polarized politics of the General Assembly, seven regional organizations managed to adopt conventions expressly calling for the suppression of terrorism between 1971 and 2000. These regional steps, plus the counterterrorist cooperation of police and intelligence agencies, no doubt benefited from the political and legal foundation laid by the global conventions produced by the world body.

The events of 9/11 gave further impetus to efforts in the Assembly, led by India, to draft a comprehensive convention against all aspects of terror- ism. This remains, however, an elusive goal. As discussed below, it appears unlikely that the drafting issues can be resolved until substantial progress has been made toward a durable peace in the Middle East. Terrorism, it seems, must still be addressed in pieces at the UN.[11]

The biggest piece of the puzzle after 9/11, of course, was dealing with the Taliban leadership and their al-Qaeda allies in Afghanistan. Security Council resolution 1368, passed unanimously the day after the attacks on the U.S. (and with France presiding over the Council), acknowledged "the inherent right of individual or collective self-defense in accordance with the Charter," words that confirmed that Council members would not seek to block a measured U.S. military response. Since neither sanctions nor fresh diplo- matic appeals could nudge the Taliban from their support for Osama bin Laden's crew, the Council was content with leaving it to the most engaged world power and its friends to carry out military measures to enforce its decisions, a pattern well established over the previous decade. The series of resolutions crafted by the Council on Afghanistan in the months following the terrorist strikes, therefore, dealt with most everything but the U.S. military action, including a tightening of the sanctions and with the human- itarian, human rights, governance, and postconflict security arrangements on which the UN would have a major voice.

The principal operational innovation of the post-9/11 period was the estab- lishment of the Counter-Terrorism Committee (CTC) in resolution 1373, approved unanimously by the Council two and a half weeks after the destruc- tion of the World Trade Center. The terms of the resolution were sweeping: All UN member states were—anywhere, anytime—to "refrain from providing any form of support, active or passive, to entities or persons involved in terrorist acts," to freeze terrorist assets, to prohibit fundraising or transferring assets on their behalf, and to deny them safe haven, passage, arms, or other material assistance. UN members were further called on to share information about possible terrorist operations and to report to the CTC about the legisla- tive and administrative steps they were taking to fulfill their obligations under the resolution. Though these measures were adopted under Chapter VII, the CTC, a subsidiary body of the Council composed of all 15 member states, was not given authority to invoke penalties or sanctions for noncompliance.

So far, under the leadership of Sir Jeremy Greenstock of the United Kingdom, the CTC has not chosen to employ naming-and-shaming techniques, though these have not been ruled out for the future. The CTC has been posting on its website the reports it receives from member states, responding privately to them about ways their implementation of 1373 provisions could be strengthened, and listing the handful of member states that have not yet reported to it. By initially taking a positive tack—identifying legislative or executive areas in which individual member states could use some capacity-building help and acting as a clearinghouse that matches those needing such assistance with those capable of supplying it—the CTC has generated substantial good will among the UN membership. Given the acute conceptual, structural, and political puzzles addressed below, however, the future of the CTC is far from assured.

CONCEPTUAL PUZZLES

National policymakers and UN officials seeking the guidance or stimulation of outside experts on how the world body might best respond to the terrorist challenge would find little intellectual nourishment. Terrorism specialists have largely ignored or denigrated the UN's efforts, other than on codification.[12] Students of the UN, on the other hand, have seen little point in researching an area of public policy to which the global organization has contributed at best modestly and which appears to entail the kind of police, intelligence, and military work for which it has been ill-suited. Though some tentative efforts to bridge these fields have commenced since 9/11, this remains a worryingly underdeveloped area of inquiry.

Several of the UN's strongest public constituencies, moreover, are distinctly uncomfortable with the prospect of its taking a more prominent place in the war on terrorism. Human rights groups have been highly critical of the CTC for not taking human rights considerations into account in its monitoring of the way states have responded to the provisions of resolution 1373. Humanitarian NGOs were initially acutely concerned about the effects of the U.S. bombing campaign in Afghanistan on the general populace and have long fretted about the humanitarian consequences of economic sanctions. Likewise, disarmament advocates caution against letting worries about the acquisition of WMD by terrorists distract attention from the larger disarmament agenda. And much of the UN membership is wary both that the costs of the war on terrorism would drain the already modest pool of resources available for development and that there will be a new round of distortions of development programs for strategic reasons, just as there had been during the Cold War.

While many in the UN would rather not talk about terrorism at all, when they do they tend to focus on "root causes." There is some preference for antiterrorist over counterterrorist rhetoric as well, since the latter is considered by some to include active defense by police, intelligence, and military assets. The Secretary-General's Policy Working Group, for instance, stated that it "does not believe that the United Nations is well placed to play an active operational role in efforts to suppress terrorist groups, to preempt specific terrorist strikes, or to develop dedicated intelligence-gathering capacities."[13] Fair enough, but the organization's self-limiting proscription on intelligence and war fighting places it in an awkward position when it comes to pronouncing on the merits of the counterterrorist actions of countries that have been victimized by terrorist violence. In the weeks following 9/11, for example, the Secretary-General put considerable emphasis on the organization's essential role in legitimizing the retaliatory strikes the U.S. was about to take.[14] But in terms of public opinion, no doubt extending well beyond that in the United States, it would have appeared ludicrous for the leader of the UN to claim that a measured and targeted response would have been unjust or unwise. Under current circumstances, it could be asked: Who is extending legitimacy to whom?

Terrorism poses a murky challenge for the UN in another way, as well. Designed by and for nation states, the world body has yet to be fully reconciled to the growing necessity of integrating non-state actors into its planning, conceptualizing, and work. Terrorist groups, unlike common profit-seeking criminals, generally seek to affect the policy choices of states. Some states, therefore, heed, employ, or sponsor terrorists as a tool of not-so-public policy. Since the UN should not deal with terrorists diplomatically and cannot deal with them coercively, its principal route to help tame them is through its member states. But because it has understandably forsaken the gathering of intelligence and needs to conduct its business with a fair degree of transparency and accountability, the UN is not well positioned to address the critical issue of state-sponsored terrorism directly. However, its norm-building efforts may help dissuade member states from aiding or abetting terrorists by raising the political costs of doing so. Even the CTC has to operate on the assumption that the member states are willing, even if not always ready, to oppose terrorism without exception. The inability of the member states to agree on a definition of what constitutes terrorism, along with their tendency to confound terrorism and counterterrorism, however, belies that assumption.

STRUCTURAL AND INSTITUTIONAL CONSTRAINTS

Organizing to deal with terrorism, especially today's global variety, poses profound structural problems for governments as well as for international institutions. The multitude of agencies that could address various pieces of the policy mosaic and the difficulties of trying to insure some modicum of coherence and coordination could be seen as easily in Washington's legislation to create a cohesive architecture for homeland security as in the UN's halting attempt to reconceptualize how best to handle such cross-cutting issues. From its earliest days, the UN has largely been faced with policy problems that are both transnational in scope and interdisciplinary in nature.

So the structural problems posed by terrorism are hardly novel for the organization, yet they have proven to be quite stubborn.[15] The Secretary-General's July 1997 reform package took a few sensible steps toward coherence, most visibly through the creation of four executive committees, including one, headed by the Department of Political Affairs (DPA), on peace and security.

DPA, in turn, has been given the mantle of serving as the UN system's focal point for dealing with terrorism. This seems logical enough, but three caveats are in order: (1) DPA, as a result of an earlier reform, is divided geographically, which makes good sense for addressing the UN's traditional concerns for regional conflict resolution and peacekeeping but less so for understanding global terrorist networks; (2) DPA has received no increment of staffing or funds for taking on its relatively new terrorism mandate; and (3) there is no office within DPA for addressing terrorism, nor are there any plans to create one. Political pressures, both bureaucratic and intergovernmental make it very difficult to shift resources even within departments, much less between them. DPA has considered requesting the addition of a single staffer, at a modest P-3 level, to handle its terrorism responsibilities, but has thus far hesitated even to seek such a modest increment. It is not at all evident, in other words, that there will be anything resembling a focal point within the UN's focal point on terrorism.

The Terrorism Prevention Branch (TPB) in Vienna is only slightly more robust, as it remains the only part of the system that has terrorism in its title or that has any regular budget posts devoted to the issue. Prior to the events of 9/11, the TPB boasted all of two mid-level (a P-5 and a P-4) staff—somewhat less than the prevention of terrorism would seem to warrant and require. Ten months after the attacks, the Secretary-General asked the General Assembly to approve an increment of three professionals and two support staff to fulfill the TPB's new mandate for administrative and legislative capacity-building in states, such as those identified by the CTC, that require such assistance.[16] Almost six months later, in December 2002, the Assembly gave its seemingly somewhat reluctant approval.[17] The TPB, it should be noted, is part of Vienna's Office for Drug Control and Crime Prevention (ODCCP), tasks which apparently require 400 posts compared to the handful for terrorism. There is certainly a logic to the UN's efforts to link these issues—a product of the 1997 reform—but at headquarters ODCCP is linked to Legal Affairs rather than to Political Affairs, the alleged focal point. The latter, of course, provides staff support for the Security Council and its newfound interest in terrorism.

Speaking of the Council, where does the CTC fit into this bureaucratic maze? Basically, it doesn't. It is staffed by about a half-dozen outside and short-term experts, with important back-up from the chair's government, to this point the United Kingdom. It is financed through a fund for special political missions rather than the UN's regular budget. As Sir Jeremy Greenstock has lamented, in terms of secretariat support, "the CTC tends to be allocated the resources that are left over when everything else has been covered."[18] While this vague bureaucratic relationship may permit greater autonomy in the short run, in the long run it could make the CTC vulnerable to complaints that its operations have never been approved by the General Assembly, the only body under the Charter authorized to allocate funds or establish posts.

POLITICS, POLITICS, POLITICS

Everything in the UN may not be politics, but nothing, it seems, is ever far from it. Only through a political lens can the course of its history, concepts, and structure be understood. In the case of terrorism, politics first strangled and then perverted its consideration by the intergovernmental bodies. The looser political calculus of the 1990s permitted a period of experimentation and some tentative steps towards finding an operational role for the world body. In some respects the drama of 9/11 and its aftermath promised to raise the struggle against terrorism above partisan and polarizing politics in the UN, as well as in the United States, at least for a while. But rather than replacing the old politics with something qualitatively different, the new intensity of the war on terrorism has simply magnified some existing concerns and reaffirmed some old worries. Today the mix indeed looks different, but, even as their configuration changes, the individual elements have a ring that is more familiar than welcome.

At this point, politics on three levels—global, regional, and institutional— threaten to derail, or at least slow, the advances of counterterrorism in the UN agenda. The key factors are likely to be, respectively, American power, developments in the Middle East, and institutional inertia. The United States has long been the driving force behind the effort to engage the UN in the fight against terrorism. This has been both a plus and a minus. As noted earlier, most countries view their terrorist troubles as domestic issues, and they would prefer that the rest of the UN do the same. While the United States has had its share of domestic terrorists, its prominence (some would say arrogance), alliance with Israel, and far-flung presence around the world guarantee that it will be a prime target of those who want to change either the world or the Middle East through violence, wherever they are based. Tempting American targets are everywhere, as are those with a grudge against its image or its policies.

The very primacy of American power, to which its politicians and pundits never tire of drawing the world's attention, paradoxically makes it a more attractive and vulnerable target. Its unique power position also complicates its relationships with other countries and groups within the UN context. They are understandably wary of being dominated, or of seeming to be dominated, by the last superpower. Likewise, they are ambivalent about whether the UN should be used primarily to constrain or harness the expression of American power (the subtext of the 2002–2003 Council debate on the use of force in Iraq).[19] Others, having far less of this asset, are particularly reluctant to see the unilateral projection of U.S. military power, yet very cautious at the same time about giving the UN's legal blessing for military adventures it cannot control.[20] From Washington's perspective, on the other hand, the balance of political power outside the UN usually looks more favorable and permissive than that within its walls. These strategic and doctrinal asymmetries are, if anything, magnified by the seemingly open-ended nature of the war on terrorism, especially as it has been cast by President Bush. Though, in this author's view, the Bush administration has not been particularly unilateralist or exceptionalist in its response to the events of 9/11, the prevalent perceptions in western Europe and elsewhere, colored by Washington's go-it-alone policies on other issues, has been decidedly otherwise.[21] None of this, of course, makes it any easier to define or implement an assertive and dynamic role for the UN in the global campaign against terrorism.

Though Asia, Latin America, and Europe have produced their share of terrorists and suffered repeatedly from their acts, nothing drives global terrorism like the cruel politics of the Middle East. This could have been said with confidence at any point over the past four decades. Unless something dramatic and constructive occurs to break the cycle of violence and despair, the same could easily be projected for the foreseeable future as well. Arab-Israeli tensions, moreover, have also infected and distorted UN deliberations on terrorism. As noted earlier, both the Security Council's consideration of specific terrorist acts and the General Assembly's attempts to define the phenomenon have been repeatedly frustrated by deep differences over the rights and wrongs of that conflict.

The Israeli use of military force to counter terrorism, according to Arab diplomats, constitutes "state terrorism," while the frequency of Palestinian suicide bombings and Israeli reprisals has made it hard to distinguish between preemption and retaliation. As in Sri Lanka, Kashmir, and Northern Ireland, one side of the conflict has sought to legitimize attacks on civilians as a necessary tactic of their political struggle against the established order and a militarily more powerful adversary. The regular use of terrorist tactics—in this case suicide bombings—has once again been rationalized by sympathizers and supporters from abroad in an extension of the wars-of-liberation rhetoric that precluded substantial progress on developing antiterrorist norms through the 1970s and 1980s. By bending to such pressures and to the politics of bloc voting in its intergovernmental organs, the United Nations is in danger of losing the moral high ground on those critical issues of law, human rights, and peaceful settlement that demand an unambiguous rejection of terrorist acts as unacceptable regardless of the political cause. It is not enough for the Secretary-General to take the high road if the actions or nonactions of intergovernmental bodies serve to undermine established norms against terrorism.

The UN has not been, and will not be, the central player in efforts to bring peace to the Middle East, but it can do a number of things to put itself in a position of greater credibility so that it can serve as a reasonably impartial mediator or peace-keeper, as needed, down the road. There have been some positive steps in recent years, including the overtures that Kofi Annan has made to the Israelis, the arrangements to give Israel at least a temporary place in a regional group, and, earlier, the Assembly's reversal of the Zionism-racism resolution. In December 2002, the Security Council—over Syrian objections—took a step toward lifting the unspoken taboo on mentioning Israeli or Jewish victims of terrorism in Council resolutions.[22] Prior to that point, they were only acknowledged in statements by the president of the Council. While a modest step, this move offers a ray of hope that the Council may be trying to position itself to be a bit more outspoken about the consequences of terrorism in or stemming from the Middle East.

Even if these two sets of international political hurdles could be overcome, old-fashioned, garden-variety bureaucratic politics would still present some formidable obstacles to a more proactive UN role in fighting terrorism. At points in its history, the UN system has been able to adapt to changing circumstances and new opportunities. Decolonization, peacekeeping, the environment, and women's rights come to mind. But this has only been possible in the absence of strong opposition from any significant group of member states. Also, it has usually meant adding new responsibilities, units, posts, and funding, given resistance to replacing existing ones. And it has obviously been easier when the additional roles did not entail taking on tasks that seemed out of place with the UN's institutional culture, i.e., its sense of what it does best and what it stands for.[23] As noted above, for example, many in the organization have been distinctly uncomfortable with attempts over the past decade to reassert the provisions of Chapter VII for coercive enforcement.

What is often seen from the outside as bureaucratic inertia may be regarded by insiders as a valiant defense of the organization's traditions, values, distinct working methods, and comparative advantages. The UN secretariat, in that sense, has not rejected the notion that the world body should make a contribution to the struggle against terrorism. Rather, it has been inclined to say that it already is making a unique contribution by dealing with the variety of developmental, social, economic, and governance problems that could be considered the "root causes" of terrorism. In their view, in other words, the appropriate place for the world body is to bolster the soft side of counterterrorism as well as to remind powerful member states not to rely too heavily on military and coercive means of addressing the overt symptoms of this deeper malady.

CONCLUSIONS

Skeptics might ask, of course, why there has been a surge in global terrorism if the UN has been doing the right things all along. Is it tenable for the UN to say that it only wants to walk the soft side of the street but nevertheless wants to have some degree of control over what happens on the other side as well? The UN, in that regard, remains an incomplete organization, one that practices only parts of its Charter. The more powerful member states, moreover, seem to find this not only an acceptable state of affairs but one that is quite compatible with their own selective approaches to the world body and its Charter, especially in sensitive areas like dealing with terrorism.

Likewise, there is nothing particularly surprising about a lack of coherence in the UN's architecture for tackling a new, or even old, priority. Such problems are endemic to its politics, history, scope, membership, and ambitions. What is telling, however, is how little interest either key member states, including those most keen on counterterrorism, or the Secretary-General have demonstrated in trying to realign the system so that it could tackle this challenge sensibly and efficiently. Not unexpectedly, this core institutional issue is one of the few topics on which the Policy Working Group had nothing to say.

This capsule history of the UN's struggles to cope with terrorism suggests, on the one hand, that the organization does not need to be a prisoner of its unpromising past and, on the other hand, that high expectations about its future role in counterterrorism are unwarranted. When viewed over time, the UN's political and institutional capacity to contribute to this cause has evolved in positive and, recently, innovative directions. Moreover, when assessed by the standard of its past record, the UN's response to the events of 9/11 deserves relatively high marks. Yet, the persistence of the serious conceptual, institutional, and political constraints described above suggests that progress will only be made incrementally.

An unpredictable factor, the actions of the terrorists themselves, could affect the ultimate scenario in unforeseen ways. If they continue to focus their assaults on the United States and Israel, then other member states will be under less domestic pressure to get the UN to respond vigorously and forcefully than if attacks of the scale of those on New York and Washington are carried out in western European or Asian capitals. The terrorists, true to form, remain the wild card.

NOTES

1. Secretary-General Kofi A. Annan, *"We the Peoples": The Role of the United Nations in the 21st Century* DPI/2106 (New York: United Nations, March 2000): 40, 43, 44, and 46.
2. United Nations, *Report of the Policy Working Group on the United Nations and Terrorism*, A/57/273, S/2002/875, (August 6, 2002): Annex, 4 (para 11).
3. League of Nations, *Convention for the Prevention and Punishment of Terrorism* L.546(1).M.383(1).1937.V (Geneva, November 16, 1937); and, for the draft convention on the ICC, see League of Nations, *Committee for the International Repression of Terrorism* C.222.M.162.1937.V (Geneva, April 26, 1937): Appendix II.
4. League of Nations, Committee for the International Repression of Terrorism, *Report to the Council Adopted by the Committee on January 15th, 1936* A.7.1936.V (Geneva, February 10, 1936): 3.

5. League of Nations, *Proceedings of the International Conference on the Repression of Terrorism*, C.94.M.47.1938.V (Geneva, November 1–16, 1937): 50.

6. League of Nations *International Repression of Terrorism, Draft Conventions, Observations by Governments, Series III* A.24(b).1936.V (Geneva, February 21, 1938): 2.

7. For accounts of the UN's growing involvement, see Chantal de Jonge Oudraat, "The UN and Terrorism: The Role of the UN Security Council" and M.J. Peterson, "Using the General Assembly," in *Terrorism and the United Nations: Before and After September 11th*, eds. Jane Boulden and Thomas G. Weiss (Bloomington, IN: Indiana University Press, forthcoming 2003) and Edward C. Luck, "Trouble Behind, Trouble Ahead?: The UN Security Council Tackles Terrorism," in *The United Nations Security Council* ed. David M. Malone (Boulder, CO: Lynne Rienner Publishers, forthcoming 2003).

8. Sydney D. Bailey, "The UN Security Council and Terrorism," *International Relations*, 9(6) (December 1993): 536 and U Thant, *View from the UN* (Garden City, New York: Doubleday, 1978), 302–308, 317–318.

9. See Martha Crenshaw, "Current Research on Terrorism: The Academic Perspective," *Studies in Conflict and Terrorism*, 15(1) (January–March 1992); Bruce Hoffman, "Terrorism Trends and Prospects," in *Countering the New Terrorism*, eds. Ian O. Lesser, et al. (Santa Monica, CA: The Rand Corporation, 1999); and Walter Enders and Todd Sandler, "Transnational Terrorism in the Post-Cold War Era," *International Studies Quarterly*, 43 (1999).

10. For assessments of these cases, see Chantal de Jonge Oudraat, op. cit. and David Cortright and George A. Lopez, *The Sanctions Decade: Assessing UN Strategies in the 1990s* (Boulder, CO: Lynne Rienner Publishers for the International Peace Academy, 2000): 107–133.

11. Many experts on terrorism would seem to prefer this, in fact, to treating the phenomenon as a singular, cohesive, and global movement. See, for example, Paul R. Pillar, *Terrorism and U.S. Foreign Policy* (Washington, DC: Brookings Institution Press, 2001): 50–56.

12. A review of post-1995 articles in *Terrorism and Political Violence*, the leading journal in the field, by Martha Crenshaw found none devoted to the UN or international cooperation. "The 'Terrorism Studies' Community and the UN Role in Counter-Terrorism," paper prepared for the Project on the United Nations and Terrorism, the Center on International Organization, Columbia University (May 2, 2002).

13. *Report of the Policy Working Group*, op. cit., para. 9, p. 4.

14. "Secretary-General, Addressing Assembly on Terrorism, Calls for 'Immediate, Far-Reaching Changes' in UN Response to Terror," Press Release SG/ SM/ 7911, (October 1, 2001).

15. Twelve different units, spread among New York, Vienna, and Geneva, were represented on the Secretary-General's Policy Working Group, which received reports from eight subgroups on different facets of the problem.

16. Report of the Secretary-General, *Strengthening the Terrorism Prevention Branch of the Secretariat*, A/57/152, (July 2, 2002). Also see the Fifth

Committee's draft resolution, "Strengthening the Terrorism Prevention Branch of the Secretariat," A/C.5/57/L.47 (December 12, 2002).

17. A/C.5/57/L.47, op. cit.

18. On the trust fund, see Security Council, 4453rd meeting, S/PV.4453 (January 18, 2002): 4. For quotation, see Security Council, 4512th meeting, S/PV.4512 (April 15, 2002): 4.

19. Edward C. Luck, "Old Realities, New Opportunities," *Mixed Messages: American Politics and International Organization, 1919–1999* (Washington, D.C.: Brookings Institution Press, 1999), 280–306 and "Making the World Safe for Hypocrisy," *The New York Times,* 22 March 2003, A11.

20. Robert Kagan, "Power and Weakness," *Policy Review* (June and July 2002): 3–28.

21. Edward C. Luck, "The United States, Counter-Terrorism, and the Prospects for a Multilateral Alternative," in *Terrorism and the UN* eds. Boulden and Weiss, op. cit.

22. Julia Preston, "In a First, UN Notes Israeli Dead in Terror Attack in Mombasa," *New York Times,* (December 14, 2002), A5; Edith M. Lederer, "UN Condemns Mombasa Terrorist Attacks," *Toronto Star,* (December 14, 2002), A27; and Louis Meixler, "UN Condemns Blasts in Argentina, London, But Doesn't Mention Targets," *Associated Press,* (July 29, 1994).

23. The Policy Working Group, composed of top UN officials leavened by a few independent experts, including this author, described a series of roles for the UN that would speak to its traditions and values but also would push forward a bit on assisting the effort to deny terrorists the means to carry out acts of terrorism, as called for in resolution 1373. A/57/273.

CHAPTER 7

UN SANCTIONS: A GLASS HALF FULL?

Andrew Mack and Asif Khan*

INTRODUCTION

By the end of the 1990s, following a series of embarrassing failures, the utility of the UN Security Council's two primary collective security enforcement mechanisms—military force and sanctions—was being subjected to increasingly serious critique both in the research and in the policy communities. Resort to force by the Security Council in the second half of the 1990s was constrained both by doubts about its efficacy, following the debacle in Somalia, and by the reluctance of member states to put the lives of their citizens at risk in distant UN operations where no perceived vital national interests were at stake. The increase in the resort to sanctions in the 1990s should be seen in this light—as a substitute for, as well as a precursor or complement to, the use of force.

Prior to 1990 the Security Council imposed sanctions regimes on only two occasions, on Rhodesia and South Africa. The 1990s saw a dramatic surge in UN-imposed sanctions regimes, with the Security Council invoking Chapter VII to impose a variety of economic and political sanctions, travel bans, and arms embargoes on both governments and nongovernmental actors (e.g., UNITA in Angola). Sanctions were imposed on Afghanistan, Angola, Ethiopia and Eritrea, Haiti, Iraq, Liberia, Libya, Rwanda, Sierra Leone, Somalia, South Africa, Sudan, and the former Yugoslavia. In the cases of Angola, Ethiopia and Eritrea, Haiti, South Africa, Southern Rhodesia, Sudan, and the former Yugoslavia, sanctions have been fully lifted, whereas in the case of Libya, they were suspended. In the case of Iraq, sanctions have been lifted, with the exception of some prohibitions related to the sale or supply to Iraq of arms and related *materiel*.

How effective have these regimes been? This question is less easy to answer than might be imagined, not least because what the ostensible rationale for actions were and what the real reasons were sometimes differed radically. The UN lacked the resources to undertake its own "lessons learned" review of its sanctions regimes and no comprehensive scholarly studies were produced in this period either. Indeed, it was not until the new millennium that the first comprehensive study of the efficacy of the UN sanctions in the 1990s was published.[1]

UN sanctions, of course, only amount to a small percentage of the total. More than one hundred sanctions regimes, mostly unilateral, were imposed during the twentieth century. The most comprehensive, most heavily cited, and influential study of the efficacy of these regimes was produced by the International Institute of Economics (IIE) in 1990.[2] The IIE study found that sanctions failed to achieve even "partial success" in coercing desired changes in target regime behavior in 66 percent of 115 cases between World War I and 1990. Moreover, the failure rate increased over time as the global economy became more open. Between 1973 and 1990, only one in four sanctions regimes achieved even partial success. The major reason for the overwhelmingly negative assessment of the efficacy of sanctions evident in almost all studies is that success in coercing target states to change their behavior has become *the* criterion of effectiveness. But while coercing compliance is clearly an important (albeit rarely achieved) goal, critics tend to forget that sanctions often seek to realize other objectives as well—from stigmatizing and containing transgressor states to serving as instruments of prevention and deterrence. No studies have systematically examined the effectiveness of sanctions in realizing these latter goals.

The most damaging charge against sanctions, particularly comprehensive sanctions, is that they impose widespread suffering on ordinary people, while leaving the regimes they target not only relatively unscathed but also sometimes enriched and strengthened. In part as a consequence, almost all studies today argue for one variant or other of what have come to be known as "smart sanctions," that is, those sanctions intended to target regimes, not peoples. The effect, though not the intent, of a number of recent sanctions regimes, most notably in the case of Iraq, has been the reverse. Peoples have been harmed far more than regimes.

The Efficacy of Sanctions

The only real disagreement in the contemporary sanctions literature relates to the *degree* to which sanctions fail as an instrument for coercing changes in the behavior of target states. No study argues that sanctions are, *in general,* an effective means of coercion, although individual sanctions regimes can and sometimes do succeed. Part of the difficulty in making judgments about the efficacy of sanctions arises from disagreements about what constitutes "success" even with respect to coercion. For example, supporters of sanctions argue that the comprehensive sanctions imposed on the Federal Republic of Yugoslavia (FRY) played an important role in coercing Slobodan Milosevic to agree to the 1995 Dayton Accords. Critics argue that sanctions were of negligible import, that the Bosnian Serbs were losing their war against Croatia and the Bosnian Muslims, and that it was this fact, together with the use of NATO military force, that determined the successful outcome of the talks. Dayton suited the FRY because it froze the status quo and prevented a greater Bosnian Serb defeat. Military force, not sanctions, was the decisive factor. In reality, the relative impact of sanctions and war on Milosevic's decision making will likely never be known. Sanctions were probably a contributory factor in determining the outcome of the Dayton negotiations, but they were certainly not a sufficient condition for success—and probably not a necessary one either.

The Yugoslavia case exemplifies the difficulty of determining the relative impact of sanctions on outcomes that have multiple causes, but this is by no means the only methodological problem raised by the sanctions literature. Supporters of UN sanctions, for example, argue that pessimistic findings of the International Institute of Economics study are of little relevance to the UN because a large number of the cases examined in the IIE study involved unilateral sanctions, mostly by the United States. The UN, by contrast, only imposes sanctions multilaterally, and multilateral sanctions, so it is argued, are inherently more effective than unilateral sanctions.

The logic of this argument is clear enough; whether UN multilateral sanctions are *in practice* more effective than unilateral sanctions is less so. Strongly enforced sanctions by a superpower like the United States against a small country that is dependent on U.S. trade, aid, and investment may well be more effective than weakly implemented multilateral sanctions. The United States has demonstrated the efficacy of economic coercion (of which sanctions are but a special case) on many occasions. Moreover, the actual success rate of the UN's multilateral sanctions in the 1990s is hardly encouraging. The UN recognizes this fact and over the past several years has been actively canvassing ways to make sanctions both more effective and less costly in human terms.

Why Sanctions Regimes Fail

One of the core assumptions of traditional sanctions theory is that the pain inflicted by sanctions on citizens of a target state will cause them to pressure their government into making the changes demanded by the sanctioning body. But, at least in authoritarian states, the assumption that "civilian pain leads to political gain" suffers from an obvious drawback. Those who bear the brunt of the sanctions have no power to influence policy; those in power tend to be relatively unaffected. From this it would seem to follow that sanctions directed against multiparty states, where there is some possibility of domestic pressure being brought to bear against the government, would be more effective than those levied on authoritarian states. One recent study provides suggestive evidence that this is, in fact, the case.

Using more demanding criteria for success than those of the International Institute of Economics study, Kim Richard Nossal found only 14 cases out of more than 100 in which sanctions were completely successful. What was remarkable about his finding was that in 86 percent of the small number of cases in which sanctions had "worked," the targeted state had a functioning multiparty electoral system. Sanctions against authoritarian states failed in more than 98 percent of the 100-plus cases.[3] Insofar as UN sanctions have been directed primarily against authoritarian states, the potential significance of this finding is obvious.

Sanctions may strengthen the regimes they seek to coerce. When trade embargoes are imposed on a target state, the sanctions-induced scarcity of goods causes prices to rise, often dramatically. Between 1990 and 1995, price increases for basic commodities of around 1000 percent a year were not uncommon in Iraq. The consequences were predictable. First, the poor who could afford least suffered terribly. Second, the economic independence of the middle class, a building block for democratization and source of potential resistance to the regime, was destroyed. Third, regime members and their allies who controlled the black market profited hugely. Elizabeth Gibbons has argued that the imposition of sanctions on Haiti created a perverse economic interest in their perpetuation amongst the very regime members they were targeted against.[4]

In Iraq, efforts by the international community to relieve the suffering of the people had a further perverse effect. Regime control over much of the food and medical supplies distributed under the oil-for-food program has increased the dependence of the people on the state and further undermined civil society, while providing an additional lever of control and coercion for the regime.

Sanctions bodies, rather than the target regime, may be blamed for sanctions-induced suffering. The "pain-leads-to-gain" assumption of traditional sanctions theory also assumes that it will be the regime, not the sanctioning body, that will be blamed for the privations imposed. In reality, sanctions often increase popular support for the regimes against which they are targeted, especially when the state controls the media and can guarantee that its "spin" on who is responsible for the sanctions-induced hardship gets the widest hearing. The so-called "rally round the flag" phenomenon is true of authoritarian as well as democratic regimes.

Failure to compensate for third-party costs may encourage cheating. Sanctions, by definition, impose disproportionately high economic costs on the economic partners of target states, but despite calls from the UN General Assembly for these costs to be borne more equitably by the international community, this almost never happens. Where little or no assistance is available, disadvantaged states will have an incentive to break sanctions and renew their traditional economic relationships to avoid harm to themselves.

Some provision for third-party compensation has been made in those cases where the implementation of sanctions regimes has engaged the interests of major powers, notably in Iraq and the former Yugoslavia. No such aid has been forthcoming in the case of the African sanctions regimes. Here and elsewhere, demands for compensation have generally been ignored by the wealthy states.

Implementation, monitoring, and enforcement problems can undermine sanctions regimes. Many critics assume that because sanctions rarely succeed, there must be some inherent flaw in sanctions strategy. But failure in many cases has been due to the inadequate monitoring and enforcement of sanctions regimes. In the case of Rhodesia, for example, sanctions busting took place on such a massive scale that exports actually *rose* after sanctions were imposed.

If it is indeed the case that the failure of many sanctions regimes is due to lack of enforcement, one might be tempted to assume that sanctions would work if only they were implemented seriously. This is a superficially attractive argument, but it ignores the fact that the difference in the way sanctions are implemented is not accidental. The level of resources allocated to monitoring, assessing, and enforcing sanctions is a function of the degree to which the perceived interests of major powers are engaged; it may be politically impossible to implement sanctions successfully when they are not. Thus, implementation of UN sanctions directed against African states, where the major powers have only minor interests at stake, generated so little effort that the regimes in question have been described by one UN insider as "atrophic." By contrast, quite extraordinary efforts have been devoted to the sanctions imposed on Iraq, where the perceived vital interests of major powers—particularly the United States and United Kingdom—were engaged.

But even when there *is* serious commitment to the regime in question, most studies point to the need for improvements in UN planning, monitoring, assessment, and enforcement procedures. A 1996 report prepared for the Carnegie Commission on Preventing Deadly Conflict noted that major problems in monitoring and enforcing economic sanctions had become glaringly apparent to professionals both within the UN and national governments.[5] Little has changed since, and many subsequent reports have stressed the need for greater technical expertise to guide the work of the Security Council's sanctions committees. As David Cortright and George Lopez note in *The Sanctions Decade*, the UN's ability to enforce sanctions has been "woefully inadequate."[6] UN officials and Security Council members concede that this is the case but note the difficulty in persuading member states to allocate the needed resources.

THE HUMANITARIAN ISSUE

Numerous recent studies have pointed out that sanctions, and in particular comprehensive sanctions, are not a nonviolent alternative to armed force. Like war, they can result in death and suffering, even though all UN sanctions regimes exempt food and medicines. Unlike war, however, the casualties are all on one side. The human suffering associated with some sanctions regimes has become a major political issue both within the United Nations Organization (UNO) and in the wider international community.

The most politically sensitive question, namely, the level of sanctions induced deaths, is difficult to resolve because of real problems in obtaining reliable data. In the Iraqi case, which has generated the most concern, media and some NGO reports have sometimes cited Iraqi government claims of one-million-plus deaths attributable to sanctions, notwithstanding the obvious need for caution in using data from such a source. But in 1999 a careful Columbia University epidemiological study, which did not rely on Iraqi data, indicated that *at least* 100,000, and more likely over 200,000, children below the age of five died between August 1991 and March 1998, *over and above the number that would be expected to die in normal times.* Three-quarters of these excess deaths were attributable to sanctions.[7] This is more than the total number of Iraqis killed in the first Gulf War when the overwhelming majority of casualties were combatants.

The primary responsibility for these deaths clearly lies with the regime. Iraq's deliberately obstructive tactics meant that humanitarian aid under the oil-for-food program did not start reaching those in need until March 1997, despite the fact that the Security Council had made provision for such aid as early as 1991. But critics of the Security Council have argued that once it had become clear that the regime would do nothing to prevent the sanctions-induced starvation of Iraqi children, then Council members had to share at least part of the responsibility for the continued suffering.

Few doubt today the considerable tension that can exist between the Security Council's pursuit of political goals via sanctions and the UN's parallel commitments to the human rights provisions of the UN Charter. As Secretary-General Kofi Annan noted in his 1998 *Annual Report on the Work of the Organization,* "The international community should be under no illusion . . . humanitarian and human rights policy goals cannot easily be reconciled with those of a sanctions regime."[8] When comprehensive sanctions regimes are imposed and effectively enforced, it is difficult to avoid major suffering and severe social dislocation. The impact of sanctions on the Iraqi economy was so large, for example, that it dwarfed any and all relief programs. Moreover, while the post–March 1997 flow of food and medicine under the oil-for-food program reversed the rise in the under-five mortality rate, it did not arrest the insidious decline in the economic development infrastructures of Iraq, in the education and public health systems, and in the institutions of civil society. These may be the most serious long-term cost of sanctions to Iraqi society and are one reason why the current post-war reconstruction program is so expensive.

Critics argue that where comprehensive sanctions generate great human suffering and destroy the social fabric of a target state without achieving their political goals, support for them will decrease and the UN's moral authority will be under-mined.

MEASURING SUCCESS AND FAILURE

As noted earlier, most studies on the efficacy of sanctions ignore the fact that they may do more than simply seek to coerce states to change their behavior. In fact the variety of goals, other than coercion, that the Security Council may pursue by imposing sanctions is considerable. A complete list would include the following:

- Stigmatizing a transgressor state and, in so doing, signaling the international community's opposition to aggression, terrorism, gross violations of human rights, and other major transgressions of international law and norms.
- Containing a target state even when there is little expectation that the measures imposed will lead to the desired change in its behavior. This was clearly a central U.S. concern with respect to Iraq. Sanctions helped contain Iraq militarily by preventing it from spending tens of billions of dollars to rebuild its conventional military capability.
- Deterring other would-be violators of international laws and norms and deterring repeat violations by the target state. Even sanctions that do not succeed in changing the behavior of the transgressor state may contribute to deterrence.
- Serving as an instrument of prevention. A sanctions regime that includes an effective arms embargo will help prevent force modernization and expansion in the target state. Economic sanctions that reduce gross domestic product (GDP) levels may force reductions in defense expenditure. Both may reduce the capacity, and hence the incentive, for aggression.
- Building support for the use of force by ensuring that it not only is, but is seen to be, a measure of last resort. In this sense sanctions can be seen as a crucial rung in an escalating program of coercive measures.
- Responding to the political imperative to "do something," in which the use of force is ruled out and in which mere verbal condemnation would be seen to be insufficient.
- *Not* lifting sanctions may also serve domestic political interests. It is clear, for example, that even though the Clinton administration came to regard sanctions on Iraq as largely ineffective, it felt constrained by the anticipated political costs from doing much to ameliorate their humanitarian impact.

Reviews of the utility of sanctions occasionally note these additional roles that sanctions may play but almost never examine them in any detail. To the extent that they fail to do so, they present an unduly pessimistic assessment.

ENHANCING THE EFFECTIVENESS AND REDUCING THE HUMAN COSTS OF UN SANCTIONS

Most reviews and studies of the Security Council's sanctions machinery and implementation and monitoring processes have offered both criticism and detailed proposals for improvement. Some have argued for quite radical structural change, such as the creation of a UN Sanctions Agency or for the General Assembly to play a major role in sanctions implementation and enforcement.

On the critical issue of the impact of sanctions in terms of human suffering, major reports commissioned by the UN's Department of Humanitarian Affairs, published in 1995 and 1997, proposed a wide range of reforms. Both studies recommended that humanitarian impact assessments be conducted before and after sanctions are imposed. Few would disagree, but the central problem is again one of resources. The question of assistance to third parties has been addressed by both the General Assembly and the Secretariat. In 1998 an ad hoc experts group was set up by the Department of Economic and Social Affairs to examine practical measures of assistance to third-party states affected by sanctions. The recommendations have been presented to the General Assembly, but few observers believe that the resources will be found to implement them.

Inducements or "Positive Sanctions"

Over the past decade, numbers of academic studies have drawn attention to the use of inducements as a means of helping secure compliance with UN resolutions. Inducement strategies on their own are neither realistic nor appropriate. Sanctions are imposed in response to gross violations of international law. Simply offering inducements to states to return to compliance with their legal obligations would create a "moral hazard," rewarding illegal behavior. But many students of sanctions argue that sanctions regimes are generally biased too far towards coercion and pay too little attention to the use of inducements *as a complement* to coercive measures. A more effective strategy, they argue, would embrace positive as well as negative sanctions.

The historical and some game-theoretic evidence suggests that mixed strategies work better than coercive strategies on their own. For example, a recent study by Gitti Armani that examined some 22 cases of inducement and coercive strategies intended to change state behavior found that mixed strategies were three times more effective in promoting desired changes in state behavior than coercive measures alone.[9] In 1993 Australian Foreign Minister Gareth Evans made the case for a "tit-for-tat," carrot-and-stick strategy, arguing that sanctions should be progressively lifted as the target regime moved towards compliance with UN resolutions.[10] Evans noted that Commonwealth sanctions on South Africa were based on this conditionality principle. In a similar vein, in 1997 the General Assembly also called for the "progressive" lifting of sanctions as an inducement to compliance.

The case of the UN sanctions regime imposed on Libya in 1992 provides further suggestive evidence for the utility of inducements as a complement to coercion, though declining oil prices were also a factor. For years Tripoli had steadfastly refused to comply with UN demands to hand over two Libyan suspects to either Scottish or U.S. authorities. The Libyans were wanted for their alleged role in the 1988 Lockerbie air disaster. Libya argued that its citizens would not get a fair trial in Scotland, where the downed plane had crashed. Only in 1998, when the United States and United Kingdom eventually conceded that the trial could take place elsewhere, was the long process set in motion that eventually led to the suspects being handed over.

Smart Sanctions

Today few dispute that sanctions are, to use Kofi Annan's words, a "blunt instrument," notwithstanding the measures introduced to alleviate their impact in terms of human suffering. One response to these concerns has been a rapid growth in support for the idea of "targeted," or "smart" sanctions. "Smart" sanctions, like "smart" weapons systems, are supposedly precision targeted and designed to reduce "collateral damage;" that is, they are designed to coerce regimes without imposing major harm on ordinary citizens. Normal commercial trade would not be stopped under a smart sanctions regime, though particular categories of imports and exports might well be. Targeted sanctions may include:

- The freezing of overseas financial assets of government and regime members;
- Specific trade embargoes on arms, luxury goods, etc;
- Flight and travel bans;
- Political sanctions intended to stigmatize the target regime, including diplomatic isolation and withdrawal of accreditation; and
- Denial of overseas travel, visas, and educational opportunities to regime members and their families.

The suspension of credits from national governments and from international institutions like the UN, the World Bank, and the International Monetary Fund and the denial or limitation of access to overseas financial markets have also been identified as possible smart-sanction options. However, unless targeted very carefully, such sanctions risk having the same harmful consequences as across-the-board trade sanctions. The advantages claimed for smart sanctions are considerable.

- They are morally appropriate: when directed against authoritarian states, the regime feels most of the pain, not the people.
- Minimizing human costs is not only a desirable goal in itself; it also makes the UN less vulnerable to charges that it subverts its own humanitarian commitments by imposing sanctions regimes that harm the innocent.
- Minimizing human costs also makes it more difficult for target regimes to rally foreign and domestic support against sanctions, as Iraq sought to do with some success.
- Because smart sanctions do not normally disrupt nonmilitary trade, they minimize costs to third-party states, reduce incentives to cheat, and thus make it easier to sustain the sanctions regime in the long term.
- In denying target regimes the black-market opportunities provided by comprehensive sanctions, smart sanctions reduce perverse incentives for elite members to benefit from sanctions.

- By reducing the need for humanitarian assistance, smart sanctions deny regimes the opportunities to extend their control over the population through control over the disbursement of aid.
- By reducing the impact on social infrastructures, smart sanctions also reduce long-term damage to educational and health systems and to the institutions or proto-institutions of civil society.

The appeal of smart sanctions is obvious, but they confront a number of difficulties. First, sanctions theory suggests that the greater the costs of sanctions to the regime, the greater the probability of compliance. Because they hit harder, comprehensive sanctions should, in principle, be far more effective than more selective targeted sanctions.[11] Second, monitoring and implementing limited trade bans is in some ways even more difficult than across-the-board trade bans, but the international community has not been very imaginative in this regard. Time-consuming and expensive border and ship searches may not be the only way to prevent "sanctions busting." A market-incentive approach, as opposed to a regulatory one, could be more effective. Such an approach could involve rewards for information leading to the detection of sanctions violators. Fines imposed on violators could form a pool for the payment of rewards. This idea is similar in principle to the concept of "citizen verification" of arms control agreements that has some support in the arms control community and to the activities of human rights organizations that are in the forefront of human rights monitoring. Other creative ideas, such as passing legislation that would invalidate the insurance coverage of sanctions-busting companies, have been proposed but not yet implemented.

The third general problem with "smart" sanctions relates to the option that has generated the most interest and has the greatest potential economic impact, namely, freezing the overseas financial assets of governments and of regime members. An oft-cited example of the effectiveness of this approach is the freezing of Iranian financial assets in the United States during the Iranian hostage crisis in 1980, but this case is of little relevance to the UN. The Security Council never imposes sanctions immediately; there is always debate that will forewarn transgressor regimes that sanctions may be applied. Moreover, many in the UN believe as a matter of principle that target states should be warned before sanctions are imposed. The net effect is that regimes under threat of sanctions will always have time to withdraw any overseas assets liable to be frozen before sanctions are implemented. "Targeting is difficult," one commentator dryly observed, "if there is nothing to target."

If sanctions are to be preceded by pre-assessment of their likely human impact as a number of reform proposals have suggested, then the warning time will be lengthened and opportunities to evade the financial sanctions increased still further. Freezing the overseas financial holdings of target regimes and elite members will be further hampered if fund ownership is disguised (thus negating the utility of namerecognition/searching software packages) or if the accounts are located in recalcitrant tax havens.

Supporters of comprehensive sanctions point out that, unlike financial sanctions, across-the-board trade embargoes, which are the sanctions with the greatest potential impact, cannot be evaded by forewarning. But nor can the suspension of credit, aid, and foreign investment—all options in the "smart" sanctions portfolio. However, sanctions against individuals cannot succeed or fail unless they are first attempted, and it is interesting to note in this context that during the 1990s the Security Council *never* mandated compulsory financial sanctions against individual members of a transgressor state. In Haiti the assets of individuals belonging to the regime *were* specifically targeted, but the Security Council resolution only "urged" states to freeze the funds in question. The resolution was not legally binding on member states.

Smart sanctions are certainly not the panacea that some of their less reflective advocates seem to believe, but nor are the problems they confront insuperable. A second Swiss-government-sponsored meeting on financial sanctions in Interlaken in March 1999 examined the key critiques of targeted financial sanctions and found them wanting. Thus, while financial assets can be readily moved electronically, their movements can be traced. If foreign currencies are repatriated to the sanctioned state, they cannot be seized by the international community, but neither can they be used by the target state without again sending them abroad, when they are again vulnerable to tracing and seizure. Notwithstanding the problems, financial sanctions were technically feasible, the experts concluded, and much could be learned from international experience in combating money laundering. The difficulties were not technical but political—securing the commitment to what needed to be done.

Following the Swiss-funded "Interlaken Process," Germany launched the Bonn/Berlin Process in 1999, which convened expert groups to examine how to improve arms embargoes and travel bans. The German program was succeeded in turn by the Stockholm Process, funded by Sweden, which focused on how targeted sanctions will be implemented and monitored. A report from this latter working group was presented to the Security Council early in 2003.

CONCLUSION

History suggests that only when the interests of major powers are engaged will sufficient economic and political resources be made available to enforce comprehensive sanctions effectively. But, as Iraq has so forcibly reminded us, effective enforcement can cause great suffering, and even sanctions whose impact is devastating do not necessarily achieve compliance. While "targeted" sanctions undoubtedly have a lesser impact than comprehensive sanctions because they focus on regimes rather than peoples, they also have far lower human and third-party costs. They are politically easier to initiate and to sustain in the long term and less likely to bring the sanctions instrument into disrepute. But even the most enthusiastic proponents of smart sanctions agree that more work is needed to evaluate their potential.

Among analysts there is broad agreement that sanctions should be seen as a tool of policy, not a substitute for it. To be effective, a sanctions regime must be guided by a coherent and comprehensive political strategy, one that seeks broad international support for the regime and minimization of the human costs it will inevitably incur. Such regimes should be implemented, monitored, and assessed with the aid of highly professional staff, while consideration should be given to the selective use of inducements as well as coercion. Unfortunately, these simple requirements are almost never met in practice.

Despite their critiques of current UN practice, none of the academic studies, nor even the most critical of the NGOs, argue that sanctions should be abandoned as an instrument of UN policy. Indeed, there is a widespread consensus that, when confronting major transgressions of international law, the international community needs an instrument of suasion that lies between mere diplomatic censure, on the one hand, and war, on the other. For this purpose there is no real alternative to sanctions. Major reform is needed, not wholesale rejection.

NOTES

* The views expressed herein are those of the authors and do not necessarily reflect the views of the United Nations.

1. David Cortright and George A. Lopez, *The Sanctions Decade: Assessing UN Strategies in the 1990s* (New York: Lynne Rienner, 2000).
2. Gary C. Hufbauer, Jeffrey J. Schott, and Kimberley Ann Elliot, *Economic Sanctions Reconsidered: History and Current Policy,* 2nd ed. (Washington, D.C.: Institute for International Economics, 1990). A revised and more up-to-date study was published in 1999. The broad findings of the earlier study were confirmed. See Cortright and Lopez (Note 1 above), 15.
3. Kim Richard Nossal, "Liberal-Democratic Regimes, International Sanctions and Global Governance," in *Global Governance and Enforcement: Issues and Strategies* ed. Raimo Väyrynen (Lanham, M.D.: Rowman and Littlefield, 1999), 127–149.
4. Elizabeth Gibbons, *Sanctions in Haiti: Human Rights and Democracy Under Assault,* Center for Strategic and International Studies, Washington Papers 177 (Westport, CT: Praeger, 1999).
5. John Stremlau, *Sharpening International Sanctions: Towards a Stronger Role for the United Nations* (New York: Carnegie Commission on Preventing Deadly Conflict, November 1996).
6. Cortright and Lopez, 5.
7. Richard Garfield, *Morbidity and Mortality Among Iraqi Children from 1990 to 1998: Assessing the Impact of Economic Sanctions* (Notre Dame, IN: Joan B. Kroc Institute for International Peace Studies, University of Notre Dame and Fourth Freedom Foundation, March 1999). Available at http://www.fourthfreedom.org/sanctions/garfield.html.
8. See United Nations, *Annual Report on the Work of the Organization* A/53/1, para. 64. Available at http://www.un.org/Docs/SG/Report98/con98.htm.

9. Gitty M. Armani, "A Larger Role for Positive Sanctions in Cases of Compellence?" Working Paper no. 12 (Los Angeles, CA: Center for International Relations, University of California, May 1997).

10. Gareth Evans, *Cooperating for Peace* (Sydney: Allen and Unwin, 1993).

11. Iraq's persistent defiance of the UN in the face of the most effective (in terms of impact) sanctions regime ever imposed on a modern state is not what sanctions theory would predict—or can easily explain. Even though individual regime members may have benefited from the sanctions-stimulated black market, there can be no doubt that the reduction in Iraq's material power that came with a halving of the Iraqi gross domestic product and the denial of arms imports would have been a serious blow to the regime.

CHAPTER 8

INTERNATIONAL TRIBUNALS AND THE CRIMINALIZATION OF INTERNATIONAL VIOLENCE

Joanne Lee and Richard Price*

INTRODUCTION

What difference does international criminal law make to global security, and what contributions has the United Nations made to international criminal law? The establishment through the UN of international criminal tribunals for the former Yugoslavia (ICTY) and Rwanda (ICTR), its role in initiating tribunals in East Timor, Sierra Leone, and Cambodia, and the rapid coming into force of the International Criminal Court represent revolutionary developments in how the world attempts to deal with war and crimes against humanity. While the Nuremberg and Tokyo military tribunals after World War II provided a major shift in the paradigm of legal responsibility for conduct in war from states to individuals, the more recent tribunals symbolize a decisive move away from the perception of "victors' justice" towards a more universal mechanism for ensuring accountability for atrocities committed during wartime and even peacetime. In doing so, these courts have overcome a number of obstacles that skeptics over the years have argued would prevent the effective operation or even existence of such international courts. Observers of international law and war had long maintained that the diverse legal systems and cultures around the world present an insuperable obstacle to the creation of a permanent international criminal court. There has also been a long tradition of critics of the ad hoc international criminal tribunals, first at Nuremberg and Tokyo and then in the former Yugoslavia and Rwanda. This chapter offers an overview of those criticisms and argues that, while significant problems exist, many of the worries of critics have progressively fallen by the wayside as the generation and application of international criminal law has reached successively novel milestones. We argue that this process, while incomplete and with significant shortcomings, represents the increasing criminalization of international and even domestic violent conflict and repression. This process has challenged traditional notions of the sovereign rights of states, giving a more prominent role to international law and institutions, including the UN, in the most sensitive of political issues faced by states—namely, the use of force.

AD HOC TRIBUNALS

While the Nuremberg and Tokyo tribunals of the 1940s gave defeated leaders a relatively novel chance to defend their actions in a court of law instead of facing summary execution, the tribunals were still tarred with the brush of "victors' justice." Representatives from four governments (all later to become permanent members of the Security Council) took a mere six weeks to draft the Nuremberg Charter, based on crimes that had already been documented by the Commission for the Investigation of War Crimes established by the United States and the United Kingdom, even though there was very little agreement at the time as to what could constitute a "war crime" under international law.[1] Thus, one of the earliest tasks of the fledgling UN was to recognize explicitly the important benchmarks set by the tribunals in terms of unacceptable conduct in warfare. The UN's successive adoption of the Genocide Convention (1948), the Geneva Conventions on the Laws of War (1949), and the Principles of Law Recognized by the Nuremberg Charter (1950) appeared to usher in a new era of consensus on what constituted "crimes against the peace and security of mankind." However, no agreement could be reached on how to enforce these international criminal laws independently of the Security Council's political mandate under the UN Charter. Numerous attempts were made to finalize a statute for a permanent international criminal tribunal, but these ultimately all foundered over the definition of the "crime of aggression." In the subsequent context of Cold War hostilities, it was unacceptable to both sides that an independent judicial institution should be able to make such a subjective evaluation of their conduct. Thus, critics had grounds to maintain that war crimes law was not really law at all, but the naked exercise of power dressed up as law. Criticisms of the impotency of international law were overdrawn in the sense that the modern laws of war have had a very palpable impact on the shape of war over the past century, both in terms of the conduct of combatants in conflict and the fact that war crimes law was still applied throughout the post World War II period through national courts and military tribunals. Still, the basic point about the very integrity of the laws of war and the impartiality of their application could not be dismissed.

Thus, the establishment of the ICTY and ICTR in 1993 and 1994 represented unprecedented milestones in the history of UN efforts to deal with its original central mission, namely, the limitation and prevention of war. These tribunals marked the first time the modern international community had sanctioned broadly international criminal courts to hold individuals responsible for the alleged perpetration of three core categories of international crimes: war crimes, genocide, and crimes against humanity. Moreover, they represented an adept legal response to the changing nature of warfare, insofar as they also dealt with noninternational conflicts rather than solely the traditional legal and political paradigm of interstate conflict. The very establishment of the tribunals themselves through the UN—they were created by Security Council resolutions[2]—crossed a novel threshold in efforts to hold perpetrators responsible for war crimes by institutionalizing a mechanism for the more broadly international interpretation and application of international humanitarian law. The tribunals thus responded to the foremost criticism that has bedevilled the laws of war throughout their history, namely, the absence of more universally sanctioned international mechanisms to apply and enforce laws that were not solely in the hands of a victorious belligerent to a conflict. From a broad historical perspective on the history of war, the revolutionary significance of this development attained through the UN cannot be exaggerated. But even as the ICTY and ICTR embodied a positive answer from the UN to the existential criticism of the laws of war, other serious second-generation criticisms soon emerged about their likely effectiveness and consequences.

"Politicized" Tribunals and Selectivity

Critics of the efficacy of international war crimes law point to the fact that tribunals were established for Bosnia and Rwanda but not for numerous other candidates. Those on the left who distrust U.S. power and those on the right who dislike international law have both criticized the tribunals as politicized in this sense of selectivity, thus questioning their legitimacy.[3] Other critics have suggested that overtly political considerations were paramount when the ICTY refused to launch an investigation of NATO's bombing of Serbia,[4] charges echoed in the accusations of "victors' justice" made by former President of Serbia Slobodan Milosevic.

If international war crimes law is to meet a reasonable test of impartiality, should not numerous tribunals have been established elsewhere? In a sense, of course, the establishment of the International Criminal Court (ICC) statute in 1998 and its rapid coming into force in July 2002 embodies the international community's multilateral response to this charge and effectively lays it to rest. However, the ICC has no mandate to apply retroactively, and thus atrocities committed before its coming into force fester in a legal lacuna. The UN has responded in piecemeal fashion to this lacuna by attempting to establish other international criminal tribunals. In Sierra Leone a special court has been created under a mandate given the UN Secretary-General by the Security Council, supported by voluntary contributions from UN members.[5] The negotiations produced a hybrid court that involves the UN and local officials who will try those most responsible for the brutality. In East Timor atrocities committed after the referendum in 1999 by pro-Indonesian militia have been left to either domestic courts or the Special Panel for Serious Crimes, set up in 2000 by the UN Transitional Administration in East Timor (UNTAET).

The special court consists of mixed panels of international and East Timorese judges, who will use as their guideline the Rome Statute of the ICC.[6] After more than five years of fitful negotiations, the model of negotiating the establishment of a UN/ local mixed tribunal finally appeared to achieve success in June of 2003 in Cambodia, where agreement was reached on the existence of a tribunal to bring to justice members of the Khmer Rouge.

Without question, the establishment by the UN of war crimes tribunals or failures to do so were political in the important sense that Cold War era ideological and geopolitical divisions were largely responsible for the paralysis of the Security Council until the fall of the Berlin Wall and resulting new-found activism of the Security Council in the 1990s. With the establishment of the ICTY, the charge of politicization shifted from indictments of victors' justice to the suspicion that the international community as represented by the UN only cared about the West (conflicts in Europe). However, the enlarged membership of the UN after decolonization meant that, after establishing the ICTY, the Security Council could not avoid dealing with humanitarian tragedies in the global south as well, such as Rwanda and the other ad hoc tribunals. Conversely, then, after the establishment of tribunals in Rwanda, Sierra Leone, and East Timor, and ultimately the ICC, we can expect some critics from the left will charge instead that the regime of international criminal law is a new form of legal neocolonialism. At the same time, the realist view is that the ICC, in particular, is a (largely failed) attempt by the weak to restrain the strong. That these critics cannot both be right is telling and indeed suggests that the establishment of international criminal courts by the UN since the end of the Cold War occupies something of a middle ground between a tool of great power hegemony and an effective challenge to it. That is, if international criminal justice, at least as pursued through the UN, is what states make of it, some states have attempted with no small success to make it more broadly legitimate than the Nuremberg and Tokyo tribunals.

Efficacy

A major source of resistance to the establishment of international criminal tribunals has been the fact that many states have been leery to establish legal mechanisms that could someday be turned upon themselves. In addition, those critical of the ICTY and ICTR argued that such tribunals were doomed to be ineffective at best and counterproductive at worst. Even some of the governments that supported the creation of the ICTY at the Security Council did so with the expectation it was not to work too well. Gary Bass argues that the tribunal was intended by many countries who approved its creation at the Security Council to be merely another kind of reprimand, not an actual functioning court with defendants in the dock, and as such "the tribunal was built to flounder."[7] Indeed, many who were sympathetic to the cause of the tribunal lamented its lack of success in arresting and prosecuting war crimes suspects,[8] leading even supporters to conclude that though laudable the tribunal was destined to an ineffective role of a "farcical marionette" with little prospect of even gaining jurisdiction over any suspects.[9]

How, then, have the tribunals measured up to this harsh skepticism? In part this depends upon the criteria for success. The most straightforward criteria is effectiveness in obtaining and prosecuting indicted suspects, while the larger question points to how well the tribunals have served the broader interests of justice, peace, and stability. The initial skepticism of the effectiveness of the ICTY was certainly warranted given that the ICTY had no independent police or military force of its own, and there was no willingness to arrest war crimes suspects on the part of the UN or NATO governments, who contributed their forces to the various international missions in the former Yugoslavia.[10] This resistance was due to military reticence to engage in "mission creep" and policing,[11] fear in the military that their troops would suffer reprisals and thus concern by politicians that their citizens would be killed in missions abroad that had dubious domestic support. Two developments began to change this, however. First was the use of sealed (secret) indictments by the second ICTY prosecutor, Louise Arbour, who replaced Richard Goldstone in October 1996. The innovation of secret indictments was a brilliant maneuver, since when secret indictments were delivered to NATO troops in Bosnia, their governments could no longer hide behind the excuse that indicted suspects were in hiding and well armed (thus making any arrest attempt likely to incur unacceptable casualties). At the same time, NATO governments faced the embarrassing threat by Arbour that the indictments could be made public if NATO refused to arrest attainable war crimes suspects. The impact of the ICTY here represents an independent effect of the UN tribunals as actors in their own right, not simply beholden to the wishes of UN member states. The second development was the May 1997 election in Britain of the Blair government, which gave chief tribunal supporter Madeline Albright (U.S. Secretary of State) some strong allies committed to arresting war crimes suspects.

The anemic record of arrests of ICTY suspects began to change with a raid by British troops in July 1997. By December 2002, 29 cases had been completed. Of the outstanding 76 public indictees that remain, 55 are currently in proceedings while 21 remain at large. While two of the most sought after suspects—Radovan Karadzic and Radko Mladic—remain at large, the success rate of detention of suspects, including, most notably, the former President of Serbia Slobodan Milosevic, goes well beyond what is necessary to deflate the core contention of critics of the tribunal—namely, that it was doomed to be an ineffective paper tiger. Indeed, bringing Milosevic, the former head of state, before a UN-established international criminal tribunal is nothing less than a revolutionary development in the criminalization of war.

The ICTR has indicted 73 suspects, 61 of whom have been detained, including numerous top leaders, such as the former foreign and defense ministers, the former chief of staff of the Rwandan army, and Jean Kambanda, the former prime minister, who became the first former head of government to be convicted for such crimes. Even more so than with the ICTY, then, the success of the ICTR in gaining custody of most of its indictees, including those in the highest positions of responsibility, goes well beyond the level of failure expected by tribunal skeptics. This is not to say that the tribunal is without significant problems, namely, its relative lack of resources (compared with ICTY) and corruption allegations. Still, the ICTR is further notable for milestones in international jurisprudence, including the first judgment and sentencing by an international court for the crime of genocide (the Akayesu and Kambanda cases) and the first prosecutions for rape as a crime against humanity (also Akayesu).

Those who study the role of international institutions often look to their success in affecting the behaviour of other major actors (in this case, states and militias) to determine their influence. But the constructivist literature on international institutions and norms also tells us to look at their effects in shaping actors' identities and interests. Beyond putting war criminals in the dock, these tribunals have given additional impetus to the pursuit of war criminals in national courts and internalization of the international standards embodied in the tribunals' jurisprudence. This has occurred in third-party states, most notably Belgium, whose enactment of universal jurisdiction legislation facilitated the trial and conviction of four nuns for their part in the Rwandan genocide.[12] It has also occurred in Rwanda and the former Yugoslavia itself, though to greatly varying degrees. The complementary jurisdictional regime of the ICC is also motivating many states finally to implement their existing treaty obligations to prosecute those accused of genocide and war crimes as well as the more recently defined "crimes against humanity."[13]

In the debate between proponents and opponents of the likely prosecutorial success of criminal tribunals, then, the opponents' initial advantage has gradually given way. This is not to presumptively conclude, however, that the tribunals can simply be judged a success for justice. The ICTR indicted only the higher level officials involved in the 1994 slaughter of up to 800,000 people, creating resentment in Rwanda since those most responsible for the genocide would not be subject to the death penalty. The ICTY under Goldstone began with a strategy of indicting lowly war criminals to build up cases against higher officials, though that strategy was later mostly abandoned in preference for targeting higher officials with greater responsibility. In the end, both tribunals have confined themselves to indicting a relatively small number of war crimes suspects, leaving over-stretched Rwandan national courts to deal with the hundreds of thousands of individuals suspected of participating in massacres, while an estimated minimum of 7,000 war criminals roam free in the former Yugoslavia.[14] The question thus remains: Have UN criminal tribunals adequately served the larger interests of justice and stability in places like Rwanda and the former Yugoslavia?

Tribunals as a Deterrent

Skeptics have challenged the ability of international criminal tribunals to deter the commission of atrocities.[15] Proponents of the tribunals, on the other hand, particularly human rights advocates, have maintained that peace and stability are impossible unless the cycle of impunity for atrocities is broken by punishment, thus providing a deterrent against future crimes.[16] As is often the case with trying to prove the causes of recent nonevents, the empirical evidence to this point is relatively scant. The dispensing of international justice on African soil for the first time through the ICTR did not adequately persuade subsequent extremists from Sierra Leone or Uganda to moderate their behaviour, though there is some anecdotal evidence from Congo and Burundi that militia leaders curtailed ethnic attacks.[17] Further research remains to determine whether the prospect of ad hoc trials for atrocities in contexts like East Timor would have dampened the levels of violence once the willingness of the Security Council to establish such tribunals was established.

In the Balkans, the fact that the massacre at Srebrenica occurred two years after the establishment of the ICTY has been taken as strong evidence that the ICTY failed to achieve one of its key objectives of deterring atrocities, as has Milosevic's later campaign in Kosovo. To be sure, the barren first years of the ICTY provided no reason for the parties to the conflict to take the tribunal seriously. There is some evidence of very limited deterrent successes from the threat of war crimes trials, including Karadzic evacuating the Omarska camp, the improvement of prison conditions and release of prisoners, and Goldstone's claim that Croatian soldiers in Krajina were restrained due to fear of indictment.[18] The better test for the deterrent capacity of the ICTY is whether its threat of indictment and trials was effective once the tribunal actually began to gain custody of suspects and put them on trial. Did Milosevic in fact modify his behaviour over Kosovo in an attempt to avoid his own indictment? Or conversely, did he judge that the likelihood of eventual ICTY indictment put him in a position of having nothing to lose, making the situation worse (a standard realist criticism of tribunals)? While we can only speculate at this point, one could surmise that the threat of indictment somewhat restrained Milosevic's brutality in Kosovo, and it was the NATO bombings that gave him nothing to lose by threatening the military defeat of his regime. Alternatively, Milosevic might have calculated that the chief threat of the NATO campaign was that it might lead to his arrest as an indicted war criminal, and thus the threat of an ICTY indictment in fact fostered atrocity rather than prevented it. In either case, it cannot be concluded that the UN-fostered criminalization of war and atrocity merely represented a paper tiger that was not taken seriously: International criminal law matters.

While the ability of the ad hoc UN tribunals of the 1990s to deter further atrocities likely admits at best to a few limited successes, the creation of the ICC (and the embrace of universal jurisdiction in national legislation around the world) narrows the scope of this debate in the sense that the spectre of such prosecutions has now become a de facto possibility for would-be perpetrators of atrocities. The criminalization of violent conflict in good part through the UN creation of tribunals thus threatens to bypass the previously raging debate of whether it would be better to have international criminal tribunals to deter atrocities or retain diplomatic flexibility and grant amnesties. The real remaining question is how effective they will be in deterring future would-be perpetrators of war crimes, genocide, and crimes against humanity. The ICC may have played a minor role in mitigating the recent U.S.-led "attack on Iraq": Some British parliamentarians seized on the fact that British soldiers would be subject to the ICC in order to urge Prime Minister Blair not to go to war,[19] and it certainly seems that the war was conducted with far more constraint than the Gulf War of 1991. However, the question for the most part will have to be revisited against the empirical evidence over the next decade. It is also worth bearing in mind the contention of proponents like Madeline Albright that the prevention of even a single criminal act of sufficient gravity to trigger the concern of the international community would justify such tribunals.[20] The argument that an international institution ought not be created because we cannot guarantee an immediate high rate of success is not convincing unless it can be shown that the institution is in fact highly unlikely ever to attain its objectives, that it will in fact prove counterproductive to those objectives or that some alternative is better. As Gary Bass has correctly put the matter, "Do war crimes tribunals work? The only serious answer is: Compared to what?"[21]

Do Justice Though the Heavens May Fall?

Realists criticize the legalist approach of war crimes trials as removing diplomatic flexibility, especially the granting of amnesties to leaders, that may be necessary to end bloody conflicts. Indeed, this concern was a chief source of opposition to the establishment of the ICTY and subsequent foot-dragging by UN member states in the context of cease-fire negotiations involving Karadzic and Milosevic. Is it the case that tribunals arising from conflicts embroiled in atrocities only make matters worse? What is the effect of tribunals on the longer-term interests of peace, stability, justice, and reconciliation? Some observers have contended the ICTY has had no impact whatsoever,[22] while others have pointed out the ways in which the ICTY has had a negative effect on reconciliation within Serbia in the sense of reinforcing the Serb's sense of injustice.[23]

It is clear that one of the foremost arguments made against indictments by the ICTY—that indictments and arrests would increase instability by causing reprisals and backlash—has largely not occurred. The indictment of

Karadzic actually helped U.S. cease-fire diplomacy by sidelining him in pursuit of their strategy of dealing only with Milosevic, while the later indictment of Milosevic did not prevent NATO from negotiating a cease-fire in Kosovo. Nor was there a destabilizing backlash to the arrests of war crimes suspects, even of Milosevic, contrary to the key realist argument that tribunal indictments would result in the resumption of mass violence. Serbian Prime Minister Zoran Djindic was assassinated in March of 2003, likely due to fears by Serbia's criminal gangs that they were next in the government's efforts to arrest remaining war criminals indicted by the ICTY. The response, however, has not been a resumption of civil war but a crackdown on criminals, thus furthering rather than frustrating the tribunal's purpose. In short, the evidence from the former Yugoslavia does not support—and indeed contradicts—the arguments of tribunal critics; the indictments by the ICTY did not hurt the prospects for the cessation of deadly violence nearly as much as realists contended, and they ultimately helped remove extremist politicians from the political process.

More progressive-minded critics of tribunals have contended that they represent an overly legal approach to complex conflicts and that other mechanisms such as truth commissions might better serve the long-term interests of justice and reconciliation. Such ideas have certainly been put into practice; those setting up the Special Tribunal in Sierra Leone, to cite but one of many examples, decided that a truth commission would be a necessary part of the overall process of ensuring long-term stability in the region. But no empirical evidence is available to suggest whether the tribunal alone would help achieve this stability. In South Africa, where the Truth and Reconciliation Commission was the main institution for dealing with grievances over past crimes, racial tensions are still prevalent and the country is hardly stable, suggesting that a special criminal tribunal may have contributed to long-term peace. Clearly, neither tribunals nor truth commissions by themselves provide a magic bullet to complex tragedies. But at this point, the moral argument for justice remains as strong as ever, while the empirical case against trials falls far short of calling for their abandonment. Perhaps the UN should establish a universal truth commission and/or reparations mechanism for all victims of international crimes, as is being discussed in UN committees?

THE INTERNATIONAL CRIMINAL COURT

The UN tribunals are widely credited with giving the necessary impetus to establish the ICC, which a coalition of "like-minded" states and NGOs successfully attained in July of 1998 in Rome over the objections of the United States, Israel, China, and several others.[24] Criticisms of the ICC by its opponents are as plentiful as laudatory praises by its proponents. Among the controversies that have arisen are: (1) the accusation that the Court represents an undue usurpation of state sovereignty because of its jurisdictional reach, (2) whether domestic amnesties will be taken into account by the

ICC, (3) fears that the ICC will provide an opportunity for the developed world to dominate developing countries whose national legal systems are more likely to be "unable or unwilling" to undertake successful prosecutions, (4) and also the opposite view that weaker countries will try and use it for "politically motivated" prosecutions against the powerful. And yet, within an incredibly short time frame, governments from every region of the world have signed up in order to subject their actions to the scrutiny of the ICC; the required number of treaty ratifications was reached in less than four years, suggesting unprecedented support for this new institution.[25] Due to the insistence of the U.S. delegation during negotiations for the Rome Statute, the ICC is to be funded separately and not through the general UN system and is not formally a UN organ. Still, the ICC was established under the auspices of the UN, and its operation will involve the UN in numerous respects.[26] In the limited space of this chapter, we focus on those issues that most directly engage the ability of the UN per se to respond to issues of global security.

The Security Council and the ICC

The Rome Statute provides that the Security Council can refer any "situation" to the ICC when acting under Chapter VII of the UN Charter—clearly signalling that the ICC should replace the need for the Security Council to establish separate ad hoc tribunals for each new international "situation" that arises in future. The United States and several other permanent Security Council members (P5) would have preferred that the ICC was under the complete control of the Council, so they could continue to pick and choose which international "situations" should be addressed by criminal tribunals and which ignored. But they did not get their wish. As a way of avoiding the charges of politicization and selectivity levelled against the Security Council-established ad hoc tribunals, any state party to the statute can also refer a "situation" to the court for investigation, and the prosecutor can initiate his own investigations with the approval of a three-judge, pre-trial chamber. However, without a referral from the Security Council, the court can only investigate crimes committed either on the territory or by a national of a party to the statute.[27]

Article 16, the Rome Statute also requires the ICC to defer any investigation or prosecution for 12 months whenever so requested by the Security Council acting under Chapter VII of the UN Charter. This provision was intended to allay some of the concerns of P5 members by providing for some "diplomatic flexibility," for example, where arrest warrants could hamper delicate peace negotiations by preventing key actors from travelling to those negotiations. Article 16 was also inserted as a way of virtually guaranteeing that no single government could impose its political agenda on the ICC because it requires all permanent members of the Security Council, as well as a majority of nonpermanent members, to agree to make the request to the court.

However, contrary to repeated U.S. fears that the ICC would be put to "politicized" use against its interests,[28] experience has shown how the United States can use Security Council politics to squash even hypothetical cases. On June 30, 2002, in a 14 to 1 vote, the United States vetoed the renewal of the UN's peacekeeping mandate in Bosnia over concerns that U.S. peace-keepers would become subject to the jurisdiction of the ICC from July 1, 2002, when the Rome Statute entered into force. Because Bosnia was a party to the statute, anyone committing an ICC crime on Bosnian territory, including UN peace-keepers, theoretically could be prosecuted by the ICC from that date. The United States used its veto because it failed to gain support from any other Security Council member for additional wording it was recommending for inclusion in the mandate renewal, which would provide permanent, blanket ICC immunity to any "current and former officials and personnel from a contributing state not a party to the Rome Statute acting in connection with these operations."[29]

The United States and the United Kingdom then allegedly joined forces to convince the rest of the Council members that they could not survive the threatened withdrawal of the United States's 25 percent contribution to the UN peacekeeping budget. The opposition to the United States on this issue was near-universal and vociferous. Over the course of the furious bargaining that took place, Kofi Annan took the unusual step of protesting U.S. actions to U.S. Secretary of State Powell. On July 3 the Preparatory Commission of the ICC (Prepcom) held a special plenary session where unanimous opposition to the U.S. position was voiced on behalf of approximately 120 states. At the request of Canada, the Security Council took the highly unusual step of convening an open session on the issue, in which statements were heard on behalf of 72 countries, most harshly and correctly condemning the U.S. efforts as amounting to an illegal usurpation of treaty law by the Security Council. Similarly, NGOs vehemently criticized this resolution as a violation of international law, since Chapter VII of the UN Charter mandates the Security Council to act only when there is a threat to or breach of international peace and security or an act of aggression. It was this U.S.–contrived "crisis" in peacekeeping that was the pretext for invoking Chapter VII.

By taking sides with the United States, the United Kingdom effectively ruined any chance of united EU opposition on the issue or even presenting a united front with ICC states parties (the United Kingdom is a party). The United States and United Kingdom on July 12 successfully pressured the Security Council to adopt unanimously Resolution 1422, which states that the ICC "shall for a twelve-month period starting 1 July 2002 not commence or proceed with investigation or prosecution of any case" involving personnel from non-state parties to the Rome Treaty involved in operations "established or authorized" by the UN "unless the SC decides otherwise."[30] In practice, the United States gained little insofar as its soldiers were minimally exposed to potential indictments as UN peace-keepers (704 personnel out of a total of some 45,000 UN peace-keepers); in principle this was a notable— if so far temporary—victory for the realpolitik unilateralism of the Bush administration in its efforts to render itself immune from the ICC and to manipulate the UN and ICC through the Security Council. While some NGOs expressed relief that the adopted resolution was much weaker than initial resolutions and does not have great practical value, they also recognized that the resolution violated the Rome Statute and the UN Charter, demonstrating the power of unilateralist U.S. diplomacy against the other member states of the Security Council, and indeed the coalition of member states of the ICC. Security Council Resolution 1422 was renewed by a Security Council vote in June 2003, while the United States continued to pressure every government in the world to sign bilateral agreements with it, providing complete immunity to U.S. nationals and others from surrender to the ICC in order to shield their senior officials from possible future prosecution by the ICC.

The UN and the Crime of Aggression

Such power plays are at the root of concerns about the place of the crime of aggression in the ICC's armory. To the disappointment of many non-P5 states, the ICC will only be able to prosecute this crime when an acceptable definition and a mechanism to bring such a case before the ICC are adopted at a treaty review conference some time after July 1, 2009.[31] A Working Group on the Crime of Aggression (WGCA) met numerous times during the ICC Prepcom sessions but failed to reach agreement on any key issues except for a recommendation that all interested governments should continue to debate the issues under the auspices of the ICC ASP.[32] Some of these issues go to the heart of the UN's role in global security, and several states are arguing that the UN should therefore be hosting the discussions. But with the United States so opposed to the ICC, it is highly unlikely that UN resources will be allocated to host any such discussions. Among the plethora of complex issues to resolve is the role of the Security Council, if any, when the ICC wishes to prosecute someone for a crime of aggression. Under article 39, UN Charter, the Security Council is supposed to "determine the existence of any . . . act of aggression." However, in almost 50 years of existence, the Council has rarely identified an "act of aggression," not even when Iraq invaded Kuwait in 1990. So, should the ICC have to wait until the Security Council identifies an "act of aggression" before anyone can be held responsible for the "crime of aggression" when the Council is highly unlikely to make such a determination, especially if a leader of one of the P5 governments is being accused? These debates have now centered around Article 24 of the Charter, whether the "primary responsibility" of the Council to make such determinations in order to maintain international peace and security is really "primary" or in fact "exclusive," as several P5 representatives have argued.

Such issues are paramount since, even when cases start coming within the ambit of the ICC, it will still need to rely on substantial cooperation from the international community, especially the most powerful actors. Without some form of military intervention to control such situations as the current conflicts in Democratic Republic of Congo or Colombia, the ICC would be foolish to try and arrest persons residing in those territories, or to try and gather evidence of atrocities other than from refugees who have left the scene. Only when current "situations" are ready to be addressed by the international community will the ICC be able to take its proper place as the "court of last resort," for situations in which no other judicial institution is willing and able to prosecute the perpetrators of "the most serious crimes of concern to the international community as a whole." Thus, the current power struggles in the Security Council are being watched closely by all those concerned about the prospects for the world's latest addition to the global security apparatus.

CONCLUSION

A revolutionary development in how the world deals with violent conflict has been the increasing criminalization of war and atrocities; that is, the increasing turn to genuinely international legal regimes to hold individuals—not just states—responsible for war crimes, genocide, and crimes against humanity. This criminalization of violent conflict has eroded traditional boundaries of sovereignty by gradually removing the requirement that such crimes need to occur in the context of interstate conflict to be the proper concern of the community of states. Now internal massacres or atrocities and not just interstate war may warrant international legal intervention. Landmarks in this process have been achieved through the UN, culminating in the ICC. One of the important results has been the inclusion of rape and other sexual crimes as new categories of international crimes, a natural progression from the UN's role in promoting human rights such as gender equality.

The ICC was not always intended to have jurisdiction over such overtly "political" crimes as the use of force in war. In that sense, the expanding reach of international criminal law into war and civil conflicts reflects not only an historic accomplishment of the UN and international law but at the same time the failure of the UN *political* system to adequately maintain peace and security. Indeed, the vehemence of the Bush administration's assault on the ICC might be taken as flattering, reflecting a clear awareness of just how important a development this is. But what ought we to think about the viability of international criminal tribunals in face of opposition by the United States and other powers?

First, realist theory tells us that international institutions are but a reflection of the interests of great powers. Indeed, this is partially true: The ICTY would not have happened without the United States, and key arrests would not have taken place without the intervention of military powers. The ICTR would not have happened without the ICTY, and the creation of the ICC was not only unlikely without the tribunals but also reflects a number of key concessions to the United States that were not unraveled when the United States voted against the Rome Statute. So to some extent the criminalization of war and atrocity confirms the realist insistence that the most powerful institutions reflect and require participation of the most powerful states.

But the tribunals also partially confirm an institutionalist logic that such creations often go beyond the interests of their powerful state creators to have independent effects of their own that insinuate themselves more deeply in international society. Moreover, the powerful coalition of like-minded states who are keen supporters of the ICC endowed it with features the United States and other powers did not want (particularly the independent prosecutor). The importance of the United States in ensuring the apprehension of suspects in the former Yugoslavia importantly underscores what will be lost without United States participation in the ICC, but in other contexts in which U.S. pressure has not been so strongly at play, successes still occurred (Rwandan arrests, role of United Kingdom in Balkans arrests). Those states most supportive of the ICC (including all EU member states) will ensure that it will not be a moribund institution even in the face of resistance and even obstructionism by the Untied States, India, and other key nonparticipating states, though clearly its effective domain will be constricted in the face of full frontal attacks by great powers.

Still, to the extent that the above is true, it actually points to a reason why we could expect more de facto compliance with international criminal law by the United States than its hostile rejection of the ICC suggests. The ICC does in fact represent a good many U.S. interests, but it also represents more: namely, U.S. values and norms that are shared with many other states based upon a belief in the rule of law. The important shortcomings in the regulative power of the UN-created criminal tribunals that follow from the opposition of key states will be offset to no small extent by the constitutive effects of the jurisprudence of the tribunals and legitimacy bestowed upon war crimes law. Thus, even to the extent that the UN is best seen most of the time as but the expression of the will of its member states, the UN has in turn affected the will of those member states. The evolving jurisprudence of UN institutions has created law that has been internalized by states who will remain the prime enforcers of that law. Let us not forget that by intention it is likely that most of the criminal trials of international concern will take place in national courts, not the ICC.

NOTES

*   The authors thank David Malone, Michael Barnett, and the other authors of this volume for their comments on earlier versions of this chapter.
1. Apart from some post-WWI treaties outlawing certain methods of warfare, e.g., use of poisonous gases.
2. UNSC Resolutions 827 and 955.

3. See Gary Bass, *Stay the Hand of Vengeance: The Politics of War Crimes Tribunals* (Princeton: Princeton University Press, 2000), 329.

4. See *Complaint to the International Criminal Tribunal for the Former Yugoslavia* (Professor Michael Mandel, Osgoode Hall Law School, Toronto, Canada, May 6, 1999) at: http://jurist.law.pitt.edu/icty.htm

5. UNSC Resolution 1315 (August 14, 2000).

6. Asahi Shimbun, "Asia Must Make its Own Human Rights Stand," *ICC Digest* 525 (April 6, 2002).

7. See Bass, 207, 213, 222.

8. See, for example, Theodore Moran, "Answering for War Crimes," *Foreign Affairs* 76(1) (January/February 1997), 8.

9. Bland, "An Analysis," 267.

10. These were UNPROFOR (1992–1995), IFOR (December 1995–December 1996) and SFOR (December 1996–present).

11. Brigadier General Huib van Lent (Netherlands) (Sarajevo, June 14, 2002).

12. Although the Belgian parliament recently revised the legislation so that only persons actually present in Belgium can be indicted, thereby passing on potentially embarrassing diplomatic problems to the new ICC.

13. For example, Canada's *Crimes Against Humanity and War Crimes Act* of July 2000.

14. Udo Janz, United National High Commissioner for Refugees (Sarajevo, June 14, 2002); Jacques Klein, UN special representative for Bosnia-Herzegovina (Sarajevo, June 14, 2002).

15. Christopher Rudolph, "Constructing an Atrocities Regime: The Politics of War Crimes Tribunals," *International Organization* 55(3) (September 2001): 655–691.

16. M. Cherif Bassiouni, "Searching for Peace and Achieving Justice: The Need for Accountability," in *Reining in Impunity for International Crimes and Serious Violations of Fundamental Human Rights* eds. C. Joyner & M. Cherif Bassiouni (Ramonville St-Agne, France: Éditions Érès, 1998), 49.

17. Chris McGreal, "Second-class Justice System," *Manchester Guardian Weekly* (April 24, 2002) (cited from *ICC Digest* 541, Wednesday, May 1).

18. Bass, *Stay the Hand*, 294.

19. Michael Smith, "'War Crimes' Fear For British Troops," *The Daily Telegraph* (London) (November 6, 2002), 19.

20. See her speech in Bass, *Stay the Hand*, 290.

21. Bass, 310.

22. Moran on the ICTY in 1997, "Answering for War Crimes."

23. Dejan Milenković, Lawyer's Committee for Human Rights (Belgrade June 17, 2002).

24. The Rome Statute of the ICC was adopted by a nonrecorded vote of 120 in favor, 7 against, and 21 abstaining.

25. At the time of writing, the Rome Statute had 90 States Parties—almost half of all UN member states.

26. The General Assembly in September 2003 will be requested to adopt a special "Relationship Agreement" between the UN and the ICC, which

envisages a close, cooperative relationship between the various organs of the UN and the ICC.

27. See Rome Statute, Part 2.
28. John Bolton, "Courting Danger: What's Wrong with the International Criminal Court," *The National Interest* 54 (Winter 1998–1999): 60–71.
29. From text allegedly circulated on 27 June, 2002.
30. Operative paragraph 1, S/RES/1422 (2002).
31. Rome Statute, Articles 5, 121 & 123.
32. ICC-ASP/1/Res.1 (September 2002).

PART IV

THE UN AND INTERVENTION

CHAPTER 9

FROM PEACE-KEEPING TO PEACE-BUILDING: THE UNITED NATIONS AND THE CHALLENGE OF INTRASTATE WAR

Allen G. Sens

Can a self-sustaining and lasting peace be constructed in societies torn asunder by war or gross violations of human rights? This question has been one of the most pressing issues facing the United Nations (UN) since the end of the Cold War. During that time, the UN became engaged in efforts to terminate intrastate conflicts in Cambodia, Somalia, Angola, Haiti, and the former Yugoslavia, among many others. However, while traditional UN peace-keeping missions were designed to keep the peace between states, the management of intrastate conflict required keeping the peace within states. As a result, the UN began to develop a new generation of peace support activities and tasks designed to respond to the challenges of intrastate conflict: consolidating civil order and establishing the political and socio-economic conditions for sustainable peace. In effect, the UN became engaged in building peace in war-torn societies. And so, by the year 2000 UN peace operations formally involved three principal activities: conflict prevention and peacemaking; peace-keeping; and peace-building.[1] The UN, an institution devised to remove the scourge of war between states, had evolved into a primary instrument of building peace within states.

This chapter traces the origins of peace-building as it emerged from the transformation of peace-keeping and argues that a peace-building norm has emerged within the UN system. However, there are limits to the reach of this norm, as evidenced by serious conceptual criticism and challenges to the very legitimacy of peace-building itself. The chapter will then evaluate the record of peace-building efforts and conclude that only very modest results have been achieved thus far. In fact, the obstacles facing peace-building are so formidable that the ability of the UN to successfully implement such efforts must be questioned. Looking to the future, the UN should focus its efforts on strengthening the emerging peace-building norm and improving its capacity to act as a coordinating mechanism and an instrument of legitimacy for peace-building activities.

UN Peace-keeping in the Cold War Era: Keeping Peace between States

The first UN peace-keeping missions were the United Nations Truce Supervision Organization (UNTSO), established in 1948 as an observer mission to oversee an Arab-Israeli cease-fire, and the 1949 United Nations Military Observer Group in India and Pakistan (UNMOGIP). More substantial was the United Nations Emergency Force (UNEF), conceived as a response to the Suez Crisis by Canadian Secretary of State for External Affairs Lester B. Pearson, authorized by the General Assembly, and deployed in the Sinai in 1956. UN peace-keeping was an improvisation, born out of the need to respond to war between states. Peace-keeping was neither mentioned nor envisioned in the UN Charter and had no clear legal standing as it occupied a middle ground between the provisions for the peaceful settlement of disputes in Chapter VI of the Charter and the enforcement mechanisms in Chapter VII. As the former Secretary-General Dag Hammarskjold described it, peace-keeping was nestled in a nonexistent "Chapter Six-and-a-half" in the Charter. Nevertheless, peace-keeping became a key role for the UN in the maintenance of international peace and security, mounting 18 peace-keeping missions during the Cold War.

UN peace-keeping acquired a number of political and operational conventions that came to define what would later be called "traditional" peace-keeping. Peace-keeping missions were created under the authority of the UN Security Council (UNSC) or the UN General Assembly (UNGA) and were under the operational control of the Secretary-General and UN headquarters. Composed primarily of military forces of small and medium-sized UN members, missions were deployed between states in support of a cease-fire or a peace settlement. Accordingly, peace-keeping operations were to be impartial and deployed with the consent of the host state or states. Non-hostile and lightly armed only for self-defense, peace-keepers were not a coercive force. Instead, they were identified by white-painted vehicles and the now-famous "blue helmets" and "blue berets" and acted as observers and mediators at the local level to deter violence and create confidence and dialogue. While there were exceptions to these conventions (notably in the Congo, where a UN force became embroiled in a civil war), by the latter half of the Cold War there was an implicit understanding of what UN peace-keeping entailed as exemplified in missions in Cyprus, the Golan Heights, Lebanon, and the Sinai. Fundamentally, peace-keeping was about maintaining a peace between states, and the political and operational parameters of peace-keeping were firmly consistent with the Westphalian principles of state sovereignty and territorial integrity.

UN Peace-keeping in the post–Cold War Era: Responding to Civil Wars

The end of the Cold War created a sense of optimism and opportunity for the UN. A surge in intrastate conflicts and the phenomenon of "failed" or "collapsed" states around the world in the late 1980s and early 1990s became the central conflict management challenge confronting the UN system. Faced with intrastate conflicts in places such as Somalia, the former Yugoslavia, Cambodia, Angola, Mozambique, Rwanda, and Haiti, states looked to the instrument of UN peace-keeping as a mechanism for stopping or controlling civil war, human rights abuses, and the collapse of civil order. International involvement in such conflicts was driven in part by strategic interests, for in some cases there were fears that violence or instability could spread to neighboring countries and precipitate wider regional wars. However, international involvement was also driven by a reaction to human rights violations and the suffering of noncombatants as heart-rending scenes of both were displayed in the world's media, pressure was placed on governments to intervene. Large-scale humanitarian crises and human rights violations thus constituted a normative rationale for robust intervention efforts and precipitated a larger dialogue on human security and the limits of state sovereignty in a "post-Westphalian" order.

In response to the increase in intrastate conflicts, there was a surge in UN peace-keeping and UN-sanctioned intervention in civil wars and "complex humanitarian emergencies." Peace-keeping operations became more numerous and complex, involving a wide set of political, military, and humanitarian tasks. While traditional peace-keeping missions would still be established (for example, between Iraq and Kuwait and between Ethiopia and Eritrea), these "second generation" peace-keeping efforts were fundamentally different in both nature and scope. Freed from the political divisions of the Cold War, the Security Council repeatedly demonstrated its willingness to invoke Chapter VII of the UN Charter, which enabled the UN (or sanctioned coalitions or regional organizations) to intervene in intrastate conflicts and failed states under the rubric of responding to threats to international peace and security. As a result, UN peace-keeping missions were deployed within (rather than between) states into environments where host state consent was partial or absent and where there was either no peace to keep or where cease-fires were sporadic and of short duration. Once deployed, UN missions became increasingly engaged in a broad spectrum of objectives and tasks, including the maintenance of order, the protection of civilian refugees and safe areas, the disarming of soldiers, the monitoring of weapons cantonment sites, mine clearance and education, police training, and elections monitoring.

However, the high expectations for the UN as a maintainer of the peace were largely disappointed. In Somalia, local leaders defied a U.S.-led force, and UN efforts to establish a political settlement failed. In the former Yugoslavia, UN forces could not stop an ethnic conflict, and in Rwanda the UN failed to respond to a genocide that killed 800,000 people. In these and many other places, UN missions were overwhelmed by the enormity of their tasks in the midst of intrastate conflicts. These experiences discredited the UN in the eyes of many. John Ruggie, for example, accused the UN of outright strategic failure in its efforts to manage regional conflicts after the Cold War.[2] However, while it is true that the UN lacked the administrative capabilities to manage these operations effectively, the fault rests more with member states than with the organization itself. UN missions were not sufficiently equipped or mandated at the outset to operate in intrastate war conditions. The norms, doctrines, and rules of engagement developed for traditional peace-keeping missions were wholly inadequate for second-generation environments, and member states responded slowly and unevenly to this reality. Although the UN would establish 35 new missions in the 1990s (double the number created during the Cold War), the UN fell out of favor as an instrument for large-scale intervention in intrastate conflicts in the second half of the decade. This resulted in a decline in the size and scale of UN missions and the increased use of coalitions of the willing and regional organizations to conduct peace operations that had UN authorization but were conducted outside the mechanisms of the UN system.

UN PEACE-BUILDING IN THE POST–COLD WAR ERA: BUILDING THE NATION-STATE

The origins of what is now called peace-building are to be found in the convergence of three trends in international conflict management efforts. First, there was the erosion of the norm of nonintervention and the development of the concept of human security. As states demonstrated an increased willingness to intervene to stop civil wars, they also demonstrated a greater willingness to intervene within societies to establish the conditions for peace. Indeed, such interference was seen as a necessity: With the responsibility to protect human security came the responsibility to rebuild just societies. Second, intervening states had an interest in the long-term success of efforts to terminate intrastate conflicts. Peace-building, like peace-keeping, had a realpolitik dimension: It would discourage conflicts with neighboring states and external military interventions, and it provided an exit strategy. Third, peace-building generally included liberal political and economic strategies that enjoyed increasing support throughout the world.

The emergence of peace-building within the UN system was often fueled by the urgency of member states to consolidate the gains of peace settlements. While the UN had some prior exposure to national reconstruction, there was little previous experience with comprehensive packages of UN activities designed around postconflict reconstruction and social rehabilitation. Like traditional peace-keeping and second-generation peace-keeping, peace-building was an improvisation. In 1991, UN engagement in Angola and the Western Sahara included assistance with democratization and institution-building. The UN mission in El Salvador was mandated to assist with the demobilization of former combatants, elections monitoring, the promotion of human rights, and reform of the police and judiciary. In Cambodia, an ambitious mission mandate included the supervision of elections, institutional capacity building, demobilization, human rights promotion, and de-mining.

The necessity of a more systematic approach was evident as intrastate conflicts continued to demand the attention of the UN. The development of the peace-building norm in the UN was built on the intellectual origins of peace-building found in academic work on conflict management and peace research. Johan Galtung distinguished between peacemaking and peace-keeping and peace-building in the 1970s, defining the latter as "the practical implementation of peaceful social change through socio-economic reconstruction and development."[3] At the UN Boutros Boutros-Ghali's *An Agenda for Peace*, issued in 1992, was the first systematic treatment of peace-building within the UN system. In that document peace-building was defined as efforts to "identify and support structures which will tend to strengthen and solidify peace in order to avoid a relapse into conflict."[4] Through the mid-1990s, peace-building continued to develop within the UN system as second generation peace-keeping missions increased in number, scale, and scope. An Electoral Assistance Unit (subsequently renamed the Electoral Assistance Division) was established in 1992 in order to assist member states in holding elections. In Mozambique the UN mission focused its efforts on demobilization of troops, return of refugees, and democratization. The missions in Somalia and the former Yugoslavia encompassed the promotion of human rights and national reconciliation, technical assistance for reconstruction and the development of institutions, as well as the promotion of democracy, demobilization, and refugee repatriation. Missions in Georgia, Liberia, Haiti, Rwanda, and Tajikistan had peace-building activities at the very core of their mandates.

In the mid to late 1990s, peace-building became "mainstreamed" in the UN system, becoming part of the discourse of peace operations generally and field operations in particular. In the 1995 supplement to *An Agenda for Peace,* peace-building was identified as one of the principal strategies for peace and security, alongside preventive diplomacy and peacemaking, peace-keeping, disarmament, sanctions, and peace enforcement.[5] Many agencies in the UN system established or designated focal points for peace-building in order to facilitate communication, consultation, and coordination. For example, in 1994 the United Nations Development Program (UNDP) established an Emergency Response Division, tasked with developing and coordinating UNDP's role in peace-building activities. In addition, the UN established the Executive Committee on Peace and Security (ECPS), which is the most important mechanism for the coordination of peace-building activities.

In 2000 the *Report of the Panel on United Nations Peace Operations* (popularly referred to as the *Brahimi Report*) built on the themes established through the 1990s. The *Brahimi Report* noted the need for a focal point for peace-building and concluded that "the United Nations should be considered the focal point for peace-building activities by the donor community."[6] The development of peace-building within the UN system continued with the creation of peace-building offices (Liberia, Guinea-Bissau, the Central

African Republic and Tajikistan) and transitional authority missions. The offices provide assistance related to the consolidation of peace and democracy, engaging with a variety of local actors such as government ministries, national assemblies, political parties, and civil society to support peace-building efforts. The transitional authority missions established in East Timor (United Nations Transitional Administration in East Timor) and Kosovo (United Nations Interim Administration in Kosovo) were designed to establish and administer civil order in these territories in preparation for self-governance (in the case of East Timor) and local autonomy (in the case of Kosovo). To this end, the missions established local governments, assumed public administration functions, and managed policing, legal, and electoral tasks.

The development of the peace-building norm in the UN system was crowned by the establishment of a definition of peace-building by the UNSC in February 2001:

> . . . peace-building is aimed at preventing the outbreak, the recurrence or continuation of armed conflict and therefore encompasses a wide range of political, developmental, humanitarian and human rights programmes and mechanisms. This requires short and long term actions tailored to address the particular needs of societies sliding into conflict or emerging from it. These actions should focus on fostering sustainable institutions and processes in areas such as sustainable development, the eradication of poverty and inequalities, transparent and accountable governance, the promotion of democracy, respect for human rights and the rule of law and the promotion of a culture of peace and non-violence.[7]

As occurred with peace-keeping, over time a set of strategies and standard practices guiding peace-building has developed in the UN system. Something like a menu of strategies and tasks has emerged, which include:

- stabilization of the internal political and security situation;
- development of regional engagement with neighboring states and regional actors;
- demobilization, disarmament, and reintegration;
- return of refugees and Internally Displaced Persons;
- democratization (electoral assistance, capacity building, institution building);
- strengthening civil society (promotion of dialogue, conflict management training, dispute resolution mechanisms);
- capacity building and security sector reform;
- technical assistance for reconstruction and economic development;
- promotion of human rights;
- promotion of intergroup recognition and national reconciliation;
- trauma recovery;
- peace / civic education;

- de-mining and awareness; and
- promotion of regional and international economic integration.

Through the 1990s, the UNSC resolution record demonstrated the central role peace-building has played in UN efforts to respond to international conflicts. Appendix 9.1 lists the UN missions mounted since the end of the Cold War and their mandated peace-building activities and tasks. The latest incarnation of peace-building is the mission in Afghanistan; to this point the UN role in Iraq following the 2003 war has been minor and the United States was expected to retain custodianship over the rebuilding of Iraq for at least a year.

OBSTACLES TO PEACE-BUILDING: CONCEPTUAL CRITICISM AND PRACTICAL LIMITATIONS

The lack of conceptual clarity in the peace-building discourse is already legendary. However, a growing body of reflective research in the form of academic studies, mission evaluation reports, and larger critical assessments of globalization and development strategies has begun to illustrate the limitations of the strategy and the contestable nature of its core assumptions and even its legitimacy. At the heart of this criticism is a challenge to the liberalism embedded in the principles and practices of peace-building.

First, peace-building may have a serious conceptual flaw as it is built on the premise that political and economic liberalization will promote stability and consolidate peace. As Roland Paris has observed, "peacebuilding is in effect an enormous experiment in social engineering—an experiment that involves transplanting western models of social, political, and economic organization into war-shattered states in order to control civil conflict: in other words, pacification through political and economic liberalization."[8] However, the liberal economic model can widen inequalities, create economic dislocation, and consolidate the power of those who benefited from black market activities during the conflict. At the same time, political liberalization can reinforce and entrench political differences and divide peoples, as in Bosnia and Kosovo, where nationalist parties gained office in UN-supervised elections. The *Brahimi Report* noted that "elections merely ratify a tyranny of the majority" until sufficient civil-society development has taken place and a culture of human rights is established.[9] As Roland Paris has argued, "both democracy and capitalism encourage conflict and competition—indeed, they thrive on it."[10] Their values may be precisely the wrong qualities to introduce into postconflict societies without due care and diligence since they can undermine the spirit of national reconciliation.

A second challenge confronting peace-building is its own legitimacy. First, there is a concern that peace-building can entail the imposition of foreign ways. Local economic patterns, local civil society, and traditional mechanisms of conflict management and leadership may be overshadowed or disrupted by peace-building activities. In Somalia UN efforts largely ignored local conflict management mechanisms in favor of a more formal diplomatic model. The process was only marginally successful and served to undermine preexisting instruments of mediation and negotiation. As a result, there have been calls for greater local ownership of peace-building and bottom-up approaches. Gendered approaches have also made a contribution to this perspective, as there is evidence that female participation in peace-building efforts has increased the level of engagement of local women and women's NGOs in elections and political life.[11]

However, some contingencies require a "heavy footprint," and in some cases, such as Sierra Leone and Afghanistan, there may be a real need for more UN engagement rather than less. Peace-building must also show results: The seed of long-term peace is difficult to plant if euphoria turns to disillusionment as high expectations are not met, if the quality of life of the people shows no change, if the inability to absorb demobilized soldiers and refugees creates unemployment and crime, and if black market economies continue to operate.

Second, the legitimacy question is inseparable from larger concerns about the marginalization of the developing world. For some, peace-building is viewed as a component of a larger agenda of western political and economic supremacy: "Peace-building in this context becomes an inherently conservative undertaking, seeking managerial solutions to fundamental conflicts over resources and power, seeking to modernize and re-legitimize a fundamental status quo respectful, reinforcing, and reflective of national and international market-oriented political economy."[12] Developing countries are frequently suspicious of peace-building, regarding it as another manifestation of western interventionism and cultural imperialism. Opposition also stems from the view that peace-building will draw resources away from development efforts and marginalize the role of local societies in establishing a peace free from external interference by western states, international organizations, and multinational corporations. The agendas of powerful states and corporations and large international financial institutions such as the IMF and World Bank are seen as dominating the implementation of peace-building, imposing solutions on the basis of their own ideology and interests in economic liberalization without a care for social justice and human needs in the host society.

A third challenge facing peace-building efforts is the sheer magnitude of the task. Bringing conditions of positive peace to societies devastated by war is very difficult because postconflict societies often lack effective institutions of governance, have massive human security problems, and face enormous development challenges. In many cases conflicts are "frozen" by external intervention and are prone to resumption if one or more parties believe military victory is possible. This problem is exacerbated if there is a fragmented political authority in the society, if there is social opposition to peace-building activities, or if there are significant social elements or local leaders with an economic or political stake in the continuation of conflict. Stephen John Steadman has highlighted this "spoiler" problem in peace-keeping and peace-building efforts, defining spoilers as "leaders and parties who believe that peace emerging from negotiations threatens their power, world view, and interests and use violence to undermine efforts to achieve it."[13]

These problems have been complicated by environments where there is considerable demand for justice stemming from gross violations of human rights, but where local legal systems are nonexistent or of suspect effectiveness. Peace-building efforts must confront the tensions between state sovereignty and human security, universalism and relativism, and order and justice. As seen in the chapter by Price and Lee, in Bosnia the apprehension of Persons Indicted for War Crimes sparked a debate between those who favored an aggressive approach to see justice done and those who favored caution to avoid a backlash against foreign peace-keepers. In Liberia and Sierra Leone, local civil society actors accused the UN of supporting a "culture of impunity" in which perpetrators of crimes were granted amnesty for their crimes in return for their support of a political settlement. In response to the weak legal institutions facing many peace-building efforts, the *Brahimi Report* suggested the need for a "common United Nations justice package" with an "interim legal code" to be used until local applicable law could be established.[14] The UN has responded with criminal tribunals as chronicled in Price and Lee's chapter. While they have achieved some successes, they are expensive and are foreign rather than local legal instruments. Meanwhile, the money and expertise needed to rebuild domestic judicial and legal systems are in short supply.

A fourth challenge facing peace-building efforts is presented by the divergent interests and agendas of participating states. At the political level, peace-building missions are subject to UNSC approval and mandate renewal and are therefore vulnerable to bargaining and shifting political alignments among the members of the Council. This can lead to vague or unsuitable mandates which provide poor guidance for operational tasks, a problem that plagued UN missions in Somalia, the former Yugoslavia, and Rwanda. Furthermore, peace-building depends on a long-term commitment of resources and material. However, the nature of public opinion and the crisis-driven character of UN interventions raise serious concerns about the capacity of states to sustain peace-building operations. The concern of contributing states over "exit strategies" and avoidance of quagmires has led to the creation of unrealistically short operational time frames and an undue emphasis on "quick impact" projects designed to show sufficient results. "Quick impact" projects can thus turn into "temporary impact" projects and fail to serve the interests of a long-term sustainable peace. Finally, elections in donor states sometimes provide a rationale for the scaling down of a mission and a convenient exit strategy for states.[15] The timing of the 1996 elections in Bosnia, driven at least in part by electoral politics in the United States, is but one example.[16]

A fifth challenge facing peace-building is the nature of the UN system itself. There is no clear institutional home for peace-building in the UN, and because the activities of peace-building cut across the mandates and activities of so many parts of the UN system, there is a pressing need for coordination among secretariat departments, UN agencies, and non-UN actors. However, coordination efforts have been complicated by the institutional and bureaucratic rivalry that characterizes the UN, a common theme in many chapters of this volume. While peace-keeping has a political and institutional apparatus within the UN system in the form of the Special Committee on Peace-keeping and the Department of Peace-keeping Operations (DPKO), peace-building has no such apparatus. The responsibilities for peace-building are diffused through the UN. The UN Secretariat has little or no control over specialized agencies such as UNHCR and UNICEF, and there is no General Assembly mechanism to evaluate or supervise peace-building operations other than the budget-oriented Fifth Committee. There is clearly a need for a center of peace-building to educate staff, serve as a "receptacle" for lessons learned, best practices, and coordination, and as a source of information and expertise on peace-building within the UN system.

In recognizing these shortcomings the *Brahimi Report* identified the Department of Political Affairs (DPA) as the focal point for peace-building in the UN system. However, the report went on to identify the UNDP as best placed to take the lead in implementing peace-building activities. The report also called for the creation of a peace-building unit within DPA, a proposal sunk by the Administrative Committee on Budgetary Questions. Meanwhile, the problem of coordination persists. In July 2001, a review of UN peace-building support offices noted the "absence of a coherent strategy for peace-building and common understanding of objectives and priorities is perhaps the single most significant obstacle to effective collaboration within the United Nations system."[17] This led to the establishment of a Plan of Action on Peace-building, which was developed to establish general guidelines on ways to coordinate peace-building efforts more effectively within the UN system. Although some friction attended these efforts, through day-to-day practice considerable progress has been made on interdepartmental communication and consultation. By any measure, coordination is much improved from the conditions that prevailed in the mid-1990s, though considerable barriers remain.

A sixth challenge facing the implementation of peace-building efforts is the fact that in many contingencies the UN is not the only or even the primary external actor. This challenge is growing because of the proliferation of NGOs and the increasing relevance of regional organizations and international financial institutions (IFIs). An increasing number of NGOs are engaged in conflict management in war-torn societies, including Conciliation Resources, International Crisis Group, International Alert, Responding to Conflict, and Search for Common Ground. The characteristic independence of the NGO sector makes coordination with these groups quite difficult. In addition, there is a serious lack of coordination between UN agencies and IFIs. In particular, the conditionality demands of the International Monetary Fund (IMF) for economic restructuring can be damaging to the immediate prospects for social stability. For example, the IMF damaged recovery in Mozambique in 1995, when a weak government was compelled to make spending cuts that would compromise the peace settlement. Coordination with the World Bank is also critical, for the Bank is the more important actor in terms of financial resources than the UNDP. However, there is no real connection between the Bank and the UN Secretariat, although there is an increasing awareness of peace-building efforts at the Bank which recently established a postconflict unit.

At the field level, peace-building is characterized by an almost bewildering array of actors. In Kosovo, civil administration and policing was under the UN (although police training was done by the OSCE); humanitarian assistance was run largely by UNHCR; economic reconstruction was run largely by the EU and the World Bank; institution building was the responsibility of the OSCE; and security was provided by NATO. Coordination on human rights was particularly difficult in Kosovo since it involved the UN mission, the NATO security force, and the OSCE.

Finally, like virtually everything else associated with the UN, peace-building suffers from the constraints of limited financial resources. While traditional peace-keeping is funded through assessed contributions, peace-building is funded through voluntary contributions. And so, despite the increase in peace-building activities mandated by the UNSC, no additional resources have been dedicated to a specific peace-building budget. There is, however, some modest funding provided by the UNDP and the DPA. This unsystematic status of peace-building funding has resulted in uneven resource allocation, the creation of "strategic favorites" and "orphans," and a lack of sustainability.

IS PEACE-BUILDING WORKING?

Evaluating the success of peace-building is an enormous conceptual challenge. Peace-building cases vary widely, depending on the extent of UN involvement and the nature of the conflict.[18] A basic measure for the success of peace-building is the cessation of war and the prevention of recidivism into large-scale political violence or human rights abuses. However, the goal of positive peace is more demanding to achieve and harder to measure, requiring the development and consolidation of democratic governance, the rule of law, robust institutions, and a healthy civil society.

Several studies examining peace-building efforts across a sample of countries suggests that the peace-building record is on balance rather poor. One study examined twelve cases of postconflict peace settlements, finding six successes, two partial successes, and four failures of sustainable peace.[19] Roland Paris's evaluation suggests that peace-building has failed in seven out of eight cases.[20] Michael Doyle and Nicholas Sambanis examined 124 cases of terminated civil wars since 1945. Using their lenient measure of success, they judged 53 of these cases to be successes and 71 failures.[21] Fen Hampson examined five cases and found two successes, one partial success, and two failures.[22] Appendix 9.2 provides a list of post–Cold War UN missions with prominent peace-building components, indicating the achievement of a positive peace against the maintenance of a negative peace and the return of significant levels of political violence. This evaluation suggests that out of 22 cases, three can be said to have achieved a positive, self-sustaining peace. Fifteen of the cases indicate the maintenance of a negative peace, where the development of democracy, institutions, civil society, and the rule of law have not taken root. In many of these cases, a large international security force is still in place to help maintain order. Recidivism into large-scale violence occurred in eight cases. Taken together, the peace-building record has not been particularly successful in attaining the key measure of success: the building of a sustainable, positive peace. Is peace-building saddled with unrealistically high expectations? The enormity of the challenges facing peace-building and the ambitious normative goals of the enterprise may have established impossibly high standards of success and an overestimation of what international engagement can deliver to war-torn societies.

CONCLUSION: THE UN AND PEACE-BUILDING

As the UN itself has recognized, "peace-building has become and is likely to remain one of the primary challenges facing the United Nations membership . . ."[23] Peace-building is an imperative, a requirement of international efforts to respond to intrastate conflicts and gross violations of human rights with the aim of achieving a self-sustaining peace. The norm of peace-building is strong but not without its challenges both conceptually and in terms of legitimacy. The implementation of peace-building in practice is compromised by the magnitude of the challenge and by serious shortcomings and constraints. The danger is the UN system will prove incapable of adequately meeting the demands and expectations placed upon it as a preferred mechanism for peace-building. Just as the UN went through a period of retrenchment after high-profile failures of second generation peace-keeping in Somalia and the former Yugoslavia, the UN's role in peace-building may be eroded through a combination of limited resources, member state conflicts, the increased involvement of regional actors and NGOs, and a growing sense of the limits of what can be expected of the UN. Aspersions would once again be cast on the UN system, provoking a shift toward other organizational or coalition mechanisms in the pursuit of peace-building objectives. In the process another blow will have been dealt to the reputation of the UN as an instrument of international peace and security. Much of this scenario may already be unavoidable. The poor record of peace-building to date and the demonstrable unwillingness of member states to provide the political leadership and resources commensurate with the task of rebuilding war-torn societies the world over may have already set the stage for a retrenchment of UN peace-building.

However, much can be done to minimize the damage to the UN and to improve the effectiveness of future peace-building efforts. The UN should take steps to improve its capacities to act as a promoter of the peace-building norm. The UN remains well placed as the multilateral body that combines the aura of impartiality and legitimacy with the capacities required for successful peace-building coordination. This may take the form of working with a "lead nation" or coalitions in any given peace-building effort. In this "UN-plus" model, the UN provides legitimacy and normative guidance and honest broker functions while others provide political direction and the marshalling of resources.

At the political level, a peace-building working group should be established within the Special Committee on Peace-keeping. This would provide a central point for conceptual discussion and evaluation as well as practical coordination. The working group would serve to enhance support for peace-building by establishing a firmer international consensus behind peace-building among a wider set of countries. In this way, the UN could serve as a center for norm development. At the institutional level, the UN can improve its capacity as an effective coordinating mechanism and focal point for peace-building among the actors and institutions engaged in peace-building efforts. A free-standing center for peace-building with dedicated personnel should be established within DPA, tasked with keeping records on best practices and lessons learned, mission planning, and coordination and consultation. Even these modest advances at the political and institutional levels of the UN system will facilitate greater communication, consultation, and coherence on peace-building. Peace-building remains a work in progress, and although formidable obstacles must be overcome, it will endure as long as responses to intrastate conflict demand the restoration of civil order and the prospects for a peaceful future.

Appendix 9.1 UN Peace Operations since 1991: Peace-building task[24]

	Date	Stabilization of the internal political and security situation	Development of regional engagement w/ regional actors	Demobilization, disarmament, and reintegration	Return of refugees and IDPs	Democratization (electoral assistance, capacity building, institution building)	Strengthening civil society (conflict management training)	Capacity building and security sector reform	Technical assistance for reconstruction and economic development	Promotion of human rights	Promotion of intergroup recognition and national reconciliation	Trauma recovery	Peace/civic education	De-mining and awareness	Promotion of regional and international economic integration
1. UNIKOM (Iraq/Kuwait)	4/91														
2. UNAVEM II (Angola)	5/91–2/95					X									
3. MINURSO (Western Sahara)	4/91–				X	X									
4. ONUSAL (El Salvador)	7/91–4/95			X		X		X		X					
5. UNAMIC (Cambodia)	10/91–3/92													X	
6. UNTAC (Cambodia)	10/91–3/92	X		X	X	X		X		X				X	
7. UNPROFOR (Former Yugoslavia)	2/92–3/95	X													
8. UNOSOM I (Somalia)	4/92–3/93				X	X	X								
9. ONUMOZ (Mozambique)	12/92–12/94			X	X	X									

#	Mission	Location	Dates								
10.	UNOSOM II	(Somalia)	3/93–3/95	X		X	X	X		X	X
11.	UNOMUR	(Uganda/Rwanda)	6/93–9/94								
12.	UNOMIG	(Georgia)	8/93–	X	X	X			X		
13.	UNOMIL	(Liberia)	9/93–9/97	X		X	X	X		X	
14.	UNMIH	(Haiti)	9/93–6/96	X			X	X	X		
15.	UNAMIR	(Rwanda)	10/93–3/96	X		X	X	X			X
16.	UNASOG	(Chad/Libya)	5/94–6/94								
17.	UNMOT	(Tajikistan)	12/94–5/00	X	X	X	X			X	
18.	UNAVEM III	(Angola)	2/95–6/97	X				X	X	X	X
19.	UNCRO	(Croatia)	3/95–1/96	X	X	X		X	X		
20.	UNPREDEP	(Macedonia)	3/95–2/99	X				X			
21.	UNMIBH	(Bosnia)	12/95–	X	X	X	X	X		X	
22.	UNTAES	(Croatia)	1/96–1/98	X	X	X	X	X		X	X
23.	UNMOP	(Prevlaka)	2/96–12/02	X		X		X	X		

Appendix 9.1 *Continued*

Date	Stabilization of the internal political and security situation	Development of regional engagement w/ regional actors	Demobilization, disarmament, and reintegration	Return of refugees and IDPs	Democratization (electoral assistance, capacity building, institution building)	Strengthening civil society (conflict management training)	Capacity building and security sector reform	Technical assistance for reconstruction and economic development	Promotion of human rights	Promotion of intergroup recognition and national reconciliation	Trauma recovery	Peace/civic education	Demining and awareness	Promotion of regional and international economic integration
24. UNSMIH (Haiti)	7/96–7/97	X				X		X	X		X				
25. MINUGUA (Guatemala)	1/97–5/97			X		X			X	X	X		X		
26. MONUA (Angola)	6/97–2/99	X		X				X	X	X	X			X	
27. UNTMIH (Haiti)	8/97–11/97							X			X				
28. MIPONUH (Haiti)	12/97–3/00							X							
29. UNPSG (Croatia)	1/98–10/98							X							
30. MINURCA (Central African Republic)	3/98–2/00	X		X		X	X	X	X	X	X			X	X
31. UNOMSIL (Sierra Leone)	7/98–10/99	X	X	X	X		X	X	X	X	X			X	X

		1	2	3	4	5	6	7	8	9	10	11	12	13
32.	UNMIK (Kosovo)	6/99–	X	X	X	X	X	X	X	X	X	X	X	X
33.	UNAMSIL (Sierra Leone)	10/99–	X	X	X	X	X	X	X	X	X	X	X	
34.	UNTAET (East Timor)	10/99–5/02	X	X	X	X	X	X	X	X	X		X	X
35.	MONUC (Democratic Republic of Congo)	2/00–	X	X	X	X	X	X	X	X		X	X	
36.	UNMEE (Ethiopia/Eritrea)	9/00–	X	X	X					X		X	X	
37.	UNAMA (Afghanistan)	3/02	X	X	X	X	X	X	X	X	X	X	X	
38.	UNMISET (East Timor)	5/02–	X	X	X	X	X	X	X	X	X	X	X	X

Appendix 9.2 United Nations peace-building operations evaluation

	Date	Positive peace	Negative peace	Recidivism	Comments
Angola	5/91–2/99		X	X	Return to civil war in 1998–99; peace process back in place in 2002
Western Sahara	4/91–			X	Conflict unresolved
El Salvador	7/91–4/95	X			Progress in consolidation of democracy; economic and social stability
Cambodia	10/91–9/93		X		Near civil war in 1997; political repression and small-scale political violence
Croatia	3/95–1/96	X	X		Consolidation of democracy and economic and social stability
Macedonia	3/95–2/99		X	X	Violence between government and Albanian rebels in 2002
Bosnia-Herzegovina	12/95–12/02				NATO-led security force remains in place; improvement in social and economic stability; national reconciliation remains elusive
Kosovo	6/99–		X		Sporadic violence; little progress on self-governance, ethnic tolerance; NATO-led security force remains in place
Somalia	4/92–3/95			X	Continuation of clan conflicts and political divisions
Mozambique	12/92–12/94	X			Consolidation of economic and social stability and democratic governance
Rwanda	6/93–3/96		X	X	Embroiled in conflicts of Great Lakes region; little progress on national reconciliation
Georgia	8/93–		X		Little progress on settlement of conflict with Abkhazia; sporadic violence
Liberia	9/93–9/97			X	Continued violence, human rights abuses
Haiti	9/93–3/00		X		Continued political instability; little progress on economic development and alleviation of poverty
Tajikistan	12/94–5/00		X		Social and political instability; elections planned for 2005
Guatemala	1/97–5/97		X		Increases in public insecurity and human rights abuses
Central African Republic	3/98–2/00		X		Sporadic violence; political, social, and economic instability
Sierra Leone	7/98–		X	X	Continued violence, social instability
Guinea-Bissau	3/99–		X		Continued political, economic, and social instability
East Timor	10/99–		X		Elections held and new government installed; social instability; Australian-led security force remains in place
Democratic Republic of the Congo	2/00–			X	Escalation in violence in 2003
Afghanistan	3/02–		X		New government has little control over the country; sporadic violence; international security force remains in place

NOTES

1. United Nations. *Report of the Panel on United Nations Peace Operations.* A/55/305-S/2000/809 (August 21, 2000): 2.

2. John Gerard Ruggie, "The UN: Wandering in the Void," *Foreign Affairs* 72 (November/December 1993): 26–31. See also Giandomenico Picco, "The UN and the Use of Force: Leave the Secretary General out of It," *Foreign Affairs* 73 (September/October 1994): 14; and Saadia Touval, "Why the UN Fails," *Foreign Affairs* 73 (September /October 1994): 45. For a recent assessment see Dennis C. Jett, *Why Peacekeeping Fails* (New York: St. Martin's Press, 2000).

3. Johan Galtung, "Three Approaches to Peace: Peacekeeping, Peacemaking, and Peacebuilding," in *Peace, War, and Defence*—Essays *in Peace Research Vol. 2* (Copenhagen: Christian Ejlers, 1975): 282–304.

4. Boutros Boutros-Ghali, *An Agenda for Peace*, 32.

5. Boutros Boutros-Ghali, "Supplement to An Agenda for Peace" *An Agenda for Peace,* 2nd Ed. (New York, United Nations, 1995). A/50/60-S/1995/1.

6. *Report of the Panel on United Nations Peace Operations,* A/55/305 S/2000/809, 8.

7. S/PRST/2001/5 (February 20, 2001)

8. Roland Paris, "Peacebuilding and the Limits of Liberal Internationalism," *International Security* 22(2) (Fall 1997): 56.

9. *Report of the Panel on United Nations Peace Operations,* A/55/305-S/2000/809 (August 21, 2000): 8.

10. Paris, "Peacebuilding and the Limits of Liberal Internationalism," 74.

11. See Louise Olson, "Mainstreaming Gender in Multidimensional Peace-keeping: A Field Perspective," *International Peacekeeping* 7(3) (Autumn 2000): 1–16; and Richard Strickland and Nata Duvvury, *Gender Equity and Peacebuilding: From Rhetoric to Reality: Finding the Way* (Washington, D.C.: International Center for Research on Women, 2003).

12. See Alejandro Bandaña, "What Kind of Peace is Being Built? Critical Assessments from the South," in *What Kind of Peace is Being Built? Reflections on the State of Peacebuilding Ten Years after The Agenda For Peace* Working Paper No. 7, The Peacebuilding and Reconstruction Program Initiative (Ottawa: International Development Research Center, 2003): 5.

13. Stephen John Steadman, "Spoiler Problems in Peace Processes," *International Security* 22(2) (Fall 1997): 5–53.

14. *Report of the Panel on United Nations Peace Operations,* A/55/305-S/2000/809 (August 21, 2000): 14.

15. Jarat Chopra, "Introducing Peace Maintenance," in *The Politics of Peace Maintenance,* Ed. Jarat Chopra (Boulder, Col: Lynne Rienner 1998), 14.

16. See Elizabeth M. Cousens and Charles K. Cater, *Toward Peace in Bosnia: Implementing the Dayton Accords* International Peace Academy Occasional Paper Series (Boulder: Lynne Rienner, 2001), 133.

17. Report of the Joint Review Mission on the United Nations Post-Conflict Peace-Building Support Offices, DPA/UNDP (20 July 2001): 21.
18. Chester A. Crocker, "The Varieties of Intervention: Conditions for Success," in *Managing Global Chaos: Sources of and Responses to International Conflict* eds. Chester A. Crocker and Fen Osler Hampson with Pamela Aall (Washington D.C.: United States Institute of Peace Press, 1996), 297–319.
19. Stephen John Stedman, Donald Rothchild, and Elizabeth Cousens, eds., *Ending Civil Wars: The Success and Failure of Negotiated Settlements in Civil War* (Landham, MD.: Lynne Rienner publishers, 2002).
20. Paris, "Peacebuilding and the Limits of Liberal Internationalism", 54–89.
21. Michael Doyle and Nicholas Sambanis, "International Peacebuilding: A Theoretical and Quantitative Analysis," *American Political Science Review* 94 (2000): 779.
22. Fen Osler Hampson, *Nurturing Peace: Why Peace Settlements Succeed or Fail* (Washington: United States Institute of Peace, 1996).
23. The United Nations System in the New Millennium: Fostering Substantive and Operational Linkages in the Implementation of Peace, S/2001/1054 (November 7, 2001): 3.
24. Excludes UN peace-building offices mounted under authority of the Secretary-General.

Chapter 10

Refugee Protection and State Security: Towards a Greater Convergence

Gil Loescher

During recent years, refugees and asylum seekers have come to be viewed as a threat to the internal order of states and to regional, and in some cases to global, security. This new emphasis on the security dimension of refugee movements has not taken place in a vacuum but has been reflected in recent policy and academic literature on refugee issues and has been a highly visible trend in debates within both the UN Security Council and the Office of the United Nations High Commissioner for Refugees (UNHCR).[1] Despite greater recognition of the links between security and forced displacement, intervention to stem refugee flows remains highly controversial. The fact remains, however, that the regionalization of conflict and the domestic instability caused by mass forced displacement or by protracted refugee situations, if left unaddressed, are likely to have serious consequences for regional and global security. Thus, the claims of states for greater security and the claims of refugees for greater protection must be brought into better harmony if the UN and the international community are to deal with this issue more effectively in the future.

Refugee Issues and the United Nations

For the past half century, the Office of the UNHCR has been central to international debates about human rights and international responsibility, conflict resolution, preventive diplomacy, and the delivery of humanitarian assistance.[2] Among UN agencies, the Office of the UNHCR is unique. It embodies both a powerful official in the High Commissioner and a bureaucracy with over 5,000 staff worldwide. The High Commissioner has little or no political authority but is vested with considerable moral authority and legitimacy dating back not just to the office's founding in 1951 but to 1921 when Fridtjof Nansen was appointed as the first high commissioner for refugees by the League of Nations.

From its creation the UNHCR has had a conflictive relationship with states, especially with countries of refugee origin. It was created by UN member states to protect a special category of forced migrants, namely refugees. As defined in the 1951 UN Refugee Convention, refugees are people who have a well-founded fear of persecution and cannot return to their home countries for fear of placing their lives in jeopardy. States also created the office to help them resolve problems related to refugees who were perceived to create domestic instability, to generate interstate tensions, and to threaten international security. States did not establish the UNHCR because of purely altruistic motives but also because of a desire to promote regional and international stability and to serve the interests of governments. Thus, the UNHCR often walks a tightrope, maintaining a perilous balance between the protection of refugees and the sovereign prerogatives and interests of states.

In the international political system today, states remain the predominant actors. But this does not mean that international organizations like the UNHCR are completely without power or influence. Successive high commissioners quickly realized that in order to have any impact on the world political arena, they had to use the power of their expertise, ideas, and legitimacy to alter the information and value contexts in which states made policy. The UNHCR promotes the implementation of refugee norms and monitors compliance with international standards. The office also tries to influence states by introducing principled ideas, norms, and discourses into policy debates by pressing for burden sharing and collective state action and by serving as a source of legitimacy and information. At the same time, it seeks to influence domestic political issues, especially those affecting access and asylum implementation.

Throughout the past 50 years, the majority of UNHCR tactics have mainly involved persuasion and socialization in order to hold states accountable to their previously stated policies or principles. High commissioners sought to maximize their influence or leverage to affect the behavior of states towards refugees, and different high commissioners have used different strategies with varying degrees of success to accomplish these ends. In recent years they have been assisted in this activity by an ever-expanding and influential network of transnational social movements or nongovernmental organizations (NGOs). In addition to exercising moral leverage to gain influence with states, the UNHCR has repeatedly tried to link the refugee issue to states' material interests. This strategy has been particularly effective in recent years as the refugee issue became closely identified with international and regional security issues.

REFUGEES AND INTERNATIONAL SECURITY

Refugees have always had security implications for states and have influenced foreign policy and international relations. During the Cold War, refugee concerns were incorporated into the foreign policies of the United States and Western states, and the concerns of countries of first asylum were often addressed through generous burden sharing and resettlement schemes. At the same time, "refugee warriors" were armed and supported in regions of intense superpower competition to further superpower interests,[3] both during anticolonial and anti-apartheid struggles and during the regional conflicts in Southeast Asia, South Asia, the Horn of Africa, Southern Africa and Central America during the 1970s and 1980s. Since the end of the Cold War, however, refugee and migration issues have gained new salience. The question of migration as a security concern was one of a series of new security issues to arise in the early 1990s.

Broadly speaking, there exist two major types of refugee problems today. The first concerns the protection and security aspects of chronic and protracted refugee situations in the developing countries. The second involves asylum and migration flows to the developed world and the policies of deterrence and exclusion pursued by most states against these newcomers.

In recent years, states have perceived refugee movements as posing both direct and indirect security threats. The direct or external threat, posed by the spillover of conflict and armed exiles, is by far the strongest link between forced migration and state security. In the post–Cold War period, traditional notions of security and sovereignty have been challenged by the spillover of conflict and refugees into neighboring countries in Africa, the Balkans, the Middle East and South Asia. But indirect or domestic threats against a state's stability or political and cultural cohesion can also impose significant burdens on receiving states in all parts of the world. The presence of refugees can exacerbate already existing tensions and heighten intercommunal conflict, particularly when a state already has ethnic rifts of its own, a vulnerable economic or social infrastructure, or hostile neighbors. Migrants and refugees can also be perceived as a threat to the survival of a host community and undermine major societal values by altering the ethnic, cultural, religious, and linguistic composition of the host populations in both developed and less developed countries.

RECENT RESEARCH ON REFUGEES AND SECURITY

The academic research on security and refugee movements has reflected these trends in world politics. Beginning in the early 1990s, researchers raised the issue of forced migration as both a potential cause and consequence of insecurity and emphasised the "high politics" dimensions of the issue.[4] Researchers also argued that: (1) it was essential to recognize that refugee problems are not just a consequence of conflict but can also be a source of instability and insecurity; (2) mass migrations create domestic instability, generate interstate tension, and threaten regional and sometimes international security; and (3) that to reach solutions for refugees it was essential to recognize that refugee problems required not only humanitarian but also political solutions.[5]

In addition to refugees as a cause of interstate tensions, researchers portrayed forced migration as part of domestic and societal security, particularly the ways in which migration affected the issues of national and cultural identity in Western societies.[6] Refugees and asylum seekers came to be viewed as culturally and economically threatening and linked to transnational criminal and terrorist networks. Events since September 11, 2001, particularly the new risks associated with terrorist attacks based in countries of asylum, smuggling of arms, and money laundering, have made this threat even more real for states.

However, the realities of the refugee issue in the developing world, especially in Africa, were perceived to be quantitatively and qualitatively different than those in the West. A primary security objective of most developing states is the reduction of the deep sense of insecurity and vulnerability from which their regimes suffer, domestically as well as internationally. Consequently, identity threats posed by refugee influxes are more acute in weak states with a fragile ethnic balance than in politically integrated and stable states. According to some researchers,[7] a comprehensive characterization of security in the Third World must be rooted in an understanding of the complex process of state building, state legitimacy, and competition over scarce resources. By focusing on the vulnerabilities of many developing countries, it is possible to explain how the presence of refugees may result in security concerns for the state by affecting the survivability of state boundaries, state institutions, or governing elites and by weakening the capacity of states and regimes to act effectively in the realm of both domestic and international politics.

REFUGEES AS A SECURITY ISSUE AT THE UN

The importance of refugee movements for state security has also been evident in political developments at the United Nations and other security forms in recent years. The refugee issue has been accorded a much higher place on the international security agenda and has created new opportunities for the UN Security Council to respond to this problem, including the imposition of sanctions and military intervention against refugee-producing states.

The Security Council has dealt with refugee issues more often since 1991 than in any other period. In northern Iraq, Somalia, former Yugoslavia, and Haiti, international interventions in the domestic affairs of states were authorized in response to refugee flows. Following the end of the 1991 Gulf War, Iraqi suppression of a widespread revolt in northern Kurdish areas created widespread fears among the Kurds, resulting in the mass flight of some two million refugees to the Turkish border and into Iran. Civil war and famine in Somalia in 1992 displaced hundreds of thousands of civilians and caused large-scale starvation and a breakdown of civil order. The breakup of the former Yugoslavia in the early 1990s resulted in bitter civil wars among competing ethnic populations and widespread ethnic cleansing and displacement. Human rights abuses and repressive military rule drove large numbers of Haitians to flee the country by boat throughout the 1990s, causing a serious policy problem for the United States. In most of these and other cases, the UN, or regional or national forces acting with UN authorization, directly intervened in intrastate conflicts in an attempt to tackle these crises which led to mass displacement.

Moreover, forced displacements were also at the center of crises in the African Great Lakes region, Liberia, Sierra Leone, Albania, Kosovo, East Timor, and Afghanistan. In Kosovo, over 850,000 people were driven out of the country in 1999 in a massive and brutal ethnic cleansing. Later in the same year in Indonesia, gangs of armed thugs, with the active support of the military and the police, waged a campaign of terror against the East Timorese people and against UN staff who were stationed there to monitor the referendum that would confirm East Timor's independence.

As a consequence of these events during the past decade and a half, there has been increasing recognition that massive refugee flows can constitute a threat to international peace and security, and that they therefore invoke the enforcement powers of the United Nations. As a threat to peace and security, the imposition of refugees on other states falls under Chapter VII of the UN Charter and therefore legitimizes enforcement action not subject to the limits of purely humanitarian action. This link has been recognized for at least the past 17 years. As early as 1986, the report of a group of governmental experts on international cooperation to avert new flows of refugees recognized the "great political, economic, and social burdens [of massive flows of refugees] upon the international community as a whole, with dire effects on developing countries, particularly those with limited resources of their own."[8] Accordingly, it recommended intervention by the international community through the good offices of the Secretary-General, refugee prevention actions by appropriate UN bodies (including the Security Council), and better use of aid programs to prevent massive displacements. The report was subsequently endorsed by the UN General Assembly, which explicitly defined such flows as a threat to peace and security, thus opening the door to action by the Security Council under Chapter VII several years later. It should be noted that Article 2(7) of the UN Charter, calling on the UN not to intervene in states' domestic jurisdiction, specifically exempts enforcement actions taken under Chapter VII. In short, a country which forces its people to flee or takes actions which compel them to leave in a manner that threatens regional peace and security has, in effect, internationalized its internal affairs and provides a cogent justification for policymakers elsewhere to act directly upon the source of the threat.

Contemporary analysts of refugee issues have supported these interventionist actions: "When there is aggression by a state against its own minority such that the domestic issue becomes an international one and is perceived to threaten peace and security because the minority begin a mass flight, then defensive military intervention is justified."[9] Others point out that if refugee flows constitute an "internationally wrongful act" or "international crime" under the principles of state responsibility, this is also a violation of the Charter and therefore responses to it are not intervention in a state's domestic affairs.[10]

These arguments have been accompanied by changing conceptions of "threats" and "security" in interstate relations. Certain internal actions and policies—especially those triggering mass expulsions or refugee movements—have been increasingly regarded as threats by others, particularly by their neighbors. From this perspective, grievous human rights abuses are not an internal matter when neighboring states must bear the cost of having refugees forced on them. In recent years the Security Council itself has taken an increasingly inclusive view of "threats to peace" where actual hostilities remained limited largely within the territory of a single state.[11] The UN Security Council's Summit Declaration of 1992 included "non-military sources of instability in the economic, social, humanitarian and ecological fields" as threats to international peace and security, while specifying "election monitoring, human rights verification, and the repatriation of refugees" as "integral parts of the Security Council's efforts to maintain international peace and security."[12]

This new thinking is linked to changing ideas of national sovereignty.[13] While sovereignty is still regarded as a cornerstone of the international political and legal system, domestic matters previously shielded from outside interference have become open to comment and action. Since the most elementary justification for the modern state is its ability to provide reasonable security for its citizens, states that force these same citizens to flee call into question the very basis of their sovereignty. There is notably greater revulsion on the part of the international community toward using "sovereignty" to shield gross patterns of persecution and notably less hesitation in employing preemptive, as opposed to reactive, approaches to such problems.[14] Finally, there is the question of whether "sovereignty" is a consideration at all in the increasingly frequent case of "failed states" or "crises of authority" when there is no generally recognized government exercising effective authority over a state's territory.

THE LIMITATIONS ON UN-SANCTIONED INTERVENTIONS

Despite growing acceptance of the links between refugee movements, human security, and intervention, the attachment to the principle of state sovereignty remains strong among many prominent states. There exists significant objection to the right to intervene and to the use of force to resolve human security problems, like refugee crises. Moreover, the major powers, including the United States, have been highly selective about whether and to what extent they should get involved in security crises and humanitarian emergencies. State perceptions of the probability for success and considerations about costs remain significant barriers to frequent use of intervention. Finally, the voting procedures, especially the veto in the UN Security Council, represent a strong restraint against a dramatic increase in intervention. Consequently, it seems likely that intervention on human rights grounds, even when there is a clear link to security, will continue to be a highly contested issue among states. At a minimum, it seems intervention will only be considered legitimate when it operates with the authorization of the Security Council.

The terror attacks in the United States and the U.S.-led attacks against Afghanistan laid the groundwork for a series of interventions in the so-called global war against terror. The overthrow of the Taliban regime in Afghanistan was the first stage in a worldwide campaign against countries that allegedly harbored terrorist networks, including Iraq, Syria, Iran, Somalia, Yemen, Sudan, North Korea, the Philippines, and Indonesia. While the United States was able to hold together a shaky but workable international coalition in its war against Afghanistan in 2002, the U.S.-British intervention was not without controversy. A significant proportion of the world's population, particularly the Islamic world, considered the military intervention illegitimate. The extension of the armed war against terrorism linked to weapons of mass destruction in Iraq in early 2003 even more severely tested the U.S.–British coalition, not only in the Middle East and other Islamic countries but also in Russia and, most significantly, among traditional allies in Western Europe.

THE UNHCR AND THE EMERGING SECURITY DISCOURSE

At the same time that refugees came to be viewed as possibly posing threats to international security, thus providing a basis for action under Chapter VII of the UN Charter, refugees were perceived increasingly as burdens within states. In the face of growing numbers of illegal migrants and the abuse of asylum systems, Western governments became increasingly reluctant to grant asylum and enacted severe new entry controls. The closure of borders to prevent unwanted refugee and migrant influxes became much more widespread than it had been during the Cold War. In the West, in place of asylum, various forms of "temporary protection" were utilized to deal with those fleeing war and "ethnic cleansing." For developing countries, the growing numbers of displaced people entering already precarious or failing economies presented problems that threatened domestic stability and governmental authority. Diminishing donor government support for long-term refugee assistance, coupled with declining levels of development assistance and the imposition of structural adjustment programs on many poorer and less stable states, reinforced and contributed to the growing hostility toward refugees in the developing world.

In response to these global developments, most governments not only became more restrictionist in their refugee policies but also pushed for a comprehensive international policy that sought to modify the causes of refugee flows through conflict resolution, peacemaking, and peace-keeping. These policies focused on unstable, refugee-producing regions to contain refugee flows or to promote their reversal through repatriation. This was to be achieved through a series of international humanitarian operations in the 1990s that were launched by the UN Security Council and the UNHCR. During this period governments felt compelled to respond to refugee disasters, especially those covered by the media, and therefore repeatedly tasked the UNHCR to provide emergency relief aid with a view towards alleviating, preventing, or containing refugee crises within their own country or region of origin. For the world's most powerful states, the provision of humanitarian assistance was financially and politically a relatively low-risk option because it satisfied the demands of the media and public opinion for some kind of action to alleviate human suffering. But it was also used repeatedly by governments as an excuse for refusing to take more decisive forms of political and military intervention to deal with the underlying political causes of these population movements.

For the UNHCR, these shifts in attitudes about intervention made it see its own work more in terms of contributing to regional and international peace and security. The agency became more frequently involved in internal conflicts and in sharing responsibility with UN-mandated military forces for the assistance of displaced people. In an effort to take advantage of the political opportunities that the post–Cold War environment presented, the UNHCR also made a concerted effort to frame its policies in terms of interests of the major powers in resolving conflicts and refugee problems. It also demonstrated a greater interest in preventing refugee flows and in finding solutions to the political problems that created mass flight. By emphasizing the responsibilities of refugee-sending states and by labeling the mass exodus of refugees as a threat to international peace and security, UNHCR sought to legitimize its own actions to facilitate repatriations as well as UN interventions into regions of refugee origin to alleviate or even solve the causes of flight. The high priority given to humanitarian operations and the increasing recognition of a link between refugees and international security meant that the UNHCR played an increasingly important role in placing refugees on the international political agenda. Starting in 1992, the high commissioner began to report regularly to the Security Council and to regional organizations such as the Organization for Security and Cooperation in Europe (OSCE) on the potentially destabilizing effects of refugee and displacement crises.

The emergence of a new international security environment and a more assertive UN Security Council dramatically changed the way in which

UNHCR operated. During the Cold War, in-country assistance and protection of internally displaced people and victims of war was perceived to violate state sovereignty and therefore was taboo for UN agencies. In the post–Cold War period, by contrast, the UN developed a series of experimental measures, including a number of humanitarian interventions, for responding to instances of forced displacement within internal conflicts. These initiatives included the offer of temporary protection rather than full refugee status, the establishment of safe havens, cross-border deliveries of assistance, and the use of military resources for the delivery of humanitarian assistance. For UNHCR, the major change in the handling of refugee issues included an increased focus on working in countries of origin—even in countries at war—to reduce the likelihood of massive refugee flows across borders. In addition, the UNHCR was also frequently asked to take part in comprehensive and integrated UN peace-keeping or peacemaking operations that involved political and military actors of the UN.

In response to these dramatic developments, the UNHCR expanded its services to a much wider range of people who were in need of assistance. For example, "war-affected populations"—people who had not been uprooted but needed humanitarian assistance and protection—comprised a substantial proportion of UNHCR's beneficiary population during the height of the 1990's Bosnian conflict. As a result, the numbers of displaced people and war-affected populations receiving UNHCR assistance increased dramatically. Worldwide the number of people receiving UNHCR assistance increased from 15 million in 1990 to a peak of 26 million in 1996. Of this total of UNHCR's beneficiaries, refugees constituted only about 50 percent. Consequently, UNHCR expanded from a refugee organization into the UN's foremost humanitarian agency, thereby gaining a higher profile in international politics and securing more generous funding for its operations.

DISILLUSIONMENT WITH THE NEW SECURITY INITIATIVES

By the mid-1990s, however, it became evident that these innovative methods of assistance and protection had not been derived from any clearly defined strategy but had been developed in an ad hoc fashion in response to immediate security crises. As seemingly intractable conflicts continued in the Balkans, Africa, and the former Soviet Union, it was apparent that states lacked the will to initiate effective enforcement for maintaining peace and security, for empowering human rights mechanisms, or for promoting sustainable development in crisis regions. The major powers had only minimal interest in most countries with internal conflicts and humanitarian crises, and international responses to refugee crises remained more often than not reactive, self-interested, and based on ad hoc initiatives. There was no guarantee that states would intervene in situations where they were desperately needed, as in Rwanda in 1994. Bruised by their failure to restore stability in Somalia, the world's major governments and the UN chose to do nothing in the face of wanton mass killings in Rwanda. Similar concerns prevented Western governments from committing sufficient ground forces to Bosnia to defend the so-called "safe areas," including Srebrenica.

Most alarmingly, the new ad hoc initiatives also seemed to exacerbate and prolong the suffering in many cases of displaced people caught up in brutal conflicts. The UNHCR's high-profile relief efforts in Northern Iraq, Bosnia, and Rwanda underlined dramatically the inadequacy of providing protection in humanitarian relief programs in the midst of on-going civil conflicts and regional security crises. In particular, the failure to halt the genocide in Rwanda in 1994, the failure to halt the militarization of refugee camps in Zaire in 1994–96, the failure to prevent the forced repatriation of Rwandan refugees in 1996, and the failure to protect and assist the Rwandan refugees driven into eastern Zaire from late 1996 onward vividly demonstrated for UNHCR the lack of commitment on the part of states to address the underlying causes of security crises and conflicts in order to find solutions to refugee problems. The international community was all too often content to encourage UNHCR and other humanitarian organizations to deal with the humanitarian consequences of conflicts rather than to actively engage in seeking political and security solutions in intrastate wars. It became clear to UNHCR that if refugee problems were to be resolved, the international community would have to become active well beyond the mandate of UNHCR.

By the mid-1990s, the major powers, particularly the United States, perceived that the interventions of the early 1990s had overextended the UN and that in the future interventions should be much more limited and essentially restricted to the most strategically important areas of the world. As Kofi Annan acknowledged in his annual report to the UN General Assembly in 1999: "[T]he failure to intervene was driven more by the reluctance of Member States to pay the human and other costs of intervention, and by doubts that the use of force would be successful, than by concerns about sovereignty."[15] The use of armed force to stem refugee movements remains highly controversial within the international community as seen in the chapters by Thakur and Welsh.[16] The NATO intervention in Kosovo in 1999 and the debates over Iraq in 2003 demonstrate that there exist significant objection, particularly among the developing states, to the right to intervene concept and to the use of force to resolve security threats, much less refugee crises.

"HUMAN SECURITY" AND UNHCR

Disillusionment with its own shortcomings and with the failure of states to take action in the Great Lakes and other refugee-prone regions gave rise to efforts on the part of UNHCR to tone down the political elements of its security discourse, to redefine security by giving it a more humanitarian emphasis, and to develop the concept of human security as an operational tool for policy formulation and implementation.[17] Building on the notion of "human security" first introduced in the UNDP's 1994 Human Development Report[18] and later integrated into the foreign policy agendas of states such as Canada, Sweden, and Norway, UNHCR began to use the concept from the mid-1990s on as a means to establish harmony among the security concerns of states, the protection needs of forcibly displaced persons, and the security needs of the staff of international humanitarian agencies.

Throughout her term as high commissioner, Sadako Ogata stressed that her most important challenge was how to strike a balance between the principles of refugee protection and the legitimate concerns of states.[19] However, the disastrous protection crises of the Great Lakes and other operations demonstrated for UNHCR that this balance could not be achieved solely through appealing to the security interests of states. UNHCR had overestimated the extent to which the international community was willing and able to intervene in sovereign states to aid refugees and displaced people. It also became clear that the security interests of states were narrower and more self-interested than UNHCR anticipated and were not always compatible with the protection needs of refugees. Consequently, UNHCR endeavoured through advocating "human security" to show how the real security of states and the international community could only be achieved by providing security for "people."[20] In other words, UNHCR's use of human security was part of the agency's attempt to shape the interests of states in directions more conducive to refugee protection and assistance as well as to mitigate the political and financial constraints imposed upon it by its environment.

However, the concept of "human security" had its own limitations. While human security emphasized the links among human rights, physical security of individuals, and the security of states, it was so all-encompassing a concept that it did not provide UNHCR with a very useful tool with which to understand and explain the nature of refugee problems.[21] The concept also did not adequately address the disjuncture between UNHCR's emphasis on human rights and the security concerns of states affected by disruptive refugee movements. In particular, human security underplayed or ignored the security concerns of states, especially the long-term consequences of hosting large numbers of refugees. It also focused on forced migration as a consequence of conflict but ignored the fact that refugees can frequently be the cause of conflict. Consequently, human security as defined by UNHCR had a questionable utility as a framework for understanding the relationship between state security concerns and refugee protection.

THE "LADDER OF OPTIONS" AND DEMILITARIZING REFUGEE CAMPS

After the Great Lakes disaster, the international community began to debate a more structured response to address the security threats of hosting refugees, particularly the threat posed by the movement of large numbers of

refugees co-mingled with combatants in refugee camps.[22] In April 2000 the
UN Security Council (Security Council resolution 1296) requested the
Secretary-General to bring to its attention incidents involving the militarization of refugee camps and to consider taking "appropriate steps to create
a secure environment for civilians endangered by conflicts." A year later UN
Secretary-General Kofi Annan recognized the need for a military force to
keep armed combatants out of refugee settlements and recommended that
the Security Council deploy "international military observers to monitor the
situation in camps for internally displaced persons and refugees when the
presence of arms, combatants and armed elements is suspected . . . [and]
consider the range of options . . . [including] compelling disarmament of the
combatants or armed elements."[23]

The UNHCR had been particularly shocked by the lack of international
assistance it received in Rwandan refugee camps in Zaire and Tanzania to
separate out the *interhamwe* and other *genocidaires* from the civilian refugee
communities. In the Great Lakes, UNHCR protection officers were totally
ineffective in preventing the militarization of the Rwandan refugee camps.
They had neither the mandate nor the training and resources to carry out
demilitarization, and their calls for international assistance went unheeded.

To deal with such situations in the future, the UNHCR proposed a
"ladder of options," ranging from contingency planning and preventive
measures, through monitoring and policing, to forceful intervention under
Chapter VII of the UN Charter as the foundation for a new UN policy
response to the problems of insecurity in refugee camps.[24] Subsequently, the
UNHCR established stand-by arrangements with a limited number of governments for the provision of police and public security experts who were
designated as Humanitarian Security Officers (HSO) to be deployed as part
of UNHCR's emergency response teams at the beginning of refugee crises
and would work with public security institutions of receiving countries.
UNHCR also enhanced its own emergency response mechanism by participating in numerous civil-military conferences, designing training programs
for HSOs, and establishing a focal point with the UN Security forces
(UNSECOORD). Finally, UNHCR entered into discussions with the UN
Department of Peacekeeping Operations (DPKO) regarding the possible
deployment of missions to situations in which refugee-populated areas have
become militarized or where they run the risk of falling under the control of
groups suspected of genocide or crimes against humanity.

One of UNHCR's first efforts to operationalize the ladder of options was
its attempt to implement a "security package" in western Tanzania and to
move Sierra Leonean refugee camps further from the border in Guinea to
protect refugees from attacks by Sierra Leonean rebels and from retaliations
from Guinean forces. While these actions helped create greater security
for some of the refugee communities in Tanzania and Guinea, they did not
succeed in separating armed elements and other exiles from the civilian
refugee populations in these countries.[25] A similar effort by UNHCR

and DPKO in the Democratic Republic of Congo in mid-2001 to separate armed refugees from their civilian counterparts met with greater success.[26]

From these experiences it is evident that the future success of the ladder of options depends on the practical partnerships and "security packages" that UNHCR is able to form with the DPKO and governments. While discussions between DPKO and UNHCR have set the groundwork for future cooperation between the two offices, serious differences of approach and political and resource constraints remain. On the one hand, UNHCR and other humanitarian aid organizations fear that too close an association with the military compromises their impartiality and neutrality, and on the other, governments are reluctant to authorize military forces for such functions. Protection for refugees in militarized situations also depends critically on the willingness and ability of host states and countries of refugee origin to observe international humanitarian norms regarding the treatment of refugees and noncombatants.

TOWARD A CONVERGENCE OF REFUGEE PROTECTION AND INTERNATIONAL SECURITY CONCERNS

An era of relative simplicity and generosity in refugee affairs has long since passed, and we are in the midst of a more complex and difficult period. The decline in generosity and openness towards the uprooted and persecuted has occurred because of a radically different international environment. The present reality is that the Cold War interest in taking refugees from the communist world has passed with the collapse of European communism and has now been replaced by a growing state interest in keeping refugees out or in sending them back home.

Unfortunately but almost predictably, the global fight against terrorism since September 2001 has further endangered the rights of refugees and migrants around the world. Most governments, including those in Europe and North America, have introduced stringent new antiterrorist laws or have given new life to old laws once used to suppress peaceful dissent and other civil and political liberties. Asylum seekers and refugees in particular have been associated with the terrorist threat. In order to address their vulnerabilities to terrorism, governments have further tightened their immigration systems and visa regimes. Consequently, the prospects for refugee protection have declined precipitously since September 2001. Not only are refugees likely to become pawns in a geopolitical struggle in which they are redefined as agents of insecurity and terrorism, but new interventions in the Middle East or in other regions are likely to trigger yet new mass refugee flows.

Despite the dangers inherent in the new geopolitics of antiterrorism, there may be greater compatibility between protecting refugees and enforcing human rights, protecting state security interests, and promoting international order than is the current perception of most governments today. Refugee movements demonstrate the close relationship between gross human rights violations within states and threats to regional security and stability.

Ignoring this linkage in an age of globalization will simply lead to greater isolation and deprivation which can breed anger, frustration, and terrorism, among other things, and pose yet new threats to regional and international security and order. Political realism demands that higher priority be given to combating human rights violations because of their propensity to promote international instability and, hence, refugee movements. This will require incorporating, in current reevaluations of state security doctrine, greater international attention to human rights violations. It is also the case that if states remain indifferent to the plight of the world's refugees, the social and political fiber of their own societies will suffer. The way states deal with refugees speaks volumes about their human rights standards and their tolerance for ethnic and racial minorities.

Refugees are both a cause and consequence of regional and global instability and conflict, and they directly engage the interests of states all over the world. The flight of refugees is the most clear-cut expression of the spill-over effects of domestic instability and violence onto other states and into neighboring regions. More active intervention by the international community is in the long-term interest of all governments; stability and growth depend generally on controlling disruptive forced migrations. Moreover, the global refugee problem is not going to disappear soon; in fact, as we have seen in the dramatic global developments since September 11, 2001, it is assuming new dimensions that require new and different responses.

For the past half century, the UNHCR has been at the heart of many of the gravest breakdowns of social and political order and tragic human loss. The UNHCR has set standards through the international, regional, and national legal instruments and acted as a transmitter and monitor of refugee norms. Even more importantly, if UNHCR did not exist, hundreds of thousands, if not millions, of refugees would be left unassisted and unprotected. The office has tried not only to advocate and instigate changes in the behavior of states but has also attempted to influence major developments in international relations. At times some states, especially powerful ones, have not been willing to be constrained by the UNHCR, but on many occasions states have been willing to work through the office because this legitimized the state's behavior both domestically and internationally. In the process, the UNHCR has steadily increased its role as a relevant participant in policy debates at the UN and elsewhere and has demonstrated that at times international organizations matter in international relations.

NOTES

1. In drafting this chapter the author drew upon discussions with many colleagues, particularly James Milner and Anne Hammerstad.
2. Gil Loescher, *The UNHCR and World Politics: A Perilous Path* (Oxford: Oxford University Press, 2001).

3. Aristide Zolberg, Astri Suhrke, and Sergio Aguayo, *Escape from Violence: Conflict and Refugees in the Developing World* (New York: Oxford University Press, 1989).

4. Myron Weiner, ed., *Refugees and International Security* (Boulder: Westview Press, 1993); and Gil Loescher, "Refugee Movements and International Security", *Adelphi Paper 268* (London: The International Institute for Strategic Studies, 1992).

5. Gil Loescher, *Beyond Charity: International Cooperation and the Global Refugee Crisis* (New York: Oxford University Press, 1993).

6. Ole Waever, et al., *Identity, Migration and the New Security Agenda in Europe* (London, Pinter, 1993); and Barry Buzan, *People, States and Fear* (Hemel Hempstead, Herfordshire: Harvester Wheatsheaf, 1991).

7. Mohammed Ayoob, *The Third World Security Predicament: State Making, Regional Conflict and the International System* (London: Lynne Reiner Publishers, 1995); and Edward Azar and Chung-in Moon, eds., *National Security in the Third World: The Management of Internal and External Threats* (Aldershot: Hants., Elgar, 1988).

8. United Nations A/41/324, (May 13, 1986); For analysis, see Luke Lee, "Toward a world without refugees: the United nations Group of Government Experts on International cooperation to Avert New Flows of Refugees," *British Yearbook of International Law* 57 (London: H. Frowde, 1986): 317–336.

9. Howard Adelman, "The Ethics of Humanitarian Intervention: The Case of Kurdish Refugees," *Public Affairs Quarterly* 6(1) (January 1992): 75. See also Alan Dowty and Gil Loescher, "Refugee Flows as Grounds for International Action," *International Security* 21(1) (Summer 1996): 43–71.

10. Lee, "Toward a World Without Refugees," 332.

11. Lori Fisler Damrosch, "Changing Conceptions of Intervention in International Law," in *Emerging Norms of Justified Intervention,* eds. Laura W. Reed and Carl Kaysen (Cambridge, Mass.: American Academy of Arts and Sciences, 1993): 100ff.

12. *UN Security Council Summit Declaration* (New York, United Nations, 1992).

13. International Commission on Intervention and State Sovereignty, *The Responsibility to Protect* (Ottawa: International Development Research Centre, 2001). For background, see: Christopher Greenwood, "Is there a right of humanitarian intervention?" *The World Today* 49(2) (February 1993): 34–40; Nigel Rodley, ed., *To Loose the Band of Wickness: International Intervention in the Defense of Human Rights* (London: Brasseys, 1992); Lori Fisler Damrosch, ed., *Enforcing Restraint: Collective Intervention in Internal Conflicts* (New York: Council on Foreign Relations Press, 1992).

14. UNHCR also made this argument in its Year 2000 Strategy Paper: "There is also a growing recognition that state sovereignty entails responsibilities, chief amongst which is the responsibility of the state to protect its citizens and that sovereignty can no longer be invoked against international scrutiny. In this respect, the trend has developed since 1991—with the adoption of Security Council resolution 688 on Iraq—of establishing a direct causal link

between the causes of mass human rights violations, consequent forced displacements and the threat to international or regional peace and security is a welcome development." UNHCR, *UNHCR Strategy Toward 2000*, (Geneva: UNHCR, 2000): para. 36.

15. Kofi Annan, *Preventing War and Disaster: a Growing Global Challenge* (New York: UN, 1999): 21.

16. See: Nicholas J. Wheeler, *Saving Strangers: Humanitarian Intervention in International Society* (Oxford: Oxford University Press, 1999).

17. For a good discussion of UNHCR and human security see: Anne Hammerstad, "Whose Security?" *UNHCR, Refugee Protection and State Security after the Cold War* (Los Angeles: ISA Convention, 2000).

18. UNDP, *Human Development Report* (Oxford: Oxford University Press, 1994). See also Anne Hammerstad, *Refugee Protection and Evolution of a Security Discourse: The United Nations High Commissioner for Refugees in the 1990s* D.Phil Thesis (Oxford), 2003.

19. Sadako Ogata, *Humanitarian Action: Charity or Realpolitik?* (Oslo, October 21, 1997).

20. Human Security was the central theme of the United Nations Office of the High Commissioner for Refugees, *The State of the World's Refugees 1997* (Oxford: Oxford University Press, 1997) and several of the High Commissioner's speeches at the time. See, for example, Sadako Ogata, *Peace, Security and Humanitarian Action* (London, The International Institute for Strategic Studies, April 3, 1997) and *Human Security: A Refugee Perspective* (Bergen, Norway: May 19, 1999).

21. Hammerstad, "Whose Security?"

22. Hammerstad, "Whose Security?" and *Refugee Protection and the Evolution of a Security Discourse*.

23. UN Security Council, *Report of the Secretary-General to the Security Council on the Protection of Civilians in Armed Conflict* S/2001/331, (2001).

24. The "ladder of options" is described in the documents *The Security and the Civilian and Humanitarian Character of Refugee Camps and Settlements* EC/49/SC/INF.2 (January 14, 1999) and *The Security and the Civilian and Humanitarian Character of Refugee Camps and Settlements: Operationalizing the 'Ladder of Options'* EC/50/SC/INF.4 (June 27, 2000).

25. Jeff Crisp, *Lessons Learned from the Implementation of the Tanzania Security Package* EPAU/2001/05 (Geneva, UNHCR, May 2001).

26. Lisa Yu, "Separating Ex-Combatants and Refugees in Zongo, DRC: Peacekeepers and UNHCR's 'Ladder of Options,'" *New Issues in Refugee Research* Working Paper No. 60 (Geneva: UNHCR, August 2002).

CHAPTER 11

AUTHORIZING HUMANITARIAN INTERVENTION

Jennifer M. Welsh*

Among statesmen, the lovers of naked power are far less typical than those who aspire to clothe themselves in the mantle of legitimate authority; emperors may be nude, but they do not like to be so, to think of themselves so, or to be so regarded.

—Inis Claude, 1966

INTRODUCTION

This chapter focuses on the debate over who can authorize humanitarian intervention in contemporary international society. The first section examines the Security Council's role in authorizing the use of force and how in the post–Cold War period it has expanded its definition of threats to international peace and security to encompass humanitarian crises. In the next section, I analyze the legal and philosophical positions on "proper authority" and make two central claims: (1) that international law on the use of force suggests that interventions for humanitarian purposes currently require Security Council authorization; and (2) that the Council should be considered not as the "proper authority" for international society in matters of peace and security but rather as an entity whose pronouncements are "authoritative." In the process, I suggest how the authoritativeness of the Council has been weakened by questions about representation and decision making, as well as by problems of capacity and delegation. The third section focuses on the politics of authorization and identifies the actors in contemporary world politics who hold various positions on the value of and need for Council authorization. I conclude with an analysis of the implications of the debate on authorizing humanitarian intervention for our understanding of the role of the United Nations (UN) in global security and the state of global multilateralism, more generally.

As Inis Claude observed almost four decades ago, one of the major functions of the UN in international society is its role as a "collective legitimiser."[1] States (particularly democratic ones) not only take great pains to justify their foreign policies to their domestic population but also are conscious of the need for broader approval for their actions. British-led efforts in the early days of 2003 to obtain the so-called second resolution authorizing the use of force against the regime of Saddam Hussein are a powerful illustration of this trend.

While collective legitimization is not the sole preserve of the UN—other intergovernmental organizations can play this role—it has traditionally enjoyed pride of place in states' multilateral efforts to win approval. As Claude astutely noted, whether UN endorsement makes a material difference is often beside the point: "[T]he value of acts of legitimization by the United Nations has been established by the intense demand for them."[2] Whether this value is eroding is one of the key questions driving this chapter. What is clear, however, is that authorization remains one of the functions that the UN is attempting to hold onto in an era where its capacity to intervene decisively, or control events on the ground, is waning. Thus, debates about Security Council authorization for humanitarian intervention invoke the broader themes of this volume: whether the UN's value is primarily procedural—a forum for establishing and reinforcing norms—or whether it remains an important actor in its own right with the ability to address substantive issues that matter to members of international society.

AUTHORIZING THE USE OF FORCE IN INTERNATIONAL SOCIETY

The Cold War competition between the United States and the Soviet Union bore heavy responsibility for the failure of the Security Council to function as was envisaged by its creators. Before the Gulf War of 1990, the Council authorized enforcement only twice: in Korea in 1950 and to prevent the violation of sanctions in Southern Rhodesia in 1966. A new lease on life for the UN began in the late 1980s with increased UN involvement in solving conflicts in Angola, Namibia, Cambodia, and the Persian Gulf. In purely *quantitative* terms, the activity of the UN in matters of peace and security saw a remarkable increase. Whereas between 1948 and 1989 the Security Council adopted 646 resolutions (an average of 15 per year), between 1990 and 1999 it passed 638 resolutions (an average of 64 per year).[3] However, the bigger change was *qualitative*: the Security Council's ever-broadening interpretation of what constitutes threats to international peace and security. While the UN had been created to address territorial aggression by one state against another, contemporary threats to security emanate largely from *inside* states. Three main issues have seen increased consideration by the Security Council in the past two decades: civil war and intrastate conflict, the possession of weapons of mass destruction, and (the focus of this chapter) humanitarian crises.

While very few humanitarian interventions[4] occurred during the Cold War, the 1990s witnessed a series of military actions explicitly supported by humanitarian rationale.[5] However, the impetus for interventionism in the name of human rights has been tempered by the equally powerful norm of nonintervention, which remains an important organizing principle for international society. In many of the cases from the 1990s, this apparent tension between sovereignty and intervention was addressed in one of two ways: through a change in the notion of sovereignty from "sovereignty as authority" (control over territory) to "sovereignty as responsibility" (respect for a minimum standard of human rights), and through an expanded definition of what constitutes a "threat to international peace and security" under Chapter VII of the UN Charter. As a result of the first move, massive violations of human rights inside the domestic jurisdiction of a state have been transformed into a matter of international concern; as a result of the second, the UN can legitimately authorize international action to address security threats that emerge from humanitarian crises.

Alongside the widening definition of threats, however, have come nagging questions about the Security Council's authority, competency, and capacity to address them. The most prominent cases fuelling such questions include the UN's failure to mount a sufficient presence to deter genocide in Rwanda, its inability to prevent massacre of civilians in the "safe area" of Srebrenica, and the breakdown of diplomacy over the use of force against Iraq in 2003. Even in those situations where the Security Council has authorized interventions for humanitarian purposes, an uncomfortable truth has bubbled to the surface: the Council's role is limited to one of advisor. It is individual states, most notably the United States, that ultimately establish the parameters of the mission and control events on the ground.

These developments have led critics to investigate alternative mechanisms and institutions for engaging in humanitarian intervention. The main contenders, discussed below, include endorsement from the General Assembly, authorization from a regional security organization, or unilateral action by a state or coalition of states without institutional sanction. For others, the central role of the Security Council remains pivotal in cases involving the use of force. The International Commission on Intervention and State Sovereignty (ICISS) concluded: "There is no better or more appropriate body than the United Nations Security Council to authorize military intervention for human protection purposes. The task is not to define alternatives to the Security Council as a source of authority, but to make the Council work better than it has."[6] This ICISS conclusion is driven by a desire to maintain the Security Council's preeminent status within international society and to avoid any further erosion of the "social capital"[7] it draws upon to encourage the cooperation of UN member states.

This begs the question, however, as to why this social function is so important. I suggest three explanations why states and organizations seek Security Council authorization for humanitarian interventions. The first, functional argument claims that the Council, while imperfect, represents the best mechanism we have for avoiding the Hobbesian conundrum of international justice: that in a world without a Leviathan, each state defines for itself what is just and unjust. The second explanation is principled or ideational: States believe that a regulated and more predictable international system is preferable to one dominated by lawlessness, and multilateral forums such as the Security Council are perceived as key parts of the infrastructure of regulation. Third, state support for UN authorization could reflect material or power-based factors. Here, there are two possibilities: Western states, who are the most powerful, coerce other members of international society to support Security Council authorization; and/or actors who have traditionally had less weight in international society—or whose influence is declining—can have their power enhanced by working through the UN and thereby constrain the actions of more powerful states. In the following sections I evaluate these three positions and identify the different actors who hold them.

THE SOURCES OF SECURITY COUNCIL AUTHORITY

During NATO's war to prevent ethnic cleansing in Kosovo in 1999, many opponents of the bombing campaign insisted that only explicit resolutions by the Security Council constitute "proper authority" for the use of force in the international system and that such resolutions can only be justified by a clear threat to international peace and security.[8] Yet very little attention has been paid to justifying why the Council has been, and should be, the repository of this authority. Is the logic primarily utilitarian—that a mission under the blanket of UN authorization might be more efficient and effective? Or, is it more realist—that the interests and ideologies of the most powerful states (particularly the United States) are furthered by giving the Council this privileged status? Is it somehow a representative claim—that the Security Council is the embodiment of "world opinion"? Or, is the argument primarily legal—that international law on the use of force has developed around the Security Council as the key actor?

Legal Arguments: UN Charter and Practice

The debate on the legality of humanitarian intervention reached a climax over Kosovo when lawyers commenting on the case arrived at surprisingly different conclusions about the interpretation of treaties and the status of customary rules. The relevant treaty law seems clear.[9] The basic presumption of international law post-1945, according to Articles 2(4) and 2(7) of the UN Charter, is that the use of force is illegal. The qualifications to this rule are self-defense or collective security; in the latter case the Security Council may authorize the use of force if it does so explicitly through a resolution adopted under Chapter VII. Up until the 1990s, most international lawyers agreed that intervention for the purposes of humanitarianism or democracy building did not pass these two hurdles. This interpretation is strengthened by the UN Charter's context and purpose—an effort to delegitimize individual acts of war by vesting sole authority for the nondefensive use of force in the Security Council.

There are two main challenges to this legal opinion. First, a debate has emerged among international lawyers as to whether the general prohibition on the use of force enshrined in Article 2(4) should be "stretched" to accommodate other important principles of the UN such as the promotion and protection of human rights. "Restrictionist" lawyers[10] opposed to such expansion insist that Article 2(4) is a *jus cogens* rule in international society, and that it would be too massive a leap to argue that the use of force to defend human rights has acquired the same kind of status.

An alternative legal argument in favor of expanding the exceptions to Article 2(4) focuses on the accumulated state practice of intervention since the end of the Cold War. The underlying premise is that international law is not static and that the intensity and frequency of international behavior has increased the rate at which new custom is being generated. These "counter-restrictionist" lawyers[11] point to a series of cases from the 1990s as state practice supportive of a new customary rule, with statements by Western governments articulating humanitarian motives presented as evidence of an accompanying *opinio juris*. The problem with such an approach is that it privileges custom over treaty—a controversial move considering the precepts of the Vienna Convention.[12] In addition, as Ramesh Thakur suggests in his chapter for this volume, non-Western legal opinion opposes this interpretation of the customary law on intervention since it seems to suggest that certain types of practice "count" more than others—that is, the actions of Western states vs. the stated opposition from those such as China, Russia, and India.

The record of state practice produces a mixed conclusion. First, while there has been no explicit treaty or amendment to the UN Charter, the body of post-1990 practice demonstrates support—or at least toleration—for Security Council-authorized actions with a humanitarian objective. This is evident not only through the use of Security Council resolutions that authorize the "use of all means necessary" to secure humanitarian outcomes but also in the *ex post facto* UN endorsements given to interventions carried out by regional coalitions of states.[13] Nevertheless, these cases do not point to a clear conflict between sovereignty and intervention, as is commonly assumed, since most instances of Council authorized intervention for humanitarian purposes in the post–Cold War period have involved some degree of state consent (even if in some cases that consent is coerced). Finally, most examples of intervention in the post–Cold War period (Kosovo being the biggest exception) have involved Council resolutions that invoke Chapter VII—that is, a threat to international peace and security. One reading of this trend is that states are still uncomfortable asserting that a human rights violation by a government against its own people is, in itself, a sufficient justification for the use of force. The rationale is beefed up by the claim that international stability is being threatened—either through the flow of refugees or the spillover effects of civil war. Such claims have enabled traditionally noninterventionist states, such as China and Russia, to support UN action.

What about humanitarian interventions that lack explicit Security Council authorization? While the Charter sanctions unilateral action for the purposes of self-defense, the legality of other forms of military action currently hinge upon the presence of Council backing.[14] In addition, given that there is to date no provision for judicial review of Council decisions, there is no mechanism by which a dispute over Charter interpretation can be resolved. For those who have opposed the Council's tendency toward a broad interpretation of what constitutes threats to international peace and security, this conclusion is an uncomfortable one.[15]

Nevertheless, the legal authority of the Charter can be ambiguous in specific instances since there are uneasy tensions between some of its norms and principles (for example, to promote human rights and to respect domestic jurisdiction). Moreover, there has been substantial evolution and innovation in these norms through interpretation and practice. Most relevant is the evolution of international human rights norms. Indeed, on the issue of humanitarian intervention, two bodies of law must be weighed against each other: one relating to the use of force and the other to the protection of individual human rights.

In light of these ambiguities, are there any legal alternatives to Council authorization? One possibility is the General Assembly (GA). Articles 10 and 11 of the Charter, supported by the "Uniting for Peace" Resolution of 1950,[16] give the GA a general responsibility for matters of international peace and security. Should the Security Council be unable or unwilling to authorize action, the General Assembly can consider a case and make recommendations. The Assembly's decisions are not binding, however; they have the status of "recommendations" only. Furthermore, once the matter has been brought before the GA, Article 18(2) specifies that any resolution regarding maintenance of international peace and security have a two-thirds majority of UN members present and voting, making consensus very difficult to achieve. A second possibility is the endorsement of regional organizations, which are given security roles and responsibilities under Chapter VIII of the Charter.[17] Again, however, the lack of any *independent* legal authority for regional organizations should be highlighted. Article 53(1) claims that while the Council may utilize such organizations, "no enforcement action shall be taken under regional arrangements or by regional agencies without the authorization of the Security Council."

This analysis of international law on the use of force suggests that the Security Council remains the only body that can legally authorize intervention for human protection purposes, and that ad hoc coalitions of the willing, acting without UN endorsement, have dubious legal status. Nonetheless, the legal opinion on authorization is becoming increasingly unsatisfactory in the messy world of international politics, particularly in the wake of the crisis over Iraq. A number of factors have created a tension between the Security Council's *legal* authority, and its *legitimacy* in the eyes of international society: the slowness of Security Council decision making; the under-representation of key regions on the Council, the fact that Permanent Five members are shielded from intervention in their own states, and the political nature of P5 vetoes. Similarly, given questions about the UN's operational effectiveness, it is no longer enough to rely on conservative assertions about the tradition of Council authorization—that it is the best existing alternative. We must go back to first principles and ask where that authority comes from.

Philosophical Arguments: Authority and Legitimacy in International Society

Debates about Security Council authorization invite questions not just of law but of fundamental political theory. Allen Buchanan helps us understand the distinctions among three important concepts in this debate: political legitimacy, political authority, and authoritativeness. An entity has *political legitimacy*, according to Buchanan, "if and only if it is morally justified in wielding political power" (where wielding political power means exercising a monopoly, within a particular jurisdiction, in making and enforcing rules). The notion of a monopoly is critical here, for without it there could be rivals to that entity in making and applying rules. An entity has *political authority* if and only if, in addition to having political legitimacy, it "has the right to be obeyed by those who are within the scope of its rules." This definition suggests that the phrase "legitimate authority," which is so often used in discussions about the Security Council, is redundant. Authority implies legitimacy; without it, we simply have raw power. Finally, an entity is *authoritative* "if and only if the fact that it issues a rule can in itself constitute a compelling reason to comply with that rule."[18]

A number of implications flow from these distinctions. First, authoritativeness can operate outside the political realm (for example, when we take the advice of stock brokers as "authoritative") and does not necessarily imply an obligation to the entity to obey. Furthermore, political legitimacy does not necessarily entail authoritativeness. An entity could be morally justified in wielding political power but that is not to say that its utterances *in themselves* provide a good reason for compliance. Finally, political authority entails political legitimacy, but not vice versa. Whether an entity is legitimate depends only upon whether the agents attempting to wield power are morally justified. In other words, we can have good reasons to comply without any obligation to those who wield political power.

But where do those "good reasons" come from? How do we determine moral justification? This question is particularly pertinent in morally contested situations—for example, the debate in 2002–2003 as to whether the Saddam Hussein regime posed a serious threat to the United States, justifying an act of preemptive self defense. Legitimacy therefore encompasses another crucial element: validation of one's justification by others. In his comprehensive study, Thomas Franck defines legitimacy as "a property of a rule or rule-making institution which itself exerts a pull toward compliance on those addressed normatively because those addressed believe that the rule or institutions has come into being and operates in accordance with generally accepted principles of right process."[19] In short, legitimacy is something that others bestow on a state or institution's decisions and policies.

Applying this framework to Security Council authorization, a series of claims can be made. First, the Council is not a political authority in the sense described by Buchanan. As scholars like John Ruggie have shown, international regimes and institutions do not conform easily to the Weberian model of superordinates and subordinates.[20] While the Council issues binding resolutions, the practical challenge of generating consensus among the P5 frequently produces ambiguous language, which in turn leaves room for varying interpretations. Still, actors in the international system can agree on common norms and institutions without the presence of a single sovereign authority.

Instead of calling the Council the "proper authority," I would argue that it should be described as authoritative with respect to matters of peace and security. As we shall see, the presence or absence of Council resolutions is for many states the key issue in determining whether or not to participate in an intervention. Indeed, in the debate about military action against Iraq in the spring of 2003, many Western states—and their populations—based their support for war upon the condition of UN authorization.

This observation leads directly to my second claim: that states in today's international society have other compelling reasons to comply with the Council's resolutions—beyond the obligation to obey and beyond perceptions of its authoritativeness. These reasons may stem, as above, from power-political considerations. Other reasons, however, derive from legitimacy. Here, as Franck reminds us, there are two possibilities: process and purpose.

In the first case, states seek Security Council authorization and comply with its resolutions because they believe the process of multilateral decision making in the Council is just—that is, in conformity with principles of consent, participation, and collaboration—and yields solutions that can be described as being in the *collective* interest, as opposed to the interests of the most powerful. This procedural source of legitimacy for the Council has been damaged by a variety of factors, including domination by a few powerful states, political uses of the veto, and increased use of "informal consultation." Interestingly, some commentators suggested that even if a "second resolution" on Iraq had been approved by a majority of Council members in 2003, the horse-trading and political coercion necessary to achieve such a result would have damaged its legitimacy. As Ruggie argued, "the quality of a vote—including how it is achieved—also matters to the determination of legitimacy, not only the sheer numbers."[21]

A second source of legitimacy derives from the fundamental purpose of the Security Council (and UN Charter), namely, to maintain peace and security and "save succeeding generations from the scourge of war."[22] Here too, however, the Council's legitimacy has been weakened, especially with respect to new security challenges. While the Council has enjoyed some success in outlawing aggression between states, it has had much less impact in providing security for individuals inside states experiencing civil war or repression. During the debates over intervention in Iraq, critics of the UN took pains to underscore the fact that 12 years of sanctions and a series of UN resolutions had failed to end the atrocities of Saddam Hussein's regime.

The final claim is that other entities besides the UN can legitimately use force for humanitarian purposes, *as long as* their reasons for doing so are morally justifiable and validated by other members of international society. At the end of its report, ICISS warns that if the Security Council "fails to discharge its responsibility to protect in conscience-shocking situations crying out for action, concerned states may not rule out other means to meet the gravity and urgency of that situation—and that the stature and credibility of the United Nations may suffer thereby."[23]

The NATO intervention in Kosovo is the obvious candidate for applying this principle. While NATO was not considered the proper *legal* authority for engaging in humanitarian intervention, many concluded that its military campaign was legitimate.[24] This conclusion can be drawn not only on the basis of NATO's "just" cause—prevention of ethnic cleansing—but also on the fact that this cause was endorsed by the 19 members of the alliance and the majority of states in the Security Council. It is important to reiterate, however, that states or organizations acting outside the legal framework face a high bar in terms of moral argument. ICISS suggests a series of non-legal criteria that could be used to help us judge whether that bar has been met: credible evidence of the scale of the crisis, a genuine internal call for assistance, right conduct by the intervening states and organizations, and positive longer-term outcomes.

There are other compelling arguments against insisting on Security Council authorization as a necessary condition of legitimacy. First, designating the Council the forum for discussing and authorizing humanitarian intervention does not guarantee that there will be agreement over specific cases—perhaps far from it. Since the Kosovo bombing, a number of scholars and practitioners have attempted to devise criteria that could be used by the Security Council to assist its decision making in situations of humanitarian crises.[25] Many believe such a checklist would make the Council more effective and less likely to equivocate, as it did so tragically in the case of Rwanda. But as the restrictionist international lawyers would argue, any attempts to articulate legitimate instances of intervention could erode the progress made by the UN to outlaw the use of force in international society. Furthermore, the current hegemon, the United States, is strongly opposed to establishing criteria that might constrain its actions. Finally, the heart of the problem is how states and organizations operationalize criteria such as "large-scale" or "extreme" emergency. In 1999, Kosovo constituted "extreme" for some, though not for others (notably China, India, and Russia). Chechnya has not crossed the threshold for anyone, despite the fact that the level of abuse of civilians has been substantially higher than in Kosovo. In the end, checklists can only represent necessary, and not sufficient, conditions for a decision to intervene.[26]

Second, the Security Council may not be able to withstand the pressure being placed upon it. It is important to recall that the principle of non-intervention outlined in the UN Charter was not intended solely as a shield for repressive states. It also reflects a more general belief held by the drafters of the Charter that decentralized action by individual nation-states is a more effective strategy for creating order than supranationalism.[27] While the Security Council has been granted substantial powers to declare and direct, it has only rudimentary competence (legally and practically) to intervene in domestic crises. The failures after 1945 both to create the Military Staff Committee and to conclude the Article 43 agreements with states to make forces available to the UN leave the Council with very little power over the organization or conduct of the military operation. Indeed, some commentators argue that its role has been reduced from one of authorization to delegation.[28]

Finally, policymakers must confront the possibility that unilateral action can be more timely and effective, especially if undertaken by a regional power with the right mix of knowledge and capability. In the end, performance—that is, the achievement of positive humanitarian outcomes—is also a critical component of legitimacy. Three interventions from the Cold War period—Tanzania in Uganda, India in East Pakistan, and Vietnam in Cambodia—lend some support to this view. Even where Security Council authorization has been given, action has often been led by a neighboring state with a strong national as well as humanitarian interest, as in the case of Australia in East Timor. This reality, coupled with the UN's well-documented "selectivity" on the question of humanitarian intervention, suggests that the Council is used as collective legitimizer only when a state or group of states is willing to invest the political capital to bring about a broad consensus.

THE POLITICS OF AUTHORIZATION

How have the different members of international society actually approached instances of humanitarian intervention and the issue of Security Council authorization?

The Position of Developing Countries

China's position on two interventions in the post–Cold War period—Kosovo and East Timor—usefully illustrates the politics of authorization. China was adamantly opposed to the Kosovo intervention and joined with Russia in its attempt to pass a resolution condemning NATO's action,[29] while in the case of East Timor it supported the UN-authorized military mission. For China, the Kosovo intervention represented both a dangerous new tendency to internationalize "domestic issues"—such as ethnic unrest—and a raw demonstration of U.S. hegemony. East Timor, by contrast, seemed to reassert the importance of both UN authorization and state sovereignty given that Indonesia's consent was secured. The presence of these two factors is what allowed China, which has traditionally opposed the expansion of norms on intervention for humanitarian purposes,[30] to support INTERFET. While China's national interests played a part in East Timor—geographical proximity and hostility toward the Indonesian government over the treatment of the large Chinese minority in Indonesia—the contrast from the Kosovo experience is nonetheless striking.

China's concern over the precedents set during the 1990s has been echoed by other developing countries at meetings of the Nonaligned Movement and G-77. This stance against humanitarian intervention reflects two deeper concerns. The first is that the UN is expanding its peace and security agenda at the expense of its economic and social agenda (a priority for developing countries). In the process, particular states gain in security—those that are privileged enough to be in the orbit of Western interests—while the human security of millions of people in the developing world continues to suffer. The second issue, well documented by Ramesh Thakur in this volume, is the familiar concern about a new round of imperialism being camouflaged by the language of humanitarian intervention. In the context of the debate on the Russian draft resolution during the Kosovo war, the Cuban ambassador argued in the UN that "never before has the unipolar order imposed by the United States been so obvious and so disturbing."[31] For developing countries, then, Council legitimacy is underpinned by a combination of functional and ideational arguments that champion the notion of the equality of states and fight against the imposition of rules and norms by "imperial" powers.

Nonetheless, a division of international society into Western vs. developing countries on the question of humanitarian intervention is too simplistic. For example, when the General Assembly passed its resolution on Kosovo criticizing the NATO bombing campaign, 52 states opposed and 33 abstained.[32] Similarly, several developing countries that were nonpermanent members of the Security Council helped to defeat the Russian draft resolution that condemned NATO's action.[33] It is also worth noting that of the four interventions that took place without explicit Security Council authorization—Liberia (1990), Sierra Leone (1997), Northern Iraq (1991), and Kosovo (1999)—the first two were carried about by the African regional organization ECOWAS.

Western States

Predictably, Western states suspect that efforts to use the General Assembly in this capacity are part of a broader campaign to decrease the power of the

Security Council and the veto. This is undoubtedly one of the reasons behind the unwillingness of the United States and United Kingdom to explore "Uniting for Peace" in 1999, when it became clear that Russia and China would not support a Chapter VII resolution on Kosovo.[34]

Regarding the need for Security Council authorization, two broad views are articulated in the developed West. The first view, exemplified by France, insists on Council authorization. Thus, when convinced of the necessity of intervention—as they were in Northern Iraq in 1991—the French work actively within the Council chamber to secure a supportive resolution. In the case of Kosovo, France was adamant that the NATO bombing represented an exceptional case that did not set a precedent for future instances of intervention without Council authorization. This view was widely shared by other Western states, particularly Germany, Italy, and Greece, who faced substantial opposition at home to the Kosovo campaign. In the debate over Iraq in 2003, the French focus on the UN was again apparent, but in this case their efforts served to block Council endorsement in order to preserve the UN's legitimacy. In the words of Jean-Marc de la Sablie, the French UN envoy: "What would be the legitimacy of an organization which gave a rubber stamp to a war we consider not to be legitimate, which the great majority finds today not to be legitimate, and which the United States says will happen anyway? Then it would be we who were irrelevant."[35] Here we see a clear example of the functional argument in favor of UN authorization. But the French envoy's remarks also suggest a power-based rationale at work—one concerned with the preservation of French influence within the Council.

The second stance is represented by the British government, which claims that interventions for humanitarian purposes need not have express authorization from the Council if a consensus within this body proves impossible. In both Kosovo in 1999 and Iraq in 2003, the Blair government put forward a strong "just war" argument and invoked new readings of international law to support its bypassing of the UN process. While the United States took the same stance on authorization in both cases, it invested much less effort in attempting to secure Council backing or in articulating a doctrine that would persuade other states of the legality or the legitimacy of its position. Indeed, during the Iraqi crisis of 2003, George W. Bush exhibited frustration and contempt for the UN, warning that it would go the way of the League of Nations if it did not "keep its word" and enforce its resolutions. If it didn't, the United States would take on the role of sheriff. "When it comes to our security," Bush claimed, "we really don't need anybody's permission."[36]

This U.S. view on the importance and value of UN authorization reflects the fact that both the U.S. government and the American people judge the legitimacy of international institutions differently than most of their international partners,[37] with a distinctive position on both process and purpose. Rather than accepting Security Council pronouncements as the reflection of democratic consensus among equal states, the U.S. government has consistently asked *who* those states represent. Moreover, the United States has become more concerned with the viability of the one-state, one-vote rule within the UN system and how this can be made compatible with the current distribution of power.[38] Second, with respect to purpose, the United States judges the legitimacy of the Council on the basis of its ability to advance the *American* conception of what best ensures international peace and security. When that conception can be reconciled with the positions of most members of the Council, as it was in Somalia and the Balkans, the aims of the UN can be furthered. When it cannot, there are dire consequences for both international order and the legitimacy of the Security Council.

CONCLUSION

In the initial aftermath of 9/11, it appeared as though the divisive issue of humanitarian intervention would fall off the policy agenda as Western states struggled to develop a new strategy to fight terrorism. Nonetheless, there are two important ways in which humanitarian intervention connects with the broader war on terrorism. First, post–Cold War changes in the conception of sovereignty remain relevant in a post–September 11 world. The terrorist acts of 2001 brought home to Western states the reality that instability within or collapse of a state can have implications that reach far wider than that particular region. Addressing the challenges posed by so-called failed states has become a crucial plank in Western states' strategies for combating new security threats.

Second, the debate over Security Council authorization raised by humanitarian intervention has proven no less relevant in the U.S. war on terror. "Proper authority" was hotly debated during the last-ditch diplomatic efforts in March 2003 to secure a resolution authorizing the use of force against Iraq. The failure to produce one, combined with the quick and successful execution of the military campaign against Saddam Hussein's regime, only added to the chorus of voices proclaiming the Security Council's irrelevance to the pursuit of international peace and security.[39] Both the procedure and the purpose of the UN were called into question.

Even before 9/11, it was questionable whether authorization itself was really the key issue in debates about whether or not to intervene for humanitarian purposes. Indeed, as Byers and Chesterman argue, clarity on who can authorize will not make action inevitable: "States are not champing at the bit to intervene in support of human rights around the globe, prevented only by an intransigent Security Council and the absence of clear criteria to intervene without its authority. The problem, instead, is the absence of the will to act at all."[40] In the arguments over Iraq that took place between the United States and its European allies, such as France and Germany, this question of political will was the fundamental dividing line: the United States believed that the use of force was justified—not only to address the alleged Iraqi possession of weapons of mass destruction but also to bring about positive change in the politics of the Middle East. For those in Europe who opposed the war, the use of force was a symbol of diplomatic failure.

This brings us back to the original question: What are states really trying to achieve by "using" the UN? In the cases of humanitarian intervention in the 1990s, functional and ideational motivations were front and center for many states. However, the question of power was always lurking—the fear of American hegemony and the desire to play a role in international peace and security despite declining capabilities. In the lead-up to the war against Saddam Hussein, these material and power-based factors became paramount. Functional arguments about the Security Council as the "best we have" came up short in the face of failure. Moreover, ideational arguments about the value of multilateralism were challenged by the structural problems within the Council and the movement toward other forms of collective action and other mechanisms for maintaining international order.

This suggests that multilateralism within the UN framework is on the ropes. It is in danger of becoming all about form rather than substance. While at one time scholars worried that the Security Council was becoming a "deodorizer" for power politics, today there is an even greater worry: that the deodorizing function is no longer valuable. This does not mean, however, that states will cease to strive for legitimacy in the use of force for humanitarian purposes. The instrumental and substantive value of legitimacy remains indispensable. Unless those who still value the UN system can rebuild the foundations of the Council's legitimacy and enhance its authoritativeness, the United States and its "coalitions of the willing" will build their own legitimation alternatives—using new arguments about process and purpose. If they do, we will no doubt experience a transitional period where those mechanisms vie with the UN in the eyes of international society. Whether this result will enhance or detract for global security remains to be seen.

NOTES

* I would like to thank David Malone, Nicholas Wheeler, and the editors of this volume for helpful comments on an earlier version of this chapter.

1. Inis L. Claude, Jr., "Collective Legitimization as a Political Function of the United Nations," *International Organization* 20(3) (Summer, 1966): 367–379.

2. *Ibid.*, 374.

3. Simon Chesterman, *Just War? Just Peace? Humanitarian Intervention and International Law* (Oxford: Oxford University Press, 2001), 121.

4. Humanitarian intervention is defined as *coercive interference in the internal affairs of a state involving the use of armed force with the purposes of addressing massive human rights violations or preventing widespread human suffering.*

5. The most prominent cases include: Liberia (1990–92), Northern Iraq (1991), Bosnia and Herzegovina (1992–95), Somalia (1992–93), Rwanda (1994), Haiti (1994), Albania (1997), Sierra Leone (1997–present), Kosovo (1998–99), East Timor (1999), and Iraq (2003).

6. Report of the International Commission on Intervention and State Sovereignty, *The Responsibility to Protect* (Ottawa: International Development Research Council, 2001): xii.
7. Ian Hurd, "Legitimacy, Power, and the Symbolic Life of the UN Security Council," *Global Governance* 8 (2002): 35–51 (p. 35).
8. See, for example, Robert Jackson, *The Global Covenant: Human Conduct in a World of States* (Oxford, Oxford University Press, 2000).
9. Michael Byers and Simon Chesterman, "Changing the Rules about Rules? Unilateral Humanitarian Intervention and the Future of International Law," in *Humanitarian Intervention: Ethical, Legal and Political Dilemmas* eds. J.L. Holzgrefe and Robert O. Keohane (Cambridge: Cambridge University Press, 2003), 178.
10. Examples include Christine Gray, *International Law and the Use of Force* (Oxford: Oxford University Press, 2000); and Chesterman, *Just War or Just Peace?*
11. See, for example, Christopher Greenwood, "International Law and the NATO Intervention in Kosovo," *International and Comparative Law Quarterly* 49 (2000): 926–934.
12. See Byers and Chesterman, *op. cit.*
13. The Security Council gave retroactive approval to ECOWAS activity in Liberia and Sierra Leone.
14. This is the conclusion of ICISS.
15. See Michael Glennon, "The New Interventionism: The Search for a Just International Law," *Foreign Affairs* 78(2) (1999).
16. This resolution was passed during the crisis in Korea, when the return of the Soviet delegation to the Security Council (after its boycott over continued recognition of the nationalists in China) prevented any enforcement action.
17. See Article 52(1).
18. Allen Buchanan, "Political Legitimacy and Democracy," *Ethics* 112 (July, 2002): 689–719, (pp. 689–692).
19. Thomas Franck, *The Power of Legitimacy Among Nations* (New York: Oxford University Press, 1990), 24.
20. John G. Ruggie, "International Authority," in *Constructing the World Polity: Essays on International Institutionalization* (London: Routledge, 1998), 59–61.
21. John Ruggie, "Measuring the legitimacy of UN vote," *Financial Times* (March 14, 2003).
22. Preamble to the Charter of the United Nations.
23. *The Responsibility to Protect*, xiii.
24. See *The Kosovo Report: Conflict, International Response, Lessons Learned* (Oxford: Oxford University Press, 2000), 4.
25. Examples would include: Nicholas Wheeler, *Saving Strangers: Humanitarian Intervention in International Society* (Oxford: Oxford University Press, 2000); former British Foreign Minister Robin Cook, "Guiding Humanitarian Intervention," (July 19, 2000) www.fco.gov.uk/hews/speechtext.asp?3989; and ICISS, *op. cit.* The criteria usually include the presence of an extreme emergency, the use of force as a last resort, and the use of proportional means.

26. Adam Roberts, "Intervention: Suggestions for moving the debate forward," submission to *The International Commission on Intervention and State Sovereignty,* Round-table meeting (London, February 3, 2001).

27. Edward Mortimer, *A Few Words on Intervention: John Stuart Mill's Principles of International Action applied to the Post Cold War World* (John Stuart Mill Institute, 1995).

28. See Danesh Sarooshi, *The United Nations and the Development of Collective Security* (Oxford: Clarendon Press, 1999).

29. Zhang Yunling, "China: Whither the world order after Kosovo?" in *Kosovo and the Challenge of Humanitarian Intervention* eds. Albrecht Schnabel and Ramesh Thakur (Tokyo: United Nations University Press, 2000): 117–127.

30. Joining China in putting forth its "traditional" understanding of sovereignty and intervention in East Asia are North Korea, Burma, Vietnam, and Malaysia. See Chu Shulong, "China, Asia and Issues of Sovereignty and Intervention," *Pugwash Occasional Papers* (January 2001).

31. S/PV.3989 (March 26, 1999), 13.

32. See General Assembly Resolution 55/101.

33. States voting with NATO included Argentina, Brazil, Gabon, Gambia, and Malaysia.

34. Nicholas J. Wheeler, "Legitimating Humanitarian Intervention," *Melbourne Journal of International Law* 2(2) (2001): 550–568 (p. 566).

35. Cited in *Financial Times,* (March 11, 2003).

36. Cited in *Ibid.*

37. Edward Luck, "The United States, International Organizations, and the Quest for Legitimacy," in *Multilateralism and U.S. Foreign Policy: Ambivalent Engagement* eds. Stewart Patrick and Shepard Forman (Boulder: Lynne Reiner Publishers, 2001): 47–74.

38. *Ibid.,* 52, 55.

39. See, for example, Richard Perle, "United they fall," *The Spectator* (March 22, 2003), 22–26.

40. Byers and Chesterman, *op. cit.,* 202.

CHAPTER 12

DEVELOPING COUNTRIES AND THE INTERVENTION–SOVEREIGNTY DEBATE

Ramesh Thakur*

The terrain on which the conceptual and policy contest over "humanitarian intervention" has been fought is essentially normative. It takes the form of norm displacement, shifting from the established norm of nonintervention to a claimed emerging new norm of "humanitarian intervention." The United Nations lies at the center of this contest both metaphorically and literally. Its Charter encapsulates and articulates the agreed consensus on the prevailing norms that give structure and meaning to the foundations of world order, and the international community comes together physically primarily within the hallowed halls of the UN. It is not surprising, therefore, that the organization should be the epicenter of the interplay between changing norms and shifting state practice.

Much as smaller economies seek protection from the big economic powers in rules-based regimes that embed agreed codes of conduct and dispute settlement mechanisms, so the weak and vulnerable countries seek protection from the predatory instincts of the powerful—an abiding lesson of history, if ever there was one—in a rules-based world order that specifies both the proper conduct to be followed by all states and the mechanisms for reconciling differences between them. The United Nations lies at the center of, and indeed symbolizes, such an order. Those who would challenge and overthrow the existing order must therefore indicate what is their preferred alternative *system of rules, including dispute resolution;* simply rejecting an existing rule or norm, no matter how unsatisfactory, in order to overthrow an existing ruler, no matter how odious, is not enough.

Today there is only one country, the United States, with the capacity to project power around the globe (which it may, for political more than military reasons, seek to do in coalition with like-minded countries) and only one standing military defense organization with the capacity to undertake out-of-area operations, namely, NATO. Questions of the lawfulness and legitimacy of overseas military action by individual or groups of states, which in practice means the United States, NATO, or coalitions of the willing with them at the core, cannot be separated from the question of the authoritative determination of justified response; or who, under what rules of evidence and procedure, can rightfully decide on what is to be done? Reducing the entire debate just to a question of UN authorization as a necessary condition for overseas military action is simply not good enough. If UN authorization is not a necessary condition, then either we accept the resulting international anarchy and the law of the jungle in world affairs, or we spell out the preferred alternative set of rules and the institutions and regimes in which they are embedded. Logically, there are six alternatives:

1. Any one country can wage war against any other;
2. Any one coalition of states can wage war against another country or group;
3. Only NATO has such a right with respect to launching military action against a non-NATO country;
4. Only NATO has the right to determine if military intervention, whether by NATO *or any other coalition*, is justified against others outside the coalition;
5. A regional organization can take in-area military action against errant members of the organization (for example, the OAU against deviant OAU members or NATO against deviant NATO members) if they have agreed in advance to such rules of the game for governing internal relations, or if they seek and get *ex post facto* authorization from the Security Council, but not against nonmembers in out-of-area operations; and
6. Only the United Nations can legitimately authorize armed intervention.

The first and second are recipes for international anarchy. Indeed the challenge of "humanitarian intervention" arises from the increasingly clear recognition that we no longer cede the right to any one state to use massive force even *within* its borders free of external scrutiny or criticism, whether it be Serbia in Kosovo, Indonesia in East Timor, India in Kashmir or Russia in Chechnya; claims for reversing the progressive restrictions on the right to interstate armed violence will be met with even more skepticism. The third is a claim to unilateralism and exceptionalism that will never be conceded by the "international community." The fourth was unwittingly implicit in the argument that NATO's actions in Kosovo cannot be construed as having set a precedent. The assumption underlying the claim is almost breathtakingly arrogant in setting up NATO as the final arbiter of military intervention by itself *and* every other coalition. The fifth and sixth options pose the fewest difficulties, although the history of the Warsaw Pact (Hungary 1956, Czechoslovakia 1968) and that of the Organization of American States (OAS) should inject elements of caution. The UN Charter encapsulates the international moral code and best-practice international behavior. The only just and lasting resolution of the challenge of military intervention for human protection purposes would be a new consensus proclaimed and embodied within the UN forum.

This chapter examines the normative contestation between North and South,[1] with respect to the so-called challenge of humanitarian intervention. It begins with a sketch of the diffusion of the human rights norm across the world. The second and third sections address issues of normative incoherence, inconsistency, and contestation. The fourth part examines the rise and fall of developing countries as norm setters. The debate is focused mainly on the UN community in New York, although in the final section I offer some personal observations on the artificial world inhabited by UN-based diplomats.

HUMAN RIGHTS: DIFFUSION FROM THE WEST TO THE REST

International law as we know it was a product of the European states system, and international humanitarian law too has its roots essentially in Europe. In the age of colonialism, most Afro-Asians and Latin Americans became the victims of Western superiority in the organization and weaponry of warfare. The danger today is that they could continue to be the objects but not authors of norms and laws that are supposedly international.[2] But a world order in which the developing countries are norm takers and law takers, while the Westerners are the norm and law setters and enforcers, will not be viable because the division of labor is based neither on comparative advantage—Africa, Asia, and Latin America are home to some of the world's oldest civilizations with their own distinctive value-systems—nor on equity.

At the start of the twenty-first century there is neither a homogeneous international society nor a unifying normative architecture. Rather, the reality of norm variation attests to the existence of a polymorphic international society. The idea of universal rights is denied by some who insist that moral standards are always culture-specific. The historicist variant of cultural relativism holds that moral precepts cannot be understood in the abstract but must always be located in the experience of particular historical communities. If relativism is often the last refuge of human rights scoundrels, it is also true that universalism can be the first refuge of Western rights chauvinists. Risse argues that the human rights norm protects citizens from the state.[3] This is truer of Western than developing countries, where often "The role of the state is essential in the need to ensure respect for and . . . the realization of human rights."[4]

With independence and following the globalization of the norm of self-determination, the newly decolonized countries engaged simultaneously in the pursuit of state building, nation building, and economic development. Sovereignty was the critical shield behind which the triple pursuit was attempted. The path dependence of their colonial history offers a clue as to why sovereignty and its correlative norm of nonintervention are more deeply internalized in the developing country elites than their counterparts in the West. As memories of colonialism dim and become increasingly distant, the

salience of sovereignty correspondingly diminishes. Domestic groups begin
to use the international human rights norm to subject the actions of
their own governments to increasingly harsh scrutiny. In parallel with this,
fewer and fewer Western leaders are impressed any longer with charges of
neo-imperialism by historical association.

At this stage human rights advocacy groups inside the target state can
forge alliances of convenience with foreign and international counterparts.
Norm-violating governments can choose to deny the validity of global
norms and reject critics as agents or stooges of ignorant or ill-intentioned
foreigners. But if vulnerable and subjected to sufficient pressure, they may
begin to make tactical concessions in order to mollify domestic and international critics, lift aid suspensions, and so on. The discourse has shifted from
denying to accepting the validity of the norm, but rejecting specific allegations of norm violation by questioning the facts and evidence presented
by critics, or else insisting that these are isolated incidents and the cases will
be investigated and perpetrators will be punished, etc. By such a process of
"self-entrapment,"[5] the war is won though many battles might remain to be
fought.

The problem becomes more intractable when we slide across from human
rights to "humanitarian intervention."[6] Venerable commentators assert
that "[i]ntervention has become the new norm" in "a climate in which nonintervention appears as a dereliction of duty, requiring explanation, excuse or
apology."[7] The assertion is open to challenge. Contrary to what many
European governments claimed, the application of a right to humanitarian
intervention in Kosovo was not self-evidently (self-righteously?) based in law
or morality. During the UN Security Council debate on Kosovo in 1999, for
example, the Sino-Russian draft resolution condemning bombing by NATO
was defeated by a vote of twelve to three. Yet the Indian ambassador claimed
that since China, Russia, and India had opposed the bombing, the representatives of half of humanity were opposed to the action.[8]

NORMATIVE INCONSISTENCY AND INCOHERENCE

The Kosovo war was a good illustration of how different norms can come
into conflict and of the lack of institutional mechanisms for resolving such
tension in the existing world order. The norm of nonintervention is underpinned by a cluster of auxiliary norms. To replace it with a new norm of
intervention carries the risk of producing, not a norm cascade, but a burst-
ing of the dam. One of the peculiar aspects of the NATO countries' handling
of the Kosovo conflict was their stress on the formal sovereignty and territorial integrity of Yugoslavia even while violating the same. Designed to deny
any normative incoherence between state sovereignty and "humanitarian
intervention," the formula fell into the related trap of normative inconsistency. Sovereignty in effect became "fluid and contingent."[9]

Normative coherence requires compatibility among a cluster of cognate norms, for example, among the norms of the use and non-use of force, non-proliferation of weapons, arms control and disarmament, and intervention and nonintervention in the internal affairs of sovereign states. *Normative inconsistency* refers to unevenness in the application of any one particular norm, for example, nonintervention or nonproliferation (cf. Iraq, Israel, and North Korea), either in different locations or over time.

Africans and Asians are neither amused nor mindful at being lectured on universal human values by those who failed to practice the same during European colonialism and now urge them to cooperate in promoting "global" human rights norms. The displacement and ethnic cleansing of indigenous populations was carried out with such ruthless efficiency that the place of settler societies like Australia, Canada, and the United States in contemporary international society is accepted as a given. The superiority of Western ways has remained a constant theme over the past few centuries, only the universal truths of Christianity have been replaced by the universal rights of humankind. Western countries, including Australia and America, are quite happy to use Amnesty International reports as a lever with which to nudge other countries on human rights. But they are outraged at the idea that their own human rights record, for example, with respect to the condition of their indigenous peoples or the racial bias in the death penalty, might merit independent international scrutiny. This is in addition to the cynical belief by many that "American democracy requires the repression of democracy in the rest of the world"[10]—and, one might add, in international organizations like the UN.

Which rights that Westerners hold dear would they be prepared to give up in the name of universalism? Or is the concept of universalism just a one-way street—what we Westerners have is ours, what you heathens have is open to negotiation?

One hint of what the answer to the above challenge is likely to be: "[T]he diffusion of international norms in the human rights area crucially depends on the establishment and the sustainability of networks among domestic and transnational actors who manage to link up with international regimes, to alert Western [*sic*] public opinion and Western [*sic*] governments."[11] The philosophical antecedents of such beliefs lie in the eighteenth and nineteenth century theory of evolutionary progress through diffusion and acculturation from the West to the rest. The implicit but clear assumption is that when Western and non-Western values diverge, the latter are in the wrong, and it is only a matter of working on them with persuasion and pressure for the problem to be resolved and progress achieved.[12] The cognitive rigidity is shown again in "[p]ressure by Western states and international organizations can greatly increase the vulnerability of norm-violating governments to external influences."[13] Self-evidently, only non-Western governments can be norm violators; Western governments can only be norm setters and norm enforcers. The rejection of the International Criminal Court (ICC) by

Washington—described by Sweden's ambassador to the UN as reminiscent of George Orwell's immortal line in *Animal Farm* that "we are all equal but some are more equal than others"[14]—highlights the irony that the United States "is prepared to bomb in the name of human rights but not to join institutions to enforce them."[15]

In other words, even if we agree on universal human rights, they still have to be constructed, articulated, and embedded in international conventions. The question remains therefore of the agency and procedure for determining what they are; how they apply in specific circumstances and cases; what the proper remedies might be to breaches; and who decides, following what rules of procedure and evidence. Under present conditions of world realities, the political calculus—relations based on military might and economic power, not to mention the nuisance value of the media and NGOs—cannot be taken out. As far as many Afro-Asians are concerned, *that* is the problem. The resilience of the opposition to the internationalization of the human conscience lies in the fear that the lofty rhetoric of universal human rights claims merely masks the more mundane and familiar pursuit of national interests by different means. The contestation reflects competing conceptions of the good life, the proper relationship between citizen and state, historical wrongs and present rights, and correlative rights and obligations. But also embedded in the ferocity of the contestation are unequal power relations.

Besides, overriding the norm of nonintervention erodes another major contemporary norm, namely, the non-use of force to settle international disputes. Kosovo was a setback to the cause of slowly but steadily outlawing the use of force in solving disputes except under UN authorization. The argument that NATO had no intention to set a precedent is less relevant than that its actions were interpreted by others, including Russia and China,[16] as having set a dangerous precedent. Although in 2003 Europeans were strongly opposed to military action against Iraq unless authorized by the UN, Washington was surely right in recalling the example of Kosovo to the contrary.

The rule of law ideal has been diffused from the West to become an international norm. It asserts the primacy of law over the arbitrary exercise of political power by using law to tame power; the protection of the citizen from the arbitrary actions of the government by making both, and their relationship to each other, subject to impersonal and impartial law; and the primacy of universalism over particularism through the principle of equal in law, whereby persons coming before the law are treated as individuals, divorced from their social characteristics.

The Independent International Commission on Kosovo, chaired by Richard Goldstone and Carl Tham, concluded that NATO's intervention was illegal but legitimate.[17] The intervention was illegal because the use of force is prohibited by the UN Charter except in self-defense or when authorized by the Security Council. It was legitimate, nevertheless, because of the scale of human rights atrocities by the Milosevic regime, the failure of other means used to try to stop those atrocities, and the political stalemate in the Security Council created by Russia and China. But if anyone can set aside the legal outcome by privileging legitimacy over law, where is the protection against vigilante justice?[18] A normative commitment to the rule of law implies a commitment to the principle of relations being governed by law, not power. It also implies a willingness to accept the limitations and constraints of working within the law, in specific instances, against individual notions of unjust or illegitimate outcome if necessary.

The legality–legitimacy distinction rests on an implicit hierarchy of norms.[19] The international order, being a society of sovereign states, has only a horizontal system of rules derived logically from the principle of sovereign equality. If the UN Charter's proscriptions on the threat and use of force can be set aside, the justification for this must necessarily rest on the existence of a higher order of norms that override Charter clauses. The *use* of force may be lawful or unlawful; the *decision* to use force is a political act. Almost the only channel between legal authority and political legitimacy with regard to the international use of force is the Security Council. Conceding to any—and therefore every—group of states the authority to decide when political legitimacy may override legal technicality would make a mockery of the entire basis of strictly limited, and in recent times increasingly constricted, recourse to force for settling international disputes.

Unlike NATO, which unilaterally transferred the legal capacity to authorize enforcement operations from the Security Council to itself, most developing countries urge reform of the Security Council. Foreign Minister Maria Soledad Alvear of Chile, for example, while acknowledging the obligations of our "common humanity," insists that for Chile, the UN Charter "constitutes the only legal framework, the condition *sine qua non*, governing humanitarian intervention." When effective UN response to humanitarian disasters is constrained by Security Council paralysis, she added, the solution must be found in reform of the veto clause in the Council and in exploring the role that the General Assembly could play.[20]

The legitimacy of the Security Council as the authoritative validator of international security action has been subject to a triple erosion when it has been perceived as being increasingly unrepresentative in composition, undemocratic in operation, and ineffective in results. Western countries often chafe at the ineffectual performance legitimacy of the Council and question its role as the sole validator of the international use of force because of this. But if the Security Council were to become increasingly activist, interventionist, and effective, its lack of representational and procedural legitimacy, political accountability, and judicial oversight would lead many developing countries to question its authority even more forcefully.[21]

The terrorist attacks of $\frac{9}{11}$ pushed Washington into an aggressive unilateralism in pursuit of U.S. preferences and priorities, and in September 2002 Bush threw down the gauntlet of relevance at the UNSC. The dismissive attitude toward world opinion has found expression in unilateral changes in U.S. doctrines on the utility and usability of nuclear weapons. In particular, Bush promised that he will not allow the world's most dangerous weapons to fall into the hands of the world's most dangerous regimes—as judged solely and unilaterally by Washington. Therein lies the logic of preemption based in a conception of world order outside the Westphalian framework of sovereign equality. In effect Bush is saying that the gap between the fiction of legal equality and the reality of power preponderance has stretched beyond breaking point. Washington is no longer bound by such fiction. The United States will remain as fundamentally trustworthy, balanced, and responsible a custodian of world order as before—but of a post-Westphalian order centered on the United States amidst a surrounding wasteland of vassal states.

Developing countries cannot be expected to be overjoyed at such a revolutionary transformation of the foundations of world order. The Bush statement in the General Assembly in September 2002 was not an American concession to UN multilateralism, but a demand for international capitulation to the U.S. threat to go to war. But in doing so Bush presented the UN with an impossible choice between effectiveness (enforce your resolutions) and integrity (or we will do so regardless). And while demanding Iraqi compliance with the resulting Security Council Resolution 1441, Washington insisted on retaining the freedom to strike at Iraq without a follow-up resolution if necessary—in effect proclaiming exemption for itself from the same resolution.[22]

Suspicions of the whole concept of "humanitarian intervention" would have been further strengthened with comments from American columnists describing the U.S. war policy on Iraq in these terms.[23] The UN is both the symbol and the major instrument for moderating the use of force in international affairs, not sanctifying a major expansion in its permissive scope through such subjective subterfuges as preemption. It is the collective body for protecting the territorial integrity of member states within the Westphalian paradigm of national sovereignty. The choice between irrelevance (for not having the courage to enforce its decisions) and complicity (in endorsing an armed attack on the territorial integrity of the weak by the powerful) would be a fatal one for the organization. For it comes down to a choice between knowing and accepting its place as a mere speed bump or becoming road kill on the highway of power politics.

The International Commission on Intervention and State Sovereignty (ICISS) concluded that "[t]he task is not to find alternatives to the Security Council as a source of authority, but to make the Security Council work much better than it has." It therefore recommended that in all cases, Security Council authorization must be sought prior to any military intervention.[24] But even ICISS conceded that if an intervention is carried out despite the failure of Security Council authorization, and the people of the world conclude that the action was necessary and done well, then it is the authority and credibility of the UN that will suffer still further erosion.[25] Thus UN authorization is not a necessary condition of international legitimacy.

Nor is it a sufficient condition. In national systems bills passed into law by the legislature and actions of the executive arm of government can be found by judicial review to violate constitutionally guaranteed rights of citizens. In principle, Security Council resolutions could similarly violate the rights of member states guaranteed by the UN Charter. But there is no mechanism to hold the Council to independent international judicial account. Given its unrepresentative nature, there are occasional tremors of apprehension among developing countries about the potential for the UN, which they see as the best protection that the weak have against the strong in international affairs, to become instead the instrument for legitimating the actions of the strong against the weak.

There is a logical slippage between normative idealism and realpolitik in picking and choosing which elements of the existing order are to be challenged and which retained. If ethical imperatives and calculations of justice are to inform, underpin, and justify international interventions, then there is a powerful case for reforming the composition of the Security Council and eliminating the veto clause with respect to humanitarian operations. To self-censor such calls for major reform on the grounds that they are unacceptable to the major powers and therefore unrealistic is to argue in effect that the motive for intervention is humanitarian, not strategic; but the agency and procedure for deciding on intervention must remain locked in the strategic logic of realpolitik. "Eroding the existing normative basis of international society in order to provide major powers the facility to intervene selectively in the domestic affairs of weaker states ought not to form a part of the humanitarian intervention argument."[26]

NORMATIVE CONTESTATION

That is the nub of the contrasting normative worldviews of the North and South. Norms do not simply collide; they are contested, sometimes fiercely so. Normative contestation reflects the reality that the international normative architecture is polymorphic, not isomorphic. Successful norm promotion requires the attributes of norm entrepreneurship: international leadership skills. Conversely, success in vetoing or blocking the replacement of one norm with another also depends on a combination of structural power and coalition-forming skills: international "spoilership" as the corollary to international leadership.

When there are contested norms, the selection made from them will depend on the relative prominence of each, their relative compatibility or coherence with other prevailing norms, and the extent to which they fit the existing environmental conditions. Ann Florini notes that of the major norm shifts since the Second World War, two include multilateralism ("meaning that all relevant actors are expected to play by the same set of rules") and restrictions on the use of force.[27] On both counts, many developing countries have problems with jettisoning the norm of nonintervention.

An order secures habitual compliance either through perception of legitimacy, in which case it is a just order, or through fear, in which case it rests on coercion. As Ayoob notes, developing countries typically seek order within and justice between states; Western countries privilege order between and justice (that is, civil-political human rights) within states.[28] The state actor with the greatest contemporary capacity to play the roles of norm entrepreneur, enforcer, and spoiler is the United States. We begin the twenty-first century with the convergence of U.S. global dominance in military might, economic dynamism, and information technology that is without precedent in human history. To this list can be added the soft power hegemony in the major multilateral institutions, especially the International Monetary Fund and the World Bank, but including also the UN; the collective action dominance of the G7 and NATO; and the many globally influential media and NGO conglomerates located in the United States.

Because of the sustaining belief in being a virtuous power, the United States is averse to domesticating international values and norms, be they with respect to greenhouse gas emissions, the death penalty, landmines, or the pursuit of universal justice. With the United States' refusal to join the universal justice of the ICC, it is hardly surprising that many developing countries should view the moral imperialism of human rights as the handmaiden to judicial colonialism with respect to international justice through ad hoc criminal tribunals that leave the process of international law more vulnerable to the pursuit of power politics than would be possible in the ICC.

Since the international system is highly stratified, there is a high probability of interventions being seen as instruments of depredation by the strong against the weak. In particular for developing countries, they will conjure up visions of the nineteenth-century doctrine of "standard of civilization,"[29] with human rights being the new standard. But the Western construction of the new standard is ahistorical, airbrushing the role of violence in the making of most Western states. The claim of developing-country governments to monopoly over the legitimate use of violence is resisted by many armed groups from within; is the state in the contemporary developing world to be denied the right to use force against those who would challenge its authority as the lawful guardian of domestic order? And of course, outside intervention on behalf of groups resisting state authority by force encourages other recalcitrant groups in other places to resort to ever-more violent challenges since that is the trigger to internationalizing their power struggle. How seriously delayed or distorted would have been the Western state-making enterprise if the likes of Amnesty International, Human Rights Watch, the UN Human Rights Commission, and the Security Council had been monitoring their actions during the violent phases of their state making process, for example, in the U.S. civil war.[30]

THE RISE AND FALL OF DEVELOPING COUNTRIES AS NORM ENTREPRENEURS

But is anyone listening anymore to developing-country charges of double standards and hypocrisy? In the 1960s and 1970s, the heady days of the post-colonial period, international conditions favored narratives of grievance and claims for redress and assistance. The developing countries were the norm advocates and norm generators via the UN General Assembly in delegit-imizing colonialism, criminalizing apartheid, and legitimizing armed national liberation movements.[31] The central norm underpinning this triple assault on the international political status quo was that of self-determination from European colonial powers. The transnational anti-apartheid move-ment, comprising domestic, state, intergovernmental, and nongovernmental actors, was formed and sustained on the members' shared advocacy of the sibling but different norm of racial equality, which led states to redefine interests even when they had material incentives to the contrary.[32] It was the successor to the anti-slavery movement and the precursor to the global human rights movement: incidentally, with both being Western in origin.

The binding character of contracts does not rest on the reliance of one party to a contract on the word or signature of the other party. Rather, it rests on the institution of the contract itself. The same argument holds with respect to the UN Charter, which affirms and enshrines the principle of state sovereignty and the norm of nonintervention. Any one intervention does not simply violate the sovereignty of any given target state in any one instance; it also challenges the *principle* of a society of states resting on a sys-tem of well understood and habitually obeyed rules. "Cherry picking" norms and laws to suit one's partisan interests of the day will undermine respect for the principle of world order founded on law. That is to say, the normative consensus on which law rests will begin to fray and the international order will risk collapse.

The dangers of this are magnified because of the potentially competing and conflicting norms and principles at play on most controversial or impor-tant issues. Much of the twentieth century advances in globalizing norms and international law has been progressive and beneficial. But their viability will be threatened if developing countries are not brought more attentively into the process of norm formation, promulgation, interpretation, and artic-ulation, that is, if they are not made equal partners in the management of regimes in which international norms and laws are embedded. Otherwise, norms will become the major transmission mechanism for embedding structural inequality in international law, instruments and, regimes.

At the same time it is just as important that leaders of the South examine their own policies and strategies critically. If the impetus for action in international affairs usually appears to come from the North, this is partly due to a failure of leadership from the South. Canada has almost an exem-plary record in forging winning diplomatic coalitions, for example on the landmine treaty, even against the wishes of some major powers. Instead of forever opposing, complaining, and finding themselves on the losing side anyway, developing countries should learn how to master the so-called "new diplomacy" and become norm entrepreneurs. Otherwise in practice they risk simply being dismissed as the international "nattering nawabs of negativism." The Non-Aligned Movement—with 113 members, the most representative group of countries outside the United Nations itself—three times rejected "the so-called 'right of humanitarian intervention'" after the Kosovo war in 1999 and the subsequent statements from the UN Secretary-General.[33] They effectively aborted the emerging new norm at the cascade point by rejecting Kofi Annan's statement in the General Assembly in September 1999. But because the Western powers with the military capacity to carry out interventions in "the real world" believed their actions to be grounded in ethical principles, they simply circumvented the blockage in the UN forum at no political cost domestically and little internationally. The net message for the global South might well be: Move with the times, or become irrelevant.

ACKNOWLEDGING BUT NOT EXAGGERATING DIVERSITY

Neither industrial nor developing countries are united and cohesive on the tension between intervention and sovereignty. Significant differences exist between and within Africa, Latin America, and Asia. Africa has gone the farthest in rejecting sovereignty as a shield from external scrutiny. Article 4(h) of the Constitutive Act of the new Africa Union explicitly spells out the "right of the Union to intervene in a Member State" with respect to the commission of "war crimes, genocide and crimes against humanity."[34] Latin Americans, despite their history of interventions from the North, are open to interventions based on universal principles and under regional or international authority. Asia is the most stubbornly resistant to external interference. Nevertheless, nowhere in the world did ICISS find an outright and absolute rejection of intervention in favor of sovereignty.[35] Instead, we found much greater focus on issues like consistency/double standards of response, agency of authorization, and clear and consistent rules of the game—echoes of which could be heard in debates over Iraq in 2003. On balance, the desire to avoid another Rwanda (where the world stood by passively during genocide) was more powerful than the desire to avoid another Kosovo (where NATO intervened without UN authorization).

Still, the differences among developing countries should not be exaggerated, for that would risk a policy of the equivalent of divide and rule for perpetuating theoretical imperialism. Overall, "the idea of humanitarian intervention has received a generally hostile response in Asia." The reformulation of "humanitarian intervention" as the "responsibility to protect" does not "entirely override the developing world's concerns about sovereignty," and it "does not entirely succeed in separating the humanitarian imperative from the political and geopolitical constraints of a UN system that will remain dominated by the P-5."[36] This is surprising for, historically, some of the clearest examples of "humanitarian intervention" have come from Asia, such as Bangladesh in 1971 and Cambodia in 1978. Yet these were not described as "humanitarian intervention" by India and Vietnam at the time. Rather, the discourse of justification was still very much within the traditional vocabulary of self-defense and threats to national and regional security and stability. Part of India's justification was also self-defense against the "demographic aggression" by ten million refugees.

Some of the examples cited above, such as the ICC and the unfolding drama involving the U.S. wish for a regime change in Baghdad, show that depiction of a binary divide along the North-South axis is too simplistic, lacking in nuance. Europe has been as sharply divided from the United States on these issues. The key difference is that where developing countries simply oppose, the Europeans also propose creative alternatives as well that are often far more progressive than Washington's preferences. And they are able to do so because they have a strategic vision for the collective advancement of the welfare and security of their peoples, unencumbered by a reflexive resistance to initiatives that stifle progress for the sake of protecting the ruling elite's privileges. The handmaiden to new diplomacy is human security, not national or regime security.

Developing countries cannot be sanguine about the future. Calls for "humanitarian intervention" could arise from any one or more of several potential flashpoints; humanitarian carnage could be triggered by any combination of contingencies. The price of a policy of denial will be paid by the victims but also by our children tomorrow, when they too are reduced to being passive and helpless spectators to atrocities if not victims themselves. If we are going to get any sort of consensus in advance of a crisis requiring urgent responses, including military intervention, "the responsibility to protect" points the way forward. If developing-country governments and critics can move beyond their reflexive hostility and suspicion of the very word "intervention" itself, they are likely to find that "the responsibility to protect" contains all the safeguards they need and all that they are going to get with respect to threshold causes, precautionary principles, lawful authorization, and operational doctrine. The real choice is no longer between intervention and nonintervention but between different modes of intervention. Given that reality, it would be far better to embed international intervention within the constraining discipline of the principles and caution underlying "the responsibility to protect" than to risk the inherently more volatile nature of unilateral interventions.

NOTES

* This paper expresses my personal opinions and reflects my personal and professional identity at the intersection of West and East and of international

relations scholarship and the international policy community, respectively. While broadly committed to the notion of universal human rights, I also have some empathy with many developing countries' charges of self-serving interpretation and application of human rights norms by the powers that be. This paper draws on my experience as a commissioner with the International Commission on Intervention and State Sovereignty (ICISS) and its follow-up outreach activities, where we received many comments and were exposed to a full range of viewpoints.

1. Of course, the West is no more homogeneous as a cultural entity and no more unified in policy stances than is the developing world.

2. See Ramesh Thakur, "Global Norms and International Humanitarian Law: An Asian Perspective," *International Review of the Red Cross* 83(841) (March 2001): 19–44.

3. Thomas Risse, " 'Let's Argue!': Communicative Action in World Politics," *International Organization* 54(1) (Winter 2000): 1–39 at p. 5.

4. Danilo Türk, "Humanitarian Interventions: Balancing Human Rights and National Sovereignty," *International Policy Perspectives* 2002.1 (St. Louis: University of Missouri-St. Louis, January 2002): 20.

5. Risse, "Let's Argue!" 32.

6. For the argument to shift the conceptual vocabulary away from "humanitarian intervention," see *The Responsibility to Protect: Report of the International Commission on Intervention and State Sovereignty* (Ottawa: International Development Research Centre, 2001).

7. Inis L. Claude, "The Evolution of Concepts of Global Governance and the State in the Twentieth Century," paper delivered at the annual conference of the Academic Council on the United Nations System (ACUNS), (Oslo, June 16–18, 2000). Claude does note, however, that the new norm "has been no less challenged in principle and dishonored in practice than was the old norm of nonintervention."

8. See the statements to the Security Council by Kamalesh Sharma, Permanent Representative of India to the United Nations, "NATO Military Action against FRY," (March 24, 1999); and "NATO Attack on FRY," (26 March 1999).

9. Christine M. Chinkin, "Kosovo: A 'Good' or 'Bad' War?," *American Journal of International Law* 93(4) (October 1999): 841–47 at p. 845.

10. An Asian human rights activist [*sic*] quoted in Jeffrey C. Goldfarb, "Losing young allies in the war on terror," *International Herald Tribune* (IHT) (August 21, 2002).

11. Thomas Risse and Kathryn Sikkink, "The Socialization of International Human Rights Norms Into Domestic Practices: Introduction," in *The Power of Human Rights: International Norms and Domestic Change* eds. Thomas Risse, Stephen C. Ropp, and Kathryn Sikkink (Cambridge: Cambridge University Press, 1999), 5.

12. Many in developing countries watched bemusedly from the sidelines when the same attitudinal divide opened up across the Atlantic in 2003 with respect to the United States' threat of war on Iraq and the stiff resistance from European citizens. The dominant view in Washington seemed once

again to be that the European people could not possibly be right. The task was to show then the error of their ways or, failing that, to make sure that the European governments listened to the U.S. administration rather than to their own people. That the administration could be wrong was a priori beyond the realm of possibility.

13. Thomas Risse and Stephen C. Ropp, "International Human Rights Norms and Domestic Change: Conclusions," in *The Power of Human Rights* eds. Risse, Ropp and Sikkink, 277.

14. Pierre Schori, "What We Need Is a Cooperative America," IHT (August 6, 2002).

15. Chinkin, "Kosovo: A 'Good' or 'Bad' War?," 846.

16. See Alexei G. Arbatov, "The Transformation of Russian Military Doctrine: Lessons Learned from Kosovo and Chechnya" *The George C. Marshall Center Papers,* 2 (Washington D.C, 20 July 2000); and Sha Zukang as quoted in Michael R. Gordon, "China Looks to Foil Missile Defense," IHT (April 30, 2001).

17. *Kosovo Report: Conflict, International Response, Lessons Learned* (Oxford: Oxford University Press for the Independent International Commission on Kosovo, 2000).

18. On the analogy of vigilante justice, see Ingvar Carlson and Shridath Ramphal, "Air strikes: incalculable damage to peace under law," http://www.cgg.ch/kosovo.htm.

19. Hideaki Shinoda, "The Politics of Legitimacy in International Relations: A Critical Examination of NATO's Intervention in Kosovo," *Alternatives* 25(4) (October/December 2000): 515–36, at pp. 528–31.

20. Maria Soledad Alvear, "Humanitarian Intervention: How to Deal with Crises Effectively," Introductory remarks to the round table consultation of ICISS (Santiago, May 4, 2001) www.iciss-ciise.gc.ca, unofficial translation.

21. See Ramesh Thakur and Samuel Makinda, "The Asia–Pacific Region and the United Nations," *Contemporary Southeast Asia* 18(2) (September 1996): 119–134 at pp. 127–29.

22. Michael J. Glennon, "How War Left the Law Behind," *New York Times* (November 21, 2002).

23. See, for example, Jim Hoagland, "Time for Bush to Cast War Aims in Iron," *Japan Times* (28 October 2002), reprinting an article from the *Washington Post.*

24. *The Responsibility to Protect,* 49–50, paras. 6.14 and 6.15.

25. *The Responsibility to Protect,* 55, para. 6.40.

26. Mohammed Ayoob, "Humanitarian Intervention and International Society," *Global Governance* 7(3) (July/September 2001): 225–30, at p. 229.

27. Florini, "The Evolution of International Norms," 377–78 and 382–83.

28. Mohammed Ayoob, "Humanitarian Intervention and State Sovereignty," *International Journal of Human Rights* 6(1) (Spring 2002): 81–102, at pp. 98–99.

29. Gerritt W. Gong, *The Standard of "Civilization" in International Society* (Oxford: Clarendon, 1984).

30. Ayoob, "Humanitarian Intervention and International Society," 227.

31. See Robert H. Jackson, "The Weight of Ideas in Decolonization: Normative Change in International Relations," in *Ideas and Foreign Policy: Beliefs, Institutions, and Political Change* eds. Judith Goldstein and Robert O. Keohane (Ithaca: Cornell University Press, 1993), 111–38.

32. See Audie Klotz, *Norms in International Relations: The Struggle against Apartheid* (Ithaca: Cornell University Press, 1995).

33. *The Responsibility to Protect: Research, Bibliography, and Background* Supplementary volume to the Report of the International Commission on Intervention and State Sovereignty (Ottawa: International Development Research Centre, 2001), 162, 357. See also Philip Nel, "South Africa: the demand for legitimate multilateralism," in *Kosovo and the Challenge of Humanitarian Intervention: Selective Indignation, Collective Action, and International Citizenship* eds. Albrecht Schnabel and Ramesh Thakur (Tokyo: United Nations University Press, 2000), 245–59.

34. The text of the Constitutive Act is reproduced in Fasil Nahum, *Visions of Transforming Africa: The Challenge of Leadership* (Addis Ababa: 2003), 77–94.

35. See *The Responsibility to Protect: Research, Bibliography, and Background,* III.3, 349–98.

36. Amitav Acharya, "Redefining the dilemmas of humanitarian intervention," *Australian Journal of International Affairs* 56(3) (2002): 373–81 at pp. 377, 378, and 380.

PART V

INSTITUTIONAL REFORM

CHAPTER 13

THE CONUNDRUMS OF INTERNATIONAL POWER SHARING: THE POLITICS OF SECURITY COUNCIL REFORM

Mark W. Zacher*

INTRODUCTION

A central issue for global security organizations since 1815 has been the character of their central decision-making body—particularly their membership and voting rules. The 1815 Congress of Vienna established that the membership of the Concert of Europe would be confined to great powers and that decisions would only be made by unanimous votes. The Hague Peace Conferences of 1899 and 1907 introduced the large number of non-great powers into global security deliberations, and the 1907 conference even adopted the practice of passing recommendations by simple majority. At the 1919 Versailles conference that formulated the Covenant of the League of Nations, the dominant consensus was that the body responsible for security issues should be the Council composed of the five great powers and four states chosen from the rest of the membership. Also, it was agreed that resolutions from the Council would require the unanimous consent of all member states, with the exception of the accused aggressor if it were a Council member.[1]

A unique feature of the deliberations to formulate the character of the United Nations was that they occurred during a major war. One important impact of this was that the major powers that were winning the war had an overriding impact on the deliberations. These were the United States, Britain, and the Soviet Union. China and France were brought into the negotiations and very importantly into the designated group of permanent Security Council members in late 1944 and early 1945, but they did not have an important influence on the character of the UN. The remaining members of the international community did not formally enter into the deliberations until they were invited to attend the San Francisco conference in June 1945.

In 1945 all conference participants recognized that the military great powers had to have major roles in the central UN security institution.

If there were one thing that governments took from their analyses of the road to war in the 1930s, it was that the prevention and reversal of aggressive wars depended on the military strength and resolve of the great powers. However, there were some important differences among states over the voting rules of the Security Council to be composed of five permanent and six nonpermanent members. The central issue was the scope of the veto of the five permanent members (the P5) in the Council. The conference participants accepted that the passage of resolutions would require the approval of seven of the eleven members, but many wanted the veto to be limited to issues concerning the use of military force by the United Nations. The five designated permanent members all opposed this, and the Soviet Union stated it would not join the United Nations if there were a diminution in the proposed scope of the veto. The conference participants gave in to the strong stand of the designated five permanent members.[2]

Some important provisions concerning the Security Council are the following:

- The 6 nonpermanent members (10 after 1965) are elected for two-year terms (Art. 23).
- Passage of resolutions requires approval of 7 of 11 members (9 of 15 after 1966), including no negative votes of the P5 (Art. 27).
- Decisions on procedural matters (especially the convening of meetings) require 7 of the 11 members (9 of 15 members after 1965). The veto does not apply to votes on procedural issues. However, a decision on what constitutes a procedural issue is subject to the veto (Art. 27).
- The Security Council has the primary responsibility for dealing with threats to or breaches of international peace, but the General Assembly has a secondary role in this sphere and can consider particular conflicts after the Security Council has ceased dealing with them (Arts. 12, 24).
- Members of the United Nations are obligated to comply with decisions of the Security Council (Arts. 25, 39–50).
- The Security Council can invite nonmembers to participate in Council debates and shall invite a nonmember if it is a party to the dispute in question (Arts. 31, 32).
- Amendments to the UN Charter require two-thirds of the General Assembly, including the support of all of the five permanent members (Art. 108).

In order to understand the reasons for the provisions concerning the role of the great powers in the Security Council and in order to evaluate proposals for reform, it is valuable to reflect on the reasons or justifications for the provisions concerning the P5.[3] First, the founding states realized that the decisions of the Council would not be effective if they were opposed by one or several great powers. Great power opposition to UN actions in armed conflicts would lead to a serious discrediting of the organization and its lack of relevance to the control of international conflicts. At the time of the UN's founding, it was hoped that the United Nations would enjoy great success in preventing and curtailing international wars, but it was not assumed that this would be the case since the history of international politics has been dominated by great power conflicts.

Second, there was a concern that if the organization took substantive action against particular great powers, the latter would distance themselves from the United Nations and might actually leave it. Third, the general membership did not want to be directed to contribute troops to a UN force that was opposed by a great power. This would entail large casualties and could actually provoke a world war.

Since 1945 there have been periodic discussions among UN member states concerning the reform of the Security Council, and the two major negotiations were between 1962 and 1963 and 1993 and 1997. The latter negotiations, although unsuccessful with regard to any formal changes to the Charter, were much more far-reaching than the earlier ones. The failure of the 1990s deliberations is often seen as simply a product of the five permanent members' resisting any incursions on their power, but this was not the case. The failure was embedded more in rivalries among other states, especially within regional groupings, than it was in the stone-walling of the major powers—although the permanent five were certainly influential in blocking particular changes. Interestingly, there were important changes in Security Council procedures that did not concern the membership and the voting rules of the Council, and in many ways they can be seen as a kind of a substitute for the failure to agree on membership and voting issues. The purposes of this chapter are to explore the disagreements and accords that occurred in the negotiations over Security Council reform and to reflect on the prominence of different norms in the political design of the Security Council and prospects for change.

ATTEMPTS AT SECURITY COUNCIL REFORM

There were no serious attempts at reform of the Security Council from 1945 through the early 1960s due to the Cold War. The situation changed in the 1960s because of the dramatic increase of members from the developing world (from 50 in 1945 to 114 in 1963). The developing states lobbied vigorously for an increase in the number of nonpermanent members on the Security Council so as to enhance their representation. This led to a decision in 1963 to increase the number of nonpermanent members from six to ten— an amendment that came into force in 1966.[4] There was an agreement among the members of the General Assembly to divide the nonpermanent members on the following basis: five from Africa and Asia, two from Latin America and the Caribbean, one from Eastern Europe, and two from the Western Europe and Others (WEO) grouping. The agreement was made possible significantly by the fact that the addition of new permanent members was basically excluded from the negotiations.

There was a flurry of diplomatic activity concerning membership on the Council in 1979 when India proposed an increase in the nonpermanent members from ten to 14, and the Latin American countries countered with a proposal for an increase to 16. Because these proposals were rejected by all of the P5 except for China, the negotiations did not take off.[5]

The political context surrounding the issue of Security Council reform underwent a major change in the 1990s as a result of the end of the Cold War in 1989 and the dissolution of the Soviet Union in 1991. First, the Western and Eastern European countries increasingly were seen as part of a single new bloc, and their collaboration was perceived as increasing Northern power in the UN Security Council. In the words of a Malaysian representative, the end of the Cold War "in reality brought about a single Europe rather than Western and Eastern Europe."[6] The emergence of greater cooperation among the former Cold War rivals meant that "[d]eveloping states ha[d] less leverage as a result of greater cooperation among the permanents after the Cold War."[7] Second, the UN Security Council began to intervene in civil conflicts more than it had in the past, and the developing countries became very concerned about their relative lack of power to control such interventions by the Council. Third, Germany and Japan took advantage of these general pressures for Security Council reform among developing countries to press their case for permanent membership.

As a result of all these developments, many states began to discuss the need to add both permanent and nonpermanent members to the Council.[8] These sentiments eventuated in the UN General Assembly's establishing the Open-Ended Working Group on the Question of Equitable Representation of and an increase in the Membership of the Security Council and other Matters Related to the Security Council in 1993.[9] Between 1994 and 1997 it submitted several reports that reflected a lack of consensus on the key membership and voting issues (Cluster I issues) and agreement on some procedural questions (Cluster II issues). The culmination was a report with recommendations of reforms by the president of the General Assembly, Razali Ismail of Malaysia, which, however, did not attract strong support from the UN member states. In fact, it provoked strong differences. From 1998 through 2002 the Open-Ended Working Group did not meet formally, but states continued to voice their views on the issues—especially in the General Assembly. There has, in fact, been a remarkable amount of continuity in states' views over the years.[10]

On the matter of the number of new permanent and nonpermanent members, there was a general agreement that the total membership should go from the existing 15 states to between 20 and 26 states—with most countries advocating around 24. Among most countries there was accord that there should be five new permanent members. On the matter of the nonpermanent members, Britain, France, and Russia backed an additional four, but the United States originally did not want to increase the number of nonpermanent members at all. There are indications now that it is willing to entertain an increase of several nonpermanent members. China has been ambiguous on the number of permanent and nonpermanent that should be added.

Most members of the Western Europe and Others (WEO) grouping supported five permanent and three to five nonpermanent members. Eastern European countries generally supported five permanent and four or five nonpermanent. Like the Western European states, they were frequent supporters of Germany and Japan for permanent membership. However, it is noteworthy that Canada, Italy, and Spain all opposed the creation of additional permanent members. The latter two are not receptive to having three permanent members from the European Union (Britain, France, and Germany) while they do not possess this status. Italy put forward a rather unique proposal for ten nonpermanent members: each seat rotating among three states—such that there would be 30 states that would constantly be rotating on and off the Security Council.

The Non-Aligned Movement (NAM), which totals 114 states, backed five permanent and six nonpermanent but was willing to move to 11 nonpermanent members if an accord on permanent members were not possible. The great majority of the small states in the NAM realized that they would probably never be chosen as permanent members, so they were quite happy with the fall-back position of 11 nonpermanent members. The African states supported a formal OAU decision in favor of five permanent and five nonpermanent. The Latin American countries generally did not support particular numbers of new permanent and nonpermanent members. In fact, a good number of them opposed any new permanent members. Brazil, which is by far the largest Latin American country, strongly supported the addition of new permanent members since it anticipated being chosen as the Latin American appointee. It received the backing of Chile and Costa Rica, but Argentina, Uruguay, Colombia, Ecuador, Peru, Guatemala, and Cuba opposed any new permanent members.

The Asian countries adopted quite diverse positions, and very few of them actually supported particular numbers of new permanent and nonpermanent members. India and Japan both called for their selection as permanent members. Pakistan, South Korea, and North Korea strongly opposed the addition of any new permanent members, while it is highly questionable whether China would ever back permanent seats for India and Japan.

The countries that oppose the addition of new permanent members do not constitute a large number of states, but they are important countries in the Latin American, Asian, and the Western European and Other groupings. Also, there is a large number of Third World states associated with the Non-Aligned Movement who see little to be gained by increasing the number of permanent members. On the contrary, they think that they are much more likely to be chosen periodically for Security Council seats if all the additions are in the nonpermanent category.

A second issue is how permanent and nonpermanent members should be chosen. The basic division is whether it should be done by the General

Assembly or by regional groupings (with the General Assembly rubber-stamping the regional decisions). The African group is most supportive of the latter. The biggest potential problem if a proposal for regional rotation of permanent members were approved would be if regional groupings became incapable of reaching a consensus in selecting their regional candidates. Also, the P5 have indicated a real unease with leaving the selection of permanent members to the regional groupings rather than the entire General Assembly membership. Since the increase in the number of nonpermanent members from six to ten in 1966, the regional groupings have chosen the nonpermanent members on the Council, but they, of course, have not exercised the rights of permanent members.[11]

Perhaps the most contentious question in the deliberations over Security Council reform is the veto power. The two major issues are whether the veto power should be curtailed for all permanent members and whether it should be eliminated (or perhaps seriously curtailed) for new permanent members. On the former, the key proposal is that the veto should only be applicable to the use of force or a threat to use force (what are often referred to as Chapter VII issues). This proposal was backed by a large number of participants in the San Francisco conference in 1945. The designated five permanent members opposed restrictions on the scope of the veto in 1945, and they are probably more vehement on this issue now than they were a half a century ago.[12] This is certainly the case with the United States. This same perspective on the scope of the veto is shared by the three most likely additions to the group of permanent members—Germany, Japan, and India.

There are some Western countries that are strongly in favor of limiting the scope of the veto—in particular, Austria, Canada, and Spain—and there is a larger group that opposes the granting of the veto to any new permanent members. This latter group includes Canada, Italy, Spain, New Zealand, and Norway. Several Eastern European countries (Lithuania and Ukraine) want to restrict the scope of the veto for new permanent members. In the Third World grouping, the reservations with regard to the veto become expectedly much more extensive. The Non-Aligned Movement wants to limit the veto to issues concerning the use of force (Chapter VII issues) with the hope of completely eliminating it in the future, and it has also mooted the possibility of requiring two negative votes by permanent members (a double veto) to prevent passage of a resolution. This position has been echoed by the African states. With regard to the Latin American and Caribbean countries, Mexico, Costa Rica, Peru, and Jamaica support the limitation of the veto to issues concerning the use of force, but Brazil, of course, is a strong advocate of new permanent members enjoying equal veto rights with the existing five permanent members. There are several Asian countries (Singapore, Fiji, and the Philippines) that want to limit or exclude veto rights for any new permanent members.

In 1997 the two co-chairpersons of the Open-Ended Working Group conducted a survey of UN members to obtain their views on Council reform, and a substantial majority advocated an increase of both permanent and nonpermanent members. This was followed by a mediation attempt by the General Assembly president, Razali Ismail of Malaysia, who was also chairperson of the Open-Ended Working Group. He put forward a set of proposals that included: 5 new permanent members and four new non-permanent members (bringing the total to 24 states); the selection of all new members by two-thirds of the General Assembly; no veto power for the new permanent members; a request that permanent members limit their vetoes to Chapter VII issues; a requirement of 15 of the 24 votes to pass resolutions; and the maintenance of Article 108 procedures for approving amendments to the Charter (that is, two-thirds of the General Assembly including approval of all permanent members).[13] The Razali proposal might have won the backing of the P5 since the new permanent members would not get the veto power. However, Razali did not provide specific suggestions of what five states should fill the five permanent slots, and the uncertainty on this matter was clearly sufficient to kill the proposal. Of course, if Razali had actually named five states for the permanent seats, this would probably have led to even more negative reactions.

The strongest opponents to the Razali plan were the middle-sized countries that were particularly opposed to regional rivals' being selected for permanent seats and/or thought that their chances of being chosen regularly for nonpermanent seats would be greatly enhanced if all new seats were non-permanent. They formed a group of 16 states known as the Coffee Club that lobbied very actively against new permanent seats. Edward Luck, who participated in the 1997 negotiations, emerged from the deliberations with a profoundly skeptical view of the prospects for future agreement. He spoke of the "profound differences both within regions and within the ranks of the 186 Member States that are not Permanent Members," and he noted that "There is little evidence that the developing countries could present a united front behind a single formula . . . " He then concluded that "[t]he tensions, divisions and distasteful compromises of the last reform drive have left delegations, officials, specialists, and even private foundations with a mighty anti-reform hangover."[14]

Since then very little has changed. A considerable majority of UN members support an increase in permanent and nonpermanent members, but the regional neighbors of some prospective members and some small states oppose the addition of permanent members. The biggest problem relating to new permanent members is not whether they should be created, but who they should be and whether they should be given the veto. Almost all Western countries and some non-Western states back Germany and Japan. However, Russia makes its backing contingent on the inclusion of India, and China has not explicitly supported any state for permanent status. While the developing countries are great protagonists on behalf of adding permanent seats to the Security Council, they are quite divided on which of their number should be chosen. The Africans are divided with regard to Nigeria,

South Africa, and Egypt; many Latin Americans oppose Brazil; and the Asians are often quite ambivalent about India and to a lesser extent Japan. A significant number of states from the regional groupings supported what are called regional rotating seats whereby every two to four years a regional grouping would choose a different member that would exercise the rights of a permanent Security Council member. Apart from the fact that the P5 have voiced reservations about the regional groupings electing permanent members, the value of rotating regional seats would be made rather meaningless if all new permanent members were not given veto powers—and it is very doubtful whether an extension of the full veto rights to new members would obtain the necessary political support.

Along with the identity of new permanent members, the key issue concerning Security Council reform relates to the veto. The states that are the leading candidates for permanent status insist that they have all of the veto powers enjoyed by the P5, while the P5's silence has been deafening. Most developing countries support the extension of equal veto powers to new permanent members, but as is clear from the NAM's fall-back position of adding solely nonpermanent members, their support for the extension of veto powers is soft. A large number of both developing and developed states would actually go for a limitation of the permanent members' veto rights to Chapter VII issues, but the P5 are very unlikely to accept the proposal.[15]

In the short run the most likely formal change in the Security Council is an increase in nonpermanent members, but even this is not particularly likely to occur because of the strong opposition of the main candidates for elevation to permanent seats (for example, Germany, Japan, and India) and their allies. Any progress that occurs is likely to be in the realm of procedural matters concerning issues such as greater transparency, accountability, and regularized communications. Discussions have gone on with regard to these "Cluster II issues" over the past decade, and some important progress has been made. Nonmembers of the Council are increasingly invited to participate in Council meetings—particularly members of the Non-Aligned Movement and contributors to peace-keeping forces. The United States, Britain, and France also consult regularly with Germany and Japan on almost all issues since the latter complained in 1991 about paying for the Gulf War without adequate input into the deliberations. Groups of nonmember states and even NGOs are now brought into negotiations on particular issues of concern to them. These latter talks can now be initiated by one Council member, although on occasion the requests do not receive adequate backing from other members.

Communication between Council and non-Council members has also been enhanced by the distribution of Council agendas and the Council president's briefing of nonmembers and often the media after private Council sessions. It is also important to note that the permanent members are sharing more information with the nonpermanent members of the Council. This communication has been enhanced by holding retreats for all

Council members and the Secretary-General and by Council members' taking trips to problem areas. Progress in spreading and intensifying communications is not an answer to all of the concerns of nonpermanent members, non-Council members, and nongovernmental organizations, but many positive developments have occurred.[16]

Ian Hurd argues that the development of consultation procedures can, in fact, constitute an effective substitute for formal changes in the character of the Council. He notes that "external change need not reduce the Council's effectiveness even in the absence of formal change, as long as the informal practice of the Council adapts to the new environment." He also points out that "the Council's 'effective membership' . . . may be found in the pattern of consultation and opinion-taking outside the formal membership."[17]

INTERNATIONAL DECISION-MAKING NORMS AND SECURITY COUNCIL REFORM

Underlying the characteristics of the UN Security Council and the proposals for reform there lie varied weightings of norms among states. This section will start with a discussion of the nature of the key norms and the main tensions that exist between them, and it will then look at the creation of the Security Council and the reform debates in terms of these norms. The four norms concern: state autonomy, international order, power, and democratic representativeness.

The first norm is the state autonomy norm (or what some might refer to as the sovereignty norm), which has been central to the interstate system since its emergence in the seventeenth century. In the words of Inis Claude, the norm upholds "the rule that every state has an equal voice in international proceedings, and that no state can be bound without its consent."[18] It still has a central status in the international legal order, but it does not have the weight that it once did. A central manifestation of the norm is the rule of unanimity in international organizations which was central to the first global security organization known as the Concert of Europe and was given significant weight in designing the League of Nations. It is because of the continued importance of states' desire to maintain a high degree of autonomy that Robert Keohane has remarked that "Global governance . . . will have to be limited and somewhat shallow if it is to be sustainable."[19]

Another norm is the international order norm, which holds that states should seek to reduce obstacles to the development of international laws and actions by international institutions so as to facilitate the management of their interdependencies. It is seldom articulated clearly in international relations and international law texts, but it does underlie the many incursions into the rule of unanimity. Moreover, "[t]he tension between the imperatives of international interdependence and the quest to retain adequate degrees of national autonomy, appears likely to remain the basic issue of international relationships for some time to come."[20] More related to the design of international institutions is Claude's comment that "the history of international organization is the story of efforts to achieve progressive emancipation from the tradition-based rule of equality and unanimity."[21]

An issue pertaining to the facilitation of international cooperation that has been prominent in global institutions is the size of executive organs such as the UN's Security Council. James Sutterlin commented that "[t]he most forceful argument [for a small Council] and the one that retains its resonance today, was that to be an effective body in dealing with threats to the peace, the Council had to be small and capable of quick decisions."[22] The political problems inherent in promoting expeditious decision-making arrangements in a world of 191 states should not be underestimated.

The third norm can be termed the power (or effectiveness) norm. It is associated mainly with two propositions. First, legally binding decisions of international bodies as well as international laws should require the support of those states whose backing will secure their implementation. Second, voting arrangements should reflect the distribution of resources in the issue area. In the case of global security organizations, this means, first and foremost, that organization actions should enjoy the support, or at least not suffer the opposition, of any of the major military powers, and the major military powers should be able to block organizational actions. Claude remarks that equal voting power "makes for unrealism by masking the tremendous differences in the capacities, resources, interests, and involvements of states, and bestows upon lesser states a disproportionate influence in international agencies which discourages powers whose role is thus artificially minimized from taking the agencies seriously or entrusting important functions to them."[23] The requirement of unanimity for decisions of the Concert of Europe and the requirement of support by the permanent members of the League Council (minus an accused aggressor) for the identification of an aggressor state are examples of the power norm in early global security institutions. There are actually several ways that a strategic influence for great powers can be built into international institutions: selective representation on executive bodies, special majorities, and weighted voting. In our present era there is seldom strong support for weighted voting schemes—especially where there is no clear consensus on criteria for distributing votes.[24]

The next norm that is often juxtaposed against the power norm is *the democratic representativeness norm*, which means that international organization decisions and international laws should have broad support from the international society of states. This does not necessarily mean that a two-thirds or simple majority of the states must give their explicit support, but that the backing of a large group of the general membership is required for organization decisions. The tension between the power and democratic representativeness norms is very clear.

It is now valuable to reflect on the decision-making structure of the Security Council and the reform proposals in the light of these norms. First, an important stipulation in the UN Charter that supports the state autonomy norm is that states are not obligated to provide troops to UN forces unless they make a commitment to do so beforehand. There is, however, an important limitation on the state autonomy norm in the Charter that member states are obligated to comply with Security Council resolutions. This having been said, there are not likely to be more than very small groups of states that are strongly opposed to Security Council resolutions that enjoy the support of nine Council members and no negative votes by a permanent member. The actual likelihood now or in the near future that the Security Council will approve resolutions that are opposed by even a modest number of UN member states is not great, and therefore states are satisfied with the de facto protection of their autonomy offered by UN voting rules. Overall there are not likely to be any important incursions into the state autonomy norm in future Security Council reform.

Second, pertinent to the international order norm, the founding states of the United Nations, in fact, did little in 1945 to reduce the traditional barriers to collaboration. In particular, they carried over the veto power of the great powers from the League Council to the Security Council. There has been some pressure recently to reduce the scope of the veto for permanent members of the Council, but such changes (particularly concerning non-Chapter VII issues) are very unlikely because of P5 opposition.

Important issues in facilitating effective cooperation in the Security Council have been maintaining the modest size of the membership (now 15) and the small number of members with the veto power. Today preventing a significant increase in the total membership and the number of permanent members remains a real concern for many states. To quote the present Canadian ambassador to the UN: "adding vetoes would only make the Council more sclerotic. It would be the equivalent of pouring cement into the UN motor."[25] It has certainly been the case since the end of the Cold War that the small group of permanent members has made major efforts, first, to seek consensuses among themselves and between them and interested parties and, second, not to push for debates that would engender verbal battles that would hinder long-term collaboration. In part because of their small number they have been able to reduce the level of verbal and behavioral hostility in the United Nations, even if it is difficult to recognize at times.[26] The problems accompanying an increase in permanent members should not necessarily lead to a rejection of new members, but they should give states pause before jumping into adding a significant number of new Council members—especially permanent members with vetoes.

Third, the provisions concerning the Security Council have always given primacy to the power norm in that the P5 have a blanket veto power over all substantive resolutions. One cannot stress strongly enough how important this norm is in understanding what the Security Council is and what it can be. The veto power of the P5 states assures that when Security Council resolutions are approved, they have the backing of the P5 states, and it also assures that the P5 states are not alienated from the UN because the Security

Council takes action against them.[27] The arguments for an increase in the number of permanent Security Council members have focused in part on the desirability of the Security Council's ability to draw on the resources of other powerful states (especially Japan and Germany), but there is not enough concern with this problem to sustain a consensus on the expansion of permanent members. This is in part due to the fact that the major candidates for permanent seats have been brought into special consultation arrangements with the P5 on most Security Council agenda items.

Fourth, the major impetus for discussions on Security Council reform since the early 1990s has concerned the issue of the democratic representativeness of the Council membership. The Third World states have exerted considerable pressure for expansion of the Council and permanent seats, and they remain the major force for reform. Quite a few observers have also stressed that the future of the Council and the UN more broadly depends on expanding Council membership. One commented: "If the interests of the majority of member states are not more adequately represented than is now the case, it is unlikely that they will, over the long run, comply with the Council's decisions."[28] The Carnegie Commission Final Report on Preventing Deadly Conflict noted: "Every year that the Security Council continues with its present structure, the UN suffers because the increasingly apparent lack of representativeness of the Council membership diminishes its credibility and weakens its capacity for conflict prevention."[29] The main progress in recent years in promoting democratic representativeness has occurred through improving consultation between the permanent and non-permanent members of the Council and between Council members and both non-Council members and nongovernmental organizations. It is precisely in this area that progress is likely to occur in the short run.

CONCLUSION

The failure of efforts to reform the membership and voting rules of the Security Council has not been a simple product of the refusal of the five permanent members to give up power to emerging great powers and the broader UN membership. They have refused to countenance a diminution of the scope of the veto power for themselves, and their future support for the traditional veto powers for new permanent members is certainly in question. Still, some compromises on the veto powers for new permanent members might be feasible in the future. This would probably involve some additional categories of Security Council members, and while it might be very difficult to secure their acceptance, it is not out of the question.

Contrary to the perceptions of most observers, differences among members of regional groupings and the broader UN membership have been much more important in undermining Security Council reform. Regional rivalries on the selection of permanent members pose major obstacles to an accord, and the lack of interest among large numbers of countries in adding new permanent members because they cannot aspire to permanent seats is another huge hurdle. In light of these obstacles, the best chances at the moment for diffusing influence in the UN Security Council lie with enriching the network of consultation that includes a deep concern by the permanent members to take the views of the nonpermanent members of the Council as well as the general UN membership seriously.

The central normative issue on the reform agenda is democratic representativeness. The UN membership has gone from 50 to 191 states in 58 years, and it is crucial to give the large number of non-Western countries greater input in global security deliberations. This is most likely to come in the short run from the promotion of greater consultation, accountability, and transparency. In the longer run progress is more likely to take the form of permanent seats (possibly without a veto power) and more nonpermanent seats.

Progress in giving "power" its proper role in the UN Security Council is as much a matter of informal practice as it is of ascribed legal powers. The countries that possess resources comparable to present permanent members should be involved in almost all major security issues in order to secure their active participation and financial contributions. In addition, a case needs to be made, and accepted, that a just and reasonable distribution of power generally does not require the bestowal of permanent seats with full veto rights—with the exception of a few very powerful countries. New innovative ways must be found of enhancing the influence of important states and groups of states without giving these states the authority to block Council decisions.

Related to giving proper consideration to power relatives is the normative issue of shaping international decision-making structures such that they contribute to international order. Failures to realize an enhancement of the influence of both the general UN membership and those important powers not on the Council can pose obstacles to international collaboration. It is going to take some very imaginative statesmen skilled in architectural design to steer through the obstacles of strong concerns for democratic legitimacy and the mobilization of power behind international regimes. The challenges are increased by the fact that there is constant change in the distribution of power resources and in the weight that is attached to ideational values. If the adage "the best is often the enemy of the good" is an appropriate way of portraying a political problems, Security Council reform is clearly such a problem.[30]

NOTES

* I thank Alexandra Fraser for research assistance and Sam Daws, Ian Hurd, Edward Luck, David Malone, Richard Price, and Ramesh Thakur for comments and information. I would also like to thank Brian Job, the director of the UBC

Centre of International Relations, and Steven Lee and the staff of the Canadian Centre for Policy Development for assistance and support.

1. Inis L. Claude, *Swords into Plowshares: The Problems and Progress of International Organization,* 3rd ed. (New York: Random House, 1964), 15–50.
2. Claude, 51–73, 133–173; Ruth B. Russell with Jeanette Muther, *A History of the United Nations Charter: The Role of the United States* (Washington, DC: Brookings, 1958), 713–749.
3. Claude, *Swords,* 133–147; Bardo Fassbender, *UN Security Council Reform and the Right of Veto: A Constitutional Perspective* (The Hague: Kluwer Law International, 1998), 165–168; Russell, *A History of the United Nations Charter,* 440–477, 646–687, 713–749; Townsend Hoopes and Douglas Brinkley, *FDR and the Creation of the U.N.* (New Haven: Yale University Press, 1997).
4. United Nations, General Assembly Resolution 1991A (XVIII), (December 17, 1963).
5. Fassbender, 222.
6. Fassbender, 199–200.
7. Sam Daws, "Seeking Seats, Votes, and Vetoes," *The World Today* (October 1997): 256.
8. Sidney Bailey and Sam Daws, *The Procedure of the UN Security Council,* 3rd ed. (Oxford: Clarendon, 1998), 384; Bruce Russett, Barry O'Neill, and James S. Sutterlin, "Breaking the Restructuring Logjam," in *The Once and Future Security Council* Bruce Russett, ed., (New York: St. Martin's, 1997), 155; David Malone, *Decision-Making in the UN Security Council: The Case of Haiti, 1990–1997* (Oxford: Clarendon, 1998), 7–36.
9. United Nations General Assembly Resolution 48/26 (1993).
10. The information on the positions of states is derived from UN documents pertaining to the work of the Open-Ended Working Group; Edward C. Luck, *Reforming the United Nations: Lessons from a History of Progress* (New Haven, CT: Academic Council on the United Nations System, 2003), 13–16, 50–51; and Fassbender, 221–275. The key UN documents are: A/48/264 (1993) and Adds. 1, 2, 3, and 4; A/48/47 (1994); A/49/47 (1995); A/49/465 (1996); A/49.965 (1995); A/50/47 (1996), A/51/24 (1997). The 1997 Razali proposal can be found at: http://globalpolicy.org/security/reform/raz-497.htm.
11. David Malone, "Eyes on the Prize: The Quest for Non-Permanent Seats on the UN Security Council," *Global Governance* 6 (2000): 3–24.
12. Russell, *The History of the United Nations Charter,* 713–749.
13. UN doc. A/AC/.247/1997/CRP.1 (1997); Fassbender, 237; Bailey and Daws, *The Procedure of the UN Security Council,* 385; Daws, "Seeking Seats, Votes, and Vetoes," 256–259.
14. Luck, 50–51.
15. Daws, "Seeking Seats, Votes and Vetoes," 256–259; Fassbender, 165, 244, 263.
16. Bailey and Daws, *The Procedure of the UN Security Council,* 382–412; Malone, *Decision-Making in the UN Security Council,* pp. 31–34; Luck,

13–16; Ian Hurd, "Security Council Reform: Informal Membership and Practice," *The Once and Future Security Council* in Bruce Russett, ed., (New York: St. Martin's, 1997), 135–150; Harold von Riekhoff, *Canada and the United Nations Security Council, 1999–2000—A Reassessment* (Ottawa: Canadian Centre for Foreign Policy Development, Department of Foreign Affairs and International Trade, June 2002), 10–16.

17. Hurd, 137.
18. Claude, 112.
19. Robert O. Keohane, "Governance in a Partially Globalized World," APSA Presidential Address (2000), 7.
20. C. Fred Bergsten, Georges Berthoin and Kinhide Mushakoji, *The Reform of International Institutions* (New York: Trilateral Commission, 1976), 2.
21. Claude, 113.
22. James S. Sutterlin, "The Past as Prologue," in *The Once and Future Security Council* Bruce Russett, ed., (New York: St. Martin's, 1997), 4.
23. Claude, 113.
24. Stephen Zamora, "Voting in International Economic Organizations," *American Journal of International Law* 74 (1980): 590–595.
25. Paul Heinbecker, "Statement by Ambassador Paul Heinbecker to the UN General Assembly on November 16, 2000," 3. www.un.int/canada/html/s-16novheinbecker2.htm.
26. Daws, "Seeking Seats, Votes, and Vetoes," 256–259; Russett, O'Neill, and Sutterlin, "Breaking the Restructuring Logjam," 158; Malone, "When Bush Says 'Charge'!."
27. Daws, "Seeking Seats, Votes and Vetoes," 256–259.
28. Sutterlin, "The Past as Prologue," 10.
29. Quoted in Klaus Schlichmann, "A Draft on Security Council Reform," *Peace and Change* 24 (4) (October 1999): 14.
30. See also W. Andy Knight, "The Future of the UN Security Council: Questions of Legitimacy and Representation in Multilateral Governance" in *Enhancing Global Governance: Towards a New Diplomacy?* Andrew Cooper, John English and Ramesh Thakur, eds. (Tokyo: UNU Press, 2002), 19–37; Bruce Russett, "Ten Balances for Weighing UN Reform Proposals," in *The Once and Future Security Council* Bruce Russett, ed. (New York: St. Martin's, 1997), 14–26.

Chapter 14

The UN, Regional Organizations, and Regional Conflict: Is There a Viable Role for the UN?

Brian L. Job*

Introduction

By the mid-1990s the demands and perils of "second generation" peace-keeping missions threatened to overwhelm the United Nations. Lacking the necessary institutional capabilities, unable to muster the political will of members, and reeling from failed missions in Africa and Yugoslavia, the Secretary-General issued a call for regional organizations to assume a larger role in peace operations. Invoking the Charter's Chapter VIII mandate for regional organizations to contribute to peace enforcement, he envisaged a division of labor based on a capability–legitimacy relationship—regional organizations providing the manpower and the UN providing legitimacy by retaining its sole authority to sanction any use of force. Indeed, from the mid-1990s onward, the number of UN peace operations and associated personnel dropped dramatically with a corresponding rise in the number and level of non-UN missions.

However, the results of this shift were decidedly mixed. Not surprisingly, as regional institutional capacities varied so did the effectiveness of regionalized peace operations. In Africa, conditions throughout the decade deteriorated rather than improved, despite and in instances because of regional institutional engagement. In recent years the UN has sought to redress these failings by reengaging in regional peace operations. However, what was also lost during this period was the perceived "value" of UN legitimacy in the capability-legitimacy relationship. With the UN relegated to the sidelines, states and regional organizations increasingly no longer perceived the necessity of gaining prior UN sanction before undertaking the use of force. Today, therefore, the UN finds itself at a crossroads: Whether or not it retains a substantial role in regional peace operations and multilateral force deployment is uncertain—much is dependent on the policies and actions of the major powers, particularly the United States.

The chapter begins by exposing the ambivalent relationship between regional organizations and the UN established in the Charter. It proceeds next to highlight the manner in which the Secretary-General sought to recast this relationship in light of the dilemmas confronting the UN as the "new world order" collapsed. The record of peace operations is reviewed, noting the three phases of peace operations of the 1990s. Finally, considerable attention is devoted to analyzing the viability of the tradeoffs inherent in a capability-legitimacy "bargain" between the UN and regional organizations. In this regard, the future for the UN is clouded, dependent upon developing effective "hybrid" arrangements with regional institutions and upon its capacity to overcome the erosion of its role as the sole legitimizing agency for the use of force in the international order.

THE CHARTER

Drawn up over 50 years ago, the UN Charter is a document of its time. Reflecting the tensions between advocates of globalism and regionalism, as advanced by the United States and European states respectively,[1] the drafters of the Charter sought an institutional formula that both facilitated, but at the same time delimited, the role of regional organizations in conflict management, especially involving military force.[2] On the one hand the Charter (Article 24) vests responsibility for maintenance of peace and security and the ability to authorize the use of force by states in the Security Council, which is controlled through the veto power by its permanent five members. But on the other hand, Article 51, by guaranteeing states' rights to act in self-defense or in "collective self-defense," opens the door for regional organizations to use force to defend member states without prior UN authorization.

Article 52 goes on to further support the security responsibilities of regional organizations by stipulating that nothing in the Charter should preclude the "existence of regional arrangements or agencies for dealing with such matters relating to the maintenance of international peace and security as are appropriate for regional action." Thus, regional organizations enter into the Charter's architecture, as indicated above, through the sanctioning of the use of force for defensive purposes but also through the drafters' desire for a division of labor between the UN and other institutions. Article 33 calls for the parties to any dispute to "first of all seek solutions through negotiation, [etc. including] . . . resort to regional agencies or other arrangements," before bringing a dispute to the Security Council. However, in a reiteration of Article 24, the use of force by regional organizations is not to be undertaken without informing the Council of its plans (Article 54) or without obtaining the advance authorization of the Security Council (Article 53).[3]

The Charter, therefore, left unresolved key issues of responsibility regarding how regional organizations were to relate to the UN. Indeed, there is no definition in the Charter as to what qualifies as a regional organization, nor has any formal, regularized context been established for UN-regional organization consultation.[4] With regard to the critical questions of capability and legitimacy, the drafters' envisaged an institution with its own capacity to undertake military action. Certainly they did not anticipate the nature of subsequent conflicts and the exigencies of peace management operations. As for the necessity to gain legitimacy for the use of force through UN approval, the Charter's ambiguity was purposeful, reflecting the tension between states' individual demands to preserve their sovereignty and right to protect themselves (through collective defense if possible) and their desire to create an institution with sufficient moral and material weight to prevent aggression by any of their number.

THE RECORD: THE UN AS PEACE-KEEPER TO THE MID-1990S

The absence of a "lasting and well-defined relationship . . . between the UN and regional organizations" was not of particular consequence during the ensuing decades of the Cold War.[5] Apart from the alliances of NATO and the Warsaw Pact, regional organizations, such as the OAS, played minor roles in international affairs. All except the Nonaligned Movement, which never jelled into effective operational institutions, were dominated by the United States and the Union of Soviet Socialist Republics. Regional conflicts were managed by the major powers, which promoted their geopolitical advantage. When it was in their interests to resolve conflicts in the South, UN peace-keeping forces (mainly manned and managed by nonmajor power Northern states) were interposed between the fighting parties. These "traditional" UN peace-keeping operations, established to monitor arranged cease-fire agreements, operated according to principles of impartiality and nonengagement and non-use of force.[6] Regional institutions were not involved. Neither the capability nor the legitimacy of these missions was at issue—in part because UN deployments were invited by the state(s) concerned and, under Chapter VI mandates, could only use force if attacked.[7]

While this style of peace-keeping was effective within narrowly defined parameters, it was not applicable to the prototypical intrastate conflict of the 1980s—conflicts in increasing numbers and complexities involving non-state actors, weak states, and polarized societies. However, instead of devising any new mode of response to these conflicts, the UN simply undertook "de facto suspensions of PKOs."[8] Indeed, no new UN operations were mounted for the entire decade of 1978 to 1988. A variety of factors can be blamed: Lack of interest on the part of North for war-ridden Southern states, preoccupation of the superpowers with their own relations, lack of political will by UN members, and reluctance on the part of the P5 to collaborate in the Security Council. Significantly, regional organizations did not step up to respond to conflicts in their own neighborhoods.

All of this changed with the ending of the Cold War. An invigorated Security Council, no longer a prisoner of the ideologically determined veto, took up the challenges presented by the "new wars," that is, intrastate conflicts that destroyed governments, economies, and civilian life in the Balkans, the former Soviet Union, and Africa. With the backing of its permanent members as expressed through Chapter VII mandates and the deployment of their own troops—especially by the United States—the UN launched operations of unprecedented numbers and scope. Thus, in the first phase of post–Cold War peace-keeping, between 1989 and 1993, 15 UN missions were undertaken. At their height, over 78,000 troops were involved. However, the perils and failures of these "second generation" peace-keeping missions were too soon brought home. This was especially so for the United States, whose commitment to participation within the UN context was yet very new. The consequence was a shift in policy in Washington, London, Paris, and other Western capitals.

A DIVISION OF RESPONSIBILITY: THE UN
AND REGIONAL ORGANIZATIONS

Early in the 1990s, the Secretary-General realized that the UN was in an increasingly untenable position. Its institutional capabilities to organize and supervise peace missions were woefully inadequate to deal with the demands of regional conflicts. Its key members, frustrated by conflicts resistant to settlement and dangerous to their peace-keeping troops, were becoming unwilling to take on new missions or to support robust mandates for those that they did. Thus, in his 1992 *Agenda for Peace* statement, the Secretary-General turned to regional organizations for support, advocating "regional action as a matter of decentralization, delegation, and cooperation with the United Nations . . . [to] not only lighten the burden of the Council but also contribute to a deeper sense of participation, consensus, and democratization in international affairs."[9] However, no particular steps were taken in this direction.[10]

By 1995, the situation had become very serious, the tragic experiences of Somalia, Rwanda, and Bosnia having exposed the limitations of the UN and eroded its moral authority and legitimacy. In response, Boutros-Ghali reinforced his call to regional organizations. In his *Supplement to An Agenda for Peace* he outlined five forms of possible cooperation between the UN and regional organizations: consultation, diplomatic support, operational support, codeployment, and joint operations. With "operational support," the Secretary-General looked to regional organizations backing up UN operations, for example, NATO's provision of air support for UNPROFOR in Bosnia. "Codeployment" described missions in which "the regional organization carries the main burden but a small United Nations operation supports it," as in Liberia with ECOWAS and in Georgia with the CIS. "Joint operations" were to involve missions in which a regional organization and the UN shared the staffing, direction, and financing of an operation, for example, as the UN and the OAS did in Haiti.[11]

The Secretary-General, in effect, advanced the notion of a division of labor for UN-regional organization peace enforcement. Regional organizations were to provide the manpower (and indeed the financing), while the Security Council was to authorize, establish mandates, and oversee operations. In other words in exchange for capabilities, the UN would provide legitimacy.[12] The Secretary-General thus attempted to reinvigorate the provisions of Chapter VIII, mandating regional organizations to respond to regional conflicts with the Security Council sustaining its primary role in authorizing any use of force.

However, while such an arrangement appeared tenable in principle, the practical details of how it could be operationalized were never clarified. The Secretary-General glossed over these, stating that "the division of labour must be clearly defined and agreed in order to avoid overlap and institutional rivalry" but acknowledging that "political, operational and financial aspects of the arrangement [could] give rise to questions of some delicacy."[13]

THE RECORD OF THE 1990S

The first notable impact of the disillusionment with UN peace-keeping was the withdrawal from UN peace operations by the major powers and the Northern middle-power states. Table 14.1 illustrates this. In 1992 five of the

Table 14.1   Top ten country contributors of personnel to UN missions: 1992, 1997, 2002

	1992		1997		2002	
	Country	Personnel deployed	Country	Personnel deployed	Country	Personnel deployed
1	France	6,175	Poland	1,084	Pakistan	4,677
2	U.K.	3,756	Bangladesh	1,025	Bangladesh	4,211
3	Canada	3,216	Austria	831	Nigeria	3,277
4	Netherlands	2,016	Finland	780	India	2,746
5	Indonesia	1,988	Ghana	776	Ghana	2,219
6	Ghana	1,970	Ireland	733	Kenya	1,841
7	Poland	1,867	Norway	724	Uruguay	1,651
8	Nepal	1,841	Argentina	667	Jordan	1,620
9	Pakistan	1,812	Nepal	661	Ukraine	1,159
10	India	1,749	United States	644	Australia	940
	United States (#35)	461			United States (#18)	631
Total		52,308		14,879		39,652

Sources:
1992: Stockholm International Peace Research Institute, *SPIRI Yearbook 1993*, p. 61. Figures as of November 1992.
1997: "Troop and Other Personnel Contributions to Peacekeeping Operations: 1997," *Global Policy Forum*. Figures as of December 1997. Available at http://www.globalpolicy.org/security/peacekpg/data/pkotrp97.htm.
2002: "Monthly Summary of Contributions," United Nations Department of Peacekeeping Operations (DPKO). Figures as of December 2002. Available at http://www.un.org/Depts/dpko/dpko/contributors/Dec2002Countrysummary.pdf.

top ten state contributors to UN missions were Northern countries, two of these P5 states. By 2002, with the exception of Australia (in tenth spot with its contribution to the East Timor mission) and the Ukraine, no Northern state was among the top ten. UN peace-keeping missions over the course of the 1990s, with the exception of those in the Balkans, became and have remained Southern state operations.

Note, however, that there was not a general withdrawal from international peace operations by the United States, Canada, and the Europeans. There was instead a shunning of the UN and a turning to regional organizations and ad hoc "coalitions of the willing." As seen in Table 14.2, from 1994 onwards the number of ongoing, non-UN missions increased sharply; in fact after 1997 less than half of total operations were conducted by the UN. Especially dramatic was the shift in the level of effort born by key regional organizations, as set out in Table 14.2. In 1993 only 14 percent of the personnel engaged in peace operations were in non-UN-authorized missions, but within two years this level of effort was completely reversed.[14] Since 1995 personnel in "coalitions of the willing" and regional organization operations made up no less than 60 percent of the total, this figure reaching 81 percent in 1998. The division of peace-keeping labor in literal terms was transformed (in line with the Secretary-General's proposed bargain), with the UN playing a secondary role throughout this second phase of 1990s peace operations.

Figure 14.1 highlights this by displaying the aggregate levels of annual personnel commitments in UN and UN-authorized missions versus those in CIS/ Russian, NATO, and ECOWAS missions. The striking feature of this chart is the decline through the 1990s of the size and scope of UN missions,[15]

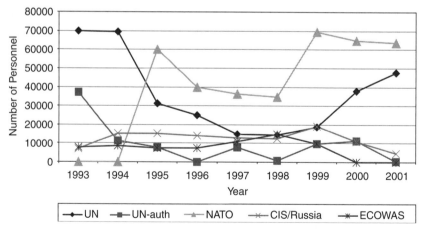

Figure 14.1 UN and regional organization peace operations, 1993–2001: numbers of personnel by type of mission.

Source: See Table 14.2.

Table 14.2 UN and Regional Organization Peace Operations, 1993–2001: numbers of missions and numbers of personnel committed

Year/organization	1993		1994		1995		1996		1997		1998		1999		2000		2001	
	#	Personnel	#	Personnel	#	Personnel	#	Personnel	#	Personnel	#	Personnel	#	Personnel	#	Personnel	#	Personnel
United Nations	20	69,961 See Note	20	69,376	24	31,096	26	24,947	25	14,907	21	14,504	24	18,572	22	37,900	18	47,402
UN-authorized missions	1	c. 37,000	2	11,189	1	7,797	0	–	2	7,925	1	800	1	9,900	1	11,285	1	200
NATO	0	–	1	–	1	60,000	1	40,000	1	36,300	2	34,800	4	69,300	2	64,700	4	63,493
WEU/EU	1	152	1	173	1	211	2	391	1	241	2	407	3	433	3	264	3	182
OSCE	5	49	4	35	10	72	11	78	12	78	14	1,171	13	2,444	12	2,708	13	1,514
CIS/Russia	3	c. 6,948	4	c. 15,500	4	7,400	4	c. 17,900	4	c. 12,350	4	12,636	4	18,928	4	11,028	3	4,577
OAU	0	–	1	47	1	65	1	1	2	20	2	23	3	38	3	–	3	62
ECOWAS	1	c. 8,000	1	8,430	1	7,269	1	7,500	1	11,000	3	14,912	3	9,600	0	–	0	–
Other	3	2,234	5	2,667	4	2,212	3	1,941	6	2,400	9	2,975	6	2,379	6	2,185	6	3,551
Total	34	124,295	47	107,370	49	116,132	53	92,753	58	85,221	58	82,228	61	131,632	55	130,074	51	120,981
Non-UN Total	14	54,334	18	37,994	23	85,036	28	67,806	37	70,314	37	67,724	37	113,060	33	92,174	33	73,579
Non-UN Total as %		43%		35%		73%		73%		82%		82%		86%		71%		61%
Non-UN, Non-UN Auth. Total	13	17,334	16	26,805	22	77,239	24	67,806	26	62,389	36	66,924	36	103,160	32	80,889	32	73,379
Non-UN, Non-UN Auth. Total as % of Total		14%		26%		66%		73%		73%		81%		78%		62%		61%

Note: Figures in the left column for each year indicate total number of missions. Figures in the right hand column for each year indicate the total number of troops, military police, and civilian police assigned to these missions.

Source: Adapted from Appendix 2A, Multilateral peace missions in annually published SIPRI Yearbook series, 1993–2002, refer to Stockholm International Peace Research Institute, *SIPRI Yearbook 1993–2002: Armaments, Disarmament, and International Security* (New York: Oxford University Press, 1993–2002).

counterbalanced by the rise in NATO-led missions, as well as the increase through to 1998 of ECOWAS operations.

Three regional actors assumed key roles during this second phase of peace operations, each seeking to preserve stability within their neighborhoods. Thus, NATO committed itself to major missions in the former Yugoslavia following the 1995 Dayton Accords. The CIS sought to keep the lid on the former Soviet empire with its operations throughout the decade in Tajikistan, Moldova, and Georgia. In western Africa, ECOWAS, through its interventions in the civil wars of Liberia (1990), Sierra Leone (1991), and Guinea-Bassau (1998), established itself as the primary peace enforcement instrument on that continent. It must be noted, however, that in each case the activities of these regional institutions were largely orchestrated by and designed to advance the interests of single hegemonic states. Thus, NATO was mobilized when the United States chose to act concerning the Balkans. Russia dominated all CIS missions, and ECOWAS served as the vehicle for Nigeria to exercise its sphere of influence.[16]

DILEMMAS OF THE CAPABILITY–LEGITIMACY BARGAIN

Regional Differences and Disparities

From the perspective of institutional capabilities, no common set of relationships across regions has emerged in terms of either the nature of UN-regional organization relations or the success of different arrangements in achieving effective results.

Of all regions only in Europe has an effective subsidiarity relationship between the UN and regional organizations evolved.[17] Over the course of the 1990s, European institutions displaced the UN. Following the failure of UN missions in the former Yugoslavia, all militarily robust peace enforcement responsibilities have since been assumed by NATO. Conflict prevention activities, defusing of minority tensions, etc. in Europe have become the purview of the OSCE, leaving the UN with a minor role in monitoring and peace-building missions.[18]

Regarding Africa the record is quite different. Neither the UN nor regional organizations, separately or in tandem, achieved much success in peace operations. In notable instances the UN failed to act; in others UN missions were undertaken with weak mandates and undelivered resources. Nor was the UN able to devolve responsibility for peace-keeping to regional institutions. The OAU, hobbled by constitutional prescriptions against intervention in member states and lacking institutional and financial resources, was constrained to conducting small monitoring and good office activities.[19] By default African subregional organizations ECOWAS and, to a limited extent, SADC emerged over the years as the primary vehicles for conflict management operations. However, ECOWAS's two major missions in Liberia and Sierra Leone were reduced to failure as well, with regional states unable to set aside their competing interests despite or because of Nigeria's strong leadership.[20] The International Peace Academy in its 2002 review offered the following bleak assessment: "These [sub-regional] mechanisms . . . reveal profound institutional weaknesses. . . . All of Africa's subregional organizations lack the financial, logistical and military resources to undertake effective military intervention."[21]

The Americas, on the other hand, living in what is generally regarded as a "zone of peace" have seen very few peace missions. Cooperation between the UN and the OAS has facilitated a variety of initiatives to calm crises and sustain peace, including observer missions for Central America and El Salvador in the early 1990s and more recently between Ecuador and Peru. The only major deployment of UN-authorized forces was in Haiti (UNMIH from 1991–96). However here, in conditions of violent civil conflict, weak state capacity, and repressive regime holders, attempts at peace enforcement by external actors proved dangerous, expensive, and largely futile—reminiscent in many ways of experiences in Africa.

With the exception of its historically large missions in Cambodia, the UN's traditional absence from Asia was maintained. Similarly, in the Middle East and in South Asia, no headway was made by either the UN or any regional initiative towards resolving their respective longstanding disputes.

The overall record has engendered substantial debate as to the relative merits of peace operations mounted by regional or subregional organizations as opposed to the UN. The distinctive characteristics of regional contexts mitigates against drawing easy generalizations. The oft-cited advantages ascribed to regionally-based institutions and actors (that is, lower costs due to proximity, ease of communication in terms of language, cultural sensitivity, local knowledge, interoperability, and direct interest in achieving a settlement to avoid spill-over effects) are both reinforced and contradicted by experience.[22]

On the other side of the coin, tendencies toward partiality and conflict of interest pervade subregional contexts and inhibit cooperation. States within a neighborhood may intervene to advance their own agendas or regional status (as has been claimed regarding Nigeria's mobilization of ECOWAS in Liberia and Sierra Leone[23]) or shy away from engagement for fear of offending or alienating a regional partner (as was seen in ASEAN states unwillingness to come forward in the East Timor crisis[24]). Interoperability, often advanced as an advantage of regional organizations, has proved to be an illusive goal even in a mission as well-resourced as NATO's 1999 Kosovo campaign.

In the final analysis, effective operational capacity comes down to financial and human resources. And, on this dimension, the disparities among regions and regional institutions are profound. Viewed in relative terms, Europe's successful peace management, for instance, is unsurprising. NATO's military budget for 2001 (paid in full) was USD 716 million; the OSCE's 2001 budget for missions and field activities was USD 156 million. In contrast, the OAU's total budget was about USD 30 million with most states in arrears and with peace operations in the OAU and ECOWAS funded on a voluntary basis.[25]

Legitimacy

It is not unexpected that legitimacy has become an increasingly problematic element in UN and regional organization relationships' peace management activities. The premise that regional organizations "with capacity but without global legitimacy" (to use McKenzie's terms describing NATO[26]) would condition their peace operations upon UN approval did not hold. While states continue to seek and value legitimation for their actions through multilateral institutions, and while the UN continues to be perceived as the primary source of such legitimization, Security Council approval is no longer regarded as a prerequisite to action in the international system.

Three trends have become apparent: First, major powers in particular have taken to acting pending formal UN legitimization. In circumstances where a state perceives its regional interests at risk or where the destruction of civilian life captures the attention of its domestic public, it will intervene forcefully and unilaterally to restore order. Usually upon doing so it then looks to the UN or a regional organization to follow on with a multilateral mission. One might term this a "leading and leaving" strategy, for example as in U.K. intervention in Sierra Leone, the U.S.-led war in Afghanistan,[27] and the U.S. coalition action against Iraq.

Second, states are increasingly satisfied to substitute the approval of regional or subregional organizations for UN legitimization of their actions. In this regard Katharina Coleman advances the idea of a "legitimacy pyramid," with UN Security Council sanction being at the top as the most desirable status to achieve.[28] Having decided to proceed with a peace enforcement action, states will seek to attain the highest "level" of legitimacy that they can. With UN approval viewed as unlikely or long delayed, states turn instead for sanction to regional or, if necessary, subregional organizations. For example, for the campaign in Kosovo, NATO endorsement was invoked when UN approval proved impossible to attain. Nigerian-led initiatives in Liberia proceeded through ECOWAS. SADC sanctioned peace operations in Lesotho and Zimbabwe. In both Africa and Europe analysts have noted "forum shopping" strategies by states who, determined to act, desire a "fig leaf" of justification from some multilateral body.[29]

Third, the strategy of seeking "retroactive legitimation" is becoming increasingly prevalent. States or regional organizations act, then look to the UN for its seal of approval. While the most controversial, recent action of this sort was NATO's campaign against Kosovo in the absence of a Security Council resolution; this is not a new strategy.[30] The Kosovo war action, however, was of particular importance because: (1) the United States was seen to have evaded the Security Council; (2) the methods employed were controversial; and (3) the cause for which force was deployed was seen by Western publics, but not Southern counterparts, to be just.[31]

Finally, the consequence of the above factors, reinforced by feelings of abandonment by the international community, is that African states have come to regard the UN as irrelevant to legitimization of regional peace enforcement operations.[32] Thus, ECOWAS explicitly refused to include requirements that its new Mechanism for Conflict Prevention either inform the UN or seek its approval for its undertakings.[33]

A THIRD PHASE: UN REENGAGEMENT IN HYBRID PEACE OPERATIONS

Thus, throughout the 1990s two parallel dangers arose to confront the UN. On the one hand, to the extent that regional organizations tended not to engage the UN in peace support missions, the UN became a less relevant actor in what the Charter drafters had envisaged as a primary responsibility—overseeing the use of force. On the other hand, to the extent that the UN became a court of last resort for intractable conflicts, the institution was left to "pick up the pieces" after regional and subregional institutions or ad hoc coalitions of states had failed, the UN faced the prospect of frustration and failure because of its own lack of resources and the absence of supportive regional contexts.

It is the latter that one fears in the UN's reengagement in Africa over the last several years. As the wars of Central Africa and Western Africa broadened to encompass regional neighbors and to ravage the lives of larger and larger proportions of the continent's civilian populations, the UN could not continue to stand aloof. However, nor could the organization mount on its own a sufficiently effective response. Thus, it has been forced to rely on willing major powers (the U.K. in Sierra Leone and France in the Ivory Coast, for instance) and to collaborate with regional organizations to cobble together its missions in Sierra Leone and more recently the Democratic Republic of the Congo. (This accounts for the sharp upturn in UN mission personnel numbers shown in Table 14.2 and Figure 14.1 for the last several years.) In doing so, the lessons of past UN experience in Africa appear to be ignored. Experts characterize these missions as "half-hearted efforts to appear to be 'doing something' rather than a genuine attempt to provide the logistical and financial support" that is necessary.[34] Malone and Wermester refer to these missions as "improvisations of last resort."[35]

LOOKING TO THE FUTURE

The post–Cold War record of deadly conflicts reveals several important trends:[36] The number of regional conflicts is in decline. Conflicts are being settled and settlements are holding. The primacy loci of conflicts, beyond the perennial Middle East and South Asia, are now in Central Africa, West Africa, and Central Asia—these three subregions mired in transnational wars across the territories of failed states.

What are implications of these trends for peace management by the UN and regional organizations? First, for the Americas and Europe, with their stronger regional institutional capacities, the prospects of future conflicts reaching a significant breakout stage in either are remote. In Europe it appears safe to conclude that a post–Cold War order has been established, held in place in the short term by a major international force presence in the Balkans and by the robust conflict prevention institutional mechanisms mandated to investigate and defuse minority-related conflict. In the Americas there has been a quite dramatic shift in regional norms. States have modified their insistence on the principles of noninterference (enshrined in the OAS Charter) and the inviolability of states to be governed as their power holders determined. But there has been a quite dramatic shift in regional norms. An Inter-American Democratic Charter has been adopted along with acceptance that OAS action is mandated whenever the democratic process within a member country is "interrupted."

In Asia an effective zone of peace has taken hold among Southeast Asian states, although eruption of major civil conflict, for example, in Indonesia, could lead to a call for UN intervention. Northeast Asia, on the other hand, remains a highly militarized environment with tense relationships hinged on the Korean Peninsula and Taiwan Straits. For the foreseeable future conflict management in this subregion will be managed by an ad hoc concert of powers, dominated by the United States.

By process of elimination, this leaves Central Africa, Western Africa, and Central Asia.[37] These, as Cilliers and Mills point out, are regional situations in which "the increasingly hollow nature of state institutions in Africa and their loss of legitimacy, coupled with Western peace-keeping disengagement" leave the UN in the breach. The overall outcome has been "two distinct tiers of peace missions—one for the developed world and another for regions such as Africa."[38] In essence the division of labor between the UN and regional organizations broke down and failed Africa. It remains to be seen whether or not recent initiatives, such as NEPAD advanced by the G-8, will translate into meaningful long-term structural change and build short-term institutional capacities to deal with peace and conflict.

But there are positive developments too. In the global context the movement towards regional security communities of democracies appears to have momentum. The Americas have made their declaration and set up regional institutional mechanisms to facilitate compliance—although their robustness remains to be tried and tested. Southeast Asia, albeit tentatively, continues to move incrementally in that direction. African states, when replacing the OAU with the new African Union (AU), have rhetorically committed themselves to this goal as well. If this trend takes hold, and with it an anticipated fall-off in regional conflicts, the future relationship between the UN and regional organizations could move closer to the subsidiary model envisaged by Boutros-Ghali and could revitalize the relevance of Chapter VIII concerning regional organizations.

However, the role of hegemons remains centrally important. As Barnett has argued, the "presence of a hegemon . . . can provide leadership through moral and material resources."[39] Its sense of identity has a strongly determining influence upon the collective identity adopted by states within the regional cohort. This raises the question of the impact of the United States upon the matters under consideration in this chapter. Certain actions and declarations of the current U.S. government have the potential to undermine in serious ways the norms underlying the UN and its role in the global legitimization of the use of force. With the Kosovo campaign the United States evaded the requirements of the Charter; with its war against the Taliban in Afghanistan the United States led an international intervention and promptly looked to get out, leaving the UN to assemble the pieces. The Bush administration's preference to act unilaterally or through contrived ad hoc coalitions does not bolster the collective identity or the role of regional organizations.

Thus much is in contention in the current international order. The UN is challenged by norms that prioritize regional distinctiveness and by norms that support unilateral behavior by major powers, both undercutting the precepts of global multilateralism. Both trends affect the development of UN-regional organization relationships. Positive economic, political, and social forces of regionalism have advanced movement towards the establishment of security communities in Europe, the Americas, and to a limited extent in Asia. However, in other regional contexts, the dilemmas of capacity and legitimacy in peace management are intensifying. The states within troubled regions, especially Africa, cannot sustain strong regional institutions and cannot contribute substantially to peace operations. On the other hand the states outside these regions that do possess the required capabilities appear unwilling to commit their political will and resources to UN peace support operations in tough regional conflict situations. Increasingly, if moved to act they are doing so unilaterally or in ad hoc coalitions of the willing, avoiding the encumbrances that are inherent in UN management, "leading" the UN and leaving it to manage the expensive, long-haul peace enforcement and peace building that must follow.

In these circumstances the UN may find itself stymied. The vision of the Charter to support the roles and responsibilities of regional organizations and simultaneously sustain the hierarchical position of the UN vis-à-vis regional organizations is in danger of unraveling. The events of the next several years, many predicated on the policies and actions of the United States as the current global power, will clarify whether or not a substantial role remains for the UN in responding to regional conflict.

NOTES

* The author acknowledges the research assistance of Robert Hartfiel. This research and writing is supported by the SSHRC and the Security and Defense

Forum program of the Centre of International Relations, UBC. The views expressed are those of the author.

1. See Inis Claude, *Swords into Ploughshares* (New York: Random House, 1983) for a recounting of the struggle between the British Foreign Office's desire to preserve a regionalized order and spheres of influence and the United States' insistence on an organization with a centralized Council of major powers in control.

2. See David Quayat, "The United Nations and Regional Organizations: A New Paradigm for Peace," *Conference of Defence Associations Institute, Second Annual Graduate Student Symposium.* www.cda-cdai.ca/symposia/1999/quayat99.htm.

3. In turn, the Council "where appropriate [is] to utilize regional arrangements or agencies for enforcement action." See Faith K. Bouayad-Agha and Boris P. Krasulin, "Report on Sharing Responsibilities in Peace-Keeping: The United Nations and Regional Organizations," Joint Inspection Unit JIU/REP/95/4 (1995) and UN Department of Peacekeeping Operations, "Cooperation Between the United Nations and Regional Organizations/Arrangements in a Peacekeeping Environment." (1999). www.un.org/Depts/dpko/lessons/regcoop.htm for further details.

4. The Charter's language of "regional agencies or other consultation mechanisms" is both encompassing and ambiguous. Regional security-related organizations are affiliated with the UN in a variety of different ways, none of which imply specific duties or responsibilities or special relationships. Four organizations have been recognized by the General Assembly "as [having] regional arrangements in the sense of Chapter VIII of the Charter"—the CSCE/OSCE, the OAS, the League of Arab States, and the OAU. (See Christopher Schreuer, "Regionalism v. Universalism," *European Journal of International Law* 6(3) (1995). Available at http://www.ejil.org/journal/Vol6/No3/art10-02.html#P58_15479) Only nine—the OAS, the OSCE, the EU, the CIS, the OAS, the Asian-African Legal Consultative Committee (AALCC), the Commonwealth Secretariat, the League of Arab States, and the Organization of Islamic Conference (OIC)—have observer status in the UN General Assembly. NATO, on the other hand, does not. As of 1999, 16 organizations, including regional (3), interregional (5), and subregional (8) organizations, were cooperating or had indicated a willingness to cooperate with the UN in peace support activities. See Bouyad for a complete list. A consultation mechanism, called for in the Secretary-General's 1992 *An Agenda for Peace,* has not been established.

5. Michael Barnett, "Partners in Peace? The UN, Regional Organizations, and Peace-Keeping," *Review of International Studies* 21(4) (1995): 411. See also Mary McKenzie, "The UN and Regional Organizations," in *The United Nations and Human Security,* eds. Edward Newman and Oliver P. Richmond (London: Palgrave, 2001), 153–55.

6. See Trevor Findlay, *The Use of Force in UN Peace Operations* (Oxford: Oxford University Press, 2002).

7. The notable exception, of course, was ONUC's (1960–64) entanglement in the civil war of the Congo—a presaging of the dilemmas and traumas to come.

8. David Malone and Karin Wermester, "Boom and Bust? The Changing Nature of UN Peacekeeping," in *Managing Armed Conflicts in the 21st Century*, eds. Adekye Adebajo and Chandra Lekha Sriram (London: Frank Cass, 2001), 39.

9. *An Agenda for Peace*, paras. 63–65.

10. In 1991 the UN General Assembly had looked to a special committee to investigate enhancing cooperation between the UN and regional organizations. Numerous initiatives involving committees, studies, commissioned reports, consultations, etc. have followed since without significant results. See Bouayad–Agha and the UN Department of Peacekeeping Operations.

11. In each of these three cooperating relationships, UN authorities were to have a role in determining force deployment. Quayat, 6.

12. Andrew Knight utilizes the term "subsidiarity model" as well. However, he refers to an ideal relationship between the UN and regional organizations rather than existing conditions. See W.A. Knight, "Towards a Subsidiarity Model for Peacemaking and Preventive Diplomacy: Making Chapter VIII of the UN Charter Operational," *Third World Quarterly* 17(1) (1996): 31–52.

13. *Supplement to An Agenda for Peace*, para 86.

14. Note the distinction between UN and UN-authorized missions. The latter operate with a UN mandate but are organized and commanded by a state or coalition of states as opposed to being under UN command. The largest of these has been the UNITAF mission in Somalia in 1993 with over 37,000 troops, followed by the MNF in Haiti and Operation Turquoise in Rwanda in 1994. The latest, large UN-authorized mission was INTERFET, under Australian command, in East Timor in 1999.

15. The large UN missions in the early 1990s were in Somalia (1993), Cambodia (1994), and Haiti (1995).

16. The exception being in Guinea-Bassau, where Nigeria was not involved.

17. Regarding conflict management in Europe, see for instance, Kelvin Ong, "Conflict Prevention and Management of Conflicts in Europe," *International Peace Academy Workshop Report* (2001) www.ipacademy.org and Emeric Rogier, "The Organization for Security and Co-Operation in Europe: Characteristics, Concepts and Capacities," (Netherlands Institute of International Relations "Clingendael," Conflict Research Unit, 2002).

18. As for 2002, the UN had three peace-keeping missions in Europe: UNMIK in Kosovo, UNMOP in Prevlaka, and UNMIBH in Bosnia-Herzegovina.

19. The OAU has become the African Union (AU), a regional institution with more robust ambitions. Here the OAU acronym will be utilized when referring to the institution's past activities.

20. For a review of African regional institutions, see the International Peace Academy, "The Infrastructure of Peace in Africa: Assessing the Peacebuilding Capacity of African Institutions," *International Peace Academy Project Report* (2002) www.ipacademy.org, Bjorn Moller, "Conflict Prevention and Peace-Building in Africa," (Copenhagen Peace Research Institute, 2001); Eric G. Berman and Katie E. Sams, *Peacebuilding in Africa: Capabilities and Culpabilities* (Geneva: UNIDIR, 2000); and Jakkie Cilliers and Greg Mills,

eds., *From Peacekeeping to Complex Emergencies* (Johannesburg: South African Institute of International Affairs, 1999).

21. IPA, *The Infrastructure of Peace in Africa*, 23.

22. See Brian Job, "Alliances' and Regional Security Developments: The Role of Regional Arrangements in the United Nations' Promotion of Peace and Stability," in *New Millennium, New Perspectives: The United Nations, Security, and Governance*, eds. Ramesh Thakur and Edward Newman (Tokyo: The UN University Press, 2000), 126–127; as well as Barnett, 424; and McKenzie for discussions of the putative advantages of regional organization engagement. Also, note Thomas G. Weiss, ed., *Beyond Subcontracting: Task-Sharing With Regional Security Arrangements and Service Providing NGOs* (New York: St. Martin's Press, Inc., 1998).

23. See Adekeye Adebajo and Chris Landsberg, "Back to the Future: UN Peacekeeping in Africa," in *Managing Armed Conflicts in the 21st Century* eds. Adekeye Adebajo and Chandra Lekha Sriram (London: Frank Cass, 2001).

24. See Allan Dupont, "ASEAN's Response to the East Timor Crisis," *Australian Journal of International Affairs* 54(2) (2000):163–70.

25. See Job, 126; Shiela Coutts, "Regionalization of Peace Operations," *International Peace Academy Workshop Report* (2002), 10–11. www.ipacademy.org; and Connie Peck, *Sustainable Peace: The Role of the UN and Regional Organizations in Preventing Conflict* (Lanham, Maryland: Rowman and Littlefield Publishers, Inc, 1998), 221.

26. McKenzie, 165.

27. The argument is made that the war on Afghanistan was in self-defense and in response to attack thus not requiring UN approval.

28. Katharina Coleman, Princeton University, interview January 2003, Vancouver.

29. These include Ong, 1; with reference to Europe, Coleman (per note 12 above) and Adekeye Adabajo (interview, February 2003, New York) with reference to Africa.

30. In the late 1970s, for instance, Nigeria intervened in Chad without the approval of the OAU, which in turn mobilized a coalition of regional states. UN approval followed months later. See Quayat, 4 for details.

31. Thus the Independent International Commission on Kosovo (2000) concluded that this action, while illegal, was justified. See Independent International Commission on Kosovo, *Kosovo Report: Conflict, International Response, Lessons Learned* (Oxford: Oxford University Press, 2000).

32. See Adebajo and Landsberg, 164.

33. See Coleman, "Launching Peace Enforcement Operations through African Sub-Regional Organizations: The Case of ECOWAS" (2003).

34. Adebajo and Landsberg.

35. Malone and Wermester, 37.

36. See Monty G. Marshall and Ted Robert Gurr, "Peace and Conflict 2003: A Global Survey of Armed Conflicts, Self-Determination Movements and Democracy" (Center for International Development and Conflict Management, University of Maryland, 2003). www.bsos.umd.edu/cidcm/CIDCMpeace.pdf.

37. Conflicts that occur within any of the major powers, including regional powers such as India, Nigeria, and Brazil, will not come onto the international agenda. The 9/11 incident has served to solidify these geopolitical realities, especially concerning Russia and China, with little prospect for UN, OSCE, or other regional institutional peace-related activities in these territories.
38. Cilliers, vii.
39. Barnett, 422.

CHAPTER 15

HUMAN SECURITY: AN OPENING FOR UN REFORM

Lloyd Axworthy*

As the authors of this volume were gathering to look at the role of the United Nations (UN) in global security, the organization itself was in the midst of a major test of that role in the debate and decisions on Iraq. In some ways the debate over Iraq reinvigorated the UN, and for a short time the UN occupied center stage in world diplomacy. Following Hans Blix and Mohammed Elbaradei's second reports to the Security Council was a spectacle quite uncommon to Security Council sessions; addresses were made with passion and resolve, heated discussions, and intense debate—diplomatic sparring at its best. In the aftermath newspaper headlines effectively captured this seeming importance: "UN Can Still Put on a Grand Show," "The Rattle of Sabers Grows a Bit Fainter in a Fiery UN Debate."[1] The eyes of the world became focused on the drama unfolding at the Security Council as proponents of war battled it out with those who argued for time and patience.

Given the vociferous stance of the Bush administration in support of war, having the issue redirected to the Security Council was in itself a small victory for multilateralism. However, the counter to this is the view that U.S. war plans since August had planned for a mid-March attack, and thus going to the UN was simply an indulgence the Bush administration could afford. Moreover, even though U.S. officials had gone to great lengths to obtain UN authorization, it became quite clear early on that a decision to proceed with military action in Iraq would not be contingent on the approval of the world body. For the Bush administration a UN resolution was considered "useful but not necessary."[2] Sure enough, attempts to work within the UN were abandoned as dissent from a number of key states proved an insurmountable barrier to prospects for a second resolution. The war began and the UN faded into the sunset, given short shrift and a minor role in the post-conflict reconstruction.

This seriously hurt the credibility of the organization. In a global survey of 20 countries conducted two months after war's end, majorities or pluralities in most countries believed that the UN was now less important than before the Iraq imbroglio. It had lost relevance, confirming President Bush's self-fulfilling claim.[3]

The role of the UN throughout the Iraq crisis was something of an anomaly. On the one hand there was an attempt to strengthen the UN by working within UN decision-making channels and forcing Iraq to comply with Security Council resolutions. Global citizens who made their voices heard in public opinion polls and street demonstrations, cautioning their government not to go to war without the sanctioning of the UN, reaffirmed the centrality of the organization in global peace and security. On the other hand, key states were sidelining the organization through manipulation and bullying, trying to relegate it to a decorative role on the periphery of international action. We could easily say that it was both the best of times and the worst of times for the UN—renewed optimism coupled with the threat of irrelevance looming in the background.

What the Iraq crisis did reveal is a United Nations held captive to the most potent tensions in contemporary global politics. Aside from the inconsistencies that arise from engaging the UN while simultaneously reserving the right to circumvent its authority were the conflicting objectives of key states. Although rhetorical support for disarmament was present, the latent objective of some was and had always been regime change. The contradictory posture towards disarmament in North Korea despite the fact that it posed a much more serious threat than Iraq, as discussed in Nina Tannenwald's chapter, provides evidence of what the underlying objectives were in Iraq. For others the central objective was, first and foremost, ensuring the safety and well being of innocent Iraqi civilians.

The clash over objectives seen in the case of Iraq—regime change versus protection of civilians—has become a common feature of international relations. It arises from a gulf in the realm of security perception and practice and has a striking impact on multilateral bodies such as the UN. Proponents of traditional security tend to focus on the state and exhibit a general disdain for tying their hands in multilateral arrangements—precisely what occurred in the case of Iraq. Innocent lives and the authority of the UN became expendable objects in the pursuit of regime change in Iraq, bolstering a doctrine of preemptive self-defense and a counterterrorist campaign that goes well beyond any proper interpretation of the UN Charter.

Human security offers a remarkably different interpretation of multilateral arrangements. Instead of perceiving such arrangements as a hindrance, proponents of human security consider multilateral institutions essential components of international order. In an era of heightened insecurity from a multitude of threats, international rules, cooperative arrangements, and a respect for international law are indispensable elements in the protection of individual rights and security. As both an architect and conveyor of international rules and norms, the UN is seen not simply as a *recommended* path towards security but a fundamental *prerequisite* of international peace, justice, and stability.

The attack by coalition forces on Iraq has left the UN in a rather precarious position. The UN is now faced with a dual challenge from the vicious networks of dictators, terrorists, and criminals on one hand and enthusiasts of preemptive self-defense on the other hand. Both display a marked disdain for international law, multilateral arrangements, and international rules—in essence, everything the UN stands for. Yet, in a world confronted with genocide, poverty, the spread of HIV/AIDS, and environmental catastrophes, a strong UN is desperately needed to counter these and other threats. The reality is, however, that the UN was not designed to deal with contemporary security threats and must therefore adjust to these new global conditions accordingly.

Various reform proposals have been proffered as a means to strengthen the organization, yet none have captured the volume of momentum necessary to incite meaningful change. This chapter will explore how human security initiatives can strengthen the United Nations by creating an opening for UN reform.

Traditional Security

Historically, international order has depended on the widespread adoption of a few essential norms, namely territorial recognition and nonintervention. Implicit in these norms is an overarching respect for state sovereignty, the mutual assurance of noninterference in states' domestic affairs. Since the creation of our modern state-system, sovereigns have been free to exercise power within their respective jurisdictions as they saw fit. Thus, a precedent was established early on whereby the treatment of individuals within states' juridical boundaries was considered to be an immaterial concern.

So engrained are these basic tenets of international conduct that they have persisted unabated for over three centuries and have had an immense impact on the practice of international law and the creation of international institutions. Of utmost concern to creators of international institutions and practices of international law was the place of the nation-state in international society. The state and the state alone was seen as the only relevant entity in international affairs, as the principal subject of international law and the only acceptable member of international organizations. Other actors were simply irrelevant on the international stage. Where individuals did matter, it was particularly a question of their respective citizenship—that is, to which state they belonged.

The UN is no exception to the rule. The members of the UN are not NGOs, donor agencies, human rights groups, transnational corporations, or individuals but nation-states. According to the creators of the organization, its central purpose was to ensure the "territorial integrity and political independence" of member states,[4] a tribute to the sovereignty norm. However, considering the atmosphere in which the UN Charter was drafted, one can hardly dispute the perceived need to reiterate the principles of sovereignty and nonintervention. Fresh in the minds of the Charter's authors was the onslaught of Nazi Germany on the European state system.

As many of the authors in this volume have noted, the UN faced a difficult inaugural period. Cold war politics and the veto resulted in a rather dormant role for the UN throughout the first five decades of its existence. Alternatively, international peace and security were held in check by the alliance systems maintained by the superpowers. The end of the Cold War hinted at the enormous potential for the UN in a new era, particularly with the universal condemnation of Iraq's aggression in Kuwait—a classic example of interstate aggression. The P5's unanimous agreement on responding to Iraq's aggression was certainly cause for optimism. Unfortunately, the Gulf War became the exception to UN activity in the post–Cold War era.

THE HUMAN SECURITY ALTERNATIVE

The predominance of intrastate wars has altered traditional conceptions of security and international order. Most, if not all, of the most rudimentary assumptions underlying international relations have been called into question, not least of which is the nature of war. Throughout the 1990s, 65 of the estimated 79 episodes of conflict occurred within developing countries, and over half of the bottom 47 countries on the Human Development Index are still suffering from the aftermath of violent conflict.[5] The links between low-level economic growth and violent conflict have become all too obvious.

The nature of contemporary war has been particularly problematic for civilians. The traditional distinction between soldier and civilian has been permanently erased. According to some statistics, the casualty rate for civilians in war have reached an alarming 90 percent, a sharp increase from an estimated 65 percent during WWII and even more remote from the five percent rate at the beginning of the twentieth century.[6] The targeting of innocent civilians is not some unintended outcome of conflict but a deliberate strategy of belligerents. The influx of small arms and light weapons into situations of instability has facilitated the ease with which civilians have become embroiled in hostilities, sometimes as direct participants. A disturbing trend has been the sharp increase in child combatants serving in government forces as well as armed rebel groups.[7]

It was difficult for policy makers, accustomed to the intricacies of competing ideologies, alliance systems, and proxy wars, to fashion an effective response to the intrastate wars of the 1990s. To make matters worse, it was not simply decision makers who were stymied by this unforeseen shift in global politics—the treasured institutions that we theoretically should have been able to turn to were ill equipped for the tasks ahead.

The UN Charter was fashioned in response to interstate wars and therefore was silent on the issue of civil conflicts. The central problem since the end of the Cold War has been how to define security in an era where civil conflicts are on the rise, particularly when domestic issues have historically evaded international consideration. However, adhering to the characterization of intrastate war as a purely domestic matter has become increasingly problematic given the significant potential for destabilization that can result from the spillover of conflict and refugee influxes into neighboring countries, as exemplified in Gil Loescher's chapter on the crucial linkage between refugees and global security. The other chapters in this volume testify to the plethora of challenges facing the UN in addressing and adapting to these threats. As the authors in this volume demonstrate, the UN was effectively paralyzed in terms of its mandate, structure, and operational capacity. Ottawa, like many other capitals, realized that a new approach was imminent. By the time I assumed the post of foreign minister, it was becoming clearer that the security of individuals would have to be redressed. It was with this sentiment in mind that Canada embraced the human security approach—the idea of "putting people first."[8]

The human security approach represents an important shift in the way to view global politics. It endeavors to modify the lens through which security is viewed—from the level of the state to the level of the individual. Yet it is not simply a question of adjusting our lenses—it is also a matter of broadening one's definition of security. Human security is much more than the absence of military threat; it includes the security against economic privation, an acceptable quality of life, and a guarantee of fundamental human rights. It recognizes the links between environmental degradation, population growth, ethnic conflicts, and migration. By acknowledging the vast array of issues threatening individual security, the human security approach is entirely consistent with the complexities of our current global reality and in this sense goes beyond the simplified and outdated version of traditional security.

The first time I used the language of human security was in September of 1996 during an address to the UN General Assembly. The United Nations seemed like the logical venue in which to introduce this important concept. In fact, human security became the platform of our 1997 campaign launch to win a seat on the Security Council. Once on the Council we actively promoted the principles of human security under the banner of "Protection of Civilians."

HUMAN SECURITY INITIATIVES: AN OPENING FOR SUBSTANTIVE UN REFORM

In recent years popular discontent with international organizations has intensified. Of particular concern is the lack of transparency, absence of international accountability, and an overall disregard for democratic principles. Moreover, the state-centric nature of international organizations, following the scriptures of traditional security, has led to a disconnect between these institutions and the vulnerable populations they are meant to serve. Globalization has heightened the democratic deficit in international structures, and the need for genuine reform is obvious.

The 2002 UNDP report *Deepening Democracy in a Fragmented World* remarks on this widespread disillusionment with international institutions: "Protests and cries of frustration have hit the streets in both industrial and developing countries reflecting concerns that marginalized and less powerful people and states are losing out because of how global security and economic affairs are managed." According to the report, these antiglobalization protests are "symptomatic of an almost universal belief that global cooperation must do a better job of preventing and managing a host of issues."[9]

The UN is certainly no exception. Failure to deliver on its post–Cold War promises dealt a severe blow to UN credibility. The problems that arose were endemic to the organization's structure, bureaucracy, ambiguous mandate, and operational incapacity. As criticisms of the organization augmented, so too did proposals for UN reform, particularly of the UN Security Council, the organization's principal decision-making body. Having spent a great deal of my tenure as foreign minister working within UN structures, I am no stranger to the need for UN reform. What I came to realize during my years in office was how human security initiatives—by tackling some of the most pressing security issues hitherto excluded from international consideration—can create an opening for substantive UN reform.

Civilian Protection in Armed Conflicts

As we have seen, an indisputable reality of contemporary global politics is the heightened level of insecurity confronted by individuals. Regrettably, this intensification of individual insecurity has not yet afforded a sufficient response from the international community. This is not particularly surprising given the state-centric nature of the international system, which is reflected in international organizations such as the UN, whose membership is restricted to nation-states. Responding to the plight of individuals has created both theoretical and operational challenges for the UN.

In February of 1999 we experimented with broadening the UN's mandate beyond the realm of traditional security concerns. During our presidency of the Security Council, we held an informal debate on the issue of civilian protection in armed conflict. Subsequent to that debate we issued a strong presidential statement expressing concern "at the growing civilian toll of armed conflict" and noting "with distress that civilians now account for the vast majority of casualties in armed conflict and are increasingly directly targeted by combatants and armed elements." The statement also went on to highlight the need for a sufficient international response: "[B]earing in mind its primary responsibility for the maintenance of international peace and security, the Council affirms the need for the international community to assist and protect civilian populations affected by armed conflict."[10]

Given the gravity of the situation and lack of attention previously devoted to the plight of civilians in armed conflict, the need to explore the issue further was obvious. It was with this in mind that we called on the Secretary-General to compile a comprehensive report on the situation of civilians in armed conflict. In September of 1999, when the final report was presented, it was well received by the international community. The report contained 40 recommendations aimed at improving the physical and legal protection of civilians in situations of armed conflict.[11]

In response to the Secretary-General's recommendations, Canada pushed for the adoption of two important resolutions related to civilian protection in armed conflicts, Resolution 1265 followed by Resolution 1296. Taken together these resolutions offer the most comprehensive measures adopted by the Security Council in terms of civilian protection. Both resolutions recognize the hardships being borne by civilian populations, condemn attacks upon innocents, and commit the Security Council to act on their behalf. The resolutions created an opening for substantive UN reform by accentuating a number of issues that had hitherto been overlooked by the international community, namely, the importance of conflict prevention strategies; adequate training for peace-keepers; the impact of landmines, small arms, and light weapons on civilians; and the need to weigh the humanitarian impacts of sanctions on civilian life.

The issue of civilian protection has become an established item on the UN agenda. The Secretary-General has presented two reports on civilian protection subsequent to the 1999 version in March of 2001 and November of 2002.[12] The incorporation of civilian protection has created the necessary momentum to incite change on a number of issues. For instance, it would be difficult to imagine the adoption of Resolutions 1314 and 1379 pertaining to the protection of children in armed conflict as well as Resolution 1325 concerning the role of women in peace-building had the issue of civilian protection in armed conflict not been on the UN agenda. The incorporation of civilian protection on the UN agenda provides a useful illustration of how human security initiatives can create an opening for substantive UN reform.

The Criminalization of Mass Violence

The privileged role assigned to nation-states in international affairs has translated into impunity for individual transgressors of international law. The absence of an international instrument of accountability for war crimes has made it difficult for the UN to advance international peace and security. A positive response to this problem was made in the form of UN-established international criminal tribunals for Rwanda and the former Yugoslavia. As Richard Price and Joanne Lee note, these tribunals went beyond the imposition of "victor's justice," as was the case with the Nuremberg and Tokyo tribunals. Furthermore, the ICTR and ICTY were a testament to contemporary global realities in the sense that they dealt with intrastate wars.

Despite the significance of these tribunals with respect to punishing crimes against humanity, genocide and war crimes, they were limited as ad hoc instruments of international justice. The tribunals may have progressed past the days of "victor's justice," yet their significance was diluted with respect to the charge of selectivity. This is particularly problematic from the perspective of human security as the advancement of human security hinges upon the ability to enforce individual rights and individual security. Nothing short of a permanent instrument dedicated to advancing the rule of law could promote human security.

Although the idea of an international criminal court had been floating through policy circles and academia for decades, the urgency for this type of mechanism grew rapidly in the 1990s. The immense speed in which the Rome statute was ratified is a testament to the acknowledged need for the court. The Statute of Rome was devised with the security of the individual in mind and the responsibility of the international community to protect individuals wherever they live from those individuals and forces that threaten human life, human security, and our collective objective to live in a world that is free from violence and free from fear. The goal is a world that is free from the Milosevics, the Idi Amins, the Pol Pots, the Suhartos, the Pinochets, the Hitlers, and all others who wield political power for the benefit of themselves and the destruction of others rather than for the benefit of humankind.

The human security approach responds to the heightened level of insecurity confronting individuals in contemporary global politics and the shortcomings of traditional security. Whereas only states were considered relevant subjects of international law under the doctrine of traditional security, the ICC is mandated to prosecute individual transgressors of international law. Moreover, it is not simply episodes of interstate war that fall within the purview of the ICC but intrastate conflicts as well. By this measure, the ICC represents the first bona fide institutional expression of human security. Although the ICC is not a formal UN organ, it was created under UN auspices and will undoubtedly strengthen the UN's role in maintaining international peace and security, not to mention its functioning as a deterrent to future war crimes.

THE HUMAN SECURITY PROCESS: AN OPENING FOR PROCEDURAL UN REFORM

While the concept of human security is largely understood as a policy outcome, this is only partially accurate. Human security is much more than an outcome; it is also a process—in fact it is the process that makes the outcome a reality. As this section will demonstrate, human security initiatives not only lead to substantive UN reform, they also create an opening for procedural UN reform.

Opening up the Security Council

As noted above UN Security Council proceedings in particular have been criticized for their lack of transparency. Of concern to many are the Council's clandestine deliberations and overall absence of democracy. Advancing human security initiatives within the UN allowed us to experiment with a subtle process of Security Council reform. If civilians face a higher degree of insecurity in today's world than ever before, then naturally there is a need to understand the nature of these security threats in order to launch an effective response. Reliance on an intergovernmental process alone cannot deliver on this demand; thus, the need to open up traditional diplomatic channels typically reserved for the state to a variety of other actors is evident. During our debate in February 1999 on "the protection of civilians in armed conflict," this is precisely what we did.

While the perspectives of Council members were important, it was simply not enough to gauge the depth of this critical issue; therefore, the doors of the Security Council chambers were opened. For the first time voices heard within the UN's central decision-making body were not exclusively those of member states. Rather than limiting the discussions to member states, this debate incorporated presentations from Carol Bellamy, president of UNICEF; Cornelio Sommaruga, president of the International Committee for the Red Cross; and Olara Otunnu, UN special representative on children. A follow-up debate was held at the end of February in order to allow non-Council members the opportunity to make statements and offer recommendations on the Secretary-General's report.

Incorporating the views of other actors on this issue provided greater depth to the discussions and enhanced the substance of the Secretary-General's report. Making the diplomatic process more accessible to a host of other actors was a strategy we employed in a variety of human security initiatives. One of the most cited examples of this is the campaign to ban antipersonnel landmines.

The Ottawa Process

The prevailing view of the landmines campaign is that it sidestepped the UN and thus offers little in terms of an example of procedural UN reform. While it is true that we had to work around the paralyzed UN Conference on Disarmament in order to achieve effective action on the issue, this by no means negates UN participation in the campaign.

A much more appropriate way to view UN participation with respect to the landmine campaign, as discussed in Keith Krause's chapter, is to look upon the UN system as part of a complex network of transnational governance. According to Krause, a purely state-centric analysis that distinguishes between the domestic and international spheres can no longer account for issues on the peace and security agenda. In today's global circumstances, assessing the scope of UN activity becomes more difficult as peace and security issues increasingly require activity on multiple levels of governance. So, along with the participation of individuals and agencies within the UN system, including the support of two Secretaries-General, were the 1000 NGOs comprising the ICBL, the ICRC, nation-states, and a number of high-profile individuals.

The landmine campaign provides a practical illustration of the "process" side of human security. The APL ban would not have been possible without the Ottawa Process. The engagement of civil society actors in a process of two-track diplomacy facilitated the ease with which a treaty was drafted. The landmine campaign did not work against the UN but improved upon the Conference on Disarmament by involving a host of other actors that were necessary in order to make the ban a reality. In this way we should consider the Ottawa Process as reforming the UN Conference on Disarmament.

The Human Security Network

Apart from the immediate benefits that derive from human security initiatives are the indirect benefits of subtle reform within the UN system. With each initiative the UN process benefited from a greater level of transparency, democracy, and accountability. One aspect of the UN system that remains difficult to reform is the structure of the organization; yet it is this aspect of the UN that draws the most criticism.

As discussed in depth by Mark Zacher in his chapter, the privileged position of the veto-wielding P5 has been a problematic element of UN decision making for quite some time. But if we look closely at the human security initiatives mentioned above, one thing becomes apparent: In no way were the initiatives undertaken consistent with or supported by the policies of the P5 in general and the United States in particular. A consistent feature of many of the human security initiatives mentioned above has been the participation of a number of like-minded middle powers working in harmony towards a common goal.

This signals immense potential for a coalition of like-minded governments and NGOs to play a meaningful role in international affairs. It was precisely with these sentiments in mind that Canada established the Human Security Network—a collection of 13 middle powers from all regions of the world committed to advancing the principles of human security. No longer can we consider the politics of the P5 as a barrier to effective international action when it comes to agenda setting and advocacy. The precedent has been established and the necessity for new leadership has mounted as U.S. foreign policy continues to retreat from multilateral commitments.

THE "RESPONSIBILITY TO PROTECT": A RECONCILIATION

This chapter has explored two disparate versions of security: one that maintains the centrality of the state in international affairs and the other that is concerned for the welfare of individuals in international society. In several settings these diverse approaches play out against one another and have the effect of paralyzing effective UN action. In some cases the UN itself—given its imperfect structure, ambiguous mandate, lack of resources, and operational incapacity—exacerbates the tensions between the two approaches.

Human security is often described as the antithesis of traditional security. While the two are indeed philosophically and operationally distinct, there is a subtle connection between them worthy of recognition. Human security is not simply an alternative to traditional security; it is first and foremost a response to the shortcomings of traditional security. As we saw the post–Cold War era delivered a set of circumstances to the international community that could not be adequately addressed by a strict reliance on the practices of traditional security. The innumerable setbacks the UN has suffered in the post–Cold war era are evidence of this. This explains why human security initiatives are ideal instruments for UN reform. It is imperative to bear in mind the relationship between traditional security and human security as failure to do so results in the tendency to view the two as irreconcilable. Assessing human security as the logical consequence of the limits posed by traditional security practices allows for the possibility of reconciliation between the two.

Despite the shortcomings of traditional security approaches and the potential for human security to improve upon these approaches, resistance to human security principles remains strong. Even with the advent of nontraditional security threats, terrorism being one, nation-states are adverse to alternative security approaches. Yet it is precisely because of these nontraditional security threats that new approaches to security are so desperately needed. These concerns have come to a head over the issue of humanitarian intervention—like Kosovo in 1999—where human security approaches emphasized the humanitarian imperative and traditional security views stressed the virtues of nonintervention and state sovereignty.

An attempt to reconcile these conceptions of security was made in 1999 when the Canadian government sponsored what is arguably the most significant of its human security initiatives: the International Commission on Intervention and State Sovereignty (ICISS). As explained by ICISS participant Ramesh Thakur in his chapter, this is a broad-based, international dialogue of scholars and policy makers charged with the task of reconciling sovereignty and intervention. The debate culminated in a report that proposed an innovative redefinition of sovereignty as the "responsibility to protect." Some of the key outcomes of the debate include:

- A focus on what sovereignty obliges rather than what it endows—by this measure states can no longer harm their populations with impunity. And if for some reason a state is unwilling or unable to protect its citizens, the task falls upon the shoulders of the international community.
- International attention is focused where it is most needed—on the victim. To quote from the report: "Such a responsibility implies an evaluation of the issue from the perspective of the victim, not the intervener."

- The Responsibility to Protect is conceived as a continuum whereby the responsibility to prevent—exercising all options prior to embracing the military option—and the responsibility to rebuild—postconflict reconstruction—are crucial components of the Responsibility to Protect principle.

The ICISS corroborates the premise—established above—that human security acts as a response to the limits of traditional security. Fresh in the minds of the ICISS commissioners were the legal and political ambiguities stemming from the Kosovo crisis, not to mention the UN failures in Srebenica and Rwanda, issues that are dealt with in detail in the chapters by Thakur and Jennifer Welsh.

WHAT NEXT?

Despite the domination of the global security agenda in recent years by the war on terrorism and U.S. rejection of multilateralism, significant room remains for initiatives to be pursued at the UN. Through its resolution making, the Assembly has the power to establish prescriptive advice for the Security Council. This is nonbinding but can carry weight, as occurred with the process of de-colonization. An opportunity to mobilize the Assembly into this kind of an advocacy role arises with the recent tabling of the report of the Canadian-sponsored Commission on Intervention and State Sovereignty. The emphasis should now be on gaining strong support for an Assembly endorsement for the principle "the responsibility to protect" and for the committee's consequent recommendations for reform of the UN to meet the needs of a more robust interventionist mandate.

The UN is a natural and necessary forum for a human security agenda. The openness advocated as part of that agenda, in fact, should extend beyond the Council to all the other UN venues. The UN still has not figured out how to incorporate civil society groups into its decision making. This may be one reason why there is a decline in the UN's credibility among various publics. Working with NGOs and continued innovations in designing multilateral forums where there can be a true sense of civil participation should be a priority.

If there is to be an alternative to the anti-UN strategy followed by the present U.S. administration and the disruptive tactics of countries like Cuba in defending the status quo, there will have to be reform. The 15 million people worldwide who walked the streets demanding UN management of the disarming of Iraq was a sign of a global constituency of support.

REINVENTING THE UN

Present UN reform efforts focus on administration efficiency and coordination or on how to gain more equitable representation of regional powers on the Security Council. Neither approach really addresses the fundamentally flawed nature of a multilateral body designed around Second World War exigencies. The secretive and exclusive exercise of power by the five permanent members of the Security Council is the most obvious anachronism. The central role of the Council, its legitimacy, and credibility are marred by the present makeup and the veto. If it is to have a future as a significant place of decision making it must become both more representative and democratic and subject to more direct scrutiny and accountability to the General Assembly.

The present members are unlikely give up their privileged position, although the advent of a single foreign policy in the European Union presided over by a European foreign minister will put separate French and British status on the Council in some jeopardy. It is also possible to develop new membership criteria with larger, more significant members serving for the longer term but without the veto. The power of the veto needs to be circumscribed, narrowing its use to specified peace and security issues under Chapter VII.

Another serious consideration is how to apply more rigorous tests of membership. Should a member state be allowed to take a seat endowing some responsibility or authority if it flaunts basic UN principles resolution, shirks its financial obligations, is governed by a dictatorship, or is in violation of rights against its own citizens? Many other multilateral organizations have established codes of conduct for their members. It is time the UN did the same.

It is also important to move towards greater democratization of the Assembly. The most obvious initiative is some form of a second chamber of the Assembly. Direct election to a global body, bypassing governments, is an idea whose time is surely coming—perhaps presently slowed down by the efforts by big countries to ignore the UN or use it only when it serves their purpose. Trying to sell Assembly-direct election in today's atmospherics would need divine intervention. Nevertheless, opening up the proposal and presenting it as a legitimate long-term plan would bring some needed zest to the institution. In the meantime there is nothing to stop individual member states from experimenting on their own ways to choose their representatives through election.

More qualified membership and a stronger democratic base would enhance Assembly credibility and provide the grounds for giving it a more active role on issues of humanitarian intervention. The General Assembly could extend the notion of responsibility to protect to civilians during peacemaking missions by authorizing various forms of soft intervention; it could act when the Council freezes on peacemaking missions, it could assert a more forthcoming role in dealing with the massive terrorist threats. This is a serious new risk to world order, putting in jeopardy the fundamental rights of people and communities to live in freedom from fear. Yet Washington aided and abetted with a spurious coalition of the willing should not be the sole author on how to answer the terrorist threat. Building a global consensus based on collaboration will in the long run be a better antidote than a military strategy that is applied unilaterally.

To make this operational there will eventually have to be a standing UN constabulary that can (1) move quickly on preventive missions; (2) provide an investigative arm for the International Court; and (3) be available to protect UN humanitarian workers or aid in the dismantling of arms systems in compliance with disarmament resolutions. Right now the UN lacks its own rapid-response capability, all past efforts to establish some form of stand-by force or to have a UN constabulary have been rejected or ignored. In this respect UN members are mired in the status quo, unwilling to challenge the will of the big powers that want to keep the UN emasculated and reluctant to put up the money and commit the resources. But why should NATO have a rapid-reaction force but not the UN? The ability of the UN to act effectively, whether in responding to massacres, policing weapons inspections, or protecting UN field activities is an idea that current circumstances seem to demand. There already exists the Standby High Readiness Brigade (Shirbrig) made of ten countries that have standby units available for UN duty. They performed well in the UN mission in Ethiopia and Eritrea. Shirbrig could be a platform to build on.

Other UN agencies need reform. The Geneva-based Disarmament Commission, the Human Rights Commission, and the High Commission for Refugees—each in their own way are ailing, as other chapters in this volume document. In each of these cases national interests and power politics get in the way; too often there is studied indifference or outright bullying from the rulers of the strongest member and defiance from many of the renegade regimes. The responsibility-to-protect principle could be a catalyst for real reform by establishing different norms for state behavior and becoming the base for asserting a more robust role for the international community.

What's more, it takes the process of reform beyond war into a basic reassessment of the ways in which the responsibility to protect must be applied to economic and environmental security needs—poverty, health, resource exploitation. As we have seen from the studies in this volume, the present financial, commercial, global system promotes an imbalanced distribution in economic benefits in which unrestrained growth invariably trumps sustainable development, where the imperatives of global rules and regulations are discriminatory and insensitive to local and regional needs. All this is to say that there is much work to do in helping the UN continue to transform itself into a more effective, credible institution for global security in the twenty-first century, a task that in some ways is more, not less, necessary in an era dominated by the U.S. war on terrorism.

Notes

* I would like to thank Serena Sharma for her invaluable assistance in developing this chapter.

1. "The Rattle of Sabers Grows a Bit Fainter in a Fiery UN Debate," *New York Times* (February 16, 2003); "UN Can Still Put on a Grand Show," *New York Times* (February 15, 2003).
2. "NATO Approves Turkey Mission," *BBC News* (February 19, 2003).
3. "Views of A Changing World June 2003" (The Pew Research Center, Washington D.C., 2003), 1. www.people-press.org
4. Charter of the United Nations (Chapter I, Article 2). http://www.un.org/aboutun/charter/
5. The World Bank Group, "Breaking the Conflict Trap: Civil War and Development Policy," http://econ.worldbank.org/prr/CivilWarPRR/text-26671/
6. Save the Children, "Mothers and Children in War and Conflict," *State of the World's Mothers Third Annual Report* (2002). www.savethechildren.org/mothers/sowm02/index.shtml.
7. There are an estimated 300,000 combatants under the age of 18 serving in government forces or armed rebel groups. See Human Rights Watch Facts About Child Soldiers, http://www.hrw.org/campaigns/crp/facts.htm.
8. For more information see Department of Foreign Affairs and International Trade, Government of Canada. "Freedom From Fear: Canada's Foreign Policy for Human Security," http://www.humansecurity.gc.ca/Freedom_from_Fear-e.pdf
9. "Deepening Democracy in a Fragmented World," *UN Human Development Report 2002* "Deepening Democracy at the Global Level" (Chapter 5), 102.
10. *Protection of Civilians in Armed Conflict: Statement by President of Security Council* S/PRST/1999/6 (February 12, 1999). http://www.reliefweb.int/w/Rwb.nsf/s/D2F04D938315E9ACC125671D0063E85D
11. *Report of the Secretary General to the Security Council on the Protection of Civilians in Armed Conflict* S/1999/957 (September 8, 1999). http://odsddsny.un.org/doc/UNDOC/GEN/N99/258/15/PDF/N9925815.pdf?OpenElement
12. United Nations, *Annual Report of the UN Secretary General* (2001, 2002).

PART VI

CONCLUSIONS

CHAPTER 16

THE LEAGUE OF NATIONS REDUX?

Richard Price*

This volume has sought answers to a question that has never before been more the topic of conversation around the world: What difference does the United Nations (UN) and its multilateral institutions make in issues of global security? Has the U.S. decision to wage war against Iraq without UN authorization in March 2003 reduced it to an irrelevant debating society, as threatened by the George W. Bush administration? For defenders of the UN system, the consolation prize, at least during the Iraq crisis, was the taking of center stage in world affairs by the UN Security Council and by UN officials like weapons inspector Hans Blix as the world stood transfixed over the drama in late 2002 and early 2003. But given the inability of the UN to substantially alter the course of U.S. policy in waging war on Iraq, is not the skepticism of realpolitik ultimately warranted? Does this mean the UN will follow the ignominious fate of its predecessor, the League of Nations, a specter proffered by the Bush administration?

The unprecedented activism of the Security Council in the 1990s after decades of paralysis during the Cold War may have raised expectations so unrealistically as to set up inevitable disappointment at the failures of the UN system to effectively and consistently contain major uses of aggressive military force. While chronicling the often profound shortcomings of UN multilateralism as an effective collective security organization, the chapters of this book at the same time resist the most dire dismissals of its relevance or even existence. The UN and its Security Council have failed in that most ambitious of tasks its creators set for it—eliminating the scourge of war—and has never fully operated in the ways its most aspiring architects hoped. In addition to the prerogatives of major powers, as Andy Mack and Edward Luck demonstrate, in terms of conflict prevention or addressing terrorism this incapacity often derives from the UN's own bureaucratic barriers.[1]

Usually below the radar screen of such spectacular failures—which have more than once been pronounced as the death knell of the UN—the UN and its agencies have nonetheless managed to soldier on in ways other than marshalling its own troops, as provided for but never invoked under Article 43 of the UN Charter. Thus, as Jennifer Welsh chronicles, rather than becoming a multilateral intervener with enough of its own muscle to transcend recourse to the military option by states and other actors, the UN's niche has become the world's chief repository of authority regarding who may legitimately do so. Here the UN embodies its most characteristic role as demonstrated in the chapters in this volume, which is its legitimizing function as the best arbiter we have of acceptable conduct for the global community. Whether it be through Security Council resolutions on terrorism, the condemnation through criminal tribunals of genocide, war crimes, and crimes against humanity (and the development of corresponding jurisprudence); the dele-gitimization of the use of weapons of mass destruction embodied in the UN treaties such as the Chemical Weapons Convention or Nuclear Nonproli-feration Treaty; efforts to curtail the violent abuses of small arms or highlight the plight of the world's refugees; or treaties such as the Torture Convention, which laid the groundwork for milestones in international criminal justice like the Pinochet case, perhaps the primary role of the UN system in the security of states and persons has been as a standard setter for the tolerable use of force. Here too there are grave limits, as Welsh, Ramesh Thakur, and Mark Zacher explore, since severe questions about the representativeness and efficacy of a Security Council all too often frozen in inaction mean that even this niche the UN has carved out for itself is under severe strain and cannot at all be taken for granted by those who seemed to invest so much in UN Security Council authority during the crisis over Iraq. Still, as Fen Hampson shows, the UN is on occasion able to translate its reputational resources into more than modest successes in mediating civil wars such as in El Salvador and Cambodia and even in interstate conflict like the Iran–Iraq war.

Ultimately, however, it is on matters other than the actual prevention of war that the UN has carved out its niches that have more directly impacted the security of states and more often people from the protection of millions of refugees to the development and implementation of international war crimes law and incarceration of hundreds of war criminals to the enactment of sanctions regimes. These contributions give truth to the remark that if the UN did not exist in the world, its peoples would have to invent it. For whatever the concerns of the day for a hegemon currently averse to UN multilateralism, the fact remains that much of the rest of the world finds itself in a variety of situations where it needs help and the sole superpower may not be paying particular attention. While Iraq took the spotlight in 2002 and 2003, the UN remained engaged—with successes and failures—on multifar-ious other fronts affecting the security of many more states and peoples around the world than were the concern of the world's superpower. Thus, even as the ink for the obituaries for the UN after the U.S. war against Iraq had barely dried, the Security Council that had been so deeply divided over Iraq was authorizing UN forces to try to forestall yet further bloodshed in the Congo and the Ivory Coast.

Ultimately, to answer the question about the difference the UN makes, we have to answer two prior questions: What is the UN and what does it do?

The chapters in this volume attest to the multiplicity of roles occupied by the UN that make far too hasty any wholesale dismissal of UN multilateralism based on the Security Council's failure to stop the U.S. war against Iraq in March of 2003. This volume has identified two major kinds of roles occupied by the United Nations in issues of security: (1) as an organizational or individual agent in its own right with its own capacities, resources, limitations, and the outcomes they produce and (2) as a preeminent institutional site of social relations engaging a multiplicity of actors in processes of cooperation, persuasion, competition, and conflict—in short, a key node for the daily socializing interactions of contemporary global society, as articulated in particular by Keith Krause. In short, an adequate assessment of the UN must take into account not only its role as an agent—the individuals or organizations that carry out the UN system's own initiatives and those of states—but also its role as part of the structure of contemporary global politics—constituting its rules, procedures, and interactions.

At one end of the spectrum, and much of the time, the UN acts very much like the deliberative body it is usually understood to be in the eyes of governments around the world—that is, it is less an independent actor in its own right but more a forum for the expression of the will of its member states. In that sense criticisms of the failure "of the UN" over crises like Iraq are sometimes misplaced—as Allen Sens argues in his analysis of the very modest accomplishments of the UN in peace-keeping and peace-building, the criticism is better placed simply at the foot of governments whose polices are merely given expression at UN fora. But recourse to that analytical refinement does not escape the realist insistence that multilateral institutions like the UN are unlikely to provide what is necessary to overcome the obstacles to entrenched cooperation given the diversity of state interests and power. Realists maintain that such institutions play at best an epiphenomenal role in the realm of power politics, a view given renewed life with the startling unilateralism of the United States under the George W. Bush administration after the decade of gains of institutionalists during the post–Cold War burst of institutionalization of world politics. The boldness of recourse to unilateralism by the United States has increasingly challenged the very premise of multilateralism that undermines the institutional structure that includes the UN. Such moves as U.S. rejections of the Comprehensive Test Ban Treaty, International Criminal Court, and the verification regime for the Biological Weapons Convention among other UN initiatives are of no surprise to realists, who would simply contend that a powerful state, particularly a hegemon, will only turn to international institutions to the extent they are convenient to facilitate material interests. The dismissal of the Security Council by the United States in its war vs. Iraq gives powerful truth to this claim. Yet what is the fate, then, of multilateral initiatives not at the service of a hegemon but proceeding without it? Can these initiatives and institutions defy or at least qualify the skeptical expectation that only the dominant powers set the rules for the system? It has been nearly a decade since the onset of U.S. dominance, making stock-taking of such questions most timely and necessary.

It has also been nearly a decade since the publication of *Multilateralism Matters,* in which John Ruggie and his coauthors persuasively maintained that the character of post–World War II multilateralism owed much to the face of the U.S. regulatory state that was projected externally unto an international institutional setting.[2] But if it is right that the New Deal state of the globe's most powerful nation had a profound impact on the international institutional architecture, then surely with American hegemony, globalization, and the move to the deregulatory state similarly profound changes must be underway in the multilateral order. Just as the growth of the western welfare state occasioned a concomitant development of the international institutional structure (including the UN), does not the retrenchment of the welfare state deign deleterious implications for the UN? More than simply a reaction to the first years in office of a unilateralist Bush administration, then, more long-standing hostility towards international institutions (especially the UN) in the U.S. Senate and the embrace of fiscal conservatism even by liberal/left-leaning parties of the industrialized west suggest profound challenges for the UN. How robust and adaptable has the UN been in the face of such changes, and how adaptable is it likely to be?

U.S. attempts to secure a privileged set of rules for itself are nothing new, and the empirical analyses of the chapters in this volume speak to a variety of alternative theoretical perspectives in the study of world politics that alert us to the reasons why multilateral institutions persist even in a world dominated by a hegemon. Neoliberal rationalists provide an account for why an enormous plethora of international institutions have become a routine feature of world politics, stressing in particular the key functional roles played by such institutions in facilitating states' pursuit of joint material gains. Constructivists emphasize the role of international institutions in defining and transforming the moral values and identities that give purpose to the means of material power—that is, in defining state interests, while critical theorists charge that to the extent such institutions really matter it can only be at the price of being engaged in undue complicity with state, corporate, or other forms of hegemonic power.

Despite dramatic failures, developments on the ground over the past decade have continued to create numerous and indeed seemingly limitless functional opportunities for the UN as a niche organization. Afghanistan in the aftermath of the U.S. war on terrorism embodies a microcosm of the chief role of the UN in contemporary security, dealing as it has with Security Council authorization of the use of force, the international law of terrorism, peace-keeping and -building, de-mining, refugees, and the internally displaced, famine relief, nation building, and transitions to stable (democratic) rule. To the extent that states have an interest in addressing such situations—and they continue to do so for a variety of reasons—the UN will continue to provide a central mechanism for coordinating those interests and providing niche capabilities where those of states left to themselves are insufficiently mobilized.

The UN in its function as a forum for the expression of not only power and interest but also of moral value and identity importantly served as a focal point that engaged people around the world in something as close to a global dialogue on pressing matters of international security during 2002 and 2003 as one could imagine—hardly the secretive machinations of a few Bismarcks of the pre–World War One era and the Concert of Europe, global diplomacy looked to approximate as much as one can imagine the kind of communicative dialogue touted by many contemporary philosophers of democracy. But that the Bush administration was in the end engaged in a monologue to see if others would join its predetermined path, rather than a genuine dialogue open to be persuaded of alternative solutions for security problems global in scope, turned Bush's derisive "talk-shop" characterization of the UN into a self-fulfilling prophecy in this case. As such, Ramesh Thakur is on the mark in his chapter in stating that "[t]he Bush statement in the General Assembly in September 2002 was not an American concession to UN multilateralism, but a demand for international capitulation to the U.S. threat to go to war." Thus while defenders of multilateralism have sought to portray the very fact that the Bush administration did go to the Security Council at all as testimony to the power of its role in conferring legitimacy, it was a Pyrrhic victory at best since the resolute determination of the Rumsfeld-Cheney team not to be sidetracked by the lack of Security Council authorization in effect set up the UN for the very failure to act that the Bush administration said would mark its irrelevance. Moreover, the stark fact remained that the UN Security Council had failed to enforce its own resolutions against Iraq. As polls in the aftermath of the 2003 Iraq crisis demonstrated, all of these resulted in a serious blow to public confidence in the UN's role in the world.[3] Still, the damage done to the UN's reputation was less complete than would have been the case had it acquiesced in the demands of the superpower and ratified its war against Iraq. For it was clear that in such a situation the body would have had no credibility at all in the eyes of most of the world; the UN would be seen as nothing more than a stamp of approval for the wishes of the global military hegemon, whereas in the eyes of opponents of U.S. policy the inspections continued by Security Council Resolution 1441 had in fact adequately contained the threat posed by Saddam Hussein's pursuit of weapons of mass destruction. Credit would still have to be given, in that case, to the pressure on Iraq created by U.S. military threats, underscoring that the other member states of the UN and the United States most efficiently achieve their interests when working in tandem. The chapters in this volume make clear that the central resource of the UN in matters of security is not its operational capacity or military assets in matters affecting great power interests but its legitimacy in deciding what initiatives have the support of the international community; had the Council squandered that asset in a gambit to retrieve relevance with the current hegemon it would have left the UN with little enough to make its obituaries more rather than less prescient.

The Bush administration's challenge to the UN, however disingenuous its ulterior motives, was ultimately no mere red herring in the powerful sense that the failure to enforce its own edicts severely undercut the credibility of the UN Security Council and multilateralism and international law more generally. For if the Security Council is to be taken seriously, it must implement in legitimate fashion the binding force of its own resolutions lest the failure to do so in turn undercut the primary source of obligation, belief in the very legitimacy of the international legal system itself.[4] But the Bush administration fell short in succeeding in that challenge because its own turn to multilateralism and international law was ultimately exposed as but an instrumental one of convenience for the more fundamental goal of regime change. That is, if the crisis really were about disarmament as U.S. Secretary of State Powell had so smartly insisted it was in his presentations to the Security Council, the efficacy of the Security Council was seriously in doubt. For the architects of U.S. Iraq policy, however, confronting Iraq was not about enforcing international law but rather about a rejection of a policy of deterrence in favor of a policy of preemption and regime change. Donald Rumsfeld's inability to refrain from insisting that the U.S. war was about regime change and not compliance with international law meant the game was up, no doubt to the continued frustration of Colin Powell's efforts. Ironically, then, the self-serving U.S. challenge to the Security Council amounted to less of a challenge to the legitimacy of the UN globally than it would have had it been in fact a relatively sincere effort to bolster multi-lateral nonproliferation regimes as a way of enhancing U.S. security since few indeed regard the failure of the UN to ratify preemption and regime change as a failure to live up to its own purposes. The UN may have failed the Bush administration and his ally Tony Blair, but from the view of most of the rest of the world it succeeded at least in refusing to ratify what it decided was an unjust and illegal war and thus rescued for itself whatever remained of its tenuous role as a repository of legitimacy, a role discussed in such subtle detail by Jennifer Welsh in this volume and challenged by Ramesh Thakur in representing the views from the South.

Power is at its most efficient when it is regarded as legitimate since conformity with it becomes more voluntary and provokes less resistance.[5] Under intense U.S. military pressure, Security Council Resolution 1441 was passed unanimously in November 2002, and the result was immediate access to Iraq by UN inspectors for the first time since 1998. But this was seen by most countries as a viable strategy to pursue disarmament and containment of Iraq without war, while for the United States it was seen as providing the pretext for war. While the launching of war despite the failure of the UN to authorize it certainly dealt a blow to the Security Council, less commented upon is the fact that this U.S. decision also detracted from American power even as it exercised it in such an awesome raw display.

The U.S. dismissal of UN multilateralism as convenient but unnecessary, as detailed by Nina Tannenwald in her chapter, carried significant costs in further estranging the Bush administration from potential allies. Not only would the United States have to pay the full military bill for the war, quite unlike the Security Council—sanctioned Gulf War of 1991 in which some 50 billion dollars was paid for by Japan, Saudi Arabia, and others, but the United States found itself attempting to pay off reluctant allies to bring them along since they were unpersuaded in the rightness of the *causus belli*. Being unable to avail itself of a key benefit of the multilateral sanctioning of its policy—burden sharing—the very real material costs of this U.S. strategy of cobbling together a "coalition of the billing" means that it can hardly be claimed that the effects of the UN are nothing more than the intangible and epiphenomenal dispersions of illegitimacy conferred by an irrelevant debating society. While multilateralism has its costs of often distasteful compromise, unilateralism too has its own costs. In this way, UN member states have been able to steer something of a precarious course for the UN between the unpalatable Scylla of being a fig-leaf legitimizing superpower hegemony and the Charybdis of utter irrelevance, though this is mostly due—and will continue to remain so—to the other roles played outside this particular drama of preventing war.

Outside the microscope of Iraq, then, the chapters in this volume demonstrate the range of other activities undertaken by the UN in matters of global security. Here, too, many shortcomings are to be found by the authors. The contemporary attempt to define the global security agenda by the United States as one of a war against terrorism does not play well to the operational capacities of the UN as shown by Edward Luck. The UN role on terrorism has mostly been that emphasized by other authors in this volume: setting global norms and standards through UN-orchestrated conventions and sometimes Security Council resolutions. Luck suggests, however, that contemporary circumstances relegate the UN to mostly a role of playing catch-up when he poses the powerful rhetorical question regarding UN resolutions on the U.S. war on terror: "Who is extending legitimacy to whom?"

Still, even here it seems to this author evident that the series of Security Council resolutions on the Taliban and al-Qaeda before and after 9/11 in fact lent significant public legitimacy to the U.S.-led war against Afghanistan. The UN was not at all irrelevant in the overall effort of isolating the Taliban regime, including even from most Arab support. Despite the endless inability of UN member states to define terrorism for a convention, this was one case where virtually no state was willing to make the "freedom fighter" case. Given UN Security Council resolutions long before September 11 and Resolutions 1368 and 1373 immediately after, the U.S.-led foray into Afghanistan was not perceived as anything remotely as divisive for the global community as the U.S.-led war against Iraq. Even if the members of the UN system cannot agree on a suitable universal definition of terrorism, actors within the UN have on occasion devised an approach that amounts to: "We can't define terrorism generally but we know it when we see it," and Lockerbie and 9/11 were it.

The challenges to the adequacy of the UN system of global multilateralism in addressing issues at the top of the contemporary agenda of global security are thus profound insofar as the United States has preponderant weight in defining that agenda and doing something about it. More deeply, the proclivity of the hegemon to seek to dictate the rules of UN multilateralism or, failing that, dispense with its legalities altogether is hardly just the product of the George W. Bush administration. Whether it be the failures to pay UN dues (a treaty obligation) or efforts to carve out exceptional treatment for the United States in treaties like the ICC, the United States can and has opted out of the more instrumental restraints of UN multilateralism if sufficient discretion for its ability to act is not forthcoming. As Nico Krisch has observed, however: "Opting out, though, does not solve the problem entirely. It removes the necessity of bowing to international law's demands for greater equality, but does not provide a new instrument for bringing superior power to bear—law is not only a constraint on power, but also a tool for its exercise."[6] This benefit is especially evident in initiatives requiring the cooperation of multiple actors in a complex world, such as the coordination of sanctions, which is the kind of niche activity that does play to the strengths of the UN.

All this is not to deny that non–UN-sanctioned action—whether it be unilateral or regional, as examined by Brian Job—can in fact serve the purposes of the UN better than UN inaction as the United States and many others argued in the controversial case of NATO's 1999 intervention over Kosovo, detailed by Thakur and Welsh. This case and many others examined in this volume reveal that the importance attached to the UN (by both those who genuinely seek to harness it towards more noble purposes and those who use it more cynically to restrain others) lies as much in procedure as it does in substance. Just as for supporters of UN multilateralism as for proponents of liberal democracy, vigilantism is taken to be wrong even if it accomplishes what many may secretly applaud since in their view the prospects for long-term order and justice rest with compliance with the rule of law. Thus the uneasy tightrope walked by those who judge actions taken without UN authorization, like Kosovo, as illegal but legitimate since supporters of the U.S. war vs. Iraq could make the same claim.

Besides its most characteristic role of serving as a coordination site for the convergence of the interests of states and setting global norms, the UN system has played a prominent role as something of a moral entrepreneur in itself in helping define and carry out that agenda of concern for the world in ways that differ from that of the United States or other great powers. And it is mostly here that the UN as an organization or embodied in the individuals acting under its employ have carved the most important niche for the UN as an operational actor—every refugee given water, shelter, or medical care; every perpetrator of genocide put behind bars by UN criminal tribunals; every small arm that may be taken out of circulation that otherwise would have killed an innocent civilian; and every peace process precipitated by UN sanctions and embargoes and mediated and implemented by the UN are victories for those who would have otherwise been victims and victories also then for humanity. While the shift in the prominence of the war against terrorism on the global agenda does not play to the advantages of the UN system, as Lloyd Axworthy argues in his chapter, the UN may be well poised to address these and other dimensions of a human security agenda that are likely to go under addressed—if at all—by the United States and other great powers.

Here too the results in terms of outcomes so far have been mixed. The ad hoc criminal tribunals have had their impact and no small success in convicting war criminals, and UN treaties such as the Genocide and Torture Conventions have proven invaluable for the astonishing evolution of international criminal law, as marked most notably by the Pinochet case. The ultimate effect on reconciliation and justice within those societies is as yet ambiguous. Moreover, what do we make of an International Criminal Court produced by the UN system and championed by a coalition of like-minded states and civil society groups that leaves behind the United States, China, Russia, and India, among others? William Schabas has pointed out that the ICC might have "accomplished indirectly something that the vast majority of United Nations Member States have been unable to accomplish directly, namely the reform of the Security Council and the taming of the veto of the permanent members."[7] This indeed accounts for part of the hostility towards the court by the United States and lack of enthusiasm by other powers, but two P5 states—the United Kingdom and France—are members of the court. Further, as Price and Lee write, "the broad coalition of like-minded states most supportive of the ICC ensure that it will not be a moribund institution even in the face of resistance and even obstructionism by the United States, China, and other key nonparticipating states, though clearly its effective domain will be constricted in the face of full frontal attacks by great powers."

That characterization might be useful shorthand for the niche role of the UN in issues of global security more generally: processes and outcomes that rarely please ardent supporters yet fill in some holes that would be left by the most demanding of detractors. The limitations of the UN in successfully coordinating the interests and values of member states and effecting the purposes of the UN is embodied in the twin facts that many important initiatives are taken outside of the UN context to get something done (Landmines Convention, interventions in Kosovo and Iraq), while some outcomes are driven more by the organizational need of the UN and its member states to be seen to do something than the requirements of effective action, as Andy Knight demonstrates on arms embargoes, Allen Sens on peace-keeping, Edward Luck on terrorism, and Andy Mack and Kathryn Furlong on conflict prevention. The strains on institutionalized multilateralism in global security are plain and may well foster increasing recourse to more flexible and informal coalitions of the willing and like minded and thus promote continued institutional adaptations away from the formal mechanisms established by the victors of a war that ended over half a century ago.[8] The ability of the UN to survive the drastic international changes in global politics over the last six decades is abundant demonstration of the claim of institutionalists of all theoretical stripes that international institutions provide actors with valued tangible and intangible goods, and not always just to the powerful. But the evidence also suggests that the UN often fails to provide all or even the most important of such goods. While the role of the UN as a key actor in global security is in crisis, it is a crisis over 50 years in the making, and we are likely to continue to see more activity by the UN in an era of U.S. hegemony than under the period of sclerosis occasioned by the Cold War. This may be so since a hegemonic United States will often be successful in having UN institutions do its bidding as per critical or realist expectations, as with Security Council Resolution 1483 of May 2003 ending sanctions against Iraq while granting the United States (and United Kingdom) predominant authority in Iraq. Otherwise, the UN may be left to pursue the agendas of others so long as they do not unduly conflict with the sole superpower and with sufficient coalitions to pursue agendas that do conflict with the hegemon's wishes as with the UN-bred ICC. Those anticipating the death of an institution that too often seems to please no one are sure to be disappointed.

NOTES

* I thank Mark Zacher and the members of the International Relations and Comparative Politics discussion group at the University of British Columbia for comments on earlier versions of this chapter.

1. See Michael Barnett and Martha Finnemore, "The Politics, Power and Pathologies of International Organizations," *International Organization* 53(4) (Autumn 1999): 699–732.
2. John Ruggie, ed. *Multilateralism Matters: The Theory and Praxis of an Institutional Form* (New York: Columbia University Press, 1993).
3. Views of a Changing World 2003, The Pew Research Center for the People and the Press, accessed June 23, 2003 at http://people-press.org/reports/display.php3?ReportID=185.
4. See Christian Reus-Smit, "The Politics of International Law," in *The Politics of International Law* ed. Christian Reus-Smit (forthcoming, Cambridge University Press, 2004).
5. Reus-Smit, "Society, Power and Ethics," in ibid.
6. Nico Krisch, "More Equal Than the Rest? Hierarchy, Equality, and U.S. Predominance in International Law," (manuscript) in *U.S. Hegemony and the Foundations of International Law* ed. Michael Byers (Oxford University Press, 2003): 134.
7. William Schabas, "International Criminal Court: The Secret of its Success," *Criminal Law Forum* 12 (2001): 424.
8. On the adaptations within and around the UN system, see Ruth Wedgwood, "Unilateral Action in the UN System," *European Journal of International Law* 11(2) (2000): 349–359.

ABBREVIATIONS

ABM	Anti Ballistic Missile
ACBQ	Administrative Committee on Budgetary Questions—United Nations
ACC	Administrative Committee on Coordination—United Nations
AECA	Arms Export Control Act
APL	Anti Personnel Landmines
ASEAN	Association of Southeast Asian Nations
AU	African Union—formerly OAU
BASIC	British-American Security Information Council
BCPR	Bureau for Crisis Prevention and Recovery—United Nations Development Program
BW	Biological Weapons
BTWC	Biological and Toxins Weapons Convention
CASA	Coordinating Action on Small Arms
CICP	Center for International Crime Prevention—United Nations
CIS	Commonwealth of Independent States
CSCE	Conference on Security and Cooperation in Europe
CTBT	Comprehensive Test Ban Treaty
CTC	Counter Terrorism Committee—United Nations
CW	Chemical Weapons
CWC	Chemical Weapons Convention
DDA	Department of Disarmament Affairs—United Nations
DFID	Department for International Development—United Kingdom
DNGOs	Domestic Non-Governmental Organizations
DPA	Department of Political Affairs—United Nations
DPKO	Department of Peacekeeping Operations—United Nations
DRC	Democratic Republic of Congo
EAPC	Euro-Atlantic Partnership Council
ECOWAS	Economic Community of West African States
ECPS	Executive Committee on Peace and Security—United Nations
EU	European Union
FMLN	Farabando Marti National Liberation—El Salvador
FRELIMO	Frente de LibertaVão de Mozambique
Frente POLISARIO	Frente Popular para la Liberacion de Saguia el-Hamra y de Rio del Oro

FRY	Federal Republic of Yugoslavia
G-7/ G-8	Group of Seven/ Group of Eight
G-77	Group of Seventy-Seven
GA	General Assembly—United Nations
GDP	Gross Domestic Product
HSO	Humanitarian Security Officer—UNHCR
IAEA	International Atomic Energy Agency
IANSA	International Action Network on Small Arms
ICBL	International Campaign to Ban Landmines
ICC	International Criminal Court
ICC-ASP	International Criminal Court Assembly of States Parties
ICISS	International Commission of Intervention and State Sovereignty
ICRC	International Committee of the Red Cross
ICTR	International Criminal Tribunal for Rwanda—United Nations
ICTY	International Criminal Tribunal for the Former Yugoslavia—United Nations
IFIs	International Financial Institutions
IIE	International Institute of Economics
IMF	International Monetary Fund
INTERFET	International Force in East Timor—United Nations
IO	International Organizations
IPA	International Peace Academy
IPIS	International Peace Information Service
IPTF	International Police Task Force
ISS	Institute for Security Studies—Pretoria, South Africa
JIU	Joint Inspection Unit—United Nations
MDGs	Millennium Development Goals
MIF	Maritime Interception Force—United States
MINURSO	United Nations Mission for the Referendum in Western Sahara
MNF	Multi-National Force
NAM	Non Aligned Movement
NATO	North Atlantic Treaty Organization
NEPAD	New Partnership for African Development
NGO	Nongovernmental Organization
NPT	Nuclear Nonproliferation Treaty
NSAs	Non-State Actors
NTM	National Technical Means
OAS	Organization of American States
OAU	Organization of African Unity
ODCCP	Office for Drug Control and Crime Prevention
OECD	Organization for Economic Cooperation and Development
ONUC	UN Peacekeeping Mission to the Congo, 1961
OPCW	Organization for the Prohibition of Chemical Weapons

OSCE	Organization for Security and Cooperation in Europe
P5/ P-5/ Permanent Five	Permanent Five Members of UN Security Council
PAN	National Advancement Party—Guatemala
PKO	Peace Keeping Operation
POLISARIO	Popular Front for the Liberation of Saguia El Hamra and Río De Oro—Morocco
Prepcom	Preparatory Commission—ICC
RENAMO	Mozambican National Resistance
RUF	Revolutionary United Front—Sierra Leone
SADC	Southern Africa Development Community
SAM	Sanction Assistance Mission
SAS	Small Arms Survey
Shirbrig	Standby High Readiness Brigade—United Nations
SPLA	Sudan People's Liberation Army
START I/ II	Strategic Arms Reductions Treaty I/ II
TNGOs	Transnational Non-Governmental Organizations
TPB	Terrorism Prevention Branch
UN	United Nations
UNAMET	United Nations Mission in East Timor
UNAMIC	United Nations Advanced Mission in Cambodia
UNCD	United Nations Conference on Disarmament
UNCTAD	United Nations Conference on Trade and Development
UNDDA	United Nations Department of Disarmament Affairs
UNDG	United Nations Development Group
UNDP	United Nations Development Program
UNEF	United Nations Emergency Force
UNEP	United Nations Environment Program
UNESCO	United Nations Educational, Scientific, and Cultural Organization
UNFICYP	United Nations Peacekeeping Force in Cyprus
UNGA	United Nations General Assembly
UNHCR	United Nations High Commissioner for Refugees
UNICEF	United Nations Children's Fund
UNIDIR	United Nations Institute for Disarmament Research
UNIIMOG	United Nations Iran-Iraq Military Observer Group
UNITA	National Union for the Total Independence of Angola
UNITAF	Unified Task Force—Somalia
UNMIH	United Nations Mission in Haiti
UNMOGIP	United Nations Military Observer Group in India and Pakistan
UNMOVIC	United Nations Monitoring, Verification and Inspection Commission—Iraq
UNO	United Nations Organization
UNPROFOR	UN Protection Force—Former Yugoslavia
UNSC	United Nations Security Council
UNSCOM	United Nations Special Commission

UNSECOORD	United Nations Security Coordinator
UNSMA	United Nations Special Mission for Afghanistan
UNTAC	United Nations Transitional Authority in Cambodia
UNTAET	United Nations Transitional Administration in East Timor
UNTSO	United Nations Truce Supervision Organization
URNG	Guatemalan National Revolutionary Unity
WEO	Western Europe and others
WEU	Western European Union
WFP	World Food Program—United Nations
WGCA	Working Group on the Crime of Aggression—ICC
WHO	World Health Organization
WMD	Weapons of Mass Destruction
WTO	World Trade Organization

Notes on Contributors

Lloyd Axworthy
Lloyd Axworthy is director and CEO of the Liu Institute for Global Issues at the University of British Columbia. He is a board member of the MacArthur Foundation, Human Rights Watch, and the Lester B. Pearson College. Lloyd Axworthy's political career spanned 27 years. From 1995 to 2000 he served as minister of foreign affairs of Canada. In his foreign affairs portfolio he became internationally known for his advancement of the human security concept, in particular, the Ottawa Treaty—a landmark global treaty banning antipersonnel landmines. He published *Navigating a New World* (Knopf Canada) in the fall of 2003.

Kathryn Furlong
Kathryn Furlong is a Ph.D. student at the University of British Columbia (UBC) in the geography department, a research associate with the International Peace Research Institutes (Oslo) Conditions of War and Peace Program, and a member of the World Conservation Union's Collaborative Management Working Group. She is presently a research assistant at UBC's Centre for Human Security. Furlong has spent a year working with the Global Environmental Change and Human Security (GECHS) project at the International Peace Research Institute in Oslo (PRIO).

Fen Hampson
Fen Osler Hampson is a professor and director of the Norman Paterson School of International Affairs, Carleton University, Ottawa, Canada. He is the author/ coauthor of six books and editor/ coeditor of twenty others. His newest book (coauthored with Chester A. Crocker and Pamela Aall), *Mediating in the Danger Zone: How to Handle the World's Most Intractable Conflicts*, will be published in 2004. He is the recipient of a Jennings Randolph Senior Fellowship from the United States Institute of Peace and a Research and Writing Award from the John D. and Catherine T. MacArthur Foundation.

Brian Job
Brian Job is professor of political science and director of the Centre of International Relations at the University of British Columbia, Vancouver, Canada. Representative recent publications include: "Track 2 Diplomacy: Ideational Contribution to the Evolving Security Order," in M. Alagappa, ed. *Asian Security Order: Instrumental and Normative Features* (2002); "Canada: The Security Environment," in Charles Morrison, ed. *Asia Pacific Security Outlook 2002* (with Allen Sens); and "Assessing the Risks of Conflict in the PRC-ROC Rivalry," *Pacific Affairs*, 2000 (with Andre Laliberte and Michael Wallace). Professor Job was one of the founders and codirectors of the Canadian Consortium on Asia

Pacific Security. He is currently cochair of the region-wide Council on Security Cooperation in the Asia Pacific.

Asif Khan

Asif R. Khan has been working for the United Nations since 1995. He earned his B.A. and Master of International Affairs degrees from Columbia University. He is currently political affairs officer in the Africa division of the Department of Peace-keeping Operations at United Nations headquarters, New York and was formerly in the strategic planning unit in the executive office of the UN Secretary-General. He has also worked for the United Nations in Bosnia and Herzegovina, Kosovo, Israel and the occupied territories, and Geneva.

W. Andy Knight

Andy Knight is professor in the department of political science and the McCalla Research Professor at the University of Alberta, Edmonton, Canada. He is former vice chair of the Academic Council on the UN System, and is currently editor of *Global Governance*. His most recent books include: *Adapting the United Nations to a Post Modern World: Lessons Learned* (2001); *A Changing United Nations: Multilateral Evolution and the Quest for Global Governance* (2000); and *The United Nations and Arms Embargoes Verification* (1998). He is coeditor with Tom Keating of a forthcoming book, *Building Sustainable Peace* (Edmonton: University of Alberta Press, 2004).

Keith Krause

Keith Krause is professor at the Graduate Institute of International Studies in Geneva and director of its Program in Strategic and International Security Studies. He is the founder and program director of the *Small Arms Survey* project. His published work includes: *Arms and the State* (1992) and articles in *International Studies Quarterly, European Journal of International Relations, Review of International Studies, Global Governance, Contemporary Security Policy, Mershon Review of International Studies, Cooperation and Conflict*, and *International Journal* as well as chapters in many edited volumes.

Joanne Lee

Joanne is an Australian lawyer and is currently in the Ph.D. program, Faculty of Law, University of British Columbia. From 1998 to 2003, she has been a research associate, International Centre for Criminal Law Reform and Criminal Justice Policy (ICCLR), Vancouver, Canada. She is principal author of two editions of the *Manual on the Ratification and Implementation of the Rome Statute*—the first edition now translated into every UN language.

Gil Loescher

Gil Loescher is senior fellow for forced displacement and international security at The International Institute for Strategic Studies in London and research associate at Queen Elizabeth House, Oxford University. He recently was codirector of a transatlantic research project for the European Council on Refugees and Exiles. For 25 years he was professor of international relations at the University of Notre Dame in Indiana. Mr. Loescher's most recent books are: *The UNHCR and World Politics: A Perilous Path* (2001) and *Problems of Protection: The UNHCR, Refugees and Human Rights in the 21ˢᵗ Century* (2003).

Edward C. Luck

Edward Luck is director of the Centre on International Organization and professor of practice in international and public affairs at Columbia University. Since 2001, Dr. Luck has served as a member of the UN Secretary-General's Policy Working Group on the United Nations and Terrorism. A past president and CEO of the United Nations Association of the United States of America, his most recent book is *Mixed Messages: American Politics and International Organization, 1919–1999.*

Andrew Mack

Andrew Mack is director of the Human Security Centre at the University of British Columbia in Vancouver. He was director of strategic planning in the executive office of Secretary-General Kofi Annan at the United Nations from August 1998 to January 2001. He formerly held the chair in the international relations department in the Institute of Advanced Study at the Australian National University (1991–1998). Mack has written or edited some 11 monographs and books, and his over 50 scholarly articles have appeared in: *World Politics, Washington Quarterly, British Journal of International Studies, World Policy, Foreign Policy, Comparative Politics, Journal of Conflict Resolution, Journal of Peace Research, Security Dialogue, Arms Control, Asian Survey, Australian Journal of International Affairs,* and *Pacific Review.* In addition to producing *Human Security Report* at UBC he is chairing the multiyear International Peace Academy project on *Economic Agendas and Civil Wars.*

Richard Price

Richard Price is an associate professor of political science at the University of British Columbia. His research focuses on the development of norms in world politics, particularly norms of warfare, and constructivist international relations theory. He has authored the *Chemical Weapons Taboo* (Cornell University Press, 1997) and numerous articles in journals including: *International Organization, International Security, World Politics,* the *European Journal of International Relations,* and *Review of International Studies.*

Allen Sens

Allen G. Sens is a senior instructor in the department of political science and chair of the international relations program at the University of British Columbia. He specializes in international conflict and conflict management with an emphasis on peace-keeping and military intervention. He is coeditor of *NATO and European Security: Alliance Politics from the End of the Cold War to the Age of Terrorism* and coauthor of *Global Politics: Origins, Currents, Directions.*

Nina Tannenwald

Nina Tannenwald is Joukowsky Family Assistant Research Professor at the Watson Institute for International Studies at Brown University. In 2002–2003 she was a visiting scholar at the Centre for International Security and Cooperation at Stanford University. Her research interests focus on international norms and institutions in the security area and weapons of mass destruction. She is the author of *The Nuclear Taboo: The United States and the Nonuse of Nuclear Weapons Since 1945* (2004).

Ramesh Thakur

Professor Ramesh Thakur is vice rector of the United Nations University. He was formerly professor and head of the Peace Research Centre at the Australian National University in Canberra and professor of international relations and director of Asian studies at the University of Otago in New Zealand. He was a member of the International Commission on Intervention and State Sovereignty (ICISS). He is the author/ editor of 18 books, the most recent being *Kosovo and the Challenge of Humanitarian Intervention: Selective Indignation, Collective Action, and International Citizenship* (2000), *United Nations Peacekeeping Operations: Ad Hoc Missions, Permanent Engagement* (2001), *Enhancing Global Governance: Towards a New Diplomacy?* (2002), and *From Civil Strife to Civil Society: Civil and Military Responsibilities in Disrupted States* (2003).

Jennifer M. Welsh

Jennifer Welsh is university lecturer in international relations at the University of Oxford and a fellow of Somerville College. She has published in the areas of international relations theory and intervention and is the author of *Edmund Burke and International Relations* (1995). She has edited *Humanitarian Intervention and International Relations* (2003) and a book on Canadian foreign policy after September 11th to be published in 2004.

Mark Zacher

Mark W. Zacher is professor of political science at the University of British Columbia. He was director of the Centre of International Relations at UBC from 1971–1991. He is the author of *Dag Hammarskjold's United Nations* (1970) and *International Conflicts and Collective Security, 1946–77: The United Nations, Organization of American States, Organization of African Unity, and Arab League* (1979) and the coauthor of *Pollution, Politics and International Law: Tankers at Sea* (1979), *Managing International Markets: Developing Countries and the Commodity Trade Regime* (1988), and *Governing Global Networks: International Regimes for Transportation and Communications* (1996). He is a fellow of the Royal Society of Canada and was the associate editor of *International Organization* from 1995–1996.

I N D E X

5021